Controversies in the Acts of the Apostles

A Comparative Analysis of Controversies in Acts of the Apostles

Controversies in the Acts of the Apostles

A Comparative Analysis of Controversies in Acts of the Apostles
Copyright © David Criswell 2013

David Criswell

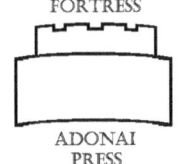

FORTRESS
ADONAI PRESS

North Charleston, S.C.

Controversies in the Acts of the Apostles

A Comparative Analysis of Biblical Controversies

David Criswell

All Rights Reserved © 2013 by David Criswell

No part of the book may be reproduced or transmitted in any form or by any means, graphic, electronic, or mechanical, including photocopying, recording, taping, or by any information storage system, without the prior permission in writing from the copyright owner.

ISBN NUMBER 0-61591-904-9

Cover Design by David Criswell

FORTRESS

ADONAI PRESS

Dallas, TX

Printed in the United States of America

Dedication

For the Lord. You are my only constant.

"We demolish every argument and pretension that sets itself up against the knowledge of God, and we take captive every thought to make it obedient to Christ" (2 Corinthians 10:5).

Preface

What was to be the sixth and final book in my Controversies series eventually became four books. *Controversies in the Acts and Epistles* grew well over six hundred pages before I had even come close to finishing it. I therefore split Acts and Epistles into two separate volumes. Two other books grew out of appendices; *The Apostles After Jesus* and *Anonymous : Who Wrote the Book of Hebrews?*

Perhaps it is just that my Controversies series on the Bible ends with seven volumes, for seven is a Biblical number. This was not intentional, but perhaps it is propitious. The book of Acts deserves its own volume for it is actually the longest book in the New Testament, just slightly eclipsing the Gospel of Matthew with 18,451 words in the original Greek compared to Matthew's 18,345.[1] It is also the only book in the New Testament to give an account of the apostles after Jesus's death and resurrection. Moreover, it is also one of the most controversial. Catholics, evangelicals, Pentecostals, Charismatics, rationalists, covenant theologians, dispensationalists, cessationists, sacramentalists, and ritualists all interpret Acts with a particular slant. This is not unusual, for historical books are the easiest to misinterpret since the context of history is too often hidden from our eyes unless we are standing back from afar. Like the saying, "you can't see the forest for the trees," many theologians bring a particular bias with them into their reading of Acts. Consequently, Acts contains more controversies than most New Testament books. Perhaps only Revelation sparks more controversy than Acts.

My approach, as with my others in the series, is modeled after 1 Peter 3:15 and 2 Corinthians 10:5. We must be "always ready to make a defense to everyone who asks" (1 Peter 3:15) and we must "demolish every argument and pretension that sets itself up against the knowledge of God, and we take captive every thought to make it obedient to Christ" (2 Corinthians 10:5). In today's world in particular antagonism against Christianity is increasing as the plague of Marxism is felt in all corners of society. Religion is viewed as the source of man's problems and the Bible is treated as mythology or legends at best. Our President, Barak Obama, even publicly claims that the Bible supports slavery (a fact I refute in *Controversies in the Epistles*) and Hollywood portrays Bible believers as tyrants, misogynists, and racists, despite the fact that the abolisionist movement was explicitly an evangelical Christian movement. Some of its leading proponents even founded Christian churches![2] Therefore it is important, now more than ever, to be able to give an answer to these lies and attacks that plague our Church today.

Sir Robert Anderson, former chief inspector of Scotland Yard, once said, "for the Christian to solve difficulties by repudiating the teaching of Christ, is like committing suicide to escape from danger."[3] Unfortunately this is exactly what many Christians do subliminally. We attempt to escape criticism of the Bible by allegorizing, dismissing, or trivializing the Bible. A thorough defense requires more thought than many are willing to give.

So here then is the fifth volume in the Controversies series, although it is the sixth that I have completed. I pray that it will benefit those who seek to understand the history of the apostles and the emergence of the church in this age.

David Criswell, November 2013

"We demolish every argument and pretension that sets itself up against the knowledge of God, and we take captive every thought to make it obedient to Christ" (2 Corinthians 10:5).

Table of Contents

Preface vii
1. Introduction 1
☦ Authroship and Background 2
2. From the Resurrection to Pentecost 5
☦ Restoring the Kingdom : Acts 1:6-7 5
☦ The Ascension and Return Promised : Acts 1:11 6
☦ How Did Judas Die? Acts 1:18-19 8
☦ The Thirteenth Apostle : Acts 1:21-26 10
3. Pentecost 23
☦ Establishing the Church 23
☦ The Tongues at Pentecost : Acts 2:3-6 33
☦ Joel in Acts : Acts 2:16-21 40
☦ Baptism and Salvation : Acts 2:38 42
☦ Signs and Wonders in Acts : Acts 2:43 49
☦ Did the Church Exist Before Penetcost : Acts 2:47 52
4. The Church in its Infancy 53
☦ Who Crucified Jesus? : Acts 4:10 54
☦ In the Name of Jesus Alone : Acts 4:12 56
☦ Were the Apostles Socialists? : Acts 4:34-35 57
☦ Ananias and Sapphira : Acts 5:1-11 64
5. The First Persecution 69
☦ "Whom You Put To Death": Acts 5:30 69
☦ Gamaliel's Counsel : Acts 5:33-45 69
☦ The Historicity of Theudas and Judas : Acts 5:36-37 70
☦ Stephen's Account of Abraham : Acts 7:4 78
☦ Stephen's Account of the Migration : Acts 7:14 81
☦ Stephen's Account of Shechem : Acts 7:16 82
☦ Stephen and the Prophecy of Amos : Acts 7:4 83
☦ Who Gave the Law? : Acts 7:53 86
☦ Stephen's Martyrdom : Acts 7:54-60 87
☦ The Scattering of the Disciples : Acts 8:1-4 88
6. The Church in Antioch 89
☦ Simon the Magician : Acts 8:9-24 89
☦ The Samaritan Pentecost and Spirit Baptism : Acts 8:15-17 98
☦ The Ethiopian Eunuch : Acts 8:27-38 103
☦ Why Do Some Modern Translations Omit This Passage? : Acts 8:37 105
☦ Philip Snatched Away : Acts 8:39-40 106
7. From Saul's Conversion to the Circumcision Debate 107
☦ The Saul Becomes Paul: Acts 9:1-9 107
☦ Saul's Early Days : Acts 9:19-31 112
☦ The Vision of Peter and Cornelius : Acts 10:9-31 114

✝ Peter and the Gentiles : Acts 11:1-20 115
✝ Herod Agrippa's Death : Acts 12:2-23 115
✝ Chronology Conflict? : Acts 13:17-22 115
8. The Circumcision Debate and the Council of Jerusalem 123
✝ The Apostle to the Gentiles : Acts 13:44-52 123
✝ Acts 14:11-18 124
✝ Herod Agrippa's Death : Acts 12:2-23 124
9. Paul's Second Journey 131
✝ Forbidden to Preach? : Acts 16:6-7 131
✝ Prophecy and Motives : Acts 16:16-19 131
✝ To An Unknown God - The Sermon on Mars Hills : Acts 17:23 135
✝ Why Did Claudius Expel the Jews : Acts 18:2 142
10. Paul's Third Journey 145
✝ The Ancient Prescript : Acts 19:0 145
✝ Baptism of the Spirit : Acts 19:1-6 146
✝ The Name of Jesus : Acts 19:13-17 147
✝ Jerusalem or Rome? Was Paul Disobeying God? : Acts 19:27 149
✝ Acts 19:24-31 153
✝ Worshipping on Sunday? : Acts 20:7 153
✝ Acts 20:22 - 21:11 158
11. Paul's Trial and the Journey to Rome 159
✝ Paul in Jerusalem: Acts 21:18 - 26:32 159
✝ Acts 22:1-6 165
✝ Supplementary Additions? : Acts 24:6-8 165
✝ Acts 26:9-19 166
✝ The Shipwreck : Acts 27:1 - 28:15 166
✝ Missing Text? : Acts 28:29 168
✝ Was Acts Finished? 169
Appendix A : The Chronology of the Acts of the Apostles 171
✝ *Chronological Chart on the Acts of the Apostles* 184
Appendix B : Peter and Rome 185
✝ Was Peter Ever in Rome? 185
✝ Was Peter Ever Bishop of Rome? 192
✝ Peter's Martyrdom 196
Appendix C : The Lives of the Apostles 201
✝ The Apostles After Christ 201
✝ The Apostles' Companions 211
✝ *Chart on the Apostles* 216
✝ *Chart on the Apostles' Companions* 217
Appendix D : The Authenticity of the New Testament 219
✝ The Canon of the New Testament 219
✝ The Authenticity and Transmission of the Text 227
✝ Conclusions 233

End Notes 236
Works Cited 258
☦   ☦   ☦

1

Introduction

The book of Acts was written by the same Luke who wrote the gospel bearing his name. Luke himself wrote as a historian. He spoke to various eyewitnesses and was himself an eyewitness to many of the events in Acts as he was a travelling companion of the apostle Paul. The book itself was commissioned for a certain Theophilus who wanted an authentic history of the apostles.

In some respects the book of Acts is more controversial than the gospels, but not for the critic so much as for the Christian. There are two reasons for this. First is the question of the nature of the church and Israel. Because of the troubled history of gentile converts and the emergence of the church as a separate entity from Jewish Messianic congregations, many have become confused about the nature of one or both. Much of Acts is about the travels of the apostle Paul who has been called the "apostle to the gentiles" (1 Timothy 2:7). It records a time when the gospel was moving from Israel to the gentile world at large. This begs the very question, "what is the church?" How is the church different from believing Israel? Has the church supplanted Israel? Are the Jews still receipients of the promises made in the Old Testament? When did the church come into being?

The second difficultly which frequently arises in Acts is that involving the use of signs and miralces, such as tongues, and whether or not they have their place in today's church. The book of Acts clearly describes great miracles and signs such as had rarely been seen in history. Some erroneously claim that miracles only took place during the times of Moses, Elijah, Jesus, and the apostles, but this is just as false as those who claim that apostles still perform daily miracles to this day. Both make assumptions about history and the Bible and project those assumptions into Biblical interpretation.

Together these make up many, but by no means all of the controversies which we will examine. In so doing I will cite authors from the church fathers down to the present, from one side of the argument to the other. I will also address debates about the accuracy of history in Acts, prophecy, alleged contradictions, and even chronology. With all these questions, the answers are mired by the fact that Acts is not a theological thesis or polemic but a history. History books are always the most difficult upon which to draw theological interpretations because the context of history itself is one which can be easily misrepresented or forgotten. For example, in the Old Testament King David had more than one wife. Many have argued that this means it was acceptable to have more than one wife in the Old Testament. In fact, this is not true. Without debating the issue itself, it is merely worth nothing that King David's actions did not necessarily reflect the law of Israel anymore than his affair with Bathsheba proves that adultery is okay. This is a common error which many make in interpreting histories. The actions of individuals do not necessarily reflect upon God's law. In the same way we must understand that the events of Acts took place in a certain context and in a time in which the world was rapidly shifting. These events took place in one of the most important times in world history, and the church was at the very center of that shift! Consequently, it is easy to assume one thing or another and read that thing into the text of a historical account, but careful exegesis must factor all the facts into the context of the passages, and this, as the reader will see, is not always an easy task.

The Authorship and Background of Acts

The Acts of the Apostles records the history of the church after the time of Jesus' death, resurrection, and ascension until the early days of Nero shortly before the Great Persecution which claimed the lives of both Peter and Paul, the two most famous apostles. It is universally recognized to have been written by Luke as a companion piece to his gospel. Said Merrill Tenney, "There can be no reasonable doubt that Acts and Luke are two volumes of the same work."[4]

In his gospel, Luke begins by saying, "it seemed fitting for me, having investigated everything carefully from the beginning, to write *it* out for you in consecutive order, most excellent Theophilus ... the exact truth about the things you have been taught" (1:3-4). Acts begins with these very words, "The first account I composed, Theophilus, about all that Jesus began to do and teach" (1:1). Hence, Acts comprises the second volume of Luke's work. The only reason that the gospel of John is placed between Luke and Acts is because the canon was arranged in such a way that the gospels were presented in the order in which they were written (see *Controversies in the Gospels* for a defense of this argument).

As for Luke himself, he was a physician (Colossians 4:14) and a traveling companion of the apostle Paul (cf. 2 Timothy 4:11, Acts). This much cannot be doubted with credulity. "Frequent use of medical terms agrees with Luke's being a physician (Col. 4:14)"[5] and the author of Acts identifies himself and the apostle Paul as "we" many times in Acts. He is believed to have been a gentile convert and, if true, would be the only gentile author of any book in the New Testament. However, some doubt that Luke was a gentile at all, but I reserve this debate for "Who Crucified Jesus : Acts 4:10" in Chapter 4, but also see Anonymous for a discussion of this subject as well.[6]

More debatable is the date of Acts' composition. "Liberal" Bible critics have long attempted to attack the early dating of the New Testament books, but none have as of yet been able to present a feasible argument for the ending of Acts unless it was composed and completed around 62 A.D. The problem is that the Acts of the Apostles ends with Paul in prison awaiting trial. This seems to many to make the book of Acts incomplete. I debate this issue more fully under Chapter 11 in the section "Was Acts Finished?" below, but shall here give a brief summary and conclusion. It is sufficient to say that there is no logical or rational argument as to how and why Luke ends the way it does unless it was written and completed at that very time. It was "complete" because everything which had thus far taken place had been completed. Luke could not record what happened to Paul after that because it had not yet taken place. All other theories fail to adequately account for this, especially the liberal attacks which make Acts a late document written by some forger many decades later.

Thus Acts was written by an eyewitness to many of the events described in Acts and a close companion of the apostles who were eyewitnesses to Jesus Himself. It was completed as the second volume of Luke's historical work around 62 or early 63 A.D. shortly before the infamous Roman persecution by Nero which claimed the lives of many apostles.

2

From the Resurrection to Pentecost

The first chapter of Acts recounts the events of Jesus's ascension. It also serves as the backdrop for the momentous change which was coming to the church, to Israel, and to the world. But this in itself is controversial, for the church, Israel, and world history are not so easily defined as some would like them to be. Nor was the change which was to come as instantaneous and complete as many believe. As we shall see, even the apostles did not fully understand what was to happen.

Restoring the Kingdom
Acts 1:6-7

> "Lord, is it at this time You are restoring the kingdom to Israel? He said to them, 'It is not for you to know times or epochs which the Father has fixed by His own authority.'"

"Is it at this time You are restoring the kingdom to Israel?" This was the simple question the apostles asked of our Lord, implying that the kingdom was to be restored to Israel as taught by all the prophets and teachers of Israel down to that day. The reader will note that Jesus's answer does not in any way appear to contradict that such a restoration will take place at the proper "time and epoch which the Father has fixed." Nevertheless, centuries of Church teaching have denied Israel any place in God's future kingdom, making this passage, or rather Jesus's answer, among the most controversial in the book of Acts.

Now some scholars have questioned the "spiritual intelligence" of the apostles for even asking this question.[7] John Calvin even went so far as to say that "their stupidity is incredible."[8] Even the famed John Lightfoot claimed that it is a "great delusion"[9] to believe that God will ever restore the kingdom to Israel, but the reader will note that in Jesus's answer "the fact that the kingdom is, indeed, to be restored to Israel is taken for granted."[10] How then can any interpreter say that Jesus left no room for national Israel? The standard answer is as follows.

Albert Barnes dodges the issue by arguing that "the question of the apostles respected the *time* of the restoration; it was not whether he *would* do it. Accordingly, his answer meets precisely their inquiry."[11] In other words, the standard answer is that "our Lord's answer is confined to this point"[12] alone. However, this is illogical and irrational for two reasons. First, Jesus could not speak about the time of "*time* of the restoration" if the restoration was never to take place! Second, if this argument were true then this would be far more troubling for it implies that Jesus would deliberately have led the apostles to believe a lie! Since their question inferred the restoration of Israel and the fulfillment of the prophecies of the Old Testament prophets, it would be unthinkable that Jesus would simply ignore this unless it is taken for granted as true. Jesus's "reply shows, however, that the gist of the inquiry was not *Israel*, but *at this time*."[13] Jesus does not deceive!

Nevertheless, Erasmus argued that the apostles "had not yet put aside the dream of an Israelite kingdom ... they did not yet understand the nature of the spiritual kingdom."[14] This idea, that the apostles "had no clear notion of the nature of that kingdom,"[15] was one promoted from the earliest of times, but was by no means universal. The church father Ephraem the Syrian, for example, believed that Jesus was telling them to "keep watch" and that the kingdom would indeed be restored to Israel when Jesus returns.[16] Richard Longenecker has opted for a median position, attempting to argue for middle ground by saying that Jesus preferred "to hold that aspect of [His] eschatological message" but ignored the question of Israel. He then argues that there is a place for Israel, but only as a part of the church "involved in some way."[17] Such ambiguity is not particularly helpful.

The best and most logical answer is the most straightforward one. Contrary to the teachings of many in the church today, Jesus's answer illustrates that "the Kingdom of God has not yet come in."[18] "The Lord does not at all contradict such a restortation in its season."[19] In fact, Jesus seems to affirm that it *will happen* in the "time and epoch which the Father has fixed." These are the words of Jesus Christ and we should take them as they stand without adding to them, nor taking away from them.

The Ascension and Return Promised
Acts 1:11

> "Men of Galilee, why do you stand looking into the sky? This Jesus, who has been taken up from you into heaven, will come in just the same way as you have watched Him go into heaven."

Once again the plain and simple words teach that Jesus will bodily return to this earth someday. Nonetheless, the Tübingen school, or so-called "liberal" scholars, have tried to paint this as a promise of Pentecost. They argue that Jesus will return in the form of the Holy Spirit at Pentecost; never mind that the Holy Spirit is a *separate* person of the Trinity. One author even calls this an "embellishing" by the angel and a "literary device" or "rhetorical" style![20] Of course another word for this would be, a "lie." Does God "embellish" the truth? Did Jesus embellish in the Upper Room when He told the apostles about the coming Holy Spirit? Are we then to believe that the angels from heaven did just that?

Gustave Dore – The Ascension – 19th Century

Despite the protests of some modern scholars, the church has always accepted that this is nothing less than a promise of the Second Coming. Ignatius, the apostolic father, uses this very verse to prove a bodily return of Jesus at the Second Coming,[21] and the church father Tertullian said that "He will come again on the clouds of heaven, just as He appeared into heaven."[22] Even some of the early medieval scholars agreed, such as the Venerable Bede, who said that Jesus would return in the very same body.[23]

Charles Spurgeon said that if you "give anybody a grain of sense" then it is must be seen as literal.[24] The promise is, as Jonathan Edwards states, that "He will come again ... by his bodily presence ... and then he will appear in that glorious kingdom."[25] Indeed, this promise was one dear to the early church in particular, for during times of persecution they took comfort that this world is not the kingdom God promised and their very farewell address, "Maranatha," comes from the Aramaic meaning "Our Lord Come."[26]

Thus the plain and simple words of the angel was that "He will return in His glorified body, accompanied with clouds."[27] "Not another and in a different way, but this same Jesus in the same way would descend for believers."[28] Even the sometimes "liberal" Albert Barnes acknowledges that Jesus will descend "in clouds as he ascended."[29] This is the promise of the Second Coming made at His ascension. It is fundamental promise of the Christian faith and cannot be abandoned without harm to Jesus Himself.

How Did Judas Die?
Acts 1:18-19 – Matthew 27:3-10

"Then when Judas, who had betrayed Him, saw that He had been condemned, he felt remorse and returned the thirty pieces of silver to the chief priests and elders, saying, 'I have sinned by betraying innocent blood.' ... And he threw the pieces of silver into the temple sanctuary and departed; and he went away and hanged himself."	"This man acquired a field with the price of his wickedness, and falling headlong, he burst open in the middle and all his intestines gushed out. And it became known to all who were living in Jerusalem; so that in their own language that field was called Hakeldama, that is, Field of Blood."

This topic was discussed previously in *Controversies in the Gospels* under Matthew 27:2-10, and I will replicate the words found therein here for convenience.

Elsewhere I have often used the analogy of a police detective reviewing differing accounts, and I have elsewhere stated that no such contradictions exist when the accounts are fully examined. On this occasion I must fully and honestly state that the resolution of the difficulty between these two verses is one that I have taken on faith alone due to the fact that I find the authors in all other areas to be credible and honest. I will not here claim that the critics are groundless in their attacks, for the two passage do indeed seem to be at odds with one another, but a resolution of the conflict is possible if we take ancient tradition as a viable witness. Let us address the issues separately.

Judas's Suicide
This is the most difficult issue, and in all honesty the only passage in the whole of the Bible which I can see as contradicting one another. Note that I do not say they *do* contradict one another, but only that I can *see* them in that way. Indeed, the apparent contradictions are obvious. The question is whether or not they can be reconciled with credibility.

Matthew records that Judas hung himself in a suicide over despair. Luke's account does not offer an exact account of what happened, but says that he fell upon rocks wherein his intestines fell out. Even many evangelicals have had problems reconciling these verses. Some have dared to speak of Matthew having relied on "creativity" and "revisions"![30] Such absurd conclusions should only be made after a man is convicted, not before!

Although we cannot be certain based strictly on the Biblical texts, there is an ancient tradition which offers a reconciliation of these passages. According to the tradition Judas hung himself with his girdle or similar article which gave way, causing his body to fall upon the rocks.[31] Others have said that "the limb broke under his weight"[32] or alternately that "the rope broke."[33] The "varying traditions"[34] are all similar in nature, and the specifics are unimportant. What is significant is that all believe that Judas had hung "himself over the ledge, [and then] then fell into the valley below."[35]

Are such legends credible? Can we hold them to be reliable? Is this really plausible or just a hackneyed attempt to reconcile the irreconcilable? If we examine Acts, we will see that this tradition is entirely likely for Luke's account in Acts does not attempt to offer a history of Judas's suicide at all. Rather Luke's account is an aside wherein God's wrath upon the "wickedness" of Judas is briefly mentioned. Matthew, however, offers a fuller history and shows Judas's despair. "Apparently his body was not discovered for some days, because it became bloated and his bowels gushed out."[36] Thus, "Acts 1:18-19 adds to our understanding."[37]

Such a tradition must be taken on faith, since it cannot be born out in the Scriptures alone, but what can be born out is the fact that Luke was a true historian (see notes on Luke 1:1-3) who researched his material and had certainly *seen* Matthew's gospel and probably even spoken to Matthew. If the account of Acts was truly contradictory to Matthew's then Luke would have known. The fact that he appears to see no difficulty is further indication that the tradition is true.

The Field of Blood
Another problem with these two accounts is less troublesome, but nevertheless confusing. Was the Field of Blood called so because it was bought with blood money or because Judas's blood was spilled upon it? Was the field bought with Judas's money or with the priests' money?

The money issue is simple. Judas threw the money back to the priests, but the priests refused to accept it. *They*, therefore, bought the field where Judas had died in *his* name. One can justly say the priests bought it, as in Matthew, or that it was "acquired ... with the price of his wickedness" (Acts 1:18). Either is equally correct.

As to the name of the field, the resolution is similar. I remember once my father and mother arguing about why my brother's middle name was "Wayne." Mom remembered him being named after a certain relative on her side, whereas dad remembered he was named after one of his relatives. *Both* are true. It was a Field of Blood because it was payed for with blood money, because Judas's blood was spilled upon it, and because it was to be a graveyard. *All* are equally true. What better name can there be?

Conclusion
The issue of the name is not troublesome as names often have multiple etymologies. In fact, traditions about the Potter's Field are intriguing and could shed even more light on the name and its multiple facets. Some believe that the Potter's Field is located in the Valley of Hinnom which is where Jeremiah prophesied the "valley of slaughter" (Jer. 7:32, 19:11) would take place and which was once an area where pagan human sacrifices took place.[38] As the burial place for Judas, it seems appropriate.

The tradition in regard to Judas's death also fits the test of validity. Although we must be careful to accept traditions which may or may not be true, there is no reason not to accept this one, for the tradition is both ancient and consistent. As in police work, when two eyewitnesses give differing accounts, any possible reconciliation of the two accounts *must* be weighed before assuming that one of the eyewitnesses is lying or in error. If the accounts can be reconciled then, barring evidence to the contrary, the eyewitness accounts must be accepted as valid and reconciled.

Interestingly enough, more debate over Judas and his motives has occurred than over his death. Erasmus merged the traditions[39] and believed Judas repented before his death,[40] but had he truly repented, he would never have committed suicide. Moreover, John 17:12 infers that Judas was damned as the "son of perdition." Despite this, some claim that Judas only betrayed Jesus because "probably he thought Christ would have prevented [the crucifixion] by a miracle."[41] Various other theories and traditions have been bandied about for ages but such traditions should be rejected because they conflict with Scripture and have no material support. The tradition of Judas's death, however, fits the Biblical stories and explains the apparent contradictions.

The Thirteenth Apostle
Acts 1:21-26

"They put forward two men, Joseph called Barsabbas (who was also called Justus), and Matthias. And they prayed ... and they drew lots for them, and the lot fell to Matthias; and he was added to the eleven apostles."

It may seem odd that this simple act of electing a new apostle is so hotly debated, but the sudden appearance of the apostle Paul, who remains one of the most famous of all the apostles (if not the most famous), has caused many to take pause and question the actions of the apostles. Were there really thirteen apostles? Were they supposed to elect an apostle to succeed Judas at all? Does Jesus alone have the authority to choose His own apostles? Did this set a pattern for apostolic succession to this very day? All these questions have emerged from the events which took place after Matthias's election, and to have a fair debate the evidences in favor of all the views must be discussed individually and fairly.

View #1 : Paul Was to Be the 12th Apostle
Judas was a follower of Christ from the beginning, and yet betrayed Him. The apostle Paul, however, began as a persecutor of the Christian faith, who turned away from his sin and became arguably the most famous of all the apostles, and yet he is often not counted among the twelve apostles. Many call him the thirteenth apostle or the "apostle to the gentiles."

This great irony of history, and of God's design, has led many to question the actions of the apostles when they elected Matthias as the replacement for Judas. They have argued that Jesus told them to wait until the coming of the Holy Spirit (cf. Acts 1:4) but they instead chose to elect by lots a replacement for Judas without waiting for the Holy Spirit. The arguments against the election of Matthias are as follows:[42]

1. There was no command from Jesus to do so
This argument is one made by inference. Jesus obviously had not given direct commands to His apostles since His ascension, and, therefore, could not have done so here. It may be argued that Jesus commanded them through the Holy Spirit, but the Holy Spirit had not descended for Pentecost was yet to come. This argument is thus tied to the fourth argument discussed below.

2. "Because Peter was habitually rash and forward"[43]
This is an argument that seems to question Peter's leadership and character. It is not so much an exegetical argument as it is one which questions Peter's judgment. By itself the argument has no merit except to point out that Peter was not above making mistakes and being premature in his actions. Moreover, it erroneously assumes that Peter was the acting force. This is debateable. Some have noted that Peter was not speaking *to* the apostles but *for* them. It was to "the *hundred and twenty*, for to them Peter spoke, and not to the eleven"[44] that Peter addressed their concerns. Nevertheless, even if it is granted that this was Peter's idea and that he was not above making rash decisions, then we must still have a better Scriptural basis for rejecting the election of Matthias.

3. Nothing else is recorded of Matthias

It is suggested that because nothing else is recorded of Matthias in the Bible, and little among the church fathers, Matthias could not have been a true apostle. Even Justus, who lost the election to Matthias, is mentioned in Colossians 4:11.[45] Does this invalidate the election? The answer is, "no." "History is equally silent as to most of the apostles."[46] Indeed, of the twelve disciples we never read another word in the Bible about Bartholomew, Thomas, or Simon the Zealot. There is also a question as to whether or not Jude was the same man as the disciple (see *Controversies in the Epistles* for this debate). Likewise, James the son of Alphaeus and Judas the son of James (also called Thaddaeus) may also be absent following this passage.

In short, Matthias' failure to appear in the rest of the Bible does not negate him as one of the twelve. If his election was invalid, then this must be deciphered elsewhere.

4. The Holy Spirit had not yet been sent

The first seemingly valid argument is that the Holy Spirit had not yet been sent and that the apostles had been told to wait. On one level this is a perfectly valid argument, but the command to wait is taken somewhat out of context. The actual passage reads, "He commanded them not to leave Jerusalem, but to wait for what the Father had promised ... the Holy Spirit" (1:4). Now it is clear that the apostles did wait in Jerusalem. Obviously they did not think that electing a new apostle was in any way a violation of this command.

Nonetheless, many have commented upon the method of the election. Because they elected Matthias by a casting of lots one commentator stated that reliance on "such methods of discovering the will of God is more like the Old Testament than the New Testament."[47] The entire idea of casting lots is equated with "chance" rather than the will of God.[48] Even Erasmus frowned upon the casting of lots, but noted that prayer was the main factor.[49] This does, however, call into question the entire decision given that the Holy Spirit had not yet come. More will be said of the use of casting lots below.

5. Paul was chosen personally by Christ

Perhaps the strongest argument made in defense of this view is that the apostle Paul was chosen not by the other apostles or by a casting of lots, but by Christ Himself. Indeed, all the apostles were chosen by Jesus Christ. Nowhere do we see any evidence that any apostle was to be chosen by anyone other than our Lord and Savior Jesus Christ. Paul, it would seem, was the perfect choice to replace a traitor who followed Christ but never knew Christ. Saul of Tarsus persecuted Jesus's followers but, as Judas betrayed Jesus, Saul betrayed the haters of Christ and became the most famous of the apostles.

Conversely many have argued that Paul was an apostle to the gentiles and not an "apostle of circumcission."[50] This argument delves heavily into the argument between covenant theologians and various dispensationalists, ranging from progressive dispensationalists to hyper-dispensationalists. For this reason, I will discuss the attempt to distinguish between the apostleship to gentiles and Jews separately below.

6. There can only be twelve apostles; not thirteen

Paul has often been called the "thirteenth apostle," but is there such a thing? Why did Peter himself state that they had to replace Judas? Could there not be eleven apostles? Anyone familiar with the Bible knows that twelve, like the numbers three and seven, is a Holy number. There were twelve tribes of Israel, from which are derived twelve stones (Exodus 39:14), twelve pillars (Exodus 24:4), twelve rods (Numbers 17:2), and many others. Only twelve times is the number thirteen found in the Bible, and none of those have symbolic significance. Nevertheless, since all the symbolic references to twelve derive from the twelve tribes themselves, this may appear to be an overstating of the case. Still, another case can be made for twelve, and only twelve.

In the book of Revelation twelve names are engraved upon the great wall of the New Jerusalem (Revelation 21). In that passage it says that twelve names are written on the gates for "the names of the twelve tribes of Israel" (21:12) and twelve names are engraved upon foundation stones for "the twelve names of the twelve apostles" (21:14). Note that there are only twelve apostles engraved upon the foundation stones. Is Paul, the most famous of the apostles, left out?

It has been noted that in early church history "some" lists omit Matthias, inserting Paul's name into the twelve.[51] The response to these critiques is that Paul was an apostle to gentiles, whereas the twelve were "apostles of circumcission,"[52] (cf. Galatians 2:8). This is the second view; that Paul was an apostle distinct from the twelve.

View #2 : Paul Was an Apostle to the Gentiles and Never One of the 12
One able commentator summarized this view in these words:

> "It is astonishing to hear able teachers of the Word talk and write of the mistake which the eleven made in the first chapter in the book of Acts in casting the lot and choosing Matthias. We have heard all kinds of criticism upon their action. They were, however, guided aright, and did *not* make a mistake, for they acted upon the Word of God in the Psalms, and in the casting of the lot they were fully authorized by the Old Testament Scriptures, and besides this, they did it in dependence on the Lord. It is also said by these brethren who see in the choosing of Matthias an error, the Lord wanted *Paul* to be the one who belongs to the twelve. This is the *worst* blunder of all. The Holy Spirit fully endorses the action of the eleven before Pentecost through Paul himself. In 1 Corinthians xv:5 we read that the risen Lord was seen by the *twelve*. In the eighth verse Paul says: 'And last of all, as to an abortion,

He appeared to me also.' It is clear from this passage that Paul does not belong to the twleve. Paul, as apostle to the Gentiles, is an apostle not from men nor through men (Gal. i:1); he received his apostleship from the risen and glorified Lord."[53]

This able argument does err in some ways. First, by mentioning Jesus's appearance to the "twelve" Paul does not in any way make a judgment upon Matthias's election. Matthias was considered one of the twelve and Paul's intention was not to debate that election, but to affirm his own apostleship in a very humble way saying, "I am the least of the apostles, and not fit to be called an apostle." The argument, therefore, has limited merit and is far from "clear." Another example of overkill is John MacArthur when he says, "Nothing in this passage indicates that this action is wrong. It is inconceivable that the Lord would allow such a crucial error ... while Paul was in no way inferior to the twelve, he was not one of their number ... the mission of the twelve was primarily to the nation of Israel, while he was the apostles sent to the Gentiles."[54] Note how MacArthur moves from a legitimate argument ("nothing in this passage indicates that this action is wrong") to an emotional assumption ("it is *inconceivable* that the Lord would allow such a crucial error"). If I had a dollar for every alleged "inconceivable" act which God allows I would be rich.

The main argument then is that "if the church had here committed a mistake, there would have been some indication in the history to that effect."[55] Because there is none, it is assumed that no such mistake took place. The second argument on behalf of this view is that Paul allegedly distinguishes himself as an apostle to the gentiles (cf. Romans 11:13).

Now it is apparent that of these two views, there are three mitigating factors which ultimately determine their validity. The first is the question of apostolic succession. Much rides on this very concept. Is there even such a thing as apostolic succession? If so, how are the successors chosen? This leads to the second question which is the question of the casting of the lots. Was this Biblical? It such a method of "chance"[56] a fair way to determine God's will? Finally, if Paul was an "apostle to gentiles" does this negate his being one of the twelve? Must there be two separate categories of apostles? To this end, what is an apostle? These are the fundamental questions that need to be answered before evaluating the two views cited above.

Apostolic Succession
The question of apostolic succession is one that has been hotly, even violently, debated for literally thousands of years. Some preachers claim to be modern day apostles and the Catholic church maintains that the pope is the successor of Peter himself and an apostle. Of course we might asks why there is only one pope rather than twelve? Obviously, this only further begs the question. At this

point it is not necessary to debate the office of the papacy, or self proclaimed apostles, but only the question of apostlolic succession in days of the apostles.

1. What is an Apostle?

Before determining how apostolic succession works, if there is such a thing, we must obviously define an apostle. Etymologically, apostle comes from αποστολος (*apostolos*) which most literally means "one who is sent," such as a missionary. In the generic sense of the term, it is a missionary or even delegate as in Philippians 2:25 where the word is usually translated as "messenger" (King James, NAS, NIV, NLT, RSV, etc). However, it is obvious that the term is used in a technical sense as a title in the Bible. The apostle Paul is very clear, for example, that the "the signs of a true apostle were performed among you with all perseverance, by signs and wonders and miracles" (2 Corinthians 12:12). Obviously this is not a mere missionary or delegate. A "true apostle" is marked by signs.

Additionally, Peter believes that he should "have accompanied us all from the time that the Lord Jesus went in and out among us - beginning with the baptism of John until the day that He was taken up from us - [and] must be a witness with us of His resurrection" (Acts 1:21-22). Now if Peter is correct then it would appear that Paul could not have been an apostle since he was not with them from the time of the baptism by John. However, Paul identified himself as "an apostle not *sent* from men nor through the agency of man, but through Jesus Christ and God the Father, who raised Him from the dead" (Galatians 1:1). Thus he affirms that he had seen the resurrected Christ.

Here then we have an apparent discrepancy in regard to apostleship. Peter wanted to select one who had "been a disciple from the beginning of Christ's ministry"[57] but Paul declared that it was Jesus Christ Himself who chose him as an apostle. Is this truly a contradiction? No, for Peter did not necessarily declare that the disciple *had* to be a disciple from the beginning; only that the apostles had decided he should be. Is this grasping at straws? No. If being an apostle required being a follower from the time of John the Baptist then the apostle Paul could not even have been the thirteenth apostle. Consequently, we can agree that an apostle must have seen the resurrected Christ, but the apostles' requirement of having been present since the baptism was in addition to the requirements for apostleship, and not synonymous with it.

One final question is whether or not the title apostle can refer to more than the twelve (or thirteen).[58] Men such as John Lightfoot and others have listed numerous passages they believe prove that an apostle can refer to others outside of the twelve. However, the verses in question are suspect. As aforementioned "apostle," when used as a verb, can refer to a missionary, but when used as a title there are no clear verses to prove otherwise. Nevertheless, it is prudent to take a quick look at these passages (see Ephesians 4:11 in *Controversies in the Epistles* for a more complete debate).

William Barclay believes that Barnabas, James the Just, Silvanus, Andronicus, and Junia were apostles,[59] but when we examine those passages closely the answer is not so clear. Romans 16:7 says that Andronicus and Junias "are outstanding among the apostles." Does this mean they were counted among the apostles? No. Most translations simply read that they "are of note among the apostles." In other words, the apostles considered Andronicus and Junias to be great men of note. They were respected by the apostles. This does not say that they were apostles.

In another passage Paul says, "we [did not] seek glory from men, either from you or from others, even though as apostles of Christ we might have asserted our authority" (1 Thessalonians 2:6). Since Silvanus is listed as a co-author with Paul, Barclay argues that Silvanus must also have been an apostle, although he curiously omits Timothy who is also listed as a co-author. Nevertheless, this is hardly proof that Silvanus was an apostle.[60] Paul includes Silvanus and Timothy with him out of humility and respect, but the passage can hardly be taken as proof that *all* of them were apostles. Paul is using the editorial "we" as he often does in various other passages. This verse is, therefore, inconclusive.

The same can be said for other passages such as Philippians 2:25. There most translations render the word *apostolon* (αποστολον) as "messenger" rather than apostle. This is because Paul is using the common form of the word, and not using it as a title. It is "your messenger," not "God's apostle." A similar passage is 2 Corinthians 8:23. Once again, there is no proof that these were apostles in the titular sense of the word.

Next we come to James the Just (Acts 14:4, 14; Galatians 1:17, 19), but as I discuss under Acts 15, there is some doubt as to whether or not James the Just is the same as James the Less. Here I will simply summarize that James was an apostle from the time of Jesus. This James was probably not Jesus's step-brother, as is often assumed. This leaves us only with Barnabas. In Acts 14:14 Luke refers to "the apostles Barnabas and Paul." Here then Barnabas does appear to bear the title, although all admit that Luke is using the word more loosely here. So does this prove that apostle, even when used as a title, may refer to more than the twelve? In fairness we can say that the word "apostle" may be used in a loose sense, but none of the passages can prove that there are more than twelve true apostles of Christ.

In summary, an apostle must be someone who had seen the resurrected Christ, who had performed miracles, and who was chosen by the Lord Jesus Himself. These three things are all required for a "true apostle" (2 Corinthians 12:12). Even if there were more than twelve apostles, *no one* can be an apostle who does not fit all three requirements.

2. Is Apostolic Succession Biblical?

Judas was not a true believer. This is apparent not only from his actions but from the Scriptures. Not only is Satan depicted as possessing Judas

(Luke 22:3, John 13:27), but Jesus Himself spoke of his apostles saying, "I guarded them and not one of them perished but the son of perdition" (John 17:12). Thus Judas was never a true apostle. Consequently, the replacement of Judas was unique. There were to be twelve apostles, not eleven. We cannot conclude then that the replacement of Judas set a pattern for apostolic succession. Indeed, one author argues that Paul may be considered a successor to James rather than Judas,[61] but this opens a can of worms. If Matthias was the successor of Judas and Paul the successor of James (who actually didn't die until after Paul was converted), then we must assume a never ending succession of all twelve apostles. Nowhere is this evident in the Scriptures. Judas's replacement (not succession) was unique in that he was never a true apostle.

Perhaps the strongest argument against apostolic succession is the very definition of "apostle" as stated above. In order to be a true apostle one must have seen the risen Lord.[62] Obviously no one since the original apostles could meet the requirements of true apostleship.

It is apparent that Judas's "succession" was a unique one time event. This event implies, however, that eleven apostles were not sufficient. There were to be twelve apostles, and only twelve. There could be no continuous succession of apostles, but the eleven were not content to allow Judas's standing as the twelfth apostle. The argument that "the subsequent appointment of Paul to the apostleship did not discredit or abrogate this decision, but simply enlarged the original number of apostles"[63] is thus invalidated for there were not thirteen true apostles, but twelve. This is why some ancient apostolic lists replace the name of Matthias name with Paul.[64] If there were only twelve, we must decide between the two, for there will only be twelve names upon the foundation stones of New Jerusalem (Revelation 21:14).

Casting the Lots
It seems apparent that there was not a pattern established for a continual succession of apostles. Nevertheless, the apostles did believe that there was a necessity of twelve true apostles. Jesus had not told them that He intended to convert Saul of Tarsus, and it is therefore not to be held against them that they decided to hold their own election from among the seventy disciples (Luke 10:1, 17). The question here is not whether or not they should have held the election, but whether or not the method in which they did so truly resulted in the efficacious will of God.

John Calvin saw this election as the duty of the chuch.[65] There was no doubt in his mind that it was required. However, some have commented that "the expression 'the lot fell upon' is not consistent with the notion of voting"[66] and that such "chance ... methods of discovering the will of God is more like the Old Testament than the New Testament."[67] The hyper-dispensationalist responds to this by stating that the Church had not yet coming into being (see

"The Establishment of the Church" debate below) and that they were still under Old Testament law. Of course that only begs the question about whether or not the apostles were "Old Testament" or "New Testament" and whether or not the Church was truly a part of the apostolic ministry. Obviously, it would be a hard argument to make that the apostles had no part in the Church.

Nonetheless, the casting of lots was not unprecedented, as alluded to by the author above. There are at least ninteen references to casting of lots in the Old Testament. The key factor should be prayer, thus while Erasmus frowned upon the casting of lots, he noted that the apostles' prayer was efficacious.[68] Indeed, prayer should be the critical factor if we are to believe that God, and not the apostles, made the final choice, and yet this begs a further question. Did the apostles limit God's choices?

In ancient Israel the priests and kings were often spoken of as consulting with the "Urim and Thummim" (cf. Number 27:21 and 1 Samuel 28:6). These were actually stones placed in the breastplate of the high priest (Exodus 28:30) and, according to tradition, the Urim and Thummim glowed in order to signify God's pleasure or displeasure.[69] However, another tradition says that there were actually three stones. One respresented "yes," another "no," and a third was "neutral."[70] However, it is more likely that one of the stones would glow for "yes" and the second for "no," but if the answer was "neither" then perhaps both stones would glow. This would insure that God's choice was not limited. Thus the priests would pray for God's counsel and receive an answer.

Here the apostles appear to follow this pattern with the exception that there is no third lot. Lots are mentioned only for Justus and Matthias. Does this mean that the apostles inadvertently limited God's choice? How could God have answered, "neither of these men is the one I choose" if the apostles only gave God two choices? This is human nature and a mistake made by even the most righteous of men. God's plan is not always our plan. I can testify that if someone had told me twenty years ago that I would be making a Christian movie in India, I would have laughed at them. At that time I did not even know a single Indian, had never seen a Bollywood movie, and was content to never leave my home of Texas. I had my own plans. God has His plans.

Paul declared that he was "an apostle not *sent* from men nor through the agency of man, but through Jesus Christ and God the Father, who raised Him from the dead" (Galatians 1:1). Matthias was an apostles chosen by lot through prayer by the eleven apostles. *If* there were to be only twelve apostles, then Paul would seem to have the greater claim, but this rest upon that very question. Could there be a thirteenth?

Apostle to the Gentiles?
The final question which must be answered is whether or not God appointed a separate apostle to the gentiles, as opposed to the other apostles. Often we see

terms thrown around like "apostle of circumcision"[71] as opposed to the "apostle to the gentiles." Obviously, we must examine the Bible to see if these phrases are Biblical and, if they are, whether or not they constitute an "enlarg[ing of] the original number of apostles."[72]

First, the term "apostle of circumcision" is taken loosely from Galatians 2:8 in which Paul declares that Peter had an "apostleship to the circumcised." This phrase is idiomatic for a ministry to Jews. Colossians 4:11 is also cited as proof wherein Paul commends "the only fellow workers for the kingdom of God who are from the circumcision." In fact, Paul does not even mention *any* of the apostles in this passage. He mentions only Tychicus, Onesimus, Aristarchus, Mark, and Justus. It is apparent that the phrase "from the circumcision" was idiomatic for "Jewish," and probably only refers to the last three names. So it is clear that Peter had a ministry to Jews, but nothing here indicates that his ministry was restricted to Jews. In fact, Acts 10 confirms that Peter was not to neglect gentile converts, and in Acts 11:1-18 Peter was confronted by Jewish Christians who were offended by Peter's ministry to the uncircumcised! Thus it appears that the "apostleship to the circumcised" found in Galatians 2:8 merely refers to the fact that Peter ministry was predominantly to Jews, not that it was restricted to Jews.

The idea of an "apostle to the gentiles" had much greater merit. The apostle Paul refers to himself in Romans as "an apostle of gentiles" (11:13), but only one other passage mentions his apostleship in direct connection with gentile ministry. That is 1 Timothy 2:7 wherein he says, "I was appointed a preacher and an apostle (I am telling the truth, I am not lying) as a teacher of the Gentiles in faith and truth." Clearly, Paul considered that his ministry was to the gentiles. He was the first of the apostles (but not the last) to reach out to the gentile world at large and to concentrate on winning pagans to Christ. In this, however, he was followed by all but two (possibly three) of the other apostles. Only the two Jameses, and possibly Matthias, never left Israel for the mission field (James the Greater because he was martyred in Jerusalem as recorded in Acts 12:2).

The Great Commission of Jesus Christ commanded to the original apostles after His resurrection that they should "go and make disciples of *all* the nations" (Matthew 28:19). It is, therefore, a mistake to argue that the original disciples were specifically apostles to Jews and that Paul was distinct in his ministry to the gentiles. It is true that Paul was the first to branch out and move away from the Israelites, and that God called him to a special ministry among the heathen. Indeed, this is one of God's great ironies for Paul was clearly the strictest and most "Jewish" of all the apostles. In Galatians 2:14 Paul recounts his confrontation with Peter wherein "I said to Cephas in the presence of all, 'If you, being a Jew, live like the gentiles and not like the Jews, how *is it that* you compel the gentiles to live like Jews?'" Thus Paul scolded Peter for "living like a gentile" while commanding gentiles to "live like Jews." Paul showed *all* the apostles who had come before him that the Great Commission was not restricted to Israel. In his own words, "to the Jew first, and then to the gentile" (Romans 1:16; 2:10).

Eventually, all but two (possibly three) of the apostles were driven away from Israel and went on to have ministries to the gentiles. It is debated whether Peter ministered to Iraq or Italy (see "Did Peter Die in Rome" for debate), but he certainly departed for the mission field. The apostle John is credited with founding the churches of Smyrna, Pergamos, Sardis, Philadelphia, Laodicea, and Thyratira,[73] all in modern day Turkey. Andrew's mission field was in modern day Turkey, Greece,[74] and even Scythia (modern day Romania and Ukraine).[75] Philip went to the people of Carthage Africa.[76] Bartholomew ministered in Syria, part of modern day Turkey, Iraq, and Iran, and even went as far as India[77] where he is credited with having translated the gospel of Matthew into their native tongue.[78] Matthew travelled to Ethiopia[79] and Egypt.[80] Thomas established a great mission field in the east reaching Carmania, Hyrcania, Bactria, Magia[81] (all in Iran and Afghanistan) and most notably becoming the father of the south Indian church.[82] Simon moved across north Africa, preaching in countries like Egypt, Cyrene, Mauritania, and Lybia[83] before becoming the first to venture to the far north and reach Britain.[84] Judas Thaddaeus ministered to Mesopotamia, Syria, Arabia, Edessa, and finally Persia.[85]

Only the two Jameses and Matthias may never left Israel. James the Greater was martyred in Judea as recorded in Acts 12:2 around 44 A.D.[86] James the "Lesser" is believed by some to have been an overseer at Jerusalem[87] and remained there until his martyrdom. Finally, of Matthias, the very man whose election is questioned by some, we read very little. It is most likely that Matthias was one of only three apostles who spent his entire missionary life in the Holy Land.[88]

What then, asks the critic, of Galatians 2:7-8 wherein Paul says:

> "I had been entrusted with the gospel to the uncircumcised, just as Peter *had been* to the circumcised (for He who effectually worked for Peter in *his* apostleship to the circumcised effectually worked for me also to the Gentiles)."

Indeed, there is no doubt that it was Paul who first ventured beyond the borders of Israel to preach the gospel. This is the very reason that he calls himself an "apostle of gentiles" (Romans 11:13), and it is equally certain that the other apostles remained to preach the gospel to the Jews of Israel to whom the gospel was offered "first" (Romans 1:16; 2:10). This is not in debate. Nor is it in debate that even after leaving Israel the apostles went "to the Jew first." What is in debate whether or not the twelve apostles were "apostles of circumcision" as distinct from an "apostle of gentiles." In this there is much debate, for why, if the twelve were to Israel alone, did Jesus command them to go *unto all the nations* (Matthew 28:19)? Why did they, in fact, leave and follow Paul's lead? Why did so many of them die in foreign lands, rather than in their own homeland? The answer is clear. Because from the very beginning Jesus planned that they should *all* (every apostle) go and preach the gospel to *"all the nations"* (Matthew 24:14). If we take the Bible at face value then it is clear that Jesus cannot return until "this gospel of the kingdom shall be preached in the whole world as a testimony to all the nations, and then the end will come" (Matthew 24:14).

Only the most extreme form of hyperdispensationalism can deny that all the apostles were commanded to preach unto gentiles as well as Jews. It was "to the Jew first, and then to the gentile" (Romans 1:16; 2:10), and not for Paul alone. If this is not so then we must believe that the apostles violated Jesus's command when they left for the mission field! We must believe that the apostles were murdered for disobedience to God, rather than suffering martyrdom in cause of the Great Commission. Worse yet, if their ministry was to Israel *alone* then we would have to say that they failed, for Israel did not convert to Christianity. Can we truly believe that the twelve apostles failed in their ministry? Are we to believe that only Paul was successful? No, they kept the Great Commission and established the church as it is known today. The apostles succeeded in planting the seeds.

Evaluation
As the reader can plainly see the preponderance of the evidence seems to favor Paul as the twelfth apostle. However, this is not a decision to be taken lightly for it is decision which is made predominantly outside of the Scriptures. The strongest argument in favor of Matthias is that "if the church had here committed a mistake, there would have been some indication in the history to that effect."[89] While true it is also clear that Luke wrote as a historian, not a theologian. He did not presume to question the apostles, for Paul himself did not seek to elevate himself or denigrate Matthias, regardless of whether or not Matthias truly was the twelfth apostle. Consequently, we cannot make too much out of this fact. Nor can we, however, emphatically say that the apostles did err.

My personal inclination is that God did indeed intend that Paul would replace Judas, for as Judas was a follower of Christ who betrayed him, Paul was an enemy of Christ who became a most faithful witness. Who would better fill the vacancy left by a traitor but a man who once persecuted our Savior? Nevertheless, until the foundation stones for New Jerusalem are laid (Revelation 21:14) we shall not conclusively know the answer, nor should we allow this debate to detract us from our duty ... to "go and make disciples of *all* the nations" (Matthew 28:19).

William Hole – Jesus Ascending to Heaven – 1905

3

Pentecost

Pentecost is a Jewish holiday commemorating the giving of the law by Moses. It follows Passover (the week in which Christ was crucified and resurrected), which commemorates the passing over of Jewish children when the final plague in Egypt slew the first-born children of the Egyptians. The Exodus took place immediately following Passover and the giving of the Law occurred seven weeks, or 49 days, later.

In the Christian church, however, Pentecost has another meaning. Just as Passover became celebrated for the resurrection of Christ, another significant even took place on the feast of Pentecost. This was the bestowing of the Holy Spirit upon all believers. The event is significant in history for many reasons, but also very controversials for an equal number of reasons. As we shall see, the bestowing of the gifts and the Holy Spirit has led to many divisions to this very day. The Pentecostal movement takes its very name from this event. Nonetheless, the first controversy is the very establishment of the church itself. What is the church? When was it formed? What is its purpose?

The Establishment of the Church

The single greatest controversy among Acts and the epistles, without question, is the question of the church and Israel. This topic will appear repeatedly throughout this book. Since I prefer exegetical deduction to eisogetical induction, I do not like to state my conclusions before reviewing the evidence for and against a particular view. However, it is necessary to define the dominant theological views which intrude upon the Scriptures and their interpretation. The first point at which they intrude is in Acts 2, because it is here that some believe the church was established, and not before, nor after.

The very question of the church begs many more questions. Questions about the Old Testament covenants (*plural*) and about the New Testament. Questions about Israel and the nations. Questions about Jews and gentiles. These questions are discussed by the apostle Paul throughout many of his epistles, and touched upon many times here in Acts. Before answering the question about when the church was established, we must know what exact the church *is*. Since there is no single Bible passage which defines church in the strictest sense of the word, it is best to deliniate the four primary doctrines which lay behind the various interpretations. Then I will look at specific issues brought up by these views. Finally, I will summarize my own conclusions, but only as a preliminary measure, for each individual passage where these topics arise must be treated *within their context*, and not interpreted to fit *any* particular theology.

The four views relating to the church and its relationship to the Old Testament covenants and/or Israel are called covenant theology, dispensationalism, hyperdispensationalism (or ultradispensationalism), and progressive dispensationalism. *Each* of these views can be traced back to the each church fathers in one respect or another. All wrongly accuse the other of being a "new" theology invented in recent years. All lie. A covenant is properly a contract. In the Bible it is often a contract or promise which God has made with some person or people. A dispensation is that which is covered under a covenant. It encompasses the time, duration, and effect of the covenant in all its aspects. Covenants and dispensations go hand in hand, yet these terms are applied to specific theologies and as a result some see them as entirely different things. In fact, they are both a part of the same thing; how God has dealt with man in history. These theologies have become important in recent years because of the restoration of Israel and the rise of interest in Last Days prophecies, but to one extent or another each and every view is as old as the Bible.

Covenant Theology

Covenant theology is very closely associated with Replacement theology. Replacement theology is that doctrine which teaches that the church has replaced Israel. Covenant theology teaches that there are only two covenants; the old and the new, and that the new replaced the old. It is obvious how the two teachings draw upon one another since the old covenants (*plural*) were made predominantly with Israel.

Covenant Theology is at best a simplification of the Biblical covenants; at worst it is an anti-Semitic heresy which makes God out to be a liar, for it is clear that many (but not all) of the Old Testament covenants were *unconditional*. The very existence of Israel today should be proof of that fact in itself, yet some people forget Paul's warning to gentiles in Romans, "do not be conceited, but fear; for if God did not spare the natural branches (Israel), He will not spare you, either" (11:20-21).

In terms of the innauguration of the church, covenant theologians tend to begin the church with the Cross itself. They argued that the church began immediately; an argument that is not in itself without merit, but again simplifies an issue which, as the reader will see, is not simple.

Ultradispensationalism

If Covenant theology is on one side of the argument, the far side of the other end is ultra or hyperdispensationalism. This is an extreme variant of traditional dispensationalism. I list this view before traditional dispensationalism because it is on the polar opposite end of covenant theology. Whereas covenant theologians see the church replacing Israel, ultradispensationalism makes a rigid and extreme distinction between the church and Israel so that the two can in no way interrelate. Ultradispensationalists are often quoted as "mainstream" dispensationalism so as to demonize dispensationalism because some (but in actuality only a few) Hyperdispensationalists go so far as to create what has been called two separate gospels; one applying to Israel, another applying to the church alone. Such extremist views are in all honesty not even mainstream among Hyperdispensationalists, but all Hyperdispensationalists do make a rigid distinction between the church and Israel that goes beyond that found in traditional dispensationalism. They also emphasize the church "mystery" in an extreme manner, so that not even a hint of the church may be found anywhere before Acts 2.

Among Hyperdispensationalists, most believe that the church began in Acts 2 with Pentecost, but others argue that it did not begin until much later, during the ministry of Paul, or even in 70 A.D. when Israel fell to the Romans. Each of these views has some merit, but ironically simplify the problem just as covenant theology does (albeit in a different manner). Making an extreme and rigid distinction between Israel and the church can often lead to as many heresies as those who deny any distiction at all. Moreover, this view must ignore the common use of the word church found in the Bible and apply a technical definition to a word which only seldom used in a technical sense.

Dispensationalism

Traditional dispensationalism acknowledges the difference between Israel and the church, but does not make the church a distinctly New Covenant entity. The early dispensationalists, such as John Darby and Sir Robert Anderson, frequently spoke of the "Jewish church" of the Old Testament, as opposed to the largely gentile church of the new.[90] For them, the church is the assembly of believers from any and all ages, whether under the old covenants (plural) or the New Covenant. However, they obviously acknowledge that the church age is different from the older dispensation in as much as God is working to convert the gentile world during Israel's chastisement. This is the key difference. Traditional dispensationalists recognize that this age is one in which Israel is chastized, but not abandoned. The church does not replace Israel, but grows its gentile fruits until Israel repents and is restored.

The reader will see that this is the view I favor, and the view which best suits the texts. Acts is a time during which the apostles were slowly coming to this knowledge. Israel is never rejected nor replaced, but gentile converts soon outnumber Jewish converts until it is clear that Israel is to again be dispersed and punished for its sins as it did once before in Babylon, but as before, she will be restored, repent, and receive all the blessings God promised to her.

Progressive Dispensationalism
For a time covenant theology and ultradispensationalism had become the dominant views. Nevertheless, no one likes to call themselves "ultra" or "hyper" anything. Consequently, ultradispensationalism became erroneously associated with traditional dispensationalism. In time two professors from Dallas Theological Seminary, once the bastion of dispensational theology, wrote a book entitled "Progressive Dispensationalism." This view borrowed heavily from George Eldon Ladd, a "conservative" covenant theologian. In essense it attempts to take the best of both worlds by claiming that God's promises to Israel are present "now" in a spiritual sense, but will be more literally present "later" to Israel in the future. It is thus a compromise position that attempts to argue for both sides. It spiritualizes certain passages in the present, while leaving room for a literal fulfillment of God's promises in the future.

What is the Church?
Obviously each of these views interprets the church in a particular way, but is that way consistent with what the Bible teaches? What exactly is the church? Is it a gentile priesthood in the time of Israel's chastizement? Is it the body of believers after the time of Christ? Is it an assembly or congregation of believers in a local city? Is it, in fact, all of these things? Or more?

The word church is found approximately 77 times in the New Testament. It comes from the Greek word εκκλησια (*ekklesia*). That word is variously translated as "congregation, assembly, gathering (of religious, political, or unofficial groups)."[91] Its most literal meaning is, therefore, an assembly or gathering of the Christian community. However, there is no doubt that the Bible uses this term, at times, in a larger sense of the word, as applying to all believers whether they are gathered together or not. In this sense, they are a congregation of God's children (both natural and adopted). This is the case when the word church is coupled with God, as in "the church of God" (cf. Acts 12:5; 1 Corinthians 10:32, 11:22; Galatians 1:13; etc.). Thus church can be synonymous with all believers or it may refer to a local assembly.

Furthermore, the Old Testament equivalent of "church" is "congregation" and the Greek *Septuagint* translation of the Old Testament uses the word εκκλησια (*ekklesia*) in place of congregation. Moreover, the NAS Bible (and others) sometimes translates εκκλησια (*ekklesia*) in the New Testament as "congregation" (cf. Acts 7:38) when it is speaking about the time of Moses. Thus the "church" of the New Testament and the "congregation" of Israel are uses in the same way. Sometimes it is a "congregation" of Jewish people gathering to meet with Moses, and at other times it is used to refer to the entire "congregation" of Israel, meaning all the people of Israel. The two terms are therefore virtually identical, save that the "church" is not made up entirely of Israelites.

It is, therefore, no wonder that John Darby refuses to translate εκκλησια (*ekklesia*) as church anywhere in his Bible translations, instead preferring "assembly." We have adopted so many assumptions about the word "church" from our local churches or teachers that we read those assumptions into the text without even thinking about it. Therefore, Darby's choice to translate the word most literally as "assembly" may be one designed to make the reader pause and think about the context, rather than reading our assumptions about the church which we absorbed as if by osmosis from childhood.

It is for this reason that, governing the context of a particular passage, I prefer not to define "church" in the general sense of the word. It is apparent that the church of today is different from that of the Old Testament, but only in a limited sense. The church includes believers from all the nations whereas the congregation of Israel was limited to Israel. Both words can be used locally of an assembly or in the larger sense of all the members of the community of believers.

Is the Church a Mystery?
The next fundamental question to this debate is whether or not the church is a "mystery." This concept of "mystery" is central to the theology of ultradispensationalism. It is also found, to a lesser degree, among traditional dispensationalists and even some progressive dispensationalists. It is therefore important to understand if this is a Biblical teaching or a theological device.

Mystery in the Old Testament
The word usually translated as "mystery" in the Old Testament is חזו (*heza*) which is literally a "revelation"[92] of a secret. It is thus a revealing something hidden. The key idea is then of something which is hidden. Indeed, the King James Bible translates חזו (*heza*) as "secret revealed."

Now this word appears primarily in the book of Daniel where it is used six times of God revealing some hidden mystery (Daniel 2:18-19, 27, 30, 47; 4:9). In five of these cases it involves a prophecy about the future, and particularly about the future gentile nations of the earth. However, it is in Daniel 9:26-27 where many see the greatest mystery of all, for in this prophecy of seventy *shevim* (week-years – a duration of seven years similar to the modern decade but composed of sevens) there appears to be a gap between the first sixty-nine *shevim* and the last *shevim*. I have discussed this prophecy in depth in *Controversies in the Prophets*, *Controversies in the Gospels*, and *Controversies in Revelation*, so I will only repeat my conclusion here. The gap between the first sixty-nine week-years and the last week-year covers the current time period, often called the "church age." Thus many see this gap as a mystery involving the church itself. Dwight Pentecost says "this interval was anticipated by Christ when He prophesied the establishing of the church (Matt. 16:18)."[93]

Thus we can say that God did not reveal all the secrets to Daniel, but we can also say that he was not ignorant of them. It was his prophecy which hinted at such an interval. He may not have been told what would happen during this interval, but he surely knew that it existed. Thus we may compare this mystery to a detective story. We are given clues, but not given all the answers. So also Daniel was given clues about the future, but not all the answers were given to him.

Mystery in the Gospels

The word mystery comes from the Greek word μυστηριον (*mysterion*). It appears only once in the gospels, that in Mark 4:11, but this is a significant verse. In that passage Jesus said, "To you has been given the mystery of the kingdom of God, but those who are outside get everything in parables." This is significant for it involves the very issue which covenant theologians and dispensationalists debate; namely, the "mystery of the kingdom of God." What is the "kingdom of God"? What is its "mystery"?

It is both important, and ironic, to note that Jesus was telling the apostles that they have been "given the mystery" which means that they *understood* the mystery. The secret had been revealed to them, but to "those who are outside" it remains a mystery. How ironic then that believers in the church today have placed themselves "outside"!

Mystery in the Pauline Epistles

The word "mystery" or "secret" appears seventeen times in the Pauline epistles, compared with five times in the rest of the New Testament (four times in the book of Revelation). Several of these passage bear a direct impact upon our debate. The first appearance is in Romans 11:25 and is about the salvation of Israel. The subject of Romans 11 is extensive and is debated in *Controversies in the Epistles*. Thus I will only quote the relevant verse as its context is discussed more fully in Chapter 3:

> "For I do not want you, brethren, to be uninformed of this mystery – so that you will not be wise in your own estimation – that a partial hardening has happened to Israel until the fullness of the Gentiles has come in" (Romans 11:25).

For those who make no distinction between the church and Israel, this verse is problematic. Is he saying that the "church" will be "hardened?" And if the "church" is "Israel" then why is Paul talking about a "hardening ... *until* the fullness of the Gentiles has come in"? Does this not mean that when the fullness of Gentiles has come in, Israel's hardening will cease? Does this not prove that the church and Israel cannot be the same? What then is the "mystery"? The conclusion of the book of Romans gives us more clear answer.

> "The revelation of the mystery which has been kept secret for long ages past, but now is manifested, and by the Scriptures of the prophets, according to the commandment of the eternal God, has been made known to all the nations ... through Jesus Christ" (Romans 16:25-27).

In other words, the mystery has been revealed through Jesus Christ "too all the nations." It is not the "church" *per se* that is a mystery but the expansion of the "Jewish Church," as Anderson and the early dispensationalists called it, to all nations and people. Does this expansion somehow negate the role of national Israel or exclude them? That is a debate reserved for Romans 11. It is sufficient to say here that the issue is not truly the *church*, but *national* Israel. Will national Israel play a role in God's future kingdom? I believe it will, but to answer that query here would be to divert from the topic. That topic is of the expansion of the church to gentiles during the period of Israel's chastizement, and of the time frame in which this took place.

When Did the Church Start?
Ultradispensationalists make every effort to pinpoint an exact moment or time in which the "church" came into existence. However, neither dispensationalists nor covenant theologians are united in their opinions on this matter. There are eight major theories on the institution of the church, but these can be categorized into five since three are but variants of one of the other views. These theories cross all theological boundaries. Advocates from almost every position will hold to one of the views listed below, although obviously some views are more popular with a particular group. Let us examine these views.

View 1. The Church Always Existed
As I have alluded several times, the Old Testament word "assembly" is translated into Greek as εκκλησια (*ekklesia*) or "church." Church is used of an congregation of believers. When coupled with "Israel" it refers to national Israel as is often the case in the Old Testament. When coupled with "God" it refers to all believers.

Some of the early dispensationalists referred to ancient Israel as the "Jewish church."[94] It is perhaps relevant that Sir Robert Anderson always put this phrase in quotation marks, but he nevertheless acccepted that the "church" is not new. He explicitly rejected the idea that Christianity was a "new" religion,[95] and in this he is absolutely correct. Christianity was not "new." It was the same religion as taught by Moses and Daniel and Isaiah and Elijah, but it was purified of traditions and expanded to include all the nations of the world.

It is therefore possible to say that the "church" always existed, but we would still have to acknowledge that something changed. No longer is the church "Jewish." It is today populated overwhelmingly by gentiles during the time of Israel's chastizement. God has not forgotten the Jews, nor national Israel (as we see in the many prophesies and promises of the Bible), but today, in this age (or dispensation), clearly something is different. We may then inquire when this change first took place. Let us then examine the other views.

View 2. The Ministry of Jesus Began the Church

Some believe that the church began with the very appearance of Jesus. Alternately, there are two variants of this view include that the church began with the Cross or with the Resurrection. Since these are all essentially the same argument, I have listed these together. In favor of these views is the fact that the word "church" appears twice in the gospel of Matthew (Matthew 16:18; 18:17), indicating that this was not some new "mystery" as of yet unreaveled. Those who say that Matthew was written at a much later time are being intellectually dishonest since Jesus either said it or he didn't. Moreover, his dealings with Samaritans (John 4:9) and a Roman centurion (Matthew 8:5-13) indicates that Jesus was not hesitant to preach to the gentiles. The strongest evidence for this view is the Great Commission in which they are commanded to "go and make disciples of *all the nations*" (Matthew 28:19).

Evidence against this view is the fact that Jesus was clearly emphasizing the gospel to the Jews. In several passages Jesus even seems derogatory of gentiles (Matthew 15:26; Mark 7:27). It is clear that while Jesus did not hesitate to accept gentiles into the fold, His ministry was to the Jews. He did not go to Rome nor step foot outside of the Holy Land all the days of His life. His ministry was to the Jew first, and then to the gentile (cf. Romans 1:16).

Logically, the appearance of the church and the Great Commission shows that Jesus was not hiding the mystery as it was revealed through Him (Romans 16:27) but neither does it prove that the "church" *began* with Jesus's ministry. Furthermore it is obvious that the church at that time was almost exclusively *Jewish*. Therefore, the gentile church cannot be said to have begun during Jesus's ministry.

View 3. The Church Begins with Pentecost (Acts 2)

One of the most popular views, particularly among many (but by no means all) ultradispensationalists, is that the "church" dates to Pentecost. Mal Couch even declares that "all admit that the church begins in Acts 2 with the outpouring and filling of the Holy Spirit."[96] While the boast of claiming that "all admit" can be discarded it is true that something significant happened in Acts 2 with the bestowing of the Holy Spirit. It was a signature event prophesied in Joel (Acts 2:17-21), but this only begs the question does it not? Ultradispensationalists claim that the church itself is a mystery not to be found in the Old Testament and yet their proof that the church began on this day is the prophecy of Joel 2 in the Old Testament! Certainly the outpouring of the Holy Spirit signifies some aspect of the New Covenant but while Mal declares that this is the "launching of the New Covenant"[97] he goes on to say that the New Covenant "will have its ultimate completion and fulfillment in the kingdom"[98] and not in the present. Thus this present age cannot be considered synoymous with the blessings of the New Covenant. Traditional dispensationalist H. A. Ironside stated that "it is folly to speak of a new covenant with the church, when no former covenant had been made with us."[99] He even goes so far as to say that "the new covenant, as such, has its place in connection with [the Jews] alone."[100]

Now I do not wish to be sidetracked into a debate upon the New Covenant, for I have discussed that in *Controversies in the Prophets*. It is sufficient to say here that "because Israel rejected the covenant in the first advent, gentiles availed themselves of the provisions (cf. Romans 9:30-33); and Israel will yet ratify it at the climax of history."[101] In short, the church is a part of the covenant but it is with Israel that the covenant is made (see notes on Romans 11 in *Controversies in the Epistles*). Having said this, we are brought back to our original query. Did the New Covenant, or the church, *begin* at Pentecost, or was Pentecost merely and important part of these institutions?

Despite its vast popularity this view has many problems. First, the word "church" is not even mentioned until Acts 5:11 (but see notes on Acts 2:47 for some translations). It is hard to argue that the "church" began at Pentecost when the "church" is not mentioned. Second, despite the fact that the people present were from all over the known world, they were still Jews, not gentiles. Peter himself declares that they were "Jews and proselytes" (Acts 2:10) meaning that even the gentiles among them had been converted to Judaism. Thus as Sir Robert Anderson remarked:

> "Their hearers were Jews, and as Jews they were addressed. The Pentecostal Church which was based upon the testimony was intensely and altogether Jewish. It was not merely that the converts were Jews, and none but Jews, but that the idea of evangelizing Gentiles never was even mooted. When the first great persecution scattered the disciples, and they 'went everywhere preaching the Word', they preached, we are expressly told, 'to none but to the Jews.'"[102]

Consequently, if we see the church as a gentile priesthood during the period of Israel's chastizement, we cannot see the church beginning here at Pentecost. The working of the Holy Spirit among the common believer is the purpose for Pentecost, but that was made "to the Jew first, but also the Greek." The "Samaritan Pentecost" also cast doubt upon this (see Acts 8:15-17). It is therefore important not to confuse Biblical exegesis with theology.

View 4. Paul Establishes the Church

Some see Paul's conversion as signaling the institution of the church (Acts 9), but this is a variant of the belief that it was Paul who established the church through his journeys and ministry. In many ways this is the strongest view for Paul makes it abundantly clear in his epistles that he was an "apostle of gentiles" (Romans 11:13). It was he who first reached out specifically to gentiles whereas Peter had to be told by God through a vision that it was permissible to reach out to gentiles (Acts 10). Yet this is also where the theory has problems, for this very passage as well as the history of the apostles proves that the other apostles did eventually reach out to the gentiles. Paul was the first, but he was by no means the only one.

Hyperdispensationalists deny that the apostles ever abandoned their ministry to the Jews, and to an extent this is true, but then neither did Paul. Paul himself said that he always went "to the Jew first, but also the Greek" (cf. Romans 1:16; 2:9-10). So also the other apostles ministered to the Jews first, but they had clearly come to the stage, following the Council of Jerusalem (Acts 15), in which they left the Holy Land and spread the gospel to all the known world. Indeed, when Thomas went to India it is believed that he first went to Kerala, India where the Jews had a community near a trade city.[103] Thomas went first to the Jews there in India, but he soon became the father of the south Indian church spreading the gospel throughout southern India. He went "to the Jew first, but also the gentiles."

Now for those who are not hyperdispensationalists, this view has few problems, for it is clear that the entire book of Acts is about the gradual shift from national Israel to the predominantly gentile church. This is, however, a view which does not cater to those who like an exact date and time, for the shift did not happen immediately. Some like to start the "church dispensation" with Paul's conversion, but one could make an equal argument for the Council of Jerusalem, for it is at that famous council wherein gentiles were finally accepted into the fold without having to formally convert to Judaism first (see Acts 15). The apostles agreed to make no further stumbling blocks against gentiles which was not Jesus Christ Himself, and history shows that it is soon after the Council of Jerusalem that most of the apostles left Israel to fulfill the Great Commission around the known world.[104]

View 5. God Shifted His Program with the Fall of Jerusalem

In 70 A.D. Jerusalem fell to the Romans. It was the ninth day of Av when the Temple was destroyed, on the very anniversary of its first destruction at the hands of Nebuchadnezzar.[105] This event, and the timing of the destruction, signalled Israel's second diaspora, which was to last almost two thousand years. Just as the Jews had been exiled under Babylon for unfaithfulness, so also they were here again exiled, but this exile was to last for almost two millennia. Eleazar, when he stood on Masada making an ill fated last stand against the Romans, himself declared, "this was the effect of God's anger against us for our manifold sins, which we have been guilty of in a most insolent and extravagant manner."[106] So the Jews themselves acknowledge that this event began the period of Israel's chastisement.

Now I have said elsewhere that what we call "the church" is in reality a gentile priesthood during the time of Israel's chastisement. Consequently, the destruction of Israel can be seen as the time at which the new dispensation began. Or can it? Clearly the fall of Israel temporarily removed national Israel from the spotlight of history until its restoration in 1948. However, it is hard to argue that the church actually began on that day since it had been in existence in one form or another for decades. Moreover, if Israel's existence could not overlap that of the church, then the church cannot exist today for in 1948 Israel became a nation again. Obviously, the church and Israel can overlap one another.

Conclusion
It is apparent that none of the views above are completely accurate although most have merit. The problem is that we are looking at the issue "theologically" rather than exegetically. Romans 11 is the best analogy possible to explain the temporary shift from national Israel to the gentile priesthood. It is apparent in Romans 11 that Israel is the tree and the church are but branches. Gentiles never replace Israel. This dispensation is not "new" in the truest sense of the word. Rather it is a time when the gentiles receive the blessings of God's grace during the time of Israel's chastizement. Like the "old" dispensation, this one will come to an end as well. John Darby put it best when he said, "the dispensation of the Gentiles has been found unfaithful ... as the Jewish dispensation was cut off, the Christian dispensation will be also."[107] This is the very reason that Paul urged us not to be arrogant "for if God did not spare the natural branches, He will not spare you, either" (Roman 11:20-21). Our own judgment day is coming, and "the times of the gentiles" (Luke 21:24) will be cut off.

So when did the church begin? The question itself is flawed. The "church" as defined in the Bible always existed, but it is *expanded* beyond Israel (which is and always will be the root of Romans 11) to include gentiles. Jesus preached it, Paul exercised it, but the fall of Jerusalem signaled the dominance of the gentile priesthood during the time of Israel's chastizement. Thus each of the views is both correct and incorrect. They arise from a misunderstanding of God's role in history. They arise from the desire of both Covenant Theologians and Dispensationalists to read the Bible into their own theology rather than extract from the Bible what it says. I consider myself a traditional dispensationalists, but only isasmuch as I find it closest to what the Bible teaches. I oppose *any* theology which serves as a template for interpreting the Bible, rather than drawing from solid exegesis.

The Tongues at Pentecost
Acts 2:3-6

> "And there appeared to them tongues as of fire distributing themselves, and they rested on each one of them. And they were all filled with the Holy Spirit and began to speak with other tongues, as the Spirit was giving them utterance ... and when this sound occurred, the crowd came together, and were bewildered because each one of them was hearing them speak in his own language."

There are two kinds of heresy. The first heresy is the most common and is found throughout history. It is compromise. In a desire to fit in or to be accepted we invariably compromise with the world or with some other element by whom we hope to be respected. The second heresy is less common, but no less heretical. It is *reactionary theology*. It responds to bad theology with faulty theology. It says, "if they are for it, I am against it."

In the early 1800s the modern Pentecostal movement began. Of course, advocates will point out that the Charismatic movement, in a general sense of the word, actually began centuries (even millenia) earlier, and this is true, but in either case, the growing popularity of the movements led some evangelicals to react against it by arguing that the "gifts of the Spirit" (c.f. 1 Corinthians 12) no longer exist. They reacted against poor theology with worse theology (see notes on 1 Corinthians 12-14 in *Controversies in the Epistles*). I have here begun with my conclusions (which I prefer not to do) because I am acutely aware that both Pentecostal/Charismatics and Cessationists (those who deny the gifts of the Spirit still exist) will both groan at my exegesis. However, it is my desire to approach this issue in the same manner which I have approached all others. I will examine only the Scriptures in question and the context thereof. In this section I will deliberately leave many questions unanswered, for they are better answered in a discussion of the book of Corinthians and elsewhere. Thus, here I will only address the question of tongues in this specific passage, and not elsewhere.

The central question here *is not*, "do the gifts of the Spirit still exist?" but rather "what are the tongues spoken in this passage and what is the context?" The reader should be aware that the answer to this question *does not* necessarily effect one's views on the tongues spoken of in Corinthians and the reader should not be distracted by such concerns. Context is what is crucial. *Nowhere is this more important than in historical passages, for history is far more easily taken out of context than doctrinal instructions.*

Theories on the Tongues of Pentecost
Before discussing the various controversies over Pentecost, it is necessary to understand the various theories and perspectives which are held concerning the events of Pentecost. Essentially six different views have been presented over the centuries.[108] Some are, as usual, variants of one another, but all will be presented for the readers' understanding.

View 1. Naturalism
Beginning in the nineteenth century the so-called "liberals" of the "Tübingen school of thought" denied the very existence of miracles. For them the act of tongues was nothing more than different disciples speaking to different people in their own tongue.[109] William Farrar, the Dean of Canterbury at the end of the nineteenth century, even declared that tongues "was not

normally a power of speaking in languages unknown to the speaker. There is not the *slightest* trace that any one of the Apostles possessed any such power."[110]

Now anyone reading the text of Acts should clearly understand that what happened was not a normal natural event. The people themselves were "bewildered" (2:6) and some mocked them, saying, "They are full of sweet wine" (2:13), but why would any say such things if they were merely different disciples speaking in foreign languages to different people? Moreover, we are told specifically in Acts that there were Parthians, Medes, Elamites, Mesopotamians, Judeans, Cappadocians, Pontans, Asians, Phrygians, Pamphylians, Egyptians, Libyans, Cyrenes, Cretans, Arabs, and Romans present (2:9-11). Since there were only twelve apostles, one might wonder how twelve apostles (who were fishmen and carpenters and the like by trade) could even know that many languages!

Obviously the naturalistic view is an invention of deism and the German Tübingen school of thought. It is clear that a miracle of the Holy Spirit was taking place. Peter considered it at least a partial fulfillment of the prophecy in Joel (see below) and the people were "bewildered" (2:6) by what was taking place. This "baptism of the Holy Spirit" (1:5; 11:16) could in no way be an ordinary event. It was the product of the Holy Spirit! We can, therefore, dismiss this view as the futile dreams of German deists.

View 2. Poetical Rhetoric

The naturalistic view is really an offshoot of a more ancient teaching. According to this view the apostles were not speaking literal languages, but poetical rhetoric of some sort.[111] As early as the sixth century men like Cassiodorus adopted a highly allegorical view that eliminated the miracle of tongues. Cassidorus said, "we must interpret tongues here as the precepts of the New Testament, for if you understand it as 'language,' how did the Jewish people hear a tongue that they did not know."[112] The answer is obviously that it was a miracle! Moreover, Acts explicitly says that the crowd was "bewildered because each one of them was hearing them speak in his own language" (2:6), thus Cassidorus makes a false assumption in declaring that it was "a tongue that they [the hearers] did not know."[113]

As with the *Naturalism view* this interpretation attempts to eliminate the miracle of Pentecost. It is flawed on numerous levels including its inability to even explain what is meant by "poetical rhetoric." How does such poetry fit with the description found in Acts? Why are the people said to hear them in their own language (2:6)? The *Poetic view* thus begs more questions than it answers and can be rejected out of hand.

View 3. Incoherent Utterances or Jubilant Expressions

Some see this as "incoherent utterances" or "jubilant expressions"[114] that do not truly express any specific words or meanings. This view is adopted from the beliefs of certain sects of the charismatic and/or pentecostal movement.

However, even if such utterances are Biblical, they are plainly not of what is spoken in Acts, for Luke states that "each one of them was hearing them speak in his own language" (2:6). This is not incoherent jargon, but an actual "language" (2:6). The people joked that the apostles were drunk not because they were babbling incoherently (2:13) but because "we hear them in our *own* tongues speaking of the mighty deeds of God" (2:11). So "there is no description here of any jargon or incoherent speech."[115]

Anthony van Dyck – Pentecost – 1618

View 4. Ecstatic Utterances or Heavenly Languages
Another offshoot of the third view is that which argues these are "ecstatic utterances" or "heavlenly languages."[116] Like the previous view, this is an outgrowth of some sects of the charismatic and/or pentecostal movement. However, it argues that these tongues are more closely associated with what is described by Paul in 1 Corinthians 12 and 13. They believe that this is a "heavenly language" unknown on the earth.

I will not address 1 Corinthians here, for it is not necessary. Leo the Great offered sufficient proof that the tongues recorded here in Acts cannot be the same as that in Corinthians for "no interpretation is used in order to understand."[117] In 1 Corinthians Paul required the use of an interpreter so that everyone would understand what was spoken (1 Corinthians 14:28). Here in Acts there was no need for "each one of them was hearing them speak in his own language" (2:6). Once again the tongues of Pentecost appears to be different from that of Corinthians.[118]

Interestingly William Barclay says "what happened at Pentecost we do not really know"[119] but then goes on to say that "there was in the early church a phenomenon which has never completely passed away. It was called *speaking with tongues* ... [which] ... Paul did not greatly approve of."[120] He then concludes that "Luke, a Gentile, had confused speaking with tongues with speaking with *foreign* tongues."[121] Thus Barclay declares that the Bible is *mistaken* to have called it "foreign" tongues! This is then an inadvertent admission that the Bible does not support the teaching of a "heavenly" language at Pentecost.

View 5. Speaking in Foreign Languages Unknown to the Speaker
The most common understanding of tongues at Pentecost is that it represents the apostles speaking in foreign languages which they did not formerly know. It has been called the "undoing of Babel."[122] Bede said that the Holy Spirit restored what Babylon had divided,[123] a sentiment echoed by Cyril.[124]

One scholar stated that "one design was to establish the gospel by means of miracles. Yet no miracle coud be more striking than the power of conveying sentiments at once into all languages of the earth. When it is remembered what a slow and toilsome process it is to learn a foreign language, this would be regarded by the heathen as one of the most striking miracles."[125] Thus new tongues means only "new to them."[126]

This theory supports all the existing evidence found in Acts, with one possible exception. If they were speaking in foreign languages then how it is said by mockers that "they are full of sweet wine" (2:13)? Why would you think someone drunk for speaking a foreign language? Moreover, the people asked, "Why, are not all these who are speaking Galileans? And how is it that we each hear *them* in our own language to which we were born?" (2:7-8). The first part of the passage might infer that they were suprised at the Galileans apparent learning in knowing foreign languages, but the later implies they were surprised to "hear" their own language. Does this not imply that what was spoken and what was heard were not the same? This has led to a sixth and final view.

View 6. A Mircale of the Hearer
Cyprian, Bede, Gregory of Nyssa, Erasmus, and many others[127] see this as a "miracle of hearing"[128] rather than speaking. Some, like John Wesley, have objected to this saying, "the miracle was not in the ears of the hearers (as some have unaccountably supposed) but in the mouth of the speakers",[129] but why does the Bible refer to the peoples' "hearing" three different times. Three times "speaking" is mentioned and three times "hearing" is mentioned. Consider that if the tongues was merely speaking in foreign languages then why were the listeners so "bewildered" (2:6), "amazed" (2:7, 12), "astonished" (2:7), and "perplexed" (2:12)? Certainly they were suprised that simple "Galileans" could do this (2:7), but this is not all. They were amazed and astonished because "we each hear *them* in our own language to which we were born" (2:8).

Now it has been argued that "other tongues" (2:4) "makes it quite unnecessary to assume a miracle in the hearers,"[130] but why? Certainly there is a miracle of speakers, but if they were all speaking foreign languages at once, how could anyone hear anything at all? I cannot even understand what is being said at parties (one reason I am not a party person) when everyone is speaking the same language at once! This fact alone explains why some joked that they were drunk. To some it sounded as if it was gibberish, but others were "perplexed" because they understand everything which was being said.

Conclusion
Based soley on the exegesis of Acts 2, it seems there was a combination of a miracle of speaking *and* of hearing. Were it solely speaking then it is unlikely that the people would have even realized that a miracle was taking place. It is true that some were surprised that Galileans were speaking, implying that they thought they were unlearned, but many were amazed that "we hear them in our *own* tongues" (2:11). Moreover the jest that they were drunk further implies that this was more than simply speaking in foreign languages, for why would anyone assume you to be drunk just for talking to people in their own language! It is apparent that what was coming out of their mouths did not appear to match what was being heard, for each heard something different. Perhaps the drunk joke was similar to the jokes we make when watching a poorly dubbed foreign film. Their mouths were not moving in conjuction with the words coming out of them.

Baptism of the Spirit
The baptism of the Spirit is discussed under Acts 8:15-17 and 19:1-6. However, its first appearance is here in Acts 2. Or is it? Some have argued that "John the

Baptist used the word 'baptize.' He is the only one who ever said it. Then all of the recounting thereafter is the 'filling' of the Holy Spirit."[131] Unfortunately, this author seemed to have missed Acts 1:5 in which Jesus Himself says "you will be baptized with the Holy Spirit." The Greek word is βαπτισθησεσθε (*baptisthesesthe*) which is the future passive indicative of "baptize." Nevertheless, John MacArthur is correct to state that "while there is no command in Scripture to be baptized with the Spirit, believers are commanded to be filled with the Spirit (Ephesians 5:18)."[132] What then are we to make of this "baptism" of the Holy Spirit?

Some sects hold that the "baptism of the Holy Spirit" is a separate event from conversion related to sanctification. Others insist with equal zeal that the "baptism of the Holy Spirit" occurs at conversion and remains for all time. Acts 19:1-6 addresses these questions in more detail, but here in Acts 2 it is apparent to all but a few that "the gift of the *Comforter* was not temporary, and this display of his power was not to be once seen and no more."[133] Further, as Charles Spurgeon remarked, "notice that 'it *sat* upon them.' It did not flicker or remove; it remained there."[134] Consequently, many believe that this baptism was "once-for-all."[135]

MacArthur said that "the purpose of the baptism with the Spirit is not to divide the body of Christ, but to unify it."[136] Unfortunately, some have used the Spirit and His gifts to divide the church. These issues are debated in Acts 8:15-17 and 19:1-6 (cf. 1 Corinthians 12:4-21; 13:8; 14:1-19; and 14:20-25). What is relevant at this point is that the baptism is here seen as a shared experience. There is no hint of believers being left out or neglected. All shared equally in the gifts that day.

Conclusion
What happened at Pentecost? Some argue that the "day when the Spirit of God was given may be considered to be the ordering of the Christian dispensation"[137] and that it was the "founding the Gospel church-state."[138] Others say that while "there had been miracles before ... now the Day of Pentecost was to be signalized by and accrediting of an organization ... on that day the church was to be demonstrated as divine."[139] Augustine believed that the Holy Spirit was given earlier (John 20:22) and Pentecost was a "double giving."[140] Certainly something unique was happening in the history of mankind, not just the church. It was the beginning of something new. Was the church founded on this day? No, but there was a profound change in God's dealing with mankind. Peter himself declared that it was a partial fulfillment of Joel's prophecy (see below). Other scholars see a connection to Isaiah 5:24 and the "tongue of fire"[141] as well.

So what were these tongues? Many believe that because Acts 2 says so little of the tongues which take place here that we should examine 1 Corinthians to understand those tongues. While this seems logical at first, it must assume that they are the same based solely upon the fact that they are both called "tongues." However, there is good reason to believe that the tongues of Acts is different from the tongues of 1 Corinthians. The most obvious is that, as Leo the Great pointed out, "no interpretation is used in order to understand"[142] (cf. 1 Corinthians 14:28). Consequently, this cannot be the same as that of Corinthians, although there is obviously a connection between the two.

Joel in Acts
Acts 2:16-21

> "'It shall be in the Last Days,' God says, 'That I will pour forth of my Spirit on all mankind; and your sons and your daughters shall prophesy, and your young men shall see visions, and your old men shall dream dreams.'"

The central question here is Joel's use in Acts, and specifically of the application of "Last Days" to the days of Peter. In full the prophecy Joel predicts that "the sun will be turned into darkness and the moon into blood before the great and awesome day of the LORD comes" (Joel 2:31), which is parallel to passages in the Olivet Discourse (Matthew 24:29; Mark 13:24; Luke 21:25) and Revelation 6:12; all of which speak of the Tribulation which shall occur immediately before the second coming of Christ. This, of course, begs the question. Since the Tribulation takes place in "Last Days" before the second coming, how can Peter apply this prophecy to his day?

Several answers have been offered; some of less value than others. As with other opinions, some of the views are a mixture. The third view, for example, necessarily draws upon the second view. Nevertheless, I list them separately for purpose of clarity.

View # 1 : Peter was Mistaken
The liberal Tübingen school of thought argues that Peter "thought the Day of Judgment as near at hand."[143] In other words, they believe he was wrong! Says one "evangelical" scholar, an apostle's "expectations about whether he would live until the Lord's return changed as he grew older."[144] Therefore, this school of thought simply argues that Peter was mistaken and erroneously believed he was living in the last days. Obviously this view rejects a normative understanding of the inspiration of the Holy Scriptures and cannot explain why Peter himself told his followers that "the Lord is not slow about His promise, as some count slowness, but is patient toward you, not wishing for any to perish but for all to come to repentance" (2 Peter 3:9). Peter even implies that the second coming might not take place for thousands of years (cf. 2 Peter 3:8). This interpretation must be rejected as speculative and disrespectful to Peter's intellect.

View # 2 : Allegorical
Because the prophecy of Joel speaks of a day in which the Lord "will display wonders in the sky and on the earth, Blood, fire and columns of smoke. And the sun will be turned into darkness and the moon into blood before the great and awesome day of the Lord comes" (Joel 2:30-31), many have a problem applying the whole of Joel's prophecy to Pentecost. This view, often incorporated into other views as well, argues that the prophecy is not to taken literally. Bede, for example, argued that the blood of Joel's prophecy stood for Jesus, the fire was Holy Spirit, and the smoke was that "produced from fire."[145] Thus they argue that the *entire* prophecy was fulfilled in the time of Pentecost and that "we are not to look for any other [fulfillment], any more than for another accomplishment of the promise of the Messiah."[146]

Some call this a "realized eschatology" which treat these passages "spiritually" and do not expect a future fulfillment.[147] The problems with this view are manifold. For one thing, no two interpreters can agree on the alleged allegorical meaning. Nor can they demonstrate similar symbolic types parallel in the Bible. I have no problem with symbols where there is a specific and clear context and parallels that render such a symbol valid. For example, when we see a dove we understand that it may symbolize, governing the context, the Holy Spirit. This we know because there are specific passages which indicate this (Matthew 3:16; Mark 1:10; Luke 3:22; John 1:32). However, without context, allegorical views tend to just be wild speculation designed to escape problematic exegesis. This view must, therefore, be rejected.

View # 3 : Last Days of the Old Dispensation
A third view draws upon the second, but with a more specific application and context. In this respect it is far superior to the second, but by no means perfect. According to this view, and its variants, the "last days" of Joel refers to either "last days of Jerusalem"[148] or the "last days of the old dispensation."[149]

This view enjoys the support of such prominent scholars as Cyril,[150] Martin Luther,[151] John Calvin,[152] John Wesley,[153] John Lightfoot,[154] and Matthew Poole.[155] The view is summarized by John Gill who says "there is no doubt with us Christians that [the prophecy] belong to the times of Christ and his apostles."[156] The prophecy that the Spirit would be poured out on "all flesh" is seen by Matthew Henry as "upon some of all sorts of men."[157] Wesley says "all flesh" provides for the inclusion of gentiles.[158] On the gift of prophecy, John Calvin argues that there are more prophets "under the gospel than under the law."[159] Naturally, they interpret the prophecy of the blood and fire allegorical as in the second view.

On some levels this view makes sense. Peter clearly was applying at least part of the prophecy to the events at Pentecost. That the prophecy refers to the "days of the Messiah"[160] is acknowledged by all. Even famed Jewish scholars such as Kimchi and Ibn Ezra apply this to Messianic age,[161] but this does not fully answer all the questions. It is obvious that part of Joel was fulfilled at this time, but as John Walvoord said, "it was quite clear that the entire prophecy of Joel was not fulfilled" at this time.[162] So it is equally clear that part of the prophecy remains to be fulfilled, but how? Can two thousand years separate the prophecy of verses 28-29 from the prophecy of verses 30-32? We must either accept 30-32 allegorically or we must accept the fourth view.

View # 4 : Last Days Embraces the Church Age

Although John Wesley appears to accept the third view, he also states that "the times of the Messiah are frequently called the Last Days, the Gospel being the last dispensation of divine grace."[163] In other words, he accepts that the term "last days" embraces a larger time period than many assume. "End times" and "last days" overlap, but are *not* synonymous. John MacArthur believes that "the term 'the last days' ... denotes the time when Messiah would come to set up His kingdom,"[164] and we now know that encompasses not one, but two comings. Thus "the last days have thus lasted nearly two thousand years."[165]

So while all agree that the prophecy relates to the "days of the Messiah,"[166] one scholars prefers the term "the pre-Messianic period" or the time before the "Parousia of Christ."[167] Another calls this the "Dispensation of the Spirit."[168] So is it possible that the "last days" of Joel 2 has lasted two thousand years? Yes. The two comings of Christ form a fundamental aspect of the Christian faith. This dispensation, or era, is called an "age of grace" not only because salvation is by grace, for it was *always* by grace, but because God has delayed judgment upon the world until the gospel has been preached to all the nations and all men have had a chance to repent. Pentecost was a partial fulfillment, but the complete fulfillment awaits the return of the Lord Jesus. Only then, in the Millennial age, will the prophecy find complete fulfillment, as J. Dwight Pentecost believes.[169]

Conclusion

The prophecy of Joel was a quick glance at the whole history of the Messianic age. It begins with the first coming, but ends with the second coming. Because he summarizes the whole era in a few passages it is little wonder that so many Jews of old assumed that there was to be but one coming. Even the apostles failed to understand that God's grace would extend the time between Jesus's resurrection and the final judgment (cf. Acts 1:7). So the "last days" began with Pentecost described in Joel 2:28 and ends with the day of wrath immediately preceding the second coming of Christ, as described in Joel 2:30-32.

Baptism and Salvation
Acts 2:38

> "Repent, and each of you be baptized in the name of Jesus Christ for the forgiveness of your sins; and you will receive the gift of the Holy Spirit."

The passage entails two issues : the mode and its effectiveness upon salvation. The two have become related through history. Indeed, the very mode of baptism has sometimes become a very contentious debate. At times in history the anabaptists (those who believed in adult baptism by immersion) were brutally persecuted for their beliefs, and not only by the Catholic inquisition, but by Protestant Reformers as well. The famous Reformer Ulrich Zwingli himself turned on some of his former students who were anabaptists, leading to the execution of some of them.[170] Martin Luther also persecuted the anabaptists.[171] One historian said that under the Calvinists of Zurich "Romanists and Anabaptists were treated with the same disregard of the rights of conscience as the Protestants in Roman Catholic countries."[172] Indeed, the Catholic inquisition deemed "re-baptism" to be a damnable heresy, equivalent to renouncing the faith, and burned them at the stake. Conversely, many have considered infant baptism to be a perversion "so horrible and unacceptable ... that it was found necessary to invent a third realm, the *Lumbus Infantum*, to which unbaptized infacts are sent."[173]

It may seem odd that such a seemingly simple ordinance has become so contorversial and a heated debate, but this tension has arisen from the doctrines and teachings surrounding baptism. So some believe that baptism is merely a symbolic and public expression of the new birth in Christ. Others believe that baptism is essential for salvation. To that end, if baptism is essential for salvation, then what of children? If children must be baptized then how can baptism be by immersion? Hence the mode of baptism has often, but not always, been tied to the belief in whether or not baptism is essential to salvation. They are not, however, the same. There are those who practice adult baptism by immersion who do not believe baptism is essential for salvation and those who do. There are those who practice infant baptism by sprinkling who believe baptism is necessary for salvation and those who do not. These are the debates which have been generated throughout the ages; influenced more by theologians than by the Bible. Let us start with the most simple argument. How was baptism performed in the Bible?

The Mode of Baptism
It is sometimes hard to even discuss such a simple thing as the mode of baptism without discussing its theological implications. For example, arguments against baptism by immersion invariably are drawn from the belief in infant baptism. Although many who now practice infant baptism do so out of the belief that it is a promise to raise a child in the ways of Christ, infant baptism may have grown out of the belief that baptism was required for salvation. I will endeavor here to restrict my arguments strictly to the Bible and how it describes baptism, reserving the theological debates for the next section.

Baptism by Immersion

The Greek word for baptism is *baptizo* (βαπτιζω) which is most literally translated "to dip repeatedly, to immerge, submerge."[174] We transliterate *baptizo* (βαπτιζω) into the English word "baptism" because of the ritual or ordinance to which it is associated, but the Greek word literally meant that people were being immersed under water. This is how John the Baptist baptized in the Jordan river. You cannot immerse someone in a baptismal font. Lest someone believe that Thayer's dictionary is biased, let us look at its use in the Bible outside of the ordinance which is at the heart of our debate.

In 2 Kings 5:14 a leper was cured by bathing himself in the Jordan river. The Greek *Septuagint* uses the word *baptizo* (βαπτιζω) to translate this passage. In Mark 7:4 the word *baptizo* (βαπτιζω) is used of the Pharisees practice of bathing after visiting the market palce. Finally, in Luke 11:38 a Pharisee was shocked that Jesus had not washed (εβαπτισθη from βαπτιζω) his hands. In each instance the word *baptizo* (βαπτιζω) is properly translated as to "bath" or "cleanse" or "wash." Even one critic of immersion admits that baptism properly means "immersion" but then argues that "it has undergone some modifiation of its etymology."[175] Nevertheless, in every instance where baptism is described as taking place in the Bible it is described as being *in* the water. John the Baptist baptized in the Jordan river (Jesus came "up *out of* the water" – Mark 1:10) and when Phillip baptized the Ethiopean eunuch the Bible states explicitly that they went down "*into* the water" (Acts 8:38). In all cases, baptism appears to have been by immersion.

Baptism is a ritual which originated from being *immersed* or bathed in water. In all cases in the Bible baptism appears to be taking place in a river or pool and sprinkling is never once mentioned anywhere in regard to baptism. How then can those who believe in sprinkling defend their position Biblically? Let us examine their arguments.

Baptism by Sprinkling (or Pouring)

Generally, the case for sprikling (or pouring) is based on an criticism of immersion. Rather than showing where baptism is done by pouring or sprinkling in the Bible, they simply argue that Jesus "coming up out of the water" (Mark 1:10) does not necessarily mean that He was immersed. "Jesus could have stepped into the shallows and had John the Baptist pour water on his head."[176] The only positive evidence they give that baptism was not by immersion is based on Acts 16:15 wherein Lydia "and her household had been baptized" and Acts 16:31. Both of these passages speak of "household baptism" which some argue must have included children.[177] Since no one would immerse a baby under water, they argue it must have done by pouring or sprinkling. Of course this pure conjecture. Nowhere is it said that they had children, let alone children who were not yet of the age of consent. So the argument in favor of pouring or sprinkling is based on a negative argument (that immersion might not be necessary) and a speculative one (that there must have been children in the households of Lydia and the guard). No other arguments have been presented to prove that baptism in the Bible was performed by any other method.

Conclusion
Based soley on the Bible, it appears that baptism was always performed by immersion under the water. No positive arguments have been made against this. Rather critics have tried to cast doubt upon baptism by immersion, but none have shown positive proof to the contrary. The real debate lies not in the mode of baptism but in the necessity of baptism. As we shall see, those who believe salvation is required for salvation must necessarily believe in infant baptism, and by default sprinkling or pouring.

Salvation By Baptism?
"Repent, and each of you be baptized in the name of Jesus Christ for the forgiveness of your sins; and you will receive the gift of the Holy Spirit." The crux of the debate here is over the relationship between being baptized and "for the forgiveness of your sins" and the reception of "the gift of the Holy Spirit." Some argue that the commands to baptize go hand in hand with salvation.

View # 1 : Water Baptism Required
Richard Lenski is perhaps one of the best known Protestant scholars who argues that baptism "bestowed the remission of sins and was thus a true sacrament."[178] This teaching is also dominant in the Catholic church under the idea of baptismal regeneration. According to the *Catechism of the Catholic Church* "Holy Baptism is the basis of the whole Christian life, the gateway to life in the Spirit ... through Baptism we are freed from sin and reborn as sons of God ... Baptism is the sacrament of regeneration."[179] This seems a mouthful based strictly on the statement, "be baptized in the name of Jesus Christ for the forgiveness of your sins; and you will receive the gift of the Holy Spirit." How do they draw this conclusion?

1 Peter 3:21 is often cited as proof that "baptism saves," but this begs the question ... which baptism? The Bible speaks about water baptism and baptism of the Holy Spirit (see notes on Acts 8:15-17). However, that the two are not synonymous is clear from Acts 8:16 wherein it is said of some disciples, the Holy Spirit "had not yet fallen upon any of them; they had simply been baptized in the name of the Lord Jesus." If water baptism saved and if the gift of the Holy Spirit were a direct result of water baptism then this statement would not be possible.

What then does 1 Peter 3:21 teach? Consider the context. In verse 20 Peter alludes to Noah's faith which saved him from the waters of the Flood. Verse 21 begins with the words, "corresponding to that." He then compares baptism to the Flood. As Noah was saved, we are saved, but is it the water that saves? Sir Robert Anderson summarizes the passage and its relation to the ritual of baptism as taught in many churches today :

> "In this matter Christendom is in direct conflict with Scripture. Christendom teaches that baptism symbolizes birth. Holy Scripture declares that it symbolizes death. Christendom teaches that it is the putting away of the filth of the flesh. Holy Scripture declares 'it is not the putting away of the filth of the flesh, but the answer of a good conscience toward God.' And in the same passage (1 Peter iii. 21) the Apostle enforces the symbolism of death, by referring to baptism as an antitype of the Flood."[180]

In other words, baptism symbolizes the death and resurrection of Christ. When we are placed under the water (by immersion) we have been buried with Christ (Romans 6:4), and as we rise from the water we symbolize the new birth (John 3:3) as Christ was resurrected from the dead. Water baptism was not a mode of salvation but rather "a public profession of their belief in Jesus as the Messiah."[181] The apostles did not believe in the practice of making "secret Christians."[182] Says John MacArthur, "Peter does not allow for any 'secret disciples.'"[183] Rather "by publicly identifying themselves as followers of Jesus of Nazareth, they risked becoming outcasts."[184] Thus "in sharp contrast to many modern gospel presentations, Peter made accepting Christ difficult, not easy."[185]

So I must agree with Dale Moody that "water baptism symbolizes the Spirit baptism."[186] The link between salvation and baptism is one of making a public profession of faith from which there could be no turning back. To make this public profession and to be baptized immediately alienated the convert from many of his friends and even family and set the enemies of Christianity against him. Baptism was thus important, but not as a means of salvation but rather as a public profession of the new birth.

What then of the clause, "be baptized in the name of Jesus Christ *for* the forgiveness of your sins"? Frank Stagg argues that a better "translation depends upon the possibility of the casual use of the Greek preposition εις followed by the accusative case."[187] He then argues that it could be better translated as "be baptized ... *on the basis* of the forgiveness of your sins."[188] As an example he cites Matthew 12:41 where it he says, "they did not repent *with the result* that Jonah preached, but *because* Jonah preached."[189] So also we are baptized *because* we have the forgiveness of sins. This is the only interpretation which can explain all the relevant passages.

View # 2 : As Baptism of the Holy Spirit

Some argue that this verse is not speaking about water baptism at all; only Spirit baptism. However, few scholars, regardless of their theological persuasion, take this argument seriously. In fact, the only "scholar" I could find who seems to make such a claim admits that water baptism is intended here but then argues that Peter departed from the teachings of Jesus, saying that Jesus never taught baptism and further claiming that Matthew 28:19 was not the authentic words of Jesus![190] Nevertheless, water baptism was clearly taught and practiced by the apostles and this is clear in passages such as Acts 8:38 where the eunuch was taken "to the water" to be baptized. This application of this argument comes from passages such as Acts 8:15-17, 19:1-6. and 11:16 and is then injected back into all other passages regarding baptism. Since I deal with spirit baptism in Acts 8:15-17 I will not discuss this here other than to say that the context of Acts 2:38 makes it perfectly clear that the act of baptism is separate from receiving the gift of the spirit. It reads, "be baptized in the name of Jesus Christ ... *and* you will receive the gift of the Holy Spirit." The two are separate. This *cannot*, therefore, be the baptism of the spirit to which this passage is alluding. The question is not whether this is spirit baptism or water baptism, but what is the relationship between water baptism and the receiving of the gift of the Holy Spirit? This is the controversy and it is this controversy which this view seeks to avoid by denying water baptism is what is spoken of here. However, avoiding a controversy does not answer the controversy.

View # 3 :Baptism as Symbol of Death and Resurrection

If we reject that baptism is required for salvation and we reject that the baptism spoken of in this passage is spirit baptism then the logical question is "what is the relationship between baptism, the forgiveness of sins, and the gift of the Holy Spirit"? As previous discussed, the language itself could be translated as "be baptized ... *on the basis* of the forgiveness of your sins."[191] It is not that we are baptized *with the result* that our sins are forgiven, but *because* our sins are forgiven.[192] So if our sins are already forgiven why be baptized at all?

John MacArthur claimes that "Peter does not allow for any 'secret disciples' ... in sharp contrast to many modern gospel presentations, Peter made accepting Christ difficult, not easy."[193] Others have equally argued that "it was equivalent to saying that they should *publicly* and *professedly* embrace Jesus Christ as their Savior."[194] Baptism was a public profession. It is "an outward manifestation of their hearts' new attitude."[195] Calvin called it a "witness."[196] Wesley saw baptism as a confession, "believing in the name of Jesus."[197]

Baptism was thus a public expression of the faith representing the death, burial, and resurrection of Jesus, and of the death of our old selves. The water may represent the earth, under which we are buried. The rising from the water represents resurrection. The apostle Peter made another comparison. He compared it to the Flood of Noah where in the wicked were drowned, but Noah was spared by his faith (1 Peter 3:21). In each case, being submerged under water represents the death of the old self. Rising from the water represents the new birth. The washing and cleansing of our sins are also represented in baptism. Thus all of these symbolize the death and resurrection of our Lord and Savior and of our burial with him (Romans 6:6).

While these are the three dominant views, a handful of other views exist as well. Stanley Toissaint, for example, sees baptism as "parenthetical."[198] He argues that the reference to baptism has no relationship to the forgiveness of sins or the gift of the Holy Spirit, but while this makes a solid theological argument, it is not a solid exegetical argument, for the grammar is fairly straightforward here. The best solution, therefore, seems to be the third view. As Christians we "must make a public profession of [our] belief in Jesus as the Messiah."[199] Such a profession of faith is a natural result of our faith and should be partaken whenever possible, but nothing consistent with the teachings of Jesus and the apostles implies that this is a requirement for salvation. To do so leads to the inevitable theological wrecks which have created the doctrine of limbo and salvation by works.

Conclusion
The command here to be baptized should neither be taken lightly, as some have done, nor perverted to a commandment required for salvation. Baptism is a public expression of faith which in the ancient world, and in many places today, literally imperils the converts life, for once baptism is undertaken the convert may be disowned by their family, persecuted, or denied basic civil rights by his government. It is no wonder that Peter does not appear to make this optional, but neither does he tie baptism to salvation as some imply. Baptism is the public profession of faith which follows conversion, but it is best compared to the Lord's Supper. We are to partake of the Lord's Supper, but are we damned if we do not? Does excommunictation damn us as the medieval church believed? No. Baptism is suppose to take place as close to our conversion as possible, but it is not a requirement for salvation. The fact that baptism was always done by immersion is proof enough of this fact. Lest anyone doubt this, I quote the Catholic church itself which admits that "The church at one time practiced immersion. This was up to the thirteenth century. The Council of Ravenna, in 1311, changed the form from immersion to pouring."[200]

It is of interest to note that this debate revolves around baptism, some have interjected other requirements for the bestowing of the Holy Spirit but, as Richard Longenecker notes, neither tongues nor laying on of hands is mentioned here, implying that neither is necessary to receive the Holy Spirit.[201] Dale Moody best summarizes this debate saying, some attempt "to relegate water baptism to the role of mere ritual and assign Spirit baptism the 'real baptism' ... Radical criticism has followed the reverse order and claimed that the primary church practiced Spirit baptism only and that water baptism came in as the glow of spiritual fervor died away. Some sacramental views say that the Spirit is imparted by water baptism ... It is more consistent ... to say that water baptism symbolizes the Spirit baptism"[202]

Baptism is, in part, a symbol of the burial of Jesus. It follows then that it must be immersion. Furthermore, it is a symbol of the washing of our sins, so this too should be by immersion. In each and every case, baptism is of believers, and therefore by those old enough to make a decision of their own free will. The doctrine of baptismal regeneration has led to the teaching of limbo and salvation by works. It is unscriptural and twist the meaning of salvation. Baptism should be undertaken as soon as possible, but it no more required of salvation than the Lord's Supper or attending church. These are duties of a Christian, but they are not essential to salvation.

Signs and Wonders in Acts
Acts 2:43

"Everyone kept feeling a sense of awe; and many wonders and signs were taking place through the apostles."

There is no question that the apostles performed many signs and wonders. In fact, 2 Corinthians 12:12 even teaches that "signs and wonders and miracles" are the marks of a "true apostle." However, both Jesus and Paul also criticized those who sought signs. It is therefore ironic that many today teach that signs and wonders are a "ministry" to be practiced in "apostolic churches." It is not uncommon to see "healing ministries" and the like around the world today. Some consider such ministries to be frauds. Others consider them a cult. Still others see them as proof that God is active in their church. In full disclosure, I will state that all of the above are both true and false. I will not here debate the teaching of "cessationism" (the belief that the gifts of the spirit no longer exist), for that is discussed in detail in *Controversies in the Epistles*. Rather it is my intent here to understand what the teachings upon signs and wonders were among Jesus and His apostles, for we cannot hope to understand signs and wonders today if we cannot even understand the context of signs and wonders in the time of the apostles!

Signs and Wonders in Apostolic Times
There can be no doubt that Jesus performed many signs and wonders such as had not been seen since the days of Moses. However, it is also true that Jesus told the Jews, "an evil and adulterous generation craves for a sign; and *yet* no sign will be given to it but the sign of Jonah the prophet" (Matthew 12:39; cf. Mark 8:12; Luke 11:29). This seems odd considering that Jesus performed so many miracles and yet the result is equally intriguing for the overwhelming majority of Jews in that day *rejected* Jesus *and* His miracles. In order to understand this irony we should look at several other relevant passages.

In the gospel of Luke we are told of Jesus cleansing ten lepers, but only one of the ten lepers came back to follow Jesus. "Were there not ten cleansed? But the nine – where are they?" (Luke 17:17) asked Jesus. He then turned to the Pharisees who sought and demanded signs (Luke 11:16; cf. Matthew 12:38;

Mark 8:11) and said to them "the kingdom of God is not coming with signs to be observed" (Luke 17:20).

How can this seeming dichotomy between the miracles of Jesus and His denials that signs shall be given be resolved? The apostle Paul himself gives us a clue, for in 1 Corinthians he scolds but Jews and gentiles. "Jews ask for signs and Greeks search for wisdom; but we preach Christ crucified, to Jews a stumbling block and to Gentiles foolishness" (1 Corinthians 1:22-23). He goes onto mock the gentile's wisdom and extols the power of Jesus which was rejected by most of those who saw. Why? Because faith is not by sight (cf. 2 Corinthians 5:7). The Jews who saw Moses part the Red Sea still feared that the Egyptian gods were more powerful and constantly lacked faith. The priests who saw Elijah's miracles refused to repent of their sins but instead persecuted Elijah. So also many of those who saw Jesus's miracles attributed them to the devil (cf. Luke 11:15)! Faith has nothing to do with seeing miracles. In fact, the greatest miracles all accompanied the greatest faithlessness on the part of those who saw. They also accompanied the greatest men of faith! This is the dichotomy and the irony. Faith is about trust. We all have it. The atheist has more of it than I ever could, for he believes that magots and slugs are our distant cousins and that the universe, which did not exist, exploded out of nothing to make something which formed stars in violation of the laws of entropy! The atheist has blind faith. The Christian has intelligent faith, but faith nevertheless. Seeing is not believing as they say. Faith is trusting in God. It is faith that pleases God; not witnessing miracles that are constantly needed to assure us of our faith.

Signs for Today
John MacArthur is a cessationist who denies that the gifts of the spirits exist today. He emphatically believes that the practice of miracles "was limited to the apostles and their close associates."[203] However, he also admits that "although the sign gift of miracles is no longer extant, God still performs miracles in response to the prayers of His people."[204] So even MacArthur admits that miracles can occur today. The question is, do they, and to what extent?

Lenski believed that "the miracles were intended to impress those that were on the outside,"[205] but Jesus and Paul implied that it was Jews who sought a sign, not gentiles (1 Corinthians 1:22; cf. Matthew 12:38-39). We cannot therefore accept that miracles were designed to attract certain people to the church. In fact, Jesus gave us the solemn warning that "false Christs and false prophets will arise, and will show signs and wonders, in order to lead astray, if possible, even the elect" (Mark 13:22 cf. 2 Thessalonians 2:9). Signs and wonders can thus be performed by false Christ as well as the true Christ. They can be used to lead people astray as well as to lead people to the Lord. I believe that this is one reason that true signs are accompanied by persecution! Elijah was persued by Ahab and Jezebel. Jesus was crucified. All the apostles were slain except for John, who was boiled in oil (see Appendix C). True signs result in persecution, but false signs often lead to adoration. This is why Simon the Magician sought the "secret" to the apostles' miracles (Acts 8). Too many of us have become like the Pharisees who felt that they needed the assurances of miracles and signs to believe, and yet their faith was impure. True faith does not need such signs, but the question still remains. Do miracles take place today?

Harold Ironside was one dispensationalists who did not believe that the gifts of the spirit had passed away, but he nevertheless held to the belief that miracles and signs are rare today. This he attributed to the separation of the purity of the ancient church and the passing of the original apostles.[206] This argument makes sense. Contrary to what some teach Moses, Elijah, and the apostolic age were not the only times to witness miracles (consider Joshua commanding the Sun to stand still). Having said that it is natural that the greatest prophets (Moses and Elijah) would perform the greatest miracles along with Jesus and His apostles. Moreover, prophecy says clearly that in the last days many will come and "will show great signs and wonders, so as to mislead, if possible, even the elect" (Matthew 24:24). So the "signs and wonders" which are performed today in a circus like atmosphere are just as likely to be those of false prophets as true prophets. In fact, the former is far more likely for the apostles themselves never made a circus of miracles, and both Jesus and Paul scolded those who sought signs.

Conclusion
Do miracles occur today? Yes. Are such miracles from God? Sometimes, but more often than not they are the signs of false prophets who set themselves up as God's spokesmen and then teach heresies such as the prosperity gospel (cf. 2 Timothy 4:3) designed to lure people away from the true gospel. "Signs ministries" are not founded in the Bible. Not even the apostles had a "ministry" of signs and wonders. Signs and wonders accompanied them because they were apostles (2 Corinthians 12:12)! Since the apostles have died off, we should not expect as many miracles or signs today. They may occur in accordance with God's will, but we are *not* to expect them as a ministry.

True miracles of God are accompanied by unbelief. This irony must be understood if we are understand the gospel itself. Our faith is not based on a constant reminder of miracles and signs, but on our trust in Jesus Christ. Faith is trust. Trust, by definition, relies on what we do not see. When our loved-one is with us we do not need to trust them. They are with us. When they are alone and we do not know what they are doing, *that* is when we must trust in their loyalty and love. The same is true of God. The greatest faith is when we rely on God even when He is silent.

Did the Church Exist Before Pentecost?
Acts 2:47

"The Lord added to the church daily such as should be saved" (KJV).

As discussed in the preceding pages, some believe that the church came into being at Pentecost. Others believe that the church developed later in the ministry of Paul. One of the arguments against a Pentecostal creation of the church is the fact that the Church is not even mentioned in Acts 2! Or is it? The King James Bible and the sixteenth century Geneva translations both contain the word "church" in this passage. However, most Bibles do not have the word. Instead most Bible have "number" (NAS, RSV, NRSV); "fellowship" (NLT); "group" (NIRV); "congregation" (Tyndale, Israeli AV); or "assembly" (Darby). This is not so much a translation issue as a textual issue. Virtually all medieval manuscripts substitute the word "church" for the generic "them." In other words, virtually all the ancient manuscripts read most literally, "the Lord added those who were saved daily *to them*." Such is the reading of the Codices Sinaiticus, Alexandrinus, Vaticanus, and Ephraemi, as well as the most ancient papyrus 74 ($\mathfrak{P}^{74}$). The variant addition of "church" probably arose from the ancient Syriac translation which inserted "church" for clarity. Contextually, it is clear that the church, as we define it today, is intended by "to them." However, the word was almost certainly not found in Acts 2:47. Consequently, to argue that the church was created in Acts 2 based on this passage is weak. The church existed inasmuch as believers assembled together and were the people of God, but we cannot read our own theological assumptions into this passage or use it as proof of one view over another. The most literal translation is the old Revised Version which reads simply, "the Lord added to them day by day those that were being saved."

4

The Church in its Infancy

It becomes clear in the book of Acts that what the apostles originally anticipated and what came to pass were not identical. This is first hinted at in Acts 1:6 where the apostles were anticipating the kingdom of God to be brought to Israel at that time, but Jesus told them that the epoch and time of this event (which He did not deny) was not to be revealed to them. The apostles therefore worked in accordance with the Will of God, but this does not necessarily mean that they understood God's Will in its entirety *at that time*. There is no doubt that as the Scriptures were written, the writers *did* understand, but Peter, for example, did not understand in those early days that gentiles did not have to be circumcised or convert to Judaism before becoming followers of Christ (see notes on The Circumcision Debate in Chapter 8). This however is the controversy, for we must grapple with the fact that the apostles may have been mistaken in some things while at the same time realizing that the Scriptures *do not* reflect an evolving view (see notes on Acts 2:16-21), as some critics claim. The Bible accurately records the deeds of the apostles even as it accurately recorded the deeds of King David who sinned against God. We cannot say that the Bible is in error or evolving because King David sinned. Nor can we say that the Bible is in error or evolving because Peter did not understand God's Will in its entirety during these early years. The epistles were written many years later when the truth had become fully revealed to them. There is no changing theology or evolution.

Having said this, it is clear that in the earliest days of the church the apostles did not yet fully understand God's intentions. They preached to Israel and formed their church in an around Jerusalem. It was not the apostles who chose to leave so much as it was God who scattered the apostles abroad. The church in its infancy was a church in growth. The apostles followed the teachings of Jesus, but Jesus did not tell them the answers to everything. He let them learn some things as we should all learn. Moreover, like children, the Lord needs to discipline the child so he is raised with an understanding of right and wrong. We see this with the case of Ananias and Sapphira.

Let us, therefore, look at the early passages of Acts and the Church in its infacy before the first persecution. We shall examine how the apostles attempted to resolve the problems of everyday life and whether or not those attempts were successful. We shall also examine the controversies in Peter's speech to the Jews and the troubles with Ananias and Sapphira.

Who Crucified Jesus?
Acts 4:10

> "Let it be known to all of you and to all the people of Israel, that by the name of Jesus Christ the Nazarene, whom you crucified, whom God raised from the dead."

The false charge of anti-semitism is often hurled at Christians. Indeed many Jews are taught that the Catholic church, with which they tend to identify with all Christians, persecuted Jews because they considered Jews to be "Christ killers." Now I address this topic in *Controversies in the Gospels* but I will also address it here in a different manner, for Acts 4:10 is used as proof that Christians allegedly consider Jews to be the killers of Christ. Nevermind that the death of Christ and His resurrection is our salvation (for the Jews think of this only as an excuse for "Christians," as they understand the word, to persecute Jews). Theologically, of course, the death of Christ is all our fault. *We* killed Christ. Historically both Jews and genties were involved in the death of Christ. Biblically, Christ came for the express purpose of dying on that Cross. The question is therefore not so much one of who killed Christ (but see *Controversies in the Gospels* for a full discussion of this debate), but whether or not Acts 4:10 truly expresses an anti-Semitic sentiment.

First it must be said that Peter, a Jew, was speaking. It is natural for Peter, as a Jew, to chastize *his* people for their role in the crucifixion. As the chosen race the Jews bore a responsibility. It was to the Jews that Jesus was revealed in the prophets and it was to the Jews that Jesus was born. It was to the Jews that Jesus exercised His ministry and it was to the Jews that salvation was first offered. It is, therefore, natural for a Jew to convict the conscience of his people for what blood guilt they might bear. But some Jews claim that Peter never said these words at all. They argue that Luke, the author, was a gentile and put these words in Peter's mouth to stiry up anti-semitism. Is this true?

As to the allegation that Luke put words in Peter's mouth, few Jews will admit to believing this as it makes the Bible author out to be a liar. The real question is whether or not Luke was a gentile, as generally believed, or whether or not he was, in fact, a Jew.

Historically, the dominant view has been that Luke was a gentile convert to Judaism. However, critics have pointed out that no extant church father specifically called Luke a gentile until St. Jerome. On the other hand, neither was he specifically called a Jew to my knowledge. Nonetheless, Jerome appears to be the first to explicitly refer to him as a gentile convert. Why? The predominant argument is based on Colossians where Paul states that Aristarchus, Mark, and Jesus called Justus "are the only fellow workers for the kingdom of God who are from the circumcision," or Jews (4:10-11). Since Aristarchus, Mark, and Jesus called Justus were the "only" Jews among his "fellow workers" it follows that Epaphras, Luke, and Demas, who were not of the circumcision, were gentiles (4:12-14).[207]

To this some answer that Luke was not properly a "fellow worker" but "was rather Paul's personal physician and historian."[208] Thus it is argued that Paul was maintaining a rigorous distinction between his fellow Jewish workers and his Jewish personal physician? The argument is weak and seems to be grasping at straws. In fact, one author admits that the Luke of Colossians is a gentile, but then argues that this is a "different" Luke from the author of Luke and Acts.[209] He bases this argument on other evidence that Luke was Jewish, and then concludes that this Luke, who was obviously a gentile, must have been a different Luke. Let us, therefore, look at this other evidence.

The best argument that Luke was a Jew is based on Acts 21:29. There Paul was falsely accused of bringing a gentile into the Temple because "they had previously seen Trophimus the Ephesian in the city with him" (21:29). Now Luke is not mentioned in this passage but based on Acts 21:17 it is *assumed* that Luke was also with them. Since only Trophimus is mentioned in verse 29, it is then assumed that Luke was a Jew.[210] However, there are two assumptions in this argument, neither of which can be proven. The first is the assumption that Luke was with them at the time of the accusations. The second is that a gentile convert to Judaism, like Luke, would exact the same outrage as Trophimus who was not a Jewish convert. Would a Jewish convert not be allowed in the Temple area? Neither assumption can be proven. In fact, Luke never once mentions himself by name in the entire book of Acts. This was his style and his humility. Whether Luke was there or not, he does not insert himself into the story. Was it only Trophimus with whom they were concerned? If we assume Luke was there, but not mentioned, might we not also assume that they leveled accusations at Luke as well but Luke, in his humility, omits himself from the story? In all cases we are engaging in speculation, and speculation is not exegesis.

There are some other arguments on both sides; both equally weak, and based on inference rather than exegesis. The two passages above seem to be the best evidence for the two respective views. The only question which remains then is the question of whether or not the Luke of Colossians might have been different from the Luke of Acts. Only David Allen seems to present any real evidence of this. He argues that Luke and Lucius are the same name and person and thus assumes that the Lucius of Acts 13:1 is Luke. Since Romans 16:21 identifies Lucius as a "kinsman," then Luke must have been a Jew.[211] Unfortunately, this has several problems. To start with Lucius is described as a Cyrene (Acts 13:1) whereas Luke is believed to have come from Antioch.[212] Although there is no Bible passage to prove which is correct, there is not a single tradition of which I am aware that Luke was a Cyrene, but rather a native of Antioch. Additionally, Paul clearly calls him Luke in Colossians (4:14), 2 Timothy (4:11), and Philemon (1:24), so we might wonder why he would call him Lucius in Romans. The theory is intriguing but pure speculation. It is not likely that Lucius and Luke were the same based primarily upon the fact that Lucius was a Cyrene.

Based solely on the Biblical evidence, Colossians 4:10-11 seems to offer the best support for the belief that Luke was a gentile. Acts 21:17-29 does not provide conclusive evidence to the contrary. Of course this only brings us back to the original accusation about anti-semitism. If Luke was a gentile, then might he not have inserted the passage to invoke anti-semitism? Logically the answer is "no." Even if we reject the inspiration of the Holy Spirit, as unbelievers obviously do, we cannot conclude that Luke, who worked with Jews in Israel for decades and worshipped a Jew, was an anti-semite. In fact, if we accept that Jerome was right in calling Luke a gentile then we would also be inclined to accept that he was been a convert to Judaism before becoming a Christian! Moreover, charges of anti-semitism are anachronistic at best. Christians and Jews did not develop an emnity for one another until many centuries later. If anything it was the Jewish hierarchy who had a resentment against Christians, which led them to persecute the early church. Christian persecution of Jews did not exist in the first century, nor has any evidence of such animosity been produced. The only argument to be made is that Acts is a forgery written centuries after the fact, but this is verifiably false, for the book of Acts is found in fragmented form in the ancient papyrii 29 ($\mathfrak{P}^{29}$), 38 ($\mathfrak{P}^{38}$), and 48 ($\mathfrak{P}^{48}$). Moreover, Acts is cited by Ignatius, Polycarp, and Clement (among others), all of whom wrote within fifty years of the time Acts was originally written![213] There can, therefore, be *no doubt* that Acts was written in the first century, long before anti-semitism developed among gentile Christians.

The fact is that Peter, a Jew, was chastising his own people. Peter's intent was not to condemn the Jews, but to call the Jews to repentance. In fact, Peter shares the blame! He had denied Christ three times when Jesus needed Him the most. Yet Jesus forgave Peter and he became one of the most famous of all apostles. This passage is not a condemnation of Jews but a call to repentance.

In the Name of Jesus Alone
Acts 4:12

> "And there is salvation in no one else; for there is no other name under heaven that has been given among men by which we must be saved."

Christians have often been accused of intolerance because we believe that Jesus alone has the power to forgive sins. It is argued that if only Jesus can forgive sins and all men are sinners then men are damned simply because they are not Christians. This, they say, is the height of intolerance. It is also a misrepresentation of the gospel message.

The words "gospel" and "evangelize" in Greek are different forms of the same word, ευαγγελιος (*evangelios*), which literally meaning "good news."

The message is that we have a savior, but with this good news comes the stark reality that we *need* a savior. The good news comes with bad news : we are all lost in sin. Men are not damned for our beliefs, for our place of origin, for our intellect, or technically even for our religion, but for our *sins*. This is not a theological nuance, it is a basic fundamental (as in fundamentalist) fact. We are condemned because of our sins, and for no other reason. The majority of religions of the world all recognize this condition, but all seek different ways to reconcile us to God through human effort. This is where Christianity differs. We believe that no human effort can ever reconcile man to God. Only Jesus can do that. The "good news" is that Jesus accepts anyone and everyone who repents and turns to Him. It does not matter if you are a Hindu, Muslim, or even an atheist. You can turn to Jesus, repent of your sins, and trust Him to transform your life. Obviously, you will no longer be an atheist, or whatever, but this is the irony of those who cry intolerance. They claim intolerance while demonizing those of us who preach the "good news" of a Jewish man from the Near East. I am not a Jew. I am not an Asian. I am a follower of Jesus Christ. It is He, and He alone, who can reconcile me to God because He was God made man (cf. John 1:1-14) for that very purpose!

Were the Apostles Socialists?
Acts 4:34-35

> "For there was not a needy person among them, for all who were owners of land or houses would sell them and bring the proceeds of the sales and lay them at the apostles' feet, and they would be distributed to each as any had need."

Were the apostles socialists? This may seem a very strange question to ask for socialism is a doctrine invented by atheists almost two thousand years after the apostles and yet it is not uncommon at all to hear socialists claim that Jesus and His disciples were early socialists. This passage is often held as proof of this "fact." Unfortunately those who make this claim fail to understand that socialism and Christian charity are not only different but at *emnity* with one another, as will be illustrated.

It has been my experience that those who hold up socialism as "Christian" are usually those who understand neither socialism nor the Bible. They are idealists who fail to understand both the nature of political socialism and the nature of sinful men. It is, therefore, necessary, to explain the fundamental elements of socialism in order to understand whether or not the Bible advocates such government institutions. First we will look at Christian charities, the Marxist ideology, and finally at the specifics of the Christian "community" here in Acts 4-5.

Christian Charity
We will begin with the simplest issue : charity. Charity is based on Christian love. It is voluntary and involves giving to those in need as we see fit. It revolves around personal responsibility, love, and accountability. It can be summarized in part by the old saying, "give a man a fish, he eats for a day. Teach a man to fish, he eats for a lifetime." Part of the Christian duty is to teach, to educate, and to give men *opportunities*. In all cases it must be done out of charity, not compulsion. Lastly, Christian charity seeks not only to care for the physical needs of man, but more importantly to care for his spiritual needs, and to bring men to Christ. The two duties are held jointly.

The Salvation Army was founded by William Booth. It was considered the epitome of Christian charity since its founding, although it is now threatened by Obamacare and similar socialist laws. Interestingly enough, Booth issued a warning on the future state of charity, saying "the chief danger of the twentieth century will be : religion without the Holy Spirit, Christianity without Christ, forgiveness without repentance, salvation without regeneration, and heaven without hell." Booth understood that Christ was central to charity.

Marxist Ideologies
Many people are under the delusion that Marxism is simply an economic ideology. I remember arguing with a socialist once about this very thing. He insisted that Marxism was only about economic policies and would "work" if everyone contributed voluntarily to the system. In this section I hope to debunk this dangerous myth, for Marxism is an ideology which is based on intrisinctly atheistic assumptions about man, about society, about family, about religion, about education, and about God. Communism cannot be divorced from these assumptions which is why every communistic country in history has been an atheistic state which persecutes Christians, creates the very poverty it claims it wants to diminish, and denies people the very liberties it professes to promote.

In short *all* Marxist ideologies seek to replace family with "society" and God with government. In order to demonstrate this I will quote from Karl Marx, Frederick Engels, and other self professed socialists. I will break down each fundamentally dangerous, and anti-Christian, precept upon which Marxism is based. The reader will see that not only is Marxism not Christian, it is *anti*-Christian.

Family in Marxism
The name of Hilary Clinton's book is "It Takes a Village." This book epitomizes the socialist view of family. In it Hilary, or at least her ghost author, draws upon the analogy of an ancient African village where the child does not belong to the mother and father alone, but to the entire village. What the book fails to tell us is that in that same culture the village chieftain is God. If he wants to "borrow" your wife for a night of sex, you cannot refuse him for your

wife does not belong to you alone, but to the village. The *family* unit did not exist in the culture to which Hilary compares her political ideology.

This is no accident. Marx and Engels did not hide their distaste for the family. Three times in the *Communist Manifesto* they speak about the "abolition of the family."[214] According to Marxism society is of more importance than family. Families are perceived to be an inherently selfish institution which can be at odds with the perceived "needs" of society. To that end, the *Communist Manifesto* promises "the dissolution of old moral bonds, [and] of the old family relations."[215] According to Frederick Engels, Communism "educates children on a communal basis, and in this way removes the two bases of traditional marriage – the dependence rooted in private property, of the women on the man, and of the children on the parents."[216] In Engels' *Communist Confession of Faith* he admits that communism may sometimes "interfere in the personal relationship between men and women or with the family."[217] Note the title of this tract. It is a "confession of faith." Atheism is based on faith; blind faith. It holds that man is supreme. It follows then that if man is supreme, he cannot sin. If man cannot sin, then it follows that he cannot be corrupted by power, which is why Communist governments invariably give totalitarian authority to state leaders. That these governments abuse that power is proof that Marxism is a lie, and that man is a sinner.

One does not have to look far in society to see the brazen attacks upon family values. Hollywood promotes the idea of families as some sort of modern household slavery. "Nontraditional" families, such as homosexual couples, are presented in a favorable light whereas traditional families are always portrayed as either dysfunctional or even abusive. Children are taught from youth that they should dream of the day they can leave the home, yet in centuries past children lived with their families until they got married, and even then they would build a new home next to their mother and father's. Marxism has made great headway in societies around the world, and as the *Communist Manifesto* promised, "the abolition of the distinction between town and country, of the family"[218] is becoming a reality.

Religion in Marxism

Families teach us to rely on others. Families are one of the primary institutions upon which God created and structured our society. Marxism hatred of family is really just an extension of its hatred of God. Karl Marx himself said, "Communism begins where atheism begins."[219] Frederick Engels declared that "communism is the stage of historical development which makes all existing religions superfluous and brings about their disappearance."[220] Communism is "inevitably atheist,"[221] which is why the *Communist Manifesto* triumphantly declares that "Communism abolishes eternal truths, it abolishes all religion, and all morality."[222] Is there any wonder why Communist governments have slaughtered more people than all the religions of human history combined? Most are executed simply for the crime of worshipping God.

Education in Marxism

Since the communist system requires a rejection of God and family, it follows that there must be a radical change in how children are brought up. Since children are born to a mother and father, it is natural that mothers and fathers (i.e. families) educate their own children. In recent years that has changed. Society now frowns upon home schooled, and even private schooled, children. There is a reason for this. Engels said that communism "educates children on a communal basis."[223] In other words, it is the government who must educate, or indoctrinate, children into the new social mores.

Probably the most famous Marxist educator in history was John Dewey, known as the father of "progressive education" which is now the basis for all public schools in America. According to Dewey education should be based on "the general principle of social control of individuals."[224] For him parents should merely be "representative and agent of the interest" of society,[225] and should have no more authority than "society" permits. The most startling statement made by Dewey explains the Marxist ideology of education perfectly; "the mere absorbing of facts and truths is so exclusively individual an affair that it tends very naturally to pass into selfishness. There is no obvious social motive for the acquirement of mere learning, there is no clear social gain."[226] In other words, education should not be about learning, but about social engineering.

This social engineering has lead to "functional illiteracy"[227] or what others have more uncharitably called "planned illiteracy." By denying children individual acheivements, he must become more dependant upon "society." He becomes dependent upon the government. Education is no longer about reading, writing, and arithmetic, but about indoctrination brought about by teaching that truths are cultural. We are constantly told that our religion and morals are a part of "western culture" but this is not true. As Allan Bloom once said, "culture and civilization are irrelevant to the truth."[228] Indeed, Europe was once a bastion of canibals, barbarians, and even human sacrifice. What changed this? What made Europe the home of colleges, universities, the Renaissance, the Reformation, science, modern democracy, abolitionism, and freedom? The answer to any honest historian is, the *truth* of Jesus Christ. Truth transcends cultures. Jesus was not a European, nor a gentile. He is relevant because He is the Truth, the Way and the Life (John 14:6). It is He who transformed pagan barbarians into the harbingers of freedom. The abolitionist movement was evangelical Christian. The end of segregation was evangelical Christian. The rise of modern democracy was evangelical Christian. A long list could follow. Truth is truth, but Marxism must teach that truth is relative, even as they teach that "every man's freedom is relative,"[229] so they teach that morality is relative.

Thus it should be apparent that for all its Utopian rhetoric, Marxism is an atheists' dream. Because they have no God, they cannot rely upon the hope of heaven or of Christ's return. The atheists' Utopia requires the suppression of all things Christian hold dear. Families must be replaced by "society," God must be replaced by the government, and schools must actively supress individual aspirations and hopes and dream for the aspirations of "society" as a whole. The "selfishness" of individuals is replaced with a government that legislates to all of society what it decress is beneficial and useful. Individuality, love, hopes, dreams, family, and faith must be crushed by Marxism. Such are the words of Marx and Engels. As the *Communist Manifesto* itself declares, "Communism abolishes eternal truths, it abolishes all religion, and all morality."[230]

The Community of Christ in Acts

Now having examined charity and Marxism, it is necessary to look specifically at Acts 4:34-35 and see what was happening. Were the apostles creating a communal society? If so, what were the precepts of this society? Did it work? Can this community be compared to socialism or used as an ideal for today? Let us look at the passage carefully.

"There was not a needy person among them, for all who were owners of land or houses would sell them and bring the proceeds of the sales and lay them at the apostles' feet, and they would be distributed to each as any had need" (4:34-35). Certainly this is an act of charity, but is it more than that. Is this a kind of communal society which was being created by the apostles. What is interesting is that what happened here did not become the standard for the early church. One author, who does see this as a sort of "religious communism" notes that the apostles eventually abandoned this practice, saying, "religious communism does not work any more than political communism, nor did it here in the Bible."[231] Why not? As one author explains:

> "It would appear that this community of goods, whatever is meant by it, was entirely confined to Jerusalem. There is no trace of it in any of the apostles, or in the Acts of the Apostles, except as regards the church in Jerusalem. On the contrary, the whole charge which is given in Scripture for almsgiving, all the rules which are laid down to the rich, the different degrees of rank recognized in Scrsipture, the warnings against covetousness, and the exhortations to benevolence, clearly demonstrate that nothing resembling a community of goods existed in the Christian church at large. Indeed, it does not seem to have continued long in Jerusalem. It was instituted to meet existing emergencies, when the church was poor, weak, and feeble; and when the circumstances of the case were altered, it was abandoned. Meyer, with whom Alford agrees, thinks that this may explain the great povery

of the church of Jerusalem – that by this method their possessions were naturally soon exhausted."[232]

Other authors have argued that the "expectation of the near approach of the second advent made them put the less value on the earthly possessions, and might have contributed to this community of goods."[233] He argues that as they realized that Jesus might not return immediately they were forced to abandon a system that depleted the very resources needed to sustain the poor. However, other commentators believe that there never was a communal system here at all. For one thing "they did not have to do it."[234] It was a purely voluntary system. Acts 5:4 "proves that there was no obligation imposed on the disciples to sell their property"[235] (but see notes on Ananias and Sapphira below). Moreover, "the language here expressly avoids saying that these men sold all they had."[236] Another author says, "the idea to be expressed is certainly not that the rich sold all of their property and thus made also themselves poor."[237]

Lawrence Browne saw this as "generalizing"[238] and John Lightfoot argued that "it cannot be taken-up for an example or precedent for the time to come"[239] based on five reasons. First, it was not a command. Nowhere are disciples required to sell their land. Ananias was not condemned for keeping his money but for lying about it (see below). Second, he argues that gentile converts could not return to their lands, and hence the lands were of no value to them. Third, based on Jesus's prophecy, he believes that they anticipated the coming destruction of Jerusalem, thus the desposal of their lands was beneifical as the lands would have been taken in the coming invasion anyway. Fourth, he saw this a provision for coming persecutions. Finally, he said "such was the state of the church at this time, as never was the like to be again."[240] Certainly there are unique circumstances involved, but this may not be a sufficient answer in itself.

I am inclined to believe that those who sold propery maintained a source of income. The selling of property did not deplete their resources, or they would have run out of money with which to feed the poor very quickly. This is one of the economic problems with socialism and welfare states. They deplete the resources which alone can sustain them, thus creating a greater poverty than they had to begin with. On the contrary, I believe that men were selling excess for the betterment of the apostolic community, but only a few, such as Barnbas, entered permanent ministry. The rest continued to work and earn money, providing charity to the poor as needed. We cannot read a communal society into these two short passages. The fact that there is nothing else in the whole of the apostles' works or writings to support communism of any kind is itself a testament to this fact. Charity is what was taking place here; not communalism.

The church did not replace the family; it supported the family. The church did not replace religion; it supported Christ. The church did not replace God; it worshipped God. All of this flies in the face of socialism, communism, and other naive attempts to merge the anti-Christian utopian myth of Marxism with Christianity. Consider the fundamental differences as stated by their own advocates and creators:

Christian Charity	Marxist Ideologies
Voluntary	Involuntary
Man is sinful, hence cannot be trusted with absolute power over other men's lives.	Religion is evil. Certain eilte men, freed from religion, are capable of making decisions for all.
Family creates a bond that overcomes much of our baser instincts (but by no means all) and is the basis for caring for those nearest to us.	"Society" replaces family. The "community" decides how to best "care" for all.
God is the master of our lives.	The "community" (government) is master.
Charity should be governed by accountable entities under the authority of God and church.	The "community" (government) should take what it needs and is an authority unto itself.
Abuses of authority can be punished by church members or government laws.	Abuses of authority cannot be punished as the state is the highest authority.
Education must center around learning and the family.	Education must teach moral relativity and make the student rely upon society. It is for indoctrination, not learning.
Christ must be the center of the charity.	Man is the center of all things.

The early Church was about Christ. Charity means "love." That is what the early charity of the Church represented; love. They did not seek to establish a communal society, a new government, an economic system, or replace the Biblical structure of the family and/or religion. They sought to glorify God and to uphold the strength of the family and the true faith. They sought to live like Christ, but Christ was not a homeless man, as some have said. He was a *missionary*. His home lay with his mother, whom He had supported and continued to support. He built up a home for her and made enough money as a carpenter to support her while He left for the mission field. Jesus was never "un-employed" or "homeless." He was a missionary who lived wherever his job took Him, even if it meant sleeping under the stars. That is charity.

Conclusion
Jesus did not make Pontius Pilate the first pope, nor did He seek to make Caesar the Messiah. Socialism, according to Marx and Engels' own words, replaces God with government. Those who misquote Jesus's "render under Caesar" forget the rest of the sentence, "render unto *God* what is ***God's***." The Church is not socialistic, but charitable. The two are in contradiction to one another. They are at odds with one another. According to the *Communist Manifesto* the aim of communism is to "abolish eternal truths, abolish all religion, and all morality."[241]

It is my estimation that not even Heaven is socialistic. We are all equal in the eyes of God, but we are not, and never were intended, to be equal in all things, for such a world would be an intollerable Hell where no man achieves, no man dreams, and no man succeeds. I will not be living in a mansion next to

Moses or Elijah. I am not worthy and if God gave me the rewards to which Moses is due, then God would *not* be a just God. We are all saved by grace, but we will not all share in the same glory as those like Moses and Elijah and the apostles who gave up everything to follow God. They will receive their glory and their rewards in heaven, and I shall not have the right to steal those rewards. So even heaven is not truly socialistic.

Ananias and Sapphira
Acts 5:1-11

> "A man named Ananias, with his wife Sapphira, sold a piece of property, and kept back *some* of the price for himself ... and Peter said, 'Ananias, why has Satan filled your heart to lie to the Holy Spirit ... While it remained *unsold*, did it not remain your own? And after it was sold, was it not under your control? Why is it that you have conceived this deed in your heart? You have not lied to men but to God.' And as he heard these words, Ananias fell down and breathed his last ... and immediately she fell at his feet and breathed her last, and the young men came in and found her dead, and they carried her out and buried her beside her husband."

There are two fundamental issues in this very controversial passage. The first is the question of what sin they committed. The second is of the very nature and meaning of their severe punishment. Ananias and Sapphira were both executed by God for a sin that in all honesty most of us have committed in some way, fashion, or form.

The Sin
There are several theories upon the sin of Ananias and Sapphira. Those who believe that these passages are about communal property maintain that they were punished for withholding some of their money. Certainly a superficial reading of the passage might lead one to believe this, but verse four refutes it once and for all. "While it remained unsold, did it not remain your own? And after it was sold, was it not under your control?" This clearly indicates that "they were not under obligation to sell their property."[242] The "giving was voluntary."[243] Another said, "His sin did not consist in retaining part of the price – he was at liberty to give or not to give, as he pleased."[244] Such is the clear statement of Peter in verse four. Moreover, "the indefinite κτητα, without the article, makes the impression that this property was only one of their possessions."[245] In other words, they had other properties which they made no pretense of selling. In any case, 5:4 makes it apparent that Ananias's sin was not in his withholding money which was "under his control." What then was the sin?

A popular view is that Ananias sold the land for "popular favor."[246] Like many millionaires in Hollywood who hire publicity agents to show them donating to charity, it is believe that Ananias was "eager for glory rather than godliness"[247] and wanted to "purchase a name for himself."[248] It was to "purchase praise and the impression of piety."[249] Certainly this was part of the sin, for there is no doubt that his motives were impure and dishonest, but Peter does not actually mention this in his condemnation, so can we consider it alone the sin? Certainly "none are so ugly in God's sight as those who flaunt a spiritual beauty they do not possess,"[250] but this is the offspring of another sin : hypocrisy.

Many believe that their sin was that of hypocrisy.[251] President Theodore "Teddy" Roosevelt had what he called the "Ananias Club" which was made up of those he considered liars and hyprocrites.[252] Others have compared Ananias's sin to the unforgiveable sin![253] Jerry Falwell declared that "there is no such a thing as a secret sin"[254] to God, but once again Peter makes no mention of this sin, however true it may be. No, these sins were known to God, but another's motive is not our concern. God will judge the motive. Here is it Peter who is acting as judge, and he makes no mention of the motives of Ananias and Sapphira, however impure they may have been.

Peter states emphatically what sin they committed. "You have not lied to men but to God." Says John MacArthur, "withholding part of the money for their own use was not a sin, as Peter clearly states in verse four ... the overt sin was lying."[255] Few people seem to even realize that lying is actually against one of the Ten Commandments. The ninth commandment is, "You shall not bear false witness against your neighbor" (Exodus 20:16). To bear false witness is to lie. Here Peter declares that Ananias was not just lying to him, but to God Himself!

Obviously the motive for lying was to cover for his own hypocrisy and to earn undeserved praise among the disciples of Christ. Nevertheless, if we are completely honest with ourselves then how many of us can say honestly that we have never tried to earn praise for ourselves which we did not deserve? How many of us have tried to take full credit for something we are only partially deserving of credit? Have we not all committed the sin of Ananias? Why then was Ananias and Sapphira executed by God? This is the greater controversy.

The Punishment
Capital punishment is considered the ultimate punishment in modern western society. It is reserved for the worst of criminals. If lying were punishable by death then all the politicians and lawyers of the world would be slaughtered in a single day. What then made Ananias and Sappira different from the rest of us? Why were they sentenced to such a harsh penalty when men like Simon the Magician were allowed to live?

Some have tried to absolve Peter of any culpibility in the deed, pointing out that it was God's judgment,[256] but why does Peter, or God, need to be absolved? Nothing in the Scriptures hints that this anything other than God's judgment at the hand of Peter. Nevertheless, the seeming harshness of the deed has been mollified in various ways. John Wesley suggested that Ananias and Sapphira were not true believers, but this is neither stated nor inferred in the Bible, nor would this mollify the act.[257] If God slew every phony believer then the world's population would be drastically decreased overnight.

Still others have tried to soften the passage by ascribing a natural death to Ananias and Sapphira. Frank Stagg claimed that "these deaths can be accounted for physiologically" as a heart attack brought on by "shock"![258] Another said that they "died of fright."[259] These are attempts to absolve God of a deed for which He needs no absolution. God alone has the right to take our life at any time for any reason. As sinners we are all subject to punishment and wrath if God so deems. Is this inconsistent with Jesus's teaching of love and forgiveness, or with the fact that Jesus died to absolve *us* of *our* sin? *That* is the question, not whether or not God was justified in His actions, which He most certainly was.

Chrysostom made special mention of Simon the Magician whose sin was greater and more brazen than that of Ananias and Sapphira. He noted that Simon did not die because the deaths of Ananias and Sapphira were not intended to be a model but "a warning to others."[260] John Pohill compared this to the sins of Achan (Joshua 7) and of Nadab and Abhu (Numbers 26:61).[261] In each case, the relatively "minor" sins were punished immediately with death; not because this was to be the punishment for all who sinned, but to serve a warning to the future generations that God's love is not an excuse to take sin lightly. The result of Ananias and Sapphira's deaths is proof of this fact.

According to Acts 5:11-13 "great fear came over the whole church, and over all who heard of these things ... and none of the rest dared to associate with them." Contrary to the popular gospel preachers of today, God was not making it is an easy choice to follow him. People were not flocking to associate with the apostles anymore. The "whole church" was seized with fear. *This* was the result, and this was what God intended. The sins of Ananias and Sapphira were no worse than those committed by many Christians today. I have no doubt that both Ananias and Sapphira will be in heaven when we get there, but their death was a stern reminder to the church that Jesus's love should not be taken for gullibility. Love should not be abused. Would we cheat on our spouse simply because we know they would forgive us? If so this would be a worse sin, for we are exploiting the love we do not deserve.

Conclusion
John Calvin compared this to the widow's two coins found in Luke 21:2-3.[262] The rich gave a little of what he had and thought he was righteous for it, but the poor woman gave everything. Ananias and Sapphira sought praise from men and lied about it. They violated the ninth commandment and bore false witness before God. They were struck dead not because they were damned nor because

all men must die for such sins, but as a stern warning to the early church that God's love is not be taken lightly or used as an excuse for libertarianism. Sin is sin and Jesus's forgiveness does not give us a license to sin. The warning was felt among the whole chuch and the message was clear : Christianity is not supposed to be easy.

Mihail Zelenskiy – Death Strikes Ananias – 1863

Harold Copping – Saul Guards the Coats – 1909

5

The First Persecution

Jesus was crucified. Before that day Jesus warned His followers, "if they persecuted Me, they will also persecute you" (John 15:20). The history of Christainity is a history of the persecution of the true church. After ten great persecutions under the Roman emperors, Constantine's conversion did not cease our persecution. Instead it came in new forms, including the medieval Inquisition whose duty it was to persecute all who owned, read, or translated the Holy Bible.[263] Persecution came from without and from within. It came from Arabia and from Europe. In the modern world the communists have slaughtered tens of millions, mostly for the crime of believing in God. Christians have borne the brunt of that persecution. Here we have a record of the first persecution and its results. It is the results, however, which are most astonishing.

The results of the first persecution proved benefical to the church. It forced the church to expand beyond Jerusalem and to begin to fulfill the Great Commission, and it also yielded a very unexpected result : the conversion of the Apostle Paul, one of the instigators of the persecutions.

"Whom You Put to Death"
Acts 5:30 – See Acts 4:10

Gamaliel's Counsel
Acts 5:33-45

> "For if this plan or action is of men, it will be overthrown; but if it is of God, you will not be able to overthrow them; or else you may even be found fighting against God."

Gamaliel was a famous Jewish leader and Pharisee. He was the grand-son of Hillel, their founder.[264] He was also the head of the Yavneh academy of learning and patriarch of the Sanhedrin.[265] One of his students at the academy was a young Pharisee named Saul, later to become the apostle Paul (Acts 22:3).

Here Gamaliel is speaking to those who sought to persecute the followers of Chirst. Although he was not a believer his words are prophetic. There is no real controversy in these words except inasmuch as they come from an unbeliever. Some have trouble grappling with the fact that unbelievers could utter prophecy, but even Caiaphas said, "it is better for you that one man die for the people, and that the whole nation not perish" (John 11:50). Of this Caiaphas, John said, "he did not say this on his own initiative, but being high priest that year, he prophesied that Jesus was going to die for the nation" (11:51). God is the author of true prophecy. He speaks through whomever He choses. Even Balaam, the false prophet, spoke God's word so that God could convey His word to unbelievers (Numbers 22). This does not mean that we should listen to false prophets, nor seek pagan prophecies to understand God. It means only that God may choose to speak to unbelievers through unbelievers, for the unbeliever rarely listens to us at all. God can do whatever He chooses, but such choices are not an excuse for us to abandon what He has told *us*.

Ultimately Gamaliel's advice was unheeded. The priests and Pharisees and others soon began their persecution, but as Gamaliel foretold, they proved only to be fighting against God. Israel was to be chastized for nearly two thousand years until its restoration, promised in both the Old and New Testaments, began in 1948.

The Historicty of Theudas and Judas
Acts 5:36-37

> "Theudas rose up, claiming to be somebody, and a group of about four hundred men joined up with him. But he was killed, and all who followed him were dispersed and came to nothing. After this man, Judas of Galilee rose up in the days of the census and drew away *some* people after him; he too perished, and all those who followed him were scattered."

The historicity of Judas the Galilean is confirmed in Josephus and by all historians. However, the Theudas of Josephus's history does not match that recorded in Acts so that Bible critics claim Luke was not only in error but guilty of ignorance. As usual the critics assumes the Bible must be in error (never Josephus) but more than this, they assume that the same Theudas is intended. In fact, there are many possible explanations which involve actual evidence rather than idle insinuation or speculation. One thing is certain, Luke wrote a decade before Josephus, so that accusations he misread Josephus may be dismissed immediately. Let us examine the historical evidence and the theories revolving around them.

Theudas
There is only one Theudas mentioned in Josephus. According to him Theudas arose in the time of the Roman procurator Fadus around 44-46 A.D.[266] He said that:

> "A certain enchanter named Theudas persuaded a great number of the people to take their belongings with them and follow him to the Jordan River. He told them he was a prophet and that he would, by his own command, divide the river and afford them an easy passage through it. And many were deluded by his words. However, Fadus did not permit

them to gain the result of this wildness, but sent a troop of horsemen out against them who, falling upon them unexpectedly, slew many of them, and took many of them captive. They also took Theudas alive, and cut off his head, and carried it to Jerusalem."[267]

Josephus then stated that "besides this, the sons of Judas of Galilee were now slain. This was the Judas who caused the people to revolt against the Romans when Quirinius came to take an account of Judea."[268] Obviously these passages run parallel to the statements of Gamaiel so that many, both Christians and Bible critics, believe they are the same event. However, the problem is two fold. First, Josephus stated that Judas of Galilee rebelled many decades earlier whereas Gamaliel explicitly says that Judas of Galilee can "after" Theudas.[269] Thus the order is reversed. Second, and more importantly, Gamaliel spoke around 33 or 34 A.D., but this revolt did not take place until a decade later around 44 A.D.![270] Obviously these two issues create major conflicts. Many theories have been put forth by Bible critics and commentators to explain these contraditions. I present the most popular and/or credible.

Theory # 1 : Luke Was in Error
The Bible critic is quick to claim that Luke was in error, but in so doing they usually invalidate their own theory. Consider that the Tübingen school of "scholars" argued that Luke's "confused dependence" led to this error.[271] They argue that because Josephus mentions the extermination of the sons of Judas of Galilee Luke mistakenly thought Judas came after Theudas rather than before him and that he did not check the dates of the rebellion so that he erroneously placed the rebellion many decades earlier. Now this sort of "critical" scholarship may sound logical at first glance, but it is nullified by its own "logic." They claim that Luke was anachronistic in his reading of Josephus and yet ignore the fact that Luke wrote the book of Acts more than a decade before Josephus wrote! The Tübingen critic is the one being anachronistic, for Luke could not have copied a book which had not been written until many years after he finished Acts!

Moreover, it is clear that Luke and Josephus could not have been referring to the same event despite the similarities. Aside from the contradictions, which alone prove they are not the same, is the fact that Gamaliel describes 400 men whereas Josephus refers to "a great number of the people" and speaks of a "turmult" immediately following in which 20,000 people were killed.[272] Furthermore, Josephus's Theudas calls himself a "prophet" and was a "magician" whereas Gamaliel's Theudas says nothing of magic. The differences in the stories are as numerous as the similarities so it is not fair to assume that they must have been the same incident.

Logically, this argument is an easy assumption but easy is neither scholarly nor often right. Luke was obviously relying on other information and not Josephus. The answer, therefore, is not to be found in Josephus, although they *may* have been referring to the same thing, but elsewhere. Consequently, another solution must sought.

Theory # 2 : Josphus's Date is in Error

A second view, counter to the critical school of thought, is that it was Josephus who erred. This was the opinion held by the esteemed John Lightfoot,[273] and it is not without evidence. According to this theory the story is correct, except that Josephus mistakenly placed Theudas under the procurator Fadus when he he should have placed him closer to the time of Judas of Galilee. The evidence for this is the extermination of the "sons of Judas of Galilee." Why would the Romans exterminate the descendants of Judas nearly a half century after the revolt (but see notes on Judas below)? It is argued that Josephus mistook this Theudas for another and the "sons of Judas of Galilee" would have been slain in the time period described by Luke and Gamaliel. Since Luke is the earlier source than Josephus, it makes sense that Luke's would be the more accurate, not that of Josephus.

This theory actually has more evidence than the first, although it is somewhat thin and speculative. If the "sons of Judas of Galilee" had participated in the revolt of Theudas's time then it is natural that the Romans would have remembered Judas and been eager to exterminate the lineage. It is not necessarily true that the sons had to have been killed near the same time as Judas. Nor can we say that the "sons" cannot be grand-children for the Hebrews word "sons" can refer to descendants as in the "son of David." This argument is, therefore, intriguing and possible, but not the best option available to us.

Theory # 3 : A Different Theudas Unknown to Us

In ancient Israel last names were not in use. Because first names were common, Jews often used nicknames or were known by their parentage or home town. This is the case with "Judas of Galilee" even though there would still have been many men named Judas from Galilee. Consequently, it is by no means certain that the Theudas Josephus mentions under Fadus is the Theudas to whom Gamaliel refers. The contradictions may be proof of that. It is then absurd to assume that they must be the same person. The problem is that there is no other Theudas found in Josephus. What solution can be found?

Matthew Poole noted that "some suppose [Theudas] a contracted name of Theodorus."[274] Of course the only Theodorus found in Josephus was in the time of the Ptolemies and seems to have no relation to Gamaliel's story. Nevertheless, one one question we might ask is "why are we looking in Josephus at all?" Granted Josephus is considered an authoritative history of the Jews at that time, but it is far from exhaustive. Consider the words of Albert Barnes:

> "Josephus has recorded many instances of insurrection and revolt. He has represented the country as in an unsettled state, and by no means

professes to give an account of 'all' that occurred. Thus, he says (Antiq., xvii. 10, section 4) that there were 'at this time ten thousand other disorders in Judea'; and (section 8) that 'Judea was full of robberies.' When this 'Theudas' lived cannot be ascertained; but as Gamaliel mentions him before Judas of Galilee, it is probable that he lived not far from the time that our Saviour was born; at a time when many false prophets appeared, claiming to be the Messiah."[275]

Having said this it is entirely possible that Josephus does mention this Theudas by a different name. Consider the words of Emil Schurer, who himself believed Luke to be in error. He said that "the name Theudas is met with also elsewhere. Θευδας is a contradction for Θεοδοσιος, Θεοδοτος, Θεοδωρος, or such like name derived from Θεος ... Even in rabbinical works we find תודוס."[276] So even the skeptic Schurer admits that Theudas is a nickname. In fact, one scholar noted that "the Hebrew word יהודה is the same as the syrian word תודה from which the names Judas and Theudas are derived."[277] Consider that the only real difference is that the "J" is replaced by the "Th." When we see that "Bill" in English is a nickname for "William," "Bob" for "Robert," and "Dick" for "Richard" this does not seem so odd. Hence, it is apparent that Theudas may have been a nickname, and possibly a nickname for the most common name in Israel; Judah or Judas. Indeed, one of Jesus's apostles, Judas Lebbæus was surnamed Thaddæus.[278]

So despite the protest of some critics, "this name was in use among the Jews, and is either the same with תודה, 'Thuda', or 'Thoda', so the Syriac version reads; one of the disciples of Christ was so called by the Jews, whose name was Thaddeus: or with תודוס, 'Thudus'; one of this name, said to be a man of Rome, is frequently mentioned in the Talmud."[279] Thus when we examine the various theories concerning the name Theudas and its possible variants it is clear that Theudas could have been known by another name which may or may not have even been mentioned in Josephus. However, Josephus is far from being the only authority on ancient Israel. The Talmud is actually of far more importance than Josephus, and the Talmud mentions several Theudases, at least one of which may be the Biblical Theudas as we shall see.

Theory # 4 : He Was the Theudas of the Talmud and the Revolt of Jannaeus

The Talmud mentions Theudas in connection with Simeon ben Sheṭaḥ, a fact which many claim is in error.[280] However, once again we see critics quick to assume error in everything but what supports their thesis. A more careful examination of the events surrounding Simeon ben Sheṭaḥ is needed before discarding the Talmud's testimony.

Who was this Simeon? He was the head of the Sanhedrin during the Ptelomies, and specifically during the reign of Alexander Jannaæus. Now Josephus neither mentions Simeon ben Sheṭaḥ nor Theudas in connection to Jannaæus but he does record a revolt against Jannaæus and other sources tell us that Simeon ben Sheṭaḥ had to flee for protection. There are several instances of revolt and rebellion under Jannæus, any one of which could have involved Theudas. The biggest revolt was followed by drastic action which Jannæus took against the Jews, including crucifying 800 and slitting the throats of their wives and children before their eyes.[281] In another instance Jannæus massacred 600 Jews who had thrown oranges at him.[282] His reign was filled with such acts and rebellions. Could Theudas have been one of these rebel leaders? The Talmud seems to think so. The similarities between the Theudas in Fadus's time and this one have led some to reject the Talmud, but this is a strange irony. Why reject the Talmud as in error? The assumption once again seems to be that there can only be one rebel named Theudas. Certainly since Theudas appears to have been a common surname, possibly for Judas, there were more than one Theudas. If not, why it is assumed that Josephus could not have erred rather than Luke and the Talmud? Does it not make more sense that Luke and Gamaliel read the Talmud rather than Josephus?

As with other speculation we cannot say that this is the Theudas Gamaliel intended. Indeed, these events took place almost eighty years before Judas of Galilee. While we do not know how long "after this man" Judas of Galilee arose, it is assumed that the two were not separated by eighty years. This theory is therefore another possibility, but lacks firm evidence.

Theory # 5 : Theudas was Judas, the son of Ezekias

The famed Archbishop Ussher argued that he had the identity of Theudas. According to Ussher, "the Hebrew word יהודה is the same as the syrian word תודה from which the names Judas and Thaddaeus are derived. The correct name is Theudas, since this Judas [son of Ezekias] seems to be none other than the Theudas of whom Gamaliel spoke."[283] This theory is supported to some extent by William Whiston, the famed translator of Josephus and pupil of Isaac Newton,[284] as well as Church historians Philip Schaff.[285]

According to Josephus "there was also Judas, the son of that Ezekias who had been head of the robbers ... This Judas, having gotten together a multitude of men of a profligate character about Sepphoris in Galilee, made an assault upon the palace and seized upon all the weapons that were laid up in it ... and he became terrible to all men, by tearing and rending those that came near him; and all this in order to raise himself, and out of an ambitious desire of the royal dignity; and he hoped to obtain that as the reward not of his virtuous skill in war, but of his extravagance in doing injuries."[286] This same Judas is again mentioned by Josephus in the "War of the Jews" where he says, "there was one Judas (the son of that arch-robber Hezekias, who formerly overran the country, and had been subdued by king Herod); this man got no small multitude together, and brake open the place where the royal armor was laid up, and armed those about him, and attacked those that were so earnest to gain the dominion."[287]

Now while Gamaliel obviously speaks of a rebel there were countless rebels at that time, so there seems little evidence other than the tentative connection of Judas to Theudas and the fact that this Judas lived in the time of Herod, close to the time when Judas of Galilee arose. The close proximity to Judas of Galilee and the name make this theory tenable, but it is suspect in most other ways for without a clear parallel we cannot say this man was Theudas anymore than one of the countless other rebels at that time.

Theory # 6 : Theudas Was Simon of Perea
One of the most intriguing theories is that this Theudas was actually Simon of Perea.[288] This Simon is mentioned by both Josephus and by Tacitus, the Roman historian.[289] According to Josephus:

> "There was also Simon, who had been a slave of Herod the king ... this man was elevated at the disorderly state of things, and was so bold as to put a diadem on his head, while a certain number of the people stood by him, and by them he was declared to be a king, and thought himself more worthy of that dignity than any one else. He burnt down the royal palace at Jericho, and plundered what was left in it. He also set fire to many other of the king's houses in several places of the country, and utterly destroyed them, and permitted those that were with him to take what was left in them for a prey; and he would have done greater things, unless care had been taken to repress him immediately; for Gratus, when he had joined himself to some Roman soldiers, took the forces he had with him, and met Simon, and after a great and a long fight ... Gratus overtook him, and cut off his head."[290]

Now more is said of this Simon in an ancient text archaeologists uncovered in Israel. It is called the "Hazon Gabriel" or "Gabriel Revelation" and dates to the end of the first century B.C., at the time of the revolt. In it this same Simon is prophesied to be resurrected from the dead in three days time.[291] Of course this did not happen and Bible critics are quick to claim that the followers of Jesus "borrowed" from this story, but it really only proves that such a prophecy of the Messiah being resurrected existed before Christ. The prophecy was not fulfilled under Simon, and none claim it was, but under Jesus Christ the true Messiah. Moreover, the attribution of this prophecy to Simon is proof that he was a false Messiah. This fits the context of Gamaliel's speech perfectly, for Gamaliel was not merely listing rebels, of whom an infinite number were available, but false Messiahs! Here then is a false Messiah who rose up in rebellion and whose followers were slain and dispersed, but this is not all. It is noteworthy that this incident took place in very close coincidence with that of Judas of Galilee.[292] Although Gamaliel is not specific, most assume that Judas arose not long after Theudas. If this is the correct interpretation, then this would again fit the Biblical story.

The problem with this theory is the connection between Theudas and Simon. We can only assume that Theudas was his nickname arising from his Messianic claims. Since θεος (*Theos*) means God, a variety of names stemmed from this word. Theodosius, Theodoric, Theophilus, and a great many others. Theudas (Theodas) could then be a Messianic title to which Simon attributed himself. This would explain why Josephus does not use the name Theudas, preferring instead his slave name of Simon. It would be like a Orthodox Jew calling Jesus "Christ," for Christ is a Greek title meaning "Messiah." An Orthodox Jew would never call Jesus the Messiah, hence they avoid the term "Christ" in all their writings. This could be the same with Simon Theudas.

The theory is plausible and the story matches even closer to that of Gamaliel than that of the Theudas of Fadus's time. However, without evidence to connect the name of Theudas to Simon of Perea this remains yet another speculative theory. It is actually one of the better theories, but nevertheless a theory alone.

In addition to these six theories are many others. Only a few are worth noting. For example, among the speculation offered is that Theudas is to be associated with Theudion, the king's brother-in-law[293] Although the connection of names does fit, nothing else in the story of Theudion does fit. Yes, he lived at the right time, but nothing is said of a rebellion or of him seeking to become king.

Yet another theory attempts to connect Theudas with Judas, the son of Saripheus, and Matthias, the son of Margalothus.[294] These men, however, made no Messianic claims and did nothing which closely matches that described in Acts. They tore down the Roman eagle, but when soldiers were sent to deal with these men and their allies, they quickly retreated. Perhaps this is why some believe the reference to Theudas's followers being "dispersed" matches this story, but contrary to Gamaliel's Theudas, Judas and Matthias were surprisingly treated with leniency by Herod who merely stripped Matthias of the high priesthood. There is nothing of their being slain with 400 men. This is, therefore, not the same story.

As the reader can see it is not easy to choose without further evidence. That all accept Judas of Galilee to be a historical figure is denied by none, so not even the Bible critic denies that this Theudas was a historical figure as well. They attempt to claim the Bible is in error based not on actual evidence, but on lack of evidence. In admitting that the stories of Josephus and Luke do not match they only prove that they are not the same story! However, if they are the same story then it is far more likely that it is Josephus who erred and not Luke, who wrote earlier. It is of significance that no Jewish critic of the New Testament made the claim that Luke erred until centuries upon centuries later. Those who lived close to the time of the apostles say nothing of it, giving further support to the fact that Luke was correct.

Which theory is correct? I cannot say with certaintly. I am inclined to reject the notion that Josephus and Gamaliel were speaking of the same man. Indeed, Gamaliel was already dead! Could Josephus have erred? Yes, but the more likely scenario is that Theudas refers to another; to one who was a false Messiah. To that end I lean toward the view that Theudas was Simon of Perea. However, Ussher's suggestion that he was Judas, son of Ezekias, is equally tempting. Perhaps the third theory, that he is unknown to us, is safest. Many times archaeology and history have unearthed proof of the Biblical stories which once were held to be fables or fiction. Countless times the Bible has proven true and the critics false. Just because we cannot prove who Theudas was at this time does not mean that the future will not establish his identity. Until that time we can take comfort in the fact that all other instances of questions about Biblical reliability have been quashed by historical revelations. Whoever this Theudas was, he was followed by a Judas of Galilee, whom all agree was real.

Judas of Galilee
Who was Judas of Galilee? According to Josephus he arose during the census of Quirinius (Cyrenius in the Latin).[295] This accords with Gamaliel's statement "in the days of the census." This is the same census of which Luke speaks in his gospel, but the events here took place after Jesus's birth and Herod's death (see *Controversies in the Gospel* for a full discussion of the census debate). Of Judas Josephus actually says very little. He is the first of the rebels which Josephus says continued until the destruction of the Temple. In *Antiquities of the Jews* he says only:

> "There one Judas, a Gaulonite, (or Galilean) ... who became zealous to draw them to a revolt, who both said that this taxation was no better than an introduction to slavery, and exhorted the nation to assert their liberty ... and the nation was infected with this doctrine to an incredible degree; one violent war came upon us after another, and we lost our friends which used to alleviate our pains; there were also very great robberies and murder of our principal men."[296]

In the W*ar of the Jews* Josephus says even less, only recording that "a certain Galilean, whose name was Judas, prevailed with his countrymen to revolt."[297] The significance seems to be that Josephus considered Judas the Galilean to be the founder of a party of Zealots, although he and his original followers "were scattered" as Acts 5:37 states.[298] The Theudas to whom Josephus refers apparently took place around 44-46 A.D. and was followed by the extinction of Judas's descendants. This connection is doubtless what has confused many readers, but it is relevant that Gamaliel does not say that Judas's followers perished along with him, but rather than "all those who followed him were scattered" (v. 37). Thus his followers did not become extinct until the time of Fadus, but they were "scattered" and of no significance in Gamaliel's day.

Conclusion
It is well known that in the time of Christ there were many false prophets and self-professed Messiahs. As Gamaliel stated all those men died and faded into history. Only Jesus remains; a testament to his Messianic credentials.

Here Gamaliel refers to two false Messiahs. The second, Judas of Galilee is known to all historians as the founder of a revolt under the Roman census that took place around the time of Herod's death. The first preceded Judas. Unless Josephus erred, as some believe, a myriad of candidates exist, but only two seem credible. Was Theudas a title give to a self-professed Messiah named Simon of Perea? The facts seem to match Gamaliel's story very closely. Alternately, Archbishop Ussher argued that Judas, the son of Ezekias, matches the story as well, and that Theudas is a Hellenization of Judas from the Syriac. I slightly favor Simon of Perear, but we may not know the answer until the Lord Himself tells us for much of history lay buried in thousands of years of sand, so that not even archaeology can reveal it all, but we have the testimony of Luke which has proven true and accurate despite countless failed attacks upon his credibility.

Stephen's Account of Abraham
Acts 7:4 – Genesis 11:32 and 12:4

> "[Abraham] left the land of the Chaldeans and settled in Haran. From there, after his father died, *God* had him move to this country in which you are now living."

Here Stephen correctly recounts the fact that Abraham moved with his father to Haran. There, in Genesis 11:32, we are told, "The days of Terah were two hundred and five years; and Terah died in Haran." We are then told in Genesis 12:4 that "Abram went forth [to Canaan] as the LORD had spoken to him; and Lot went with him. Now Abram was seventy-five years old when he departed from Haran." Many commentators, and Stephen as well, assume that Abraham then left "after his father died" (Acts 7:4). The problem is that Genesis 12:4 explicitly says that Abraham was seventy-five years old when he departed Haran, and was two hundred and five years old when he died. How is this a problem? Because Genesis 11:26 says that "Terah lived seventy years, and became the father of Abram, Nahor and Haran." This would mean that Abraham was a hundred and thirty-five years old when Terah died! How are we to resolve this?

There are two issues here. One is of what Genesis itself actually teaches. The second is what Stephen believed. In *Controversies in the Pentateuch* I thoroughly discussed the story in Genesis. I will recap my conclusions here briefly.

The Story in Genesis
There two primary solutions which have been proposed through the centuries. One of the most popular is that the statement, "Terah lived seventy years, and became the father of Abram, Nahor and Haran" does not refer to the birth of Abram, but to one of his brothers. According to this view, Abram "is first named in order of dignity (for which cause Shem is put before Ham and Japheth, and Moses before Aaron,) not in order of time."[299] That author then argues that Haran is actually the eldest and Abram the youngest.[300] He is followed in this belief by men like John Calvin,[301] James Ussher,[302] John Lightfoot,[303] Matthew Henry,[304] John Wesley,[305] and John Gill.[306] However, the natural flow of the text seems to indicate that Abraham was the first born.

The second solution, and the best, is that Genesis 11:32 is a footnote to close the genealogical passages. It is parenthetical. Augustine explains that Terah's total years are counted first "otherwise it would not be known how many years Terah lived."[307] Then "the Scripture, according to its custom, has gone back to the time which had already been passed by the narrative."[308] In other words, the fact that Terah's death is recounted before Abram's departure does not necessarily imply that Terah's death came first. Jewish scholar Ibn Ezra agrees, saying that these passages are "not chronological,"[309] as do Rashi[310] and Jewish tradition in general.[311] But Stephen departs from Jewish tradition, one author even says, "Stephen apparently departs from Biblical tradition."[312] The question is why did Stephen contradict this view?

Stephen's Account
A variety of theories have been proposed to explain why Stephen does not take the traditional Jewish interpretation.

Theory # 1 : Stephen followed the Samaritan Pentateuch
One argument is that Stephen was following "conjectural emmendation of Samaritan Pentateuch"[313] which says that Terah was only a hundred and forty-five when he died. This argument is the weakest and has many problems. First, that would make Abraham fifteen when years old when Terah died. Second, Stephen was not a Samaritan, who were in fact despised among most Jews. Third, no one suggest that the Samaritan Pentateuch is the original text, but rather than the Hebrew text is authentic. Fourth, even if he had for some odd reason borrowed from the Samaritan Bible, he would still be wrong, so this would not actually answer the fundamental question.

Theory #2 : Spiritual Death
One argument is that Stephen was not referring to Terah's physical death, but his "spiritual death."[314] Says one author, "Terah was, for all practical purposes, 'dead' to God's will and plan ... Terah was 'dead,' though he would not actually be ready for burial for perhaps another threescore years."[315] This view is generically echoed by Philo[316] and the Jewish *Midrash* which says that

"the wicked, even during their lifetime, are called dead."[317] However, this is an unsatisfying solution since the Bible gives no indication that this is the intended meaning. It reads too much into the context and condemns Terah without just cause. Furthermore, the context of Stephen's account at this stage is chronological and exegetical. There is nothing here to indicate that Stephen is implying that Terah had lost his soul. Theologically we are all spiritually dead from birth! How then can anyone say that Terah became "spiritually dead" at a hundred and forty-five? Had he lost the ability to repent? Nothing in the Bible, or in Stephen's account hints at such a notion.

Theory # 3 : Abraham Was Not the Oldest Son

As aforementioned, many believe that Abraham was not the oldest son, despite being mentioned first in the genealogy. They argue that Abraham's name is only listed first on account of his prestige.[318] This view is doubtless the most popular among Christians, but as I stated above it is not the best. The genealogy is fairly straightforward and nothing indicates that Terah was a hundred and forty-five when he became the father of Abraham. In fact, as Henry Morris points out, "if Abram himself were born when his father was [145] years old, [then why] should it have taken a special miracle for Abram to become a father when he was only an hundred years old!"[319] Although popular, this is not correct.

Theory # 4 : Stephen Was Mistaken

Many Christians mistakenly assume that if Stephen was wrong, the Bible is wrong, but this is not true. Luke here was acting as a historian. His job is not to correct a mistake Stephen *may* have made, but to accurately report what Stephen said. Consider, for example, Acts 15:1 where Luke accurately records the fact that Peter once taught the heresy that "unless you are circumcised according to the custom of Moses, you cannot be saved" (Acts 15:1). We know that Peter later repented of this, and the Bible is *clear* that Peter was wrong. The Bible is thus inerrant, as was Peter when he wrote his epistles, but this does not mean that the apostles were themselves without error in their lifetimes, let alone that Stephen could not have made a common error in a speech to the people on an issue of no particularly significance!

Conclusion

Genesis does not say that Terah died before Abraham left for Canaan, nor does Acts. Acts only says that Stephen believed Terah died first. Stephen was mistaken, *not* the Bible. This answer is therefore the best. Abraham left Haran when he was seventy-five. He was doubtless living in Canaan when news arrived of his father's death. Genesis 11:32 is parenthetical, not chronological. The book of Acts recounts the story of Stephen's martyrdom as it happened, altering nothing, including his mistaken notion that Terah had died first.

Stephen's Account of the Migration
Acts 7:14 – Exodus 1:1-5

"Joseph sent *word* and invited Jacob his father and all his relatives to come to him, seventy-five persons *in all*."

Here again Stephen is accused of error. However, the critic is sometimes so desperate to find error that he errs in his own reading. It is true that Exodus 1:5 states that "all the persons who came from the loins of Jacob were seventy in number," but this passage does not stand on its own. Let us examine the relevant passages and the theories regarding Stephen's account.

It has been pointed out that the Greek *Septuagint* translation of Genesis says "seventy-five" rather than "seventy" so many have assumed that Stephen was following the *Septuagint* account rather than the Hebrew. While this is possible, it is not in itself a solution. Where did the *Septuagint* even get this number? The answer may come from examining the relevant passages.

It has been argued that the *Septuagint* omitted the names of Jacob and Joseph, but included his seven grand-children. Alternately, some have suggested that the *Septuagint* followed Genesis 46:26 which says, "not including the wives of Jacob's sons, there *were* sixty-six persons in all," but then included the nine wives in Genesis 46:27 and Exodos 1:5.[320] In either case the numbers come out correct, but there is another explanation as well.

Genesis 46:26-27 states that "all the persons belonging to Jacob, who came to Egypt, his direct descendants, not including the wives of Jacob's sons, *were* sixty-six persons in all, and the sons of Joseph, who were born to him in Egypt were two; all the persons of the house of Jacob, who came to Egypt, *were* seventy." Exodus 1:5 repeats this number, but when we read Genesis 50:23 we find that "Joseph saw the third generation of Ephraim's sons; also the sons of Machir, the son of Manasseh, were born on Joseph's knees." All these were born *before* the death of Jacob. So while there were only seventy offspring of Jacob when he arrived in Egypt, "the five additional names given in the LXX are Machir the son, and Galaed the grandson of Manasseh, and the two sons of Ephraim, Taam and Soutalaam, with Soutalaam's son Edom."[321] In other words, those children born in Genesis 50:23 are said in tradition to be "Machir, Gilead, Shutelah, Tahen, and Eden."[322] These were all born before Jacob's death so that Stephen, and the *Septuagint*, could accurately say that there were "seventy-five people in all."

It is of interest to note that in the Dead Sea Scrolls the ancient Hebrew manuscript 4QExod[a] also contains the number "seventy-five."[323] Thus it is entirely possible that the Massoretic text is in error at this point and the original Hebrew text did read exactly as Stephen said. Since the Dead Sea Scrolls predate the Massoretic texts this is entirely possible.

Now such this tradition may or may not have been to what Stephen was alluding. It is indeed possible that Stephen was merely following the

Septugaint, which would match what we said of Stephen in Acts 7:4. Either solution is possible and neither is problematic, for Luke was again recording exactly what Stephen said, and recounting it accurately.

Stephen's Account of Shechem
Acts 7:16 – Joshua 24:32

> "They were removed to Shechem and laid in the tomb which Abraham had purchased for a sum of money from the sons of Hamor in Shechem."

Poor Stephen. His critics just can't seem to acknowledge that he knew what he was talking about. Here again the critic claims a contradiction with the Old Testament passages, but again they make only a superficial reading of an issue which is not superficial. It is true that many Bible commentators have been equally confused, for the accounts are largely parenthetical and it is easy to misinterpret their meaning, so let us, once again, look at the relevant passages carefully.

Genesis 50:13 states that Jacob's descendants "carried him to the land of Canaan and buried him in the cave of the field of Machpelah before Mamre, which Abraham had bought along with the field for a burial site from Ephron the Hittite." We also know that Joseph's bones were removed from Egypt as well, for Exodus 13:19 confirms that "Moses took the bones of Joseph with him" when he left Egypt and so were conveyed many decades later into Canaan.

Now Joshua 24:32 states that "they buried the bones of Joseph, which the sons of Israel brought up from Egypt, at Shechem, in the piece of ground which Jacob had bought from the sons of Hamor the father of Shechem for one hundred pieces of money; and they became the inheritance of Joseph's sons." Note that only Joseph is mentioned in Joshua 24:32.

So we have here three passages in the Old Testament which confirm the following:

1. Jacob's bones were taken to Canaan.
2. Joseph's bones were taken to Canaan.
3. Jacob's bones were "buried in the cave of the field of Machpelah before Mamre, which Abraham had bought."
4. Joseph's bones were "buried at Shechem, in the piece of ground which Jacob had bought from the sons of Hamor."

Now the problem is that Stephen here says "they" were buried at Shechem. Who are "they?" In Stephen's speech he says Jacob "and our fathers." Obviously this implies that Jacob is a part of those buried in Shechem, but technically it refers only to "our fathers." This is a generic passage and not a technical one. "They" refers to "our fathers," although not all of the Hebrew fathers were buried in the same place. It is not the purpose of Stephen here to give a census of which forefather was buried in which tomb, but generically to state that "they" were brought to Canaan and buried here, even as Joseph was buried at Shechem. Some have argued that that Stephen emphasized the burial grounds at Shechem because it was the homeland of the Samaritans,[324] whom many Jews despised.

In any case the story is accurate if not complete. Stephen is not giving an exhaustive history, but a summary. Technical arguments made to discredit him are frivolous and take the purpose of his speech out of context. The Hebrews' fathers were all caried up out of Egypt and laid to rest in Canaan, such as Shechem where the tomb of Joseph resides to this day.

Stephen and the Prophecy of Amos
Acts 7:43 – Amos 5:26-27

"You also took along the Tabernacle of Moloch and the star of the god Rompha, the images which you made to worship. I also will remove you beyond Babylon."	"You also carried along Sikkuth your king and Kiyyun, your images, the star of your gods which you made for yourselves. Therefore, I will make you go into exile beyond Damascus."

Here again the Bible critic claims that Stephen is misquoting the prophecy of Amos. There are two apparent conflicts. Let us start with the easiest.

Babylon Or Damascus?

According to the prophecy "I will make you go into exile beyond Damascus" (Amos 5:27), but here Stephen says "beyond Babylon." Of course Babylon is obviously "beyond Damascus" and the prophecy had long ago been fulfilled so that no one can deny that the exile in Babylon is of what Amos spoke.

Now in fairness to the critics, even men like John Calvin suggested that Babylon may have "crept in here by error."[325] Alternately Albert Barnes thought that "Damascus ... evidently denotes the eastern region, in which also Babylon was situated,"[326] but others have commented that "Stephen substitutes 'beyond Babylon' because the prophecy had been fulfilled long ago, the people having been carried so far beyond Damascus as to have been scattered even beyond Babylon."[327] Since the deportation was not limited to Damascus or Babylon, the passage cannot be said to be in error,[328] for "a deportation which took them beyond Damascus ... to Babylon."[329]

The answer to this criticism is then simple. Babylon lay beyond Damascus and the prophecy of Amos was clearly about the exile instigated Babylon. The Jews were deported, as prophesied, beyond Damascus, even as far as Babylon. Stephen is paraphrasing the prophesy because all the Jews knew and understood that they had been deported by Babylon.

The Idols Carried Away
A better question is how "Sikkuth your king and the star of Kiyyun" became "the Tabernacle of Moloch and the star of the god Rompha." This is a two part question, but first, bear in mind that Stephen was paraphrasing for the common Jew, and second, it is important to remember that we are actually dealing with three languages; Hebrew, Greek, and English, all of which have entirely different alphabets.

Tabernacle, God, or King?
The first part of the question is in regard to "the Tabernacle of Moloch" whose Old Testament parallel is various translated. One study Bible states that "Amos' unusual employment of words makes this verse the most difficult verse in the book [of Amos] to comprehend."[330] In fact, there are no fewer than five different translations of this difficult passage. The chart below shows the various translations.

King James / Webster / Darby / Douay-Rheims	"The tabernacle of your Moloch."
MKJV	"The booth of your king."
NKJV / NAS / RSV / NRSV / ESV	"Sikkuth your king."
NIV	"The shrine of your king."
ASV	"The tabernacle of your king."

Note how three different King James versions have three entirely different translations! The problem is that both the Hebrew words סכות (*s-cuth*) and מלך (*m-l-k*) can be translated various ways depending on the vowels. Because ancient Hebrew did not use vowels (the root meaning of words was always in the consonants, with vowels determined by context and use; e.g. noun, verb, adjectival use, etc.), these words can be taken in one of several ways. The first word, סכות (*s-cuth*) was translated σκηνην (*skenen*) in the *Septuagint*, which means "tablernacle," "shrine," or "booth." This is based on the Hebrew word סִכּוּת (*siccuth*) which is in turn believed to be related to סֻכּוֹת (*succoth*) which can mean "booths."[331] The problem is that סֻכּוֹת (*succoth*) is plural. Many doubt that סִכּוּת (*siccuth*) could properly be a singular word. Gleason Archer says that סִכּוּת (*siccuth*) "has a very dubious base as a common noun for 'shrine,'"[332] and thus many render it as a proper name. The problem with this is that neither A.T. Olmstead nor Robert Rogers mention any such god in their monumental histories of Babylon and Assyria.[333]

The second part of the sentence revolves around the form of the word מלך (*m-l-k*), or more precisely מלככם (*m-l-kk-m*). Now מֶלֶךְ (*melek*) is the most common word for "king" found in Hebrew. Here the כם (*kem*) suffix means "yours." Hence, "your king." However, remember again that Hebrew was written without vowel points. Context determined if a word was a proper name or not. Since the well known pagan god Moloch would also be spelled this way without vowel points, some have taken it as a proper name.

We then have three options. It could be rendered "the shrine [or tabernacle] of your king" as in the NIV, ASV, and MKJV. It could be rendered, "the shrine [or tabernacle] of your Moloch" as in the KJV, Webster, Darby, and Douay-Rheims. Or it could be rendered as "Sikkuth your king" as found in the NAS, NKJV, RSV, NRSV, and ESV.

The last, although popular, is not only conjecture but illogical, for if it is "Sikkuth" (a "god" unknown to historians) then it should read "Sikkuth your god" or "Sikkuth your idol," not "Sikkoth you king," since the king would not be an actual person. A "god" is not a king, and neither is an idol. This translation, therefore, should be rejected.

Although it is true that סכות (*siccuth*) may be a suspect word for shrine, the fact that it was so translated by the ancient Jews in the *Septuagint*, and here in the book of Acts by Stephen, should be sufficient proof that "shrine" or "tabernacle" is intended. If the word is naturally plural, then we could have no objection to "shrines." The idea that there was only one Tabernacle of Israel should not be an obstruction since the Jews were obviously not being faithful at this point. They would doubtless have had many shrines in violation of God's law. The final question is, therefore, whether or not these were shrines of the king, or shrines dedicated to the pagan god Moloch. This question is harder to answer, but not impossible. Jewish tradition supports Moloch, as this is the translation found in the *Septuagint*. However, later Massoratic vowel points clearly favored "king." Contextually, the idea of a shrine dedicated to a king is weak. This is especially true since the Israelites were being exiled for the sins of idolatry and following after false gods, the chief of which was Moloch. Since this is how Stephen and the *Septuagint* both translated the passage, it is best to agree with the older King James translation ... and Stephen.

Rompha or Kiyyun?

Here again is a translation issue rather than one of contradiction. First, in regard to the various reading the reader should be reminded that Hebrew, Greek, and English all have different alphabets, so that Kiyyon can be rendered Chiun (as in the KJV) or even Kaiwan because the "yy" can be taken either as an "iu" (Chiun) or as a "w" (Kaiwan) in English. The "hard" *ch* is the same as a "k" followed by the long "i" sound, and the last syllable can be transliterated various as either "un" or "wan." Likewise, Raiphan has various forms in Greek which in turn are variously transliterated into English leading to such diverse names as Rompha (with or without the "n" ending) and Raiphan. I will not go into detail here, but they are the same word. The only real debate is over the confusion between Kiyyon and Raiphan (or Rompha).

Some have made this matter extremely complication. Gleason Archer, for example, has made a prolonged conjecture regarding how Kiyyon became

Raiphan. He argues that similarities between Elephantine alphabet and the standard Hebrew alphabet led to a confusion as to the spelling, but this conjecture is really unnecessary.[334] The answer is really simple.

כִּיּוּן (*Kiyyon*) was the name of Saturn,[335] an Assyrian astral deity. The Greek name of Saturn is Ραιφαν (*Raiphan*).[336] Thus both names refer to the Assyrian god of Saturn.

Conclusion
Beyond Damascus lay Babylon where history records the prophesied exile took place. Here Stephen reminds the Jews that they were exiled to Babylon. This is a paraphrase of Amos. The confusion between the names of the idols has been unnecessarily complicated by some scholars, but he solution is simple. The proper translation of the first is that of "shrines to Moloch" as Stephen here states. In the second, Raiphan (or Romphan) is merely the Greek word for Saturn which is Kiyyon (or Chion) in Hebrew.

Who Gave the Law?
Acts 7:53

"You who received the law as ordained by angels."

Here is an interesting controversy. Here Stephen seems to imply that the law was given to Moses by angels, whereas the Bible appears to state that it none other the Lord God Himself who conveyed the law to Moses (cf. Exodus 20:1). In fact, it was considered heresy to attribute to angels what God alone did. Consider the heretic Cerinthus who believed that angels not only gave law but created the world![337] Surely, it is argued, Stephen was in error? If not, then how can this be reconciled?

A number of answers have been hypothesized although all are similar in nature. Some have noted that "the Jews attributed the whole deliverance of the Law, except the utterance of 'the Ten Words,' to angels (Deut. xxxiii.2 {LXX}; Ps. lxviii.17, Jos. *Antiq.*, xv.5.3) 'it was ordained *through angels* by the hand of a mediator' (Gal. iii.19)."[338] Indeed, the Septuagint adds the words, "and on His right hand were angels" to Deuteronomy 30:2.[339] Now the Hebrew reads, "at His right hand there was flashing lightning." So it appears that the Jews traditionally interpreted the lightning in some form as angels. So "it has been supposed to mean that the law was given *amidst* the various ranks of angels, being present to witness the promulgation."[340]

Others, like Lightfoot, have noted that the word "angels" literaly means "messengers."[341] So John Calvin stated that "He means that the angels were messengers of God and His witnesses in publishing the law."[342]

Still others argue that "angels" is a term used in reverence of Moses and the Israelites. Galatians 4:14 is cited as proof of such usage,[343] but an examination of these verses nullifies this argument. In Galatians Paul states that "you received me as an angel of God." This is, however, very different from saying "you who received the law as ordained by angels." Even if Moses were referred to as an angel, or messenger, it was not Moses who ordained the law. It was the Lord and His host.

So of these three opinions, the strongest is that, as John Wesley argued, "God, when He gave the Law on Mount Sinai, was attended with thousands of His angels, Gal. iii.9, Psalms lxviii.17."[344] Such was the opinion of the Jews at the time of Stephen, for this view was accepted by both Philo and Josephus in the same era.[345] This seems to be what Stephen intended here. The fact that God personally gave the Ten Commandments to Moses (Exodus 20:1) does not negate the fact that angels participated in the giving of the law as stated explicitly in both the Old Testament (Psalms 68:17) and the New (Galatians 3:19 and Hebrews 2:2).

According to Psalms 68:17, "the chariots of God are myriads, thousands upon thousands; The Lord is among them *as at* Sinai." Since Sinai is the place where the Law was given tradition, and proper exegesis, has viewed this as the presence of angels (cf. the *Septuagint* reading of Deuteronomy 30:2). The New Testament is even more clear. In Galatians 3:19 Paul said that the Law "was added because of transgressions, having been ordained through angels by the agency of a mediator." Hebrews also states that "the word spoken through angels proved unalterable" (2:2). This "word" refers to the Scriptures, of which the Law was the dominant portion.

Stephen was then completely accurate to say that "you who received the law as ordained by angels" even though all aknowledge that the Lord God was the prime factor and Law giver. The point of Stephen was not to say that God did not give the Law, but that even the angels are subject to God, thus convicting his listeners of their own rebellion against the Law which given to man with the assistance of angels who accompanied the Lord.

Stephen's Martyrdom
Acts 7:54-60

"They had driven him out of the city, they *began* stoning *him*; and the witnesses laid aside their robes at the feet of a young man named Saul."

Stephen bore the honor of being the first of tens of millions of Christian martyrs who have given their lives for their faith, and yet this verse is of far more significance than that fact alone. The honor due to Stephen was accompanied by one of the great ironies of history, and one which bears the hand of God. Saul, later to become Paul the Apostle, was there at the murder. He sanctioned it and led the early persecutions against Christians. Many years later when he stood before the Jews of Jerusalem he declared that "I persecuted *The Way* to the death" (Acts 22:4). "The Way" was the original name of the early Christians. It comes from John 14:6 where Jesus said, "I am the Way, the Truth, and the Life; no one comes to the Father except through Me." It was at Antioch some time later that we first became called Christians (Acts 11:26), which means "follower of Christ" or "belonging to Christ," and it was Paul, the one time persecutor of us, who would become one of the most important apostles in history!

The Scattering of the Disciples
Acts 8:1-4

> "Saul was in hearty agreement with putting him to death. And on that day a great persecution began against the church in Jerusalem, and they were all scattered throughout the regions of Judea and Samaria."

This scattering of the disciples is important both historically and theologically. It is said that "the blood of the martyrs is the seed of the church." Tertullian declared that "we conquer in dying. We go forth victorious at the very time we are subdued."[346] The question is, "why?" Obviously part of the reason is that it shows people what we have something worth dying for, but this is not all, for evil men also die for a cause. Part of it is how we die. Unlike suicide bombers, we do not kill for our faith but quietly lay down our lives for it. Nevertheless, there is far more to it than even this.

According to Acts 8:4 "those who had been scattered went about preaching the word." Historically it is a fact that the gospel spreads further and faster under persecution. Remember that Jesus ordered the apostles from the very beginning to "Go therefore and make disciples of all the nations" (Matthew 28:19), but the disciples naturally stayed at home and witnessed the gospel to Israel. Some believe that this was their duty, and it was certainly a part of their duty to preach the gospel " to the Jew first and also to the Greek (Romans 1:16). "Also the gentile." This was neglected by the apostles until God Himself pushed them out of Israel. There is no such thing as "if" in history. God is the author of history, but hypothetically I wonder what would have happened if Christians had never been persecuted. Would we have been subjugated along with Israel in 70 A.D.? Would we have become too comfortable in the world, as many are today, and neglected the Great Commission? Would the gospel ever have reached Rome? Like Jonah all of us are reluctant to go to hostile lands to preach the Lord's Word, but like Jonah God insures we go where He desires. The persecutions of the early church forced the church to scatter and as a result, "therefore," says Acts 8:4, "those who had been scattered went about preaching the word." The word "therefore" is significant, for it indicates that had they not been scattered by persecution they would not have preached the word abroad. This is the lesson of history, and of God's sovereignty. Even in persecution God's Will is at work!

6

The Church in Antioch

After the persecutions of Jerusalem the church headquarters moved to Antioch which lay in Syria, near the border of modern day Turkey. It rest north of Israel and was close enough to make the apostles' ministry to Israel still feasible while protecting them from overt persecution. However, they were still not entirely safe. Antioch had a large population of Jews, which actually favored the apostles who were Jewish, but with this there also came the threat from Jewish radicals, such as Saul of Tarsus.

These days were still a part of the church in its infancy, but clearly it was also a church fastly growing to maturity and in flux. With Antioch as its new base the church was forced to deal with new problems, and with a vast gentile population which they had not formerly known. It is during this time period that the apostles first began to encounter gentile converts, which would lead to the debate about circumcision years later. God was slowly pushing the apostles toward His Will.

Simon the Magician
Acts 8:9-24

> "When Simon saw that the Spirit was bestowed through the laying on of the apostles' hands, he offered them money."

The crime of "simony" is when a priest is paid money for what is his charitable duty to do for free.[347] It gets its name from Simon the Sorcerer who dared to offer bribe money to the apostles so that he could obtain the "power" of the Holy Spirit. Indeed, Simon did not understand the Holy Spirit at all. He was a sorcerer who saw it only as a source of "power," even as many modern day preachers and televangelists seem to believe.

In history Simon is called by the Latin name, Simon Magus, meaning Simon the Magician. Although he is found only in this one chapter. He is spoken of as a disciple of Phillip, and nothing in the text itself indicates that he was not, at least in his own mind, a sincere follower. However, his crime is so infamous that Simon has been demonized ever since. Legends portray him as an opponent and enemy of Christianity, and one even makes him out to be an early Luciferists who believed Jesus was the rival of God the Father![348] It is therefore important to examine the Simon of tradition and legend with the Simon of history and the Bible.

The History and Legends of Simon the Sorcerer
The story of Simon is a fascinating one which had led to countless extra-Biblical legends and traditions. Moreover, because Simon is a common name in ancient Israel, and because of the popularity of magic and sorcery in those days a number of Simons are to be found in history which may or may not be synonymous with Simon the Sorcerer. Josephus, for example, records the story of a certain Simon whom some believe was none other than Simon Magus. Although these legends only peripherally, if at all, relate to the bible, it is noteworthy to examine these histories, traditions, and legends.

Simon in Josephus

Let us begin with history, before moving into tradition and legend. Josephus records the story of a Jew named Simon who practiced magic and lived at the same time as the Simon in Acts. According to Josephus :

> "But for the marriage of Drusilla [the sister of Herod Agrippa II] with Azizus, it was in no long time afterward dissolved upon the following occasion : While Felix was procurator of Judea, he saw this Drusilla, and fell in love with her; for she did indeed exceed all other women in beauty; and he sent to her a person whose name was Simon one of his friends; a Jew he was, and by birth a Cypriot, and one who pretended to be a magician, and endeavored to persuade her to forsake her present husband, and marry him; and promised, that if she would not refuse him, he would make her a happy woman. Accordingly she acted ill, and because she was desirous to avoid her sister Bernice's envy (for she was very ill treated by her on account of her beauty), was prevailed upon to transgress the laws of her forefathers, and to marry Felix; and when he had had a son by her, he named him Agrippa."[349]

So it is that this Simon created a scandal by persuading Drusilla to divorce her husband to marry the pagan Roman governor, from whom a possible future heir was born! To be sure he was by no means the first, or even second, in line for the throne, but the royal lineage was considered tainted nevertheless. This Simon was thus infamous among Orthodox Jews, but was he Simon Magus?

William Whiston, the successor of Isaac Newton, and translator of Josephus believes "this Simon ... could hardly be that of the famous Simon ... [because he] was not properly a Jew, but a Samaritan, of the town of Gittae, in the country of Samaria."[350] Nonetheless, the problem with Whiston's assersion is that he has picked and chosen which legends to believe and which ones to reject. The truth is that the Bible says nothing about where Simon was born. We only know that he was then working in Samaria (Acts 8:9). The Bible tells us nothing more of him. Nothing is said of his ancestry or of his background except that was one who "formerly was practicing magic in the city and astonishing the people of Samaria, claiming to be someone great" (Acts 8:9).

The church father Hippolytus does record that he was from Samaria,[351] but I am inclined to believe that Josephus's Simon was Simon Magus, albeit with reservations. Simon was indeed a popular name and magic was common among the superstitious peasants. Consequently, it is possible that another Simon is intended, but the following evidence favors that this was Simon Magus.

1) He was a Jew named Simon practicing magic in Israel. Although there may have been more than one Simon who practiced magic, the Bible itself condemns sorcery. Deuteronomy 18:10-12 condemns sorcery and commands the Jews to drive all such sorcerers and magicians from the land of Israel. It is likely that Simon enjoyed the protection of Rome because of his friendship with the royal family. Consequently, despite the fact that magic was more popular in those days (cf. Acts 13:6-8), the Jews were not tollerant of magicians and it is not likely that a great many Magicians named Simon were practicing their art in Israel.

2) Simon was "claiming to be someone great" (Acts 8:9). We cannot say that practicing "magic" alone would allow Simon to make this claim, especially since the Laws of Israel condemned magic. However, if Simon was a friends with royalty, then it is logical that he would enjoy the protection of Rome and be able to call himself "great." This would also explain why he was allowed to violate the laws of Israel with apparent impunity.

3) The dates make this a probablity. Felix was procurator, or governor, of Judea from approximately 52 or 53 A.D. to 59 or 60 A.D.[352] We know that he was already married to Drusilla when Paul arrived in Jerusalem and preached to him, for Acts 24:24 mentions this same Drusilla as the wife of Felix. This means that the marriage took place sometime in the early fifties. This actually bears some impact upon the debate of whether or not Simon was a true convert (see below), but its importance here is merely that it did take place around fifteen to twenty years after Peter's confrontation. Simon was most likely still alive at this time, heightening the probability that this was the same Simon.

In short, the Simon of Josephus is probably the same as that of Simon Magus. Years after being rebuked by Peter Simon had apparently not mended his ways. This fits well with the animosity with which tradition treats Simon. Although it cannot be said as a certainty, it seems the most likely scenario.

The Founder of Gnosticism?

As we see, the Simon of history does not appear to have left a mark as a disciple of Christ. Nowhere do we read anything positive of Simon. Instead, a great many legends say that Simon was the founder of gnosticism.[353] Gnosticism was the first major cult of Christianity and is refuted in Colossians and many other epistles. Many of these epistles were even written for the expressed purpose of refuting gnostic heresies.

According to gnosticism God could not have created a world with evil in it.[354] They believe that god-like entities, called "aeons," created each other, with each being inferior to its creator, until one "aeon," called "Wisdom," sought to create another "aeon" but then "aborted" its birth at the last moment, resulting in the earth.[355] And so according to gnosticism, the earth is a mistake! Accordingly they believed that all matter is evil.[356]

Now this strange belief was merged with various forms of dualism. Orphic, Platonic, and even Persian dualism are all considered ancestral to that of gnosticism.[357] By dualism several things are intended, but here I mean that the manner in which they seperate the physical and spiritual has led to an ironic dualism in regard to our physical bodies. Some gnostics held to a strict asceticism while others engaged in a sensualistic libertinism.[358] The argument was that "if the body were only temporary, its acts were inconsequential."[359] So "what we are to do is to leave the body to its own devices and let it follow the guidance of its own passions. Thus, while some Gnostics were extreme ascetics, others were libertines."[360]

Two other aspects of gnosticism are important to understand. Like all mystery cults, gnosticism holds that their followers are bestowed with secret knowledge denied to others. The name gnostic itself comes from the Greek word γνωσις (*gnosis*) meaning "knowledge."[361] The gnostic therefore considered themselves to be superior in knowledge of spiritual matters to all who were not initiated into their sect. This is something Paul explicitly mocked in Colossians when he repeatedly referred to Jesus as the "mystery of God" (Colossians 2:2) which has been revealed to all through Him (cf. Colossians 1:26). Several times in Colossians Paul refers to both "mystery" and "knowledge" as relating to Christ alone and indicating that "true knowledge" (2:2) comes through Christ and Christ alone!

The last aspect of gnosticism which Paul also vigorously attacked was the denial of the resurrection.[362] Since gnostics believe that all flesh is evil, they cannot believe that Jesus was ever flesh and blood. For the gnostics Christ was not physical, but a messenger without a real corporal body.[363] There could, therefore, be no resurrection. This may be why John, in his gospel, explicitly states that God "became flesh and dwelled among us" (John 1:14). It is certainly why Paul and the other disciples made clear many times that Jesus came in the flesh (Hebrews 5:7; 1 John 4:2; 2 John 1:7) and was resurrected from the dead!

Our question is how did such a bizarre cult arise so early in the history of Christianity, in a nation, Israel, which was not pagan! Clearly gnosticism is a bastard child of paganism, and some see strong similarities specifically to the Egyptian religion.[364] Luciferism is also apparent in gnosticism on several levels. In fact, the "aeons" appear much more like fallen angels, than angels, in which case the earth would have been created, according to gnosticism, by demons! One legend even claims that Simon believed Jesus to be a rival of God the

Father![365] These tenets fit the doctrines of Luciferism, so how could this possibly have led so many early Christians astray?

According to Philip Schaff, it was "Simon Magus, who unquestionably adulterated Christianity with pagan ideas and practices, and gave himself out, in pantheistic style, for an emanation of God" (Acts 8:10).[366] According to Acts 8:10 it was said by Simon's followers, "this man is what is called the Great Power of God." So Simon saw himself as a mystic manifestation of God's power, not unlike certain televangelists. This is the testimony of Hippolytus who records that Simon taught all these things,[367] and then recounts the bizarre mystical interpretations of Scripture which he promoted.[368] Not unlike the modern "liberal" scholar, Simon interpreted the Bible as pure allegory and mysticism with no historical value or literal application. Certainly Simon's belief in magic came not from Judaism, in which it is condemned, but from pagan religions. Like gnosticism Simon believed in mystical powers which could be controlled and apprently purchased for a sum of money. It is not hard to see why Simon, after being rebuked by Peter, is thought to have become the founder of a Christian cult set up against the apostles. Nevertheless, this is pure speculation. If he was the Simon of Josephus then he obviously had not learned his lessons and was continuing to enhance his power and prestige among the nobilty and governing powers that be. His character is consistent with those who found cults.

Whether it is true that Simon was involved in gnosticism or not cannot be said, for we have only legends. However, such legends fit very well with the Simon who sought to purchase the power of the Holy Spirit. This wreaks of a cult leader who was seeking to glorify himself rather than God, and is all too reminiscent of some televangelists. The teachings of gnosticism cannot be tied to Simon with any certainly at all, but we can say that much of its tenets are consistent with what a man of Simon's character would teach and preach. On the other hand, the asceticism of gnosticism does not match Simon's love of money, making his association with gnosticism much less likely. I will leave the reader to make his own determination.

Simon in Rome?

Tradition and legend place Simon Magus in Rome at the time that Peter first travelled to the city. According to the apocryphal Acts of Peter, written in the middle of the second century,[369] Simon Magus came to Rome shortly after Paul was acquitted in his first trial and had departed. Having no one to confront Simon who was spreading his heresies amid the church in Rome, Peter promptly came to combat him. There they are said to have engaged in a battle of miracles with Simon including resurrecting a fish and even making a dog speak. Finally, in a battle of magic versus prayer Simon Magus is said to have levitated himself in the air, but when Peter prayed, Simon fell and broke his leg.[370] Hippolytus recorded that Simon's death came when he ordered his followers to bury him alive in a trench, promising to resurrect himself after three days.[371] Unlike Jesus, Simon's body has remained buried for two thousand years.

Now these legends are obviously a work of "historical fiction" *at best*. The over-the-top battle of miracles and similar fabrications can obviously be rejected as ancient Hollywood entertainment for the readers. However, there are a great many who believe that Simon Magus did indeed travel to Rome. The great church historian Eusebius (263-339 A.D.), repeated the story that Peter came to Rome to combat Simon Magus, but without the wild embellishments.[372]

More importantly, the famed Justin Martyr recorded the following:

> "In Claudius's time ... [Simon Magus] was deemed a god at Rome and honored as a god with a statue in the river Tiber between the two bridges, and bore this inscription, in the language of Rome : – '*Simoni Deo Sancto*' meaning 'To Simon the holy God.' And almost all the Samaritans, and a few even of other nations, worship him, and acknowledge him as the first god."[373]

Interestingly enough, the discovery of a statue in 1574 seems to support this story for its inscription read "*Semoni Sancto Deo*."[374] The problem is that "*Semoni*," as opposed to "*Simoni*," was a Sabine deity. It is thus assumed by most modern scholars that Justin made a mistake in reading the inscription and that no such statue to Simon Magus ever existed. Still, some scholars believe that "this has always seemed to us very slight evidence on which to reject so precise a statement as Justin here makes : a statement which he would scarcely have hazarded in an apology addressed to Rome, where every person had the means of ascertaining its accuracy. If, as is supposed, he made a mistake, it must have been at once exposed, and other writers would not have so frequently repeated the story as they done."[375]

Was Simon ever in Rome? Let us consider the facts. Simon was a close friend and associate of Felix the Roman governor of Judea and his wife Drusilla. Between 59 and 60 A.D. Felix was relieved of duties in Judea and replaced as procurator/governor. As a Roman it is highly probable that Felix would eventually have retired to Rome. It makes sense that Simon Magus would have at least visited his friends in Rome to continue to promote his prestige and power. Consequently, while the fanciful legends may be rejected, and rightly so, it is highly probable that Simon eventually came to Rome. Whether he was deified in a statue or confronted by Peter we cannot say, but it is very likely that he travelled to Rome and spread his heresies there.

As the reader can see, Simon Magus has become a fanciful villain in Christian traditions. One tradition suggested he used the money with which he intended buy the Holy Spirit to purchase a prostitute.[376] Underlying these legends and traditions is the true historical Simon Magus. Of him we can say little beyond the Bible, but it does appear that he was a friend of Felix and Drusilla who had not turned from his wicked way. He may have followed them to Rome at some point where he continued to spread his doctrines and teachings. Whether or not those teaching included gnosticism we cannot say for certain but the apostles' epistles demonstrate that gnosticism was a heresy which they were combating very early on in church history.

The Nature of Simon's Magic

The book of Acts says only that Simon "formerly was practicing magic" (8:9). Nothing beyond this is said although clues to the nature of the "magic" appear in 8:10 wherein his followers called him the "power of God." Many have presumed his "magic" was but magic tricks, a pretense to gain followers. Others that he practiced ritualistic pagan rituals which were called "magic" as a way of "marginalizing the practices of a ritual."[377] Still others draw a distinction between "magic" and "sorcery," as many translations read. Each is worthy of consideration.

Sorcery vs. Magic

Some translations read "sorcery" rather than "magic." The two are actually quite different. Sorcery is that branch of the "black arts" which utilizes mind-altering drugs. The Greek word for sorcery is φαρμακεια (*pharmakia*), from which we get the word "pharmacy." It can be translated either "sorcerery" or "to administer drugs."[378] In this case, the translation is unwarranted for the Greek word found in all manuscripts of Acts is μαγευων (*mageuon*) from which we get the word "magician."[379]

It has been demonstrated that socerers were popular even among Jews in those days, often posing as prophets. In one incident, very close to the time of Simon and Peter's confrontation, around 35 A.D., Pontius Pilate and soldiers confronted a sorcerer and his followers on Mt. Gerezim where they were driven away.[380] The incident illustrates that false prophets came in all forms, many in the form of sorcerers and magicians.

Some Bible commentators argue that sorcerers had a "a superior knowledge of the laws of nature, especially of chemistry."[381] However, while knowledge of chemistry was doubtless a part of sorcery,[382] that does not seem to be the case here. As aforementioned, the Greek word is not φαρμακεια (*pharmakia*) but μαγευων (*mageuon*). The two cannot be confused. It is apparent from Acts that Simon claimed to be the "power of God." This is consistent with a belief in mystic power, not traditional sorcery which used drugs to interact with the "spirit world." Sorcery would certain be a practice in keeping with gnosticism, of which Simon is alleged to have founded, but based strictly on the Bible we can only say that he was a practiced "magician," and probably not a "sorcerer."

Trickster or Magician?

The next logical question is the nature of his magic. In western society we have tended to reject all belief in occult magic. Even Christian Bible commentators often assign the court magicians of Pharaoh to mere stage magicians and hucksters. In past generations most, like John Calvin, believed that God "permits false prophets to work miracles to deceive."[383] John Wesley argued that such miracles could happen "by the power of evil angels."[384] However, in the modern age men like Charles Spurgeon now declare that such court magicians acted "by dexterous sleight of hand ... and so deceived the eye."[385] This trend has continued here in Acts. Was Simon's "so-called magic" mere "trickery"?[386]

Josephus for one denied that Simon was a true magician. In his account Simon was "one who pretended to be a magician."[387] Many modern scholars follow this belief, calling his magic mere "tricks."[388] However, "tricks" are not as easy as many assume and the crowd is rarely as gullible as we would like. Stage magicians go to sometimes incredible lengths to make their tricks appear real. Such stage acts are both expensive and require stage and lighting which Simon would not have on the streets of Samaria. Also bear in mind that Jews were not uneducated, even if they were not formally educated. "Home schooling" was taught to all Jews and learning in the synogogues was common. This is why the Jews were the bankers of medieval Europe and why they escaped the bubonic plague. They were the best educated people in Europe who kept their communities free from disease carrying vermin. The Jews are living proof that "home schooling" is the *best* education possible. Therefore, let no one fool you by telling you that the apostles were unlearned or uneducated because they were simple fishmen who had never been to college. They could all speak multiple languages, knew the Bible and Jewish tradition, and could out-think most college professors in the U.S.A. So also the common Jewish peasant was not completely gullible as some may believe, especially since their own laws forbade the practice of magic. Hence their natural inclination would be to reject charltains. Certainly there are fools everywhere, but calling Simon a mere "trickster" may be a simple "out" for modern readers.

Consider that this same issue often appears in relation to Moses combating the magicians of Pharaoh's court. Many westerners consider ourselves too enlightened to believe in magic, and many have built a theology around the idea that Satan cannot truly perform miracles. Certainly Satan's "miracles" are limited by God and inherently inferior to those of the Lord, but nothing in the Bible indicates that magicians of Pharaoh's court were mere tricksters; nor would we expect that the Pharaoh was a gullible fool who would have tollerated such.

It is of interest to note that in Acts 19:19, converts were seen burning books of magic. This indicates that the practice of magic was religious in nature, a part of pagan ritual, and that it was far more than mere "sleight of hand" and "stage tricks." It was a part of Simon's religion. While we can reject over-the-top absurdities such as levitation, it is probable that Simon's magic deeds were counterfeit miracles, in opposition to the Lord. For a brief time he appeared to turn away from such dark arts and follow Jesus, but like the seed which fell on rocks, there was no root (cf. Matthew 18:23) and Peter's rebuke did not appear to stir him to repentance. Or did it? This is the question of Simon's faith.

Simon's Faith
Based strictly upon the Bible we cannot say that Simon's faith, however immature and unsanctified, was not real. Acts 8:13 declares "even Simon himself believed." However, nowhere is the word "believed" qualified. His actions, Peter's rebuke, and the legends of Simon which followed all speak against his faith being real, and yet Simon did ask Peter, "pray to the Lord for me yourselves, so that nothing of what you have said may come upon me" (Acts 8:24). Was this repentance?

Irenaeus believed Simon faked conversion to steal magic power.[389] This cynical interpretation is again drawn from the legends of Simon as the founder of gnosticism, but there does not seem to be a doubt that Simon at least thought he believed. He is like the seed which fell on shallow dirt in Jesus's parable (Matthew 18:23). Because he had no firm root and no true repentance, he quickly fell away. Philip should not be criticized, as some have done, for accepting Simon into the fold. It is not our duty to predetermine whose faith is sincere and whose is not. Until Simon offered money for the Holy Spirit there was no reason to deny him access to the church and to the faith. Philip was a hundred percent correct to mentor Simon and it is no fault of his own that Simon fell away. We have a duty, but that duty does not give us power over other men's souls as some seem to believe.

Simon's faith was "the faith that does not save."[390] He was seeking to glorify himself rather than God. Such false miracles and power seekers are common among religious cults and a growing number of mainstream preachers in the church today. Simon is then a warning to us not to accept a preacher simply because he performs a miracle and speaks powerfully. Such false prophets were in the beginning and are prophesied to become so numerous in the Last Days that "even the elect will be deceived, if possible" (Matthew 24:24). That day has clearly come.

Conclusion
Simon Magus is one of the most fascinating characters in Christian tradition. His appearance in the Bible is so brief that we cannot ascertain much except to take warning as Luke intended. God is not for sale. The power of the Holy Spirit is not a means to an end. More importantly, false prophets have always been among us and will continue to increase until the time of the end (2 Peter 2:1; 1 John 4:1). Although I prefer the NAS translation, I love the NIV translation of 2 Timothy 4:3 which says, "for the time will come when men will not put up with sound doctrine. Instead, to suit their own desires, they will gather around them a great number of teachers to say what their itching ears

want to hear." That day has come. As Jesus declared, "false Christs and false prophets will arise and will show great signs and wonders, so as to mislead, if possible, even the elect." (Matthew 24:24). Let us beware.

The Samaritan Pentecost and Spirit Baptism
Acts 8:15-17 – See also Acts 19:1-6

> "[The apostles] prayed for them that they might receive the Holy Spirit. For He had not yet fallen upon any of them; they had simply been baptized in the name of the Lord Jesus."

I have addressed the Baptism of the Spirit to some extent in Acts 2:38 and will address it again in Acts 19:1-6. Here, however, is the question of what some have called the "the Samaritan Pentecost."[391] The debate is of whether or not the new birth and the baptism of the Holy Spirit are synonymous. Those who teach that baptism of the Holy Spirit is distinct from conversion cite this passage along with Acts 19:1-6 as proof. However, the two passages are different, and will therefore be addressed seperately.

Here it is said that "the apostles in Jerusalem heard that Samaria had received the word of God, they sent them Peter and John, who came down and prayed for them that they might receive the Holy Spirit. For He had not yet fallen upon any of them; they had simply been baptized in the name of the Lord Jesus. Then they *began* laying their hands on them, and they were receiving the Holy Spirit" (8:14-17).

The Theories on the Samaritan Pentecost
"The temporal separation of the baptism of the Spirit from commitment to Jesus and water baptism in this passage has been of paramount and perennial theological interest to many. Catholic sacramentalists take this as a biblical basis for the separation betweeen baptism and confirmation. Charismatics of various denominational persuastions see in it a justification for their dotrine of the baptism of the Spirit as a second work of grace following conversion."[392] Certainly there is something unique in this passage, but if we are going to draw an entire theological system based on a single passage, which is theologically dangerous, then we had best examine the passage thoroughly.

Of the plethora of beliefs and arguments regarding the meaning of this passage there are six that are worthy of mention. Few of them sufficiently answer all the questions, and a few create more questions than they answer, but these are the arguments which are most often put forward in the discussion of the "Samaritan Pentecost."

View # 1 : Catholic Confirmation
According to the *Catechism of the Catholic Church* confirmation is a ritual distinct from baptism.[393] Unlike baptism, which they bestow in childhood,

confirmation is usually done on older, often adult, members.[394] This passage is the passage used to justify the practice; a practice which separates baptism from confirmation by decades. According to Catholics "the people of Samaria were baptized in Christ, but did not receive the fullness of the Spirit until they were confirmed by the elders. Confirmation is a sacrament that Jesus Christ instituted within His Catholic Church to further strengthen those who have reached adulthood."[395] Hence, this view argues that "the fullness of the Holy Spirit"[396] is bestowed by an elder or priests sometime after baptism.

The problems with the Catholic sacramental view include the fact that only the apostles are mentioned, and nowhere else are priests or elders shown, discussed, or even hinted at, as being required for the blessings of the Spirit. This, and Acts 19:1-6, are the only passages which indicate that the Holy Spirit was not "bestowed" (8:18) when they first believed (but see notes on Acts 19:1-6). Consequently, it is more than inference to suggest that priests are required to anoint someone. This teaching has naturally led to theological and ethical dilemas within the church. For example, those "in danger of death" must received the rite of confirmation even if they have not attained the "age of discretion."[397] In other words, if someone dies without a priest to anoint him, and he has not been confirmed previously, the the Catholic has died without anointing! This is almost as problematic for the Catholic as dying without baptism and reflects the turmoil created by doctrines which arose out of inference rather than exegesis.

Another problem is the obvious fact that outside of Acts 19:1-6 there is no other passage which even hints at such a ritual. In fact, these two passages make special mention of the fact that these groups did not receive the Holy Spirit precisely because this was *not* the normal procedure. If the blessings of the Holy Spirit were separate from rebirth then there would not have been special mention needed. Moreover, if a priests or elder could perform this anointing then why could not Philip the Evangelist? Philip was one of the Seven Elders (Acts 6:3)! How much greater was he than a priest? Obviously the fact that Peter and John were called up from Jerusalem indicates that something unique was taking place. We must, therefore, look elsewhere for the answer.

View # 2 : Baptism of the Spirit is Separate from Rebirth

Similar to the Catholic view is that of various Charismatic sects, particularly Pentecostals. According to these sects the baptism of the Holy Spirit is distinct from the rebirth. Some believe that the Holy Spirit does indwell the believer when he is born again, but that it is the baptism of the Holy Spirit that causes us to be "filled with the Holy Spirit." This they called the "doctrine of subsequence."[398]

By their own admission, their evidences for this are only partly based on the Scripture. One Pentecostal website list a handful of verses, such as this one, but then states that "history" and "personal experience" validate their claims.[399] Despite one's claim that "the Acts accounts are unanimous"[400] they are, in fact, nothing of the sort. Moreover, the context of history and the presence of the apostles would make most people stop and question whether or not the acts of the apostles constitute a normative basis for experience. The fact that "history and experience" are used to justify an interpretation of a small handful of passages (and there are very few in question), is evidence that the Biblical support is meager. Nevertheless, there is some good evidence which may suggest a different experience from regeneration.

David Petts noted that "the baptism in the Spirit is sometimes received through the laying on of hands (Acts 8:18; 19:6), but there is no suggestion anywhere in the New Testament that apostles laid hands on people in order that they might be born again."[401] In this respect, he is completely correct. Obviously something unique was happening here (see notes below on "Laying on of Hands" for more).

Now here is one of the great ironies of theology. Cessationists are those who believe that the "gifts of the Spirit" no longer exist. They are the polar opposite of Pentecostals and Charismatics. However, on this point they are virtually identical! Although the Bible says nothing of tongues in this passage it is assumed, based on what Simon "saw" (nevermind that tongues is not something you "see") that the Spirit was accompanied "probably by some glossolalia."[402] Matthew Henry said, "the gift of tongues ... seems then to have been the most usual immediate effect of the pouring of the Spirit."[403]

The Reformer Matthew Poole commented that "it is plain that the Holy Ghost as the author of saving grace, is not here meant, for so he was fallen upon all them that did believe, for faith is the gift of God; but he was not yet beswowed upon them as the author of theose extraordinary gifts."[404] Thus both Pentecost and Cessationist are curiously argeed that this was a bestowing of gifts, probably including tongues. These arguments then touch upon the next two views, so I will leave this discussion here with simple conclusion.

A Ford is a car : not all cars are Fords. Likewise, the baptism of the Spirit is accompanied by the filling of the Holy Spirit, but not all filling of the Spirit is the baptism of the Spirit. Obviously not even King David could claim to have been filled with the Spirit his whole life (cf. Psams 51:11). No believer is "filled with the Holy Spirit" when he is in sin. The filling may or may not take place after regeneration, but it is not a permanent state. The Holy Spirit permanently resides in all believers, but is not at all times filling all believer, for the spirit is under the control of the saints (cf. 1 Corinthians 14:32). It is not demon possession. Consequently, to argue that baptism of the Spirit is a separate event from regeneration, resulting in a permanent filling of the Spirit cannot be supported anywhere in Scripture any more than it is fair to say that the filling of the Spirit necessarily takes place at regeneration for all time (although the Holy Spirit does begin to indwell the believer at that time). Both views are misguided and based on sparse Biblical support.

View # 3 : Sign Gifts; not the Holy Spirit

As noted, Pentecostals and Cessationists are curiously agreed that the bestowing of the Holy Spirit was accompanied by tongues, but here is where the similarities end. One fundamentalist says that "outward manifestations" of the Holy Spirit is all that took place here,[405] while another commentator argues that "the anarthous πνευμα denotes only some effect or actual operation of the Spirit, while το πνευμα signifies the Divine Person in general."[406] In other words, because the word "Spirit" does not have "the" before it in these passages, it is argued that Holy Spirit already resided in them, but that the work of the Holy Spirit had not yet come upon this. This accords with the Charismatic/Pentecostal view that baptism of the Spirit is separate from the regeneration, save that the Cessationist argues this was only for the time of the apostles, and not for today, but are either one correct?

To begin with, it is hard to argue that "Spirit" and "the Spirit" can be distinguished in any significant way. The grammatical argument does not work. Verse 18 supports "some *visible* manifestation"[407] taking place, but this only begs the question. Is "glossolalia,"[408] or tongues, *visible*? Nonetheless, since it is clear that some miracles were taking place it is fair to say, as Chrysostom does, that there was "the Spirit of signs."[409] Calvin, however, said that "the situation of in Acts 8 was only a temporary sign."[410] 1 Corinthians is used to support this notion (see *Controversies in the Epistles* for more on this issue), but such slender Scriptural support gives him only a slight edge over the alternative view. The Pentecostal has one passage (two if you count Acts 19-1-6), the Cessationists has one verse (1 Corinthians 13). Note that in both instances (the Pentecostal and the Cessationist) assumption overrides exegesis. To an extent this is understandable since Acts 8 stand alone in all the Bible as a unique event unparalleled elsewhere (but once again see Acts 19:1-6). It is then dangerous theology to attach to much of a normative experience to a single passage. Let us therefore look at some other explanations.

View # 4 : Laying on of Hands Required

Many have noticed that "the baptism in the Spirit is sometimes received through the laying on of hands (Acts 8:18; 19:6)."[411] Note "somtimes." The ritual laying on of hands by some is faulty. Aside from Jesus there are only two instances where laying on of hands is mentioned in the whole of the New Testament. Acts 8 and Acts 9:17 wherein Ananias laid hands upon Paul. No where else is it mentioned in connection with bestowing the Holy Spirit.[412] Some have even argued that the laying on of hands was performed only by the apostles,[413] although this is not so, for Ananias was not an apostle.

What then is the relationship between the "laying on of hands" and the baptism of the Spirit? In truth, like the issue at hand, two instances are not a solid ground upon which to reach *any* conclusion. The laying on of hands by Jesus was *not* required for all healing. In one instance, Jesus healed someone without having even met them (Luke 7:6-10)! The laying on of hands is symbolic of the authority but neither healing, nor the bestowing of the Holy Spirit, are relayed by physical means. It is simply a way of showing the authority of the one doing the deed. This is obvious by the mere fact that not everyone even met the apostles in their lifetime, so the Holy Spirit did not require some physical laying on of hands.

View # 5 : They Weren't True Believers

If the separation of baptism of the Spirit and regeneration is at one end of the spectrum then the other end of the spectrum is the idea that the Samaritans were not true believers until the apostles came. Like the Pentecostals who try to make the passage fit their own assumptions, the Fundamentalists here do the same thing. Since this is the only clear instance where separation occurs, they assume that they cannot have been true believers, as is the case in Acts 19:1-6.

Anthony Hoekema is among those who argue that the Samaritans were not true believers,[414] but the passage seems very clear on this. Acts states that "when they believed Philip preaching the good news about the kingdom of God and the name of Jesus Christ, they were being baptized, men and women alike" (8:12). Now some argue that the word "believe" does not necessarily mean saving faith. Even "the demons also believe, and shudder" (James 2:19). However, are we truly to believe Philip was baptizing none but unbelievers? Certainly a few converts, such as Simon, were not true to the faith, but can we truly believe that none of them were believers? Was Philip so ignorant of the Christian faith that he was teaching them the wrong thing? Was Philip's gospel so different from the apostles that they had to come to explain the resurrection? Obviously not. Acts is very clear that Samaritans were coming to the faith. While not all may have been sincere believers, we cannot assume that they were *all* unbelievers who then *all* instantaneous became believers upon seeing the apostles!

The Bible is very clear that the purpose for Peter and John's visit was not to preach the gospel, which they had already received, but rather "when the apostles in Jerusalem heard that Samaria had received the word of God, they sent them Peter and John, who came down and prayed for them that they might receive the Holy Spirit" (8:14-15). Something unique and not normative was taking place here.

View # 6 : A "Gentile" Pentecost

D.A. Carson argues that Luke is not "particularly interested in the question of normative order of faith, water rite, experience of the Holy Spirit, and the like."[415] He is correct. In this respect I hope the reader can agree. What was taking place at the Samaritan Pentecost was unique. This is why it has been given that title, for Pentecost took place one time in Jerusalem. It was a single event like the resurrection. What happened there should not be mistaken for a normal event. It was a prophetic event found in Joel (cf. Acts 2:16-35)! Thus it is clear that "despite all the evidence that all believers have been indwelt by the Holy Spirit (John 7:38-39; Romans 8:9; 1 Cor. 12:3b, etc.), the Samaritans did not immediately possess the Holy Spirit ... either it is a contradiction or a special exception to the way the Holy Spirit normally works."[416] So also this Samaritan Pentecost appears unique and that for some reason "the Spirit was reserved until this apostolic intervention occurred,"[417] but why?

Richard Longenecker believes that the dissension between the Jews of Judea and the Samaritans was such that had the Samaritans received the Holy Spirit under Philip's ministry there would have arisen two rival churches.[418] Stanley Toussaint said that the delaying of the Holy Spirit was "to prevent schism."[419] It is thus argued that the apostles' sanctioned the ministry of Philip to those outside of Judea.[420]

Now the reasoning appears sound, but requires some emendations. First, Samaritans were rejected by most Jews because of their mixed heritage and history, but they were not properly gentiles. They were of mixed heritage, but still of Jewish descent. Gaebelein nevertheless argued that just as Paul and the gentiles required a special dispensation from God, so also "it was divinely ordered that the gift of the Spirit in their case should be withheld till the two apostles came."[421] It is significant to note that Philip's ministry to Samaria is followed by the story of the Ethiopian Eunuch (discussed below). Consequently, although Israel was still the focus of the gospel missions, these stories indicate that the Word was moving out away from Jerusalem and was sanctioned by the apostles.

Conclusion

Acts 8:15-17 has been called the "Samaritan Pentecost" for a reason. It is a unique, one of a kind, circumstance (also see notes on Acts 15:1-31). The sanctioning of the apostles to the Samaritans was an indication that there was but one Spirit, the Spirit of God, which was to be bestowed on all believers, whether Jewish, half-blood, or gentile. Slowly the gospel was being pushed outside of Jerusalem and out into the whole world.

The Ethiopian Eunuch
Acts 8:27-38

"There was an Ethiopian eunuch, a court official of Candace, queen of the Ethiopians, who was in charge of all her treasure; and he had come to Jerusalem to worship and he was returning and sitting in his chariot, and was reading the prophet Isaiah."

The story of the Samaritan Pentecost is followed by the story of the Ethiopian Eunuch. It is a contiuation of Philip's missions beyond Jerusalem and Judea. The story illustrates the sovereignty of God and the fact that there are no accidents, for who could say that the Ethiopian's reading of Isaiah 53 at that exact moment was a mere coincident? But some have wondered why he was reading from the Hebrew Scriptures at all. Was he not from Ethiopia? Was he not a slave? How did an Ethiopia slave come to be reading the Jewish scriptures?

The history of Black Jews goes almost a thousand years before Christ, or so legend claims. The story of Solomon and Sheba is well known. The alleged seduction of the Queen of Sheba by Solomon is not. It is neither recorded in the Bible, nor by Josephus, nor the *Mishna*, nor any other legend of great antiquity, but is a legend told to every young Ethiopian child, for according to the legend, Solomon impregnated the Queen of Sheba who bore his child from whom many Ethiopians claim to be descended.[422] Thus Black Jews, or Ethiopian Jews, are converts to Judaism who claim to be descended from the line of King David. This is hotly debated to this very day and has been a source of contention today. This was likely the case in ancient Israel as well.

As to the legend itself, I will not debate except to say that it is suspect on two grounds. First, although it is true that the Queen of Sheba ruled Ethiopia which was a part of her kingdom, she may or may not have been of Ethiopian descent for her kingdom expanded to Egypt, the Sudan, and the Arabian Peninsula which was its headquarters.[423] Second, even if she were Ethiopian and did have Solomon's child (of which there is no Scriptural support), only the tiniest population of Ethiopia would truly have Jewish blood for she was but one woman and one child (assuming the legend was true).

Regardless of whether or not he was truly of Jewish blood, it is no surprise that an Ethiopian Eunuch would have been a Jewish proselyte. Nor is it a surprise that the Lord had desired the Great Commission to commence at once, and reach out into all the world. Tradition calls this eunuch Indich or Fudich.[424] He is alleged to have been the founder of the church of Ethiopia,[425] which seems logical. As a man of some prominence he would certainly have had authority to found a church with the queen's permission and if tradition is to be believed then the Ethiopian Eunuch converted the Queen, named Candice, and founded the church of Ethiopia.[426] That this story has some historical merit is clear from the fact that a queen Kandake has been discovered living near the time of the apostles.[427]

Beyond this the story has even more significance for we have already seen that the Samaritans were looked down upon by the average Jew. Here too the Ethiopian Jews were considered fake Jews. Because few Jews, if any, believe the Solomon bore Ethiopian children they look at this as an affront to the integrity of Solomon. To this very day Black Jews are often subjected to ridicule and racism. Thus Philip brought the gospel to two "mixed" races at best; perhaps even to gentiles! This was the first instance where gentiles were clearly being brought to Christ and it was to begin a debate which grew increasingly each day until the Council of Jerusalem settled the issue once and for all.

Why Do Some Modern Translations Omit This Passage?
Acts 8:37

"And Philip said, 'If you believe with all your heart, you may.' And he answered and said, 'I believe that Jesus Christ is the Son of God.'"

Many Bibles omit this verse in its entirety (NIV, RSV, ESV, and even the famed Latin Vulgate). Many others place this verse in brackets. King James only advocates argue that this is a deliberate tampering with the text and an attempt to omit this fundamental Christian doctrine. Of course one would be very hard pressed to argue that the Sonship of Christ is found only here or that believing Jesus is the Son of God as the prerequisite to baptism cannot be found elsewhere. Nonetheless, the omission of certain verses in modern day translations has left many worried about the legitimacy of modern translations and/or the Bible. Consequently, there are two issues to examine here. First, why is it omitted and was it written by Luke in the original text? Second, does it matter?

Even the New King James Bible footnotes the fact that this verse is missing from almost all ancient Greek text. In fact, while it is found in some ancient Latin and Syrian copies, the only ancient Greek text in which it is found is the Codex Laudianus 35 (E) which dates to the sixth century.[428] It is missing from the papyrii 45 ($\mathfrak{P}^{45}$) and 74 ($\mathfrak{P}^{74}$), which are two of the earliest copies of Acts. It is also missing from the ancient Codices Sinaiticus (א), Alexandrinus (A), Vaticanus (B), and Ephraemi (C). Moreover, it is missing from a great many minuscules, and is even omitted in the famed Latin Vulgate which follows the same *Textus Receptus* as the King James! Perhaps the strongest evidence in favor of the originality of the verse is the fact that it is quoted, in part, by Irenaeus, or does he? The truth is that Irenaeus confirms only that baptism was accompanied by this confession of faith. Thus Bruce Metzger argued that "the forumula πιστευω ... Χριστον was doubtless used by the early church in baptismal ceremonies, and may have been written in the margin of a copy of Acts."[429] In other words, the margin notes of scribes were mistaken by some as part of the original text. The textual evidence is thus overwhelmingly against the idea that Luke wrote these words.

The next question is then, "is this important?" Because of the importance of the Sonship of Christ some King James only advocates argue that this is an attempt to deny the Sonship. However, the Sonship of Christ is taught throughout the New Testament. If there were a conspiracy to remove Sonship then a great many other, and more clear, passages would need to be excised as well. The truth is that most translations place this verse in brackets with notes to the effect that it is missing from most ancient manuscripts. Even the New King James does so. It is best to argue the Sonship of Christ from other passages rather than from a suspect passage. The point of Acts 8 is that the Eunuch found Christ and was baptized, not to give a full description of the baptismal ritual.

Philip Snatched Away
Acts 8:39-40

> "The Spirit of the Lord snatched Philip away; and the eunuch no longer saw him, but went on his way rejoicing. But Philip found himself at Azotus."

One final debate is over this curious passage. What does it mean when it says that Philip was "snatched" away and was "found" at Azotus? Some argue that this is merely idiomatic for "was next heard of there"[430] or "he come to,"[431] but this both ignores the "snatching" and the fact that an idiom, by definition, is a common phrase, and yet the only other place where such language is employed in the New Testament is in regard to the rapture.[432] The Greek word 'ηρπασω (*harpazo*) is in Latin *rapio* from which we get the word "rapture."[433]

Certainly "'He was found' does not mean that Philip walked away."[434] The language here implies a miracle.[435] Moreover, the addendum by Luke that "the eunuch no longer saw him" (8:39) obviously indicates something unique had happened. John Calvin believed the Ethiopean had seen Philip appear and disappear.[436] Another scholar of old, J.A. Bengal, even goes so far as to claim that one of the apostles may have been taken to the New World America by this means![437] Now while such fanciful speculations may be rejected, the language employed here is obviously miraculous. Philip was "snatched" (raptured) and appeared (miraculously) at Azotus. Should we be surprised that the apostolic age was accompanied by such miracles? Truly something was happening then that has not happened since.

7

From Saul's Conversion to the Circumcision Debate

The story of Saul, or Paul, is one of the most fascinating stories in history. From the Pharisee who persecuted and killed Christians to the man who wrote most of our New Testament epistles, Paul literally changed the world. No serious historian can deny that Paul wrote the Biblical epistles which bear his name. Some have even called him "the second founder of Christianity."[438] This phrase is both inaccurate and disrespectful in several ways, but it does illustrate the vast influence which Paul has had over the centuries.

It is no surprise that Paul was not trusted by the apostles after his conversion. Paul was considered an outcast; both from his own people and from the Christians. The Pharisees considered him a traitor and the Christians were afraid of him. Paul would spend the rest of his life living in the poorest of circumstances, enduring punishment and imprisonment, making amends for his sins, but most importantly carving out the foundations for the gentile churches which exist today. At a time when the other apostles were reluctant to venture out of Judea and away from their home, Paul was an outcast who went to other outcast. He left his home and found followers where none had existed before. In this respect he was a trailblazer.

Paul was also the most educated of all the apostles. He was a man of learning who could argue with Greeks on their own ground and could quote the law to any Jew better than a lawyer. It was said of Paul that "his letters are weighty and strong, but his personal presence is unimpressive and his speech contemptible" (2 Corinthians 10:10). Nevertheless, Peter said of him, "our beloved brother Paul, according to the wisdom given him ... in all *his* letters, speaking in them of these things, in which are some things hard to understand, which the untaught and unstable distort, as *they do* also the rest of the Scriptures, to their own destruction" (2 Peter 3:15-16). So Paul was a man of learning who eventually earned the respect of the other apostles, even though he was not afraid to rebuke even Peter, which he did at the famous Council of Jerusalem, as we shall see.

Saul Become Paul
Acts 9:1-9 – Acts 22:1-6 – Acts 26:9-19

> "As he was traveling, it happened that he was approaching Damascus, and suddenly a light from heaven flashed around him and he fell to the ground and heard a voice saying to him, 'Saul, Saul, why are you persecuting Me? And he said, "Who are You, Lord?' And He *said*, 'I am Jesus whom you are persecuting, but get up and enter the city, and it will be told you what you must do.'"

It is alleged here, as elsewhere, that the stories of Paul's conversion contradict one another. Three different accounts are given by Paul, each emphasizing different aspects in different ways. In my other *Controversies* volumes I have often compared such alleged contradictions to eyewitnesses in a police investigation. On the surface the stories may appear to conflict, but when all the pieces of the puzzle are put together, the complete picture makes perfect sense. If one witness describes a black car speeding away while another describes a red car speeding away, a good detective will not assume that one of them is in error, for the facts may reveal that there were two bankrobbers in two different get-a-way cars. So also piecing together the accounts here gives us a fuller picture of Paul's conversion. Let is examine the story in each of his different aspects one by one.

The Eyewitnesses
The first line of attack is the alleged contradictions between the accounts of Paul's companions in Acts 9:1-9, 22:1-6, and 26:9-19. According to Acts 9:7 says, "the men who traveled with him stood speechless, hearing the voice but seeing no one." Acts 22:9 records this same event but says, "those who were with me saw the light, to be sure, but did not understand the voice of the One who was speaking to me." Finally, in Acts 26:14 Paul adds, "when we had all fallen to the ground, I heard a voice." Some see contradictions in this. First, in whether or not the companions fell to the ground, and second, in whether or not they had heard the voice.

As with policemen speaking to eyewitnesses, it is prudent not to jump to conclusions but to examine the facts and see whether they can be resolved in a logical manner. Only then can we accuse the witnesses of ignorance or deception. To do otherwise would harm any potential prosecution of the case.

Did They Hear a Voice?
Acts 9:7 says that the eyewitnesses were "hearing the voice, but seeing no one." In Acts 22:9 there appears to be a contradiction found in some translations as Paul says "they heard not the voice" (KJV). Now many translations render this as "they did not understand the voice" (NAS, NIV, NLT) which removes any contradiction. Critics have called this dishonest, saying that the word in both passages is from the root word 'ακουω (*akouo*).[439] Some websites have even circulated the false statement that "the Greek word 'akouo' is translated 373 times in the New Testament as 'hear,' 'hears,' 'hearing' or 'heard' and only in Acts 22:9 is it translated as 'understand.'"[440] In fact, 'ακουω (*akouo*) can be translated as "understand" in Mark 4:33, 8:18; John 7:51; 1 Corinthians 14:2; and Galatians 4:21 (cf. Matthew 13:15) to name a few.[441] Although many translations do render these passages as "hear," the idiomadic

language is clear. It means to understand. "Do you have ears, but do not hear?" (Mark 8:18). Every Greek Lexicon lists "understand" as a possible definition.[442]

Nonetheless, let us assume that "hear" is the correct translation, for it is the primary one. There still remains the fact that the Greek word for "voice" is the same for "sound." There is but one word for each. Φωνη (*phone*), from which we get the English word "phone," is therefore used for both. Consequently, the best answer is that "they heard the sound (9:7) but heard not the words."[443] They "heard the sound"[444] but could not understand the words.[445] Although Theodore Beza believed that it was "voice of Paul" which they heard,[446] it is more logical that they heard something like a "sound of thunder" or some other incomprehensive noise.[447] One thing is certain. The same author who penned Acts 9:7 penned Acts 22:9. Obviously he saw no contradiction here, and neither should we.

The answer to this part of the question is simple; they heard a sound or noise, but they could not understand what was being said.

Did They Fall to the Ground?

A second aspect is whether or not Paul's companions fell to the ground or not. In Acts 9:7 it is said that the men "stood speechless" but Acts 26:14 implies that "we had all fallen to the ground." So did the companions of Paul fall to the ground or stand speechless? Although seemingly more difficult, this is actually resolved more easily than the first issue which involved translation.

Two explanations have been offered. The first is that "stood speechless" is merely an idiomatic way of saying that they were dumfounded or "panick-struck."[448] In the same vein some say that "stood" can be to be "fixed" in a certain position, but that does not necessarily mean on one's feet.[449] Although certainly legitimate possibilities, there is a more simple explanation.

If one falls down, it does not logically follow that they never got back up. Luke is not giving an exhaustive narrative here. He is not trying to write *War and Peace*. He is simply giving a brief account of Paul's conversion, the companions being cursory to the story. As one commentator said, "at the first flash of the super earthy light, they, too fell prostrate (26:14), upon recovering, they now stand speechless."[450] In Acts 26:14 "Paul's narrations of what happened to him contain the complete account. He tells us that they were all fallen to the ground when the glory light shone out of heaven. This fact is omitted in the historical account" of Acts 9:7.[451] This makes the most sense and is the simplest explanation.

Did They See Jesus?

One final point of conflict in regard to the companions is whether or not they had actually seen Jesus. Acts 9:7 makes it clear that they "saw no one." Acts 22:9 gives a fuller description in which Paul states that "those who were with me saw the light." Of course there is a difference in seeing a light and in seeing a person. Nevertheless, some have argued that "'Seeing' is often related in Luke and Acts to perceiving God's activity ... or with understanding the significance of an event."[452] This explanation, although valid, is unnecessary. They saw only a light, but did not see or perceive Jesus within the light. That is the clear testimony of these two passages.

Paul's Command
Some have tried to argue that the words of Jesus in Acts 22:10 are somehow contradictory to what is recorded in Acts 26:16-18. In 22:10 it is only said, "get up and go on into Damascus, and there you will be told of all that has been appointed for you to do." Acts 26:16-18 however gives a fuller account wherein Jesus said, "but get up and stand on your feet; for this purpose I have appeared to you, to appoint you a minister and a witness not only to the things which you have seen, but also to the things in which I will appear to you; rescuing you from the *Jewish* people and from the Gentiles, to whom I am sending you, to open their eyes so that they may turn from darkness to light and from the dominion of Satan to God, that they may receive forgiveness of sins and an inheritance among those who have been sanctified by faith in Me."

Now common sense dictates that just because someone says "hello" in one passage does not negate the possibility that they may have said "goodbye" in another. *Neither* account is exhaustive. Each tells the reader what is relevant to the context. To suggest that Jesus could have said both of these things is not legitimate exegesis but grasping at straws. There is nothing contradictory in the words. Acts 26:16-18 is in addition to the words of Acts 9:7 and 22:10, not in contrast to them.

Was This a Miracle?
The nineteenth century rationalists denied that miracles exist. Naturally they tried to read this passage in a way that negated the obvious miracle taking place. Some argued that Paul had actually experienced an epileptic fit, to which Charles Spurgeon mockingly replied, "O blessed epilepsy, if it effects a conversion like this!"[453] Ironisde declared that "every conversion is a miracle"[454] but obviously Paul's conversion was unlike any of ours. Paul alone among post-ascension converts saw Jesus face to face. It is for this reason that he can be called an apostle. God can do anything He wants. He is not restricted by the laws of nature He Himself created. This was nothing short of a miracle.

Alleged Contradictions with Galatians
Some Bible critics have argued that Galatians 1:16-17 conflicts with Paul's account here.[455] There Paul says that after his conversion "I did not immediately consult with flesh and blood, nor did I go up to Jerusalem to those who were apostles before me; but I went away to Arabia" (1:16-17). The arguement is that in Acts he did not "immediately" go to Arabia but "consulted" with Ananias (Acts 9:17). A complete discussion of this is to be found in the next section under Acts 9:19-30, but the short answer in regard to Ananias is that Paul here

speaks of his conversion experience which obviously included the entire events and baptism by Ananias. *After* these events is when Paul went down to Arabia. Even if we are to believe that Paul was referring strictly to the event at the road to Damascus, the word "immediately" in the context of a person's life does not mean that he could not have done anything else in the first few days before leaving. When I graduated High School I "immediately" went to College. Or did I? No, I went to dinner first. Am I a liar?

In short, it is clear from Paul's statement in Galatians that he did not "go up to Jerusalem to those who were apostles before me" (1:17) but instead went to Arabia to study the Word of God (but see notes on Acts 9:19-30). Ananias baptized Paul, but was not his teacher. There is nothing in Galatians 1:16-17 that in any way contradicts the story of his conversion.

Conclusion
All eyewitness accounts are non-exhaustive. Each give a portion of the events which is of importance to them in the context of what they are addressing. Luke gives a general summary of the vision of Jesus in chapter nine, but when Paul is recounting his experience to the governor of Judea and the king, he emphasizes different points. A good detective resolves alleged conflicts. Only if there is evidence which cannot be resolved does he approach the judge or magistrate with proof of perjury. Were he to approach the judge with accusations of perjury which he cannot substantiate or upon trivial issues which no man would bother to lie about, then the judge will be inclined to reject all his pleadings in the future. This is why a good policeman works to get a complete picture, whereas a phony or corrupt officer simply twists people's words and testimonies to make them sound contradictory or libelous. The same is true here of the Bible critic.

This is not to say that the average reader does not have questions. He does, and he should. But like a good detective he seeks to resolve the situation. Here in Acts it is apparent that when Saul was struck blind his companions, after recovering themselves were struck by what was happening. They saw the light, but could not see Jesus. They heard a noise, but could not hear the words being spoken. They did not know what was happening. These men were companions of Saul, the persecutor of Christians. There is nothing more said of them in the Bible. It is likely that they were not converts. They knew that something extraordinary had happened to Paul but they did not know exactly what. Consequently, they took back the story of Paul's encounter to the enemies of Christ, but Paul later gives a fuller testimony, including the words of Jesus, to the king and governor. This is the context of the passages. This is the solution to our problems.

Saul's Early Days
Acts 9:19-30

"When he came to Jerusalem, he was trying to associate with the disciples; but they were all afraid of him, not believing that he was a disciple."

The account of Acts appears to give the impression that Paul returned to Jerusalem not too long after his conversion. However, in the book of Galatians Paul indicates that he went to Arabia and did not return for three years. He further states that when he did reach Jerusalem he spoke only to Peter and James, whereas Acts indicates that Barnabas "brought him to the apostles." As with the previous issue, a good detective does not immediately discount seemingly different testimonies until he has examined all the evidence. Let us start then with the complete passages in question. In Acts Luke records that:

"For several days [Paul] was with the disciples who were at Damascus, and immediately he *began* to proclaim Jesus in the synagogues, saying, 'He is the Son of God.' All those hearing him continued to be amazed, and were saying, 'Is this not he who in Jerusalem destroyed those who called on this name, and *who* had come here for the purpose of bringing them bound before the chief priests?' But Saul kept increasing in strength and confounding the Jews who lived at Damascus by proving that this *Jesus* is the Christ. When many days had elapsed, the Jews plotted together to do away with him, but their plot became known to Saul. They were also watching the gates day and night so that they might put him to death; but his disciples took him by night and let him down through *an opening in* the wall, lowering him in a large basket. When he came to Jerusalem, he was trying to associate with the disciples; but they were all afraid of him, not believing that he was a disciple. But Barnabas took hold of him and brought him to the apostles and described to them how he had seen the Lord on the road, and that He had talked to him, and how at Damascus he had spoken out boldly in the name of Jesus" (Acts 9:19-27).

In Galatians Paul explains what happened after his conversion, saying:

"When God, who had set me apart *even* from my mother's womb and called me through His grace, was pleased to reveal His Son in me so that I might preach Him among the Gentiles, I did not immediately consult with flesh and blood, nor did I go up to Jerusalem to those who were apostles before me; but I went away to Arabia, and returned once more to Damascus. Then three years later I went up to Jerusalem to become acquainted with Cephas, and stayed with him fifteen days. But I did not see any other of the apostles except James, the Lord's brother" (Galtians 1:15-19).

Now the key to whether or not there is a conflict is in the statement of Galatians that "I went away to Arabia, and returned once more to Damascus" (1:17). In Acts, however, the conversion experience is separated from Paul's preaching of the gospel in Damascus but a single word in the NAS, "now." In Greek the shift is more apparent, and indicates a shift in time.

The new paragraph, in the middle of verse nineteen, begins with the Greek words, "εγενετο δε μετα" (*egeneto de meta*). This unique arrangement of words is generally translated simply as "then," "and," or "now." In fact, none of these one word translations sufficiently convey the meaning. Εγενετο (*Egeneto*) is the middle aorist Greek form of "to be" meaning "to become" or "to happen." Δε (*de*) is a Greek conjunction which, according to a Greek text book, can mean "a change in temporal setting."[456] The last word in this transition phrase is which means μετα (*meta*) "after."[457] Put them together and the reader will see that they do not translate into English well. "To become ... in temporal setting ... after" would make no sense. Thus the phrase εγενετο δε μετα (*egeneto de meta*) is sometimes left completely untranslated. In fact, it clearly indicates a shift in time. Luke is not trying to give an exhaustive account but shifts from his conversion to his return to Damascus years later. This is apparent by the very fact that the Paul was "proving Jesus was the Christ" (9:22) to the amazement of those who heard he was the one who had once persecuted Christians (9:21). Obviously Paul would not have the knowledge to be able to prove Jesus was the Christ to Jews only a few days after his conversion. A shift in time has obviously taken place.

The second issue is one of the apostles. When Paul finally made it back to Jerusalem he said he "became acquainted with Cephas, and stayed with him fifteen days. But I did not see any other of the apostles except James, the Lord's brother." In the Acts account Luke says that none of the apostles wanted to associate with Paul out of fear until Barnabas brought Paul before them (9:26-27). Once again, some see a contradiction, but the resolution is not that difficult. Acts makes it clear that the apostles were all initially afraid of Paul. In Galatians Paul is, once again, giving a fuller account. Likewise, translation once again enters the picture. Although some want to draw a technical argument from Paul's statement that he "did not *see*" any of the other apostles, the Greek word ειδον (*eidon*) in the aorist tense is used. This word has a plethora of meaning. I will list them in the order given in the famed Thayer's Lexicon; "to perceive ... to discover ... to see ... to experience ... to have an interview with, to visit."[458] The normal word for "see" in Greek is βλεπω (blepo). Here the meaning is clearly to visit or to spend time with someone. One Greek dictionary reads that it means "attending to" someone.[459] Except for the brief introduction by Barnabas, Paul spent no time with the apostles, except for Peter and James.

So in summary, Acts omits Paul's journey to Arabia where he spent years studying the Word of God and learning the Scriptures all over again. It is only when he returned to Damascus that Acts again takes up his story. This "temporal shift" is very obvious in the Greek but usually left untranslated in English. The time shift is however obvious by the shift in Paul's understanding and in the people's reaction in Damascus. Upon his return to Jerusalem Paul did manage to meet with Peter and with James, but aside from the brief introduction by Barnabas he did not spend time with (ειδον) the other apostles. The point is not whether or not Paul had ever seen or been introduced to the apostles, but whether or not he had actually spend any time "attending to" the apostles.

The Vision of Peter and Cornelius
Acts 10:9-31

> "He saw the sky opened up ... and there were in it all *kinds of* four-footed animals and crawling creatures of the earth and birds of the air. A voice came to him, 'Get up, Peter, kill and eat!' But Peter said, 'By no means, Lord, for I have never eaten anything unholy and unclean.' Again a voice *came* to him a second time, 'What God has cleansed, no *longer* consider unholy.'"

Cornelius, a Roman centurion of the people who were oppressing Israel, was sent to Peter by an angel of the Lord. Peter, unaware that Cornelius' men were coming, then had a vision which opens the debate upon gentile conversion. In Judaism kosher law has specific requirements in regard to what a person can and cannot eat. The vision compares unclean foods to the "unclean" gentile whom the average Jew looked down upon.

The incident would open the floodgates in regard to the debate over gentile conversion. Even Peter's vision did not immediately settle the matter completely in his mind. Should the gentile have to convert to Judaism before becoming a Christian? Should a Christian convert have to be circumcised in accordance with the Jewish covenant? This later was particularly important. According to Acts 10:45, "all the circumcised believers who came with Peter were amazed, because the gift of the Holy Spirit had been poured out on the Gentiles also," but others "who were circumcised took issue with him, saying, 'You went to uncircumcised men and ate with them'" (11:2-3). This created an almost immediate schism. Some "made their way to Phoenicia and Cyprus and Antioch, spoke the word to no one except to Jews alone. But there were some of them, men of Cyprus and Cyrene, who came to Antioch and *began* speaking to the Greeks also, preaching the Lord Jesus" (11:19-20).

This schism would ultimately lead to the Council of Jerusalem (see Chapter 8), but it is necessary to discuss this vision because some argue that it is proof of "the abolition of Jewish ceremonial law"[460] while others see in Peter's vision a type for the church and his taken to heaven as rapture.[461] Such views tend to read too much into the dream. Clearly the dream was about gentiles. God was telling Peter to accept us without precondition. The gospel is not for some, but for all. Yet even this did not answer all of Peter's questions. What was the purpose for the law? If we are to accept without preconditions then can the Christian continue in sin? These questions are answered best by the apostle Paul in Galatians, in which he refers to the Council of Jerusalem and even contronts Peter. I will therefore only summarize. It is God who changes our hearts. The law does not make us perfect, but rather reveals our sins. The law does not save, it condemns. It is Jesus who saves us and makes us whole. The law shows us the need for Jesus, not vice versa.

Peter and the Gentiles
Acts 11:1-20 – See Acts 10:9-31

Herod Agrippa's Death
Acts 12:20-23

> "And immediately an angel of the Lord struck him because he did not give God the glory, and he was eaten by worms and died."

Herod the Great died from an acute condition which included worms, or magots, on his testicles. This story is recorded by Josephus.[462] His son, Herod Agrippa, also died of worms, although of a different sort. Apparently Agrippa died of tape worms. One scientist suggested that "Herod's death was almost certainly due to the rupture of a cyst formed by a tapeworm."[463]

This story is repeated in Josephus, save that he gives the exact date for Herod's death as five days after his blasphemy in accepting the people's claim that he was God.[464] This took place in 44 A.D., establishing the timeline for this portion of Acts. It is also important to note that "immediately an angel of the Lord struck him" (12:23) is not the same as saying "immediately he was struck dead." That Herod lingered for five days is perfectly consistent with the narrative of Acts. In fact, Luke's account here rings more true than that of Josephus wherein Agrippa gives a speech acknowledging God's wrath upon him for his sin and rebuking the people for calling him a god. Although this portion of Josephus's story may be true, it is not found in Acts and does not seem to fit. Had Herod repented and rebuked the people, he might well have lived. This is further evidence that Luke is a more reliable historian than Josephus.

Chronological Conflict?
Acts 13:17-22 – Exodus 12:40 – 1 Kings 6:1

> "The God of this people Israel chose our fathers and made the people great during their stay in the land of Egypt, and ... when He had destroyed seven nations in the land of Canaan, He distributed their land as an inheritance – *all of which took* about four hundred and fifty years."

"Chronology is the backbone of history."[465] So said a famous historian and chronologer. Without chronology history becomes a series of unrelated events, but when we can see the chronology which ties history together, we see that history is but links a chain of events which takes us from the past to the present. We see God in history.

Here is a thorny chronological problem. It is of no consequence for the average reader, but it is of importance to the historian and Bible scholar, and a target of the silly Bible critics. 1 Kings 6:1 states explicitly that it was "in the four hundred and eightieth year after the sons of Israel came out of the land of Egypt" that Solomon began to build the Temple. Exodus 12:40 states that the Israelites lived in Egypt (perhaps including Canaan - see *Controversies in the Pentateuch*) for four hundred and thirty years. Now here Acts *appears* to say that the conquest of Canaan took four hundred and fifty years! Obviously one can see the potential problem. A problem which has no fewer than seven proposed solutions, none of which is that Paul could not count.

Proposed Solutions

An uncritical critic will immediately dismiss all attempts at reconciliation, claiming that the authors were either stupid or could not count. The real historian, like the detective, searches all possibilities *before* reaching a conclusion. Seven different solutions have been offered with varying degrees of support. Some are grasping at straws while others are strong possibilities.

View # 1 : Textual Error

Some have dismissed this as an error in the Biblical copies. Martin Luther and Theodore Beza argued it should be 350 years but have *no* evidence to support this.[466] The only textual question is of the relationship of the four hundred and fifty years to the passages surrounding it. Some text do appear to have added words or shifted the word order so that the meaning would be more clear. Sir Robert Anderson even claimed that "the New Testament Revisers have corrupted the text through neglect."[467] Nevertheless, the evidence for this is highly debateable. In fact, if anything the reverse is more likely the case.

Virtually all of the most ancient Greek manuscripts ($\mathfrak{P}^{74}$, ℵ, A, B, C) contain "ως ετεσιν τετρακοσιοις και τεντηκοντα. και μετα ταυτα" which is most literally translated "which years four hundred and fifty. And after this ..." This would appear to connect the four hundred and fifty years in some way to the previous passages. However, in an attempt to resolve this problem a few late Greek manuscripts, along with the Majority text (D^2, 𝔐), rearranged the word order placing "και μετα ταυτα" ("and after this") before the four hundred and fifty years, thus associating the four hundred and fifty years with what follows. This has led to three different translation variants as we shall see.

The evidence obviously favors that it should be placed with verse nineteen. Of all the Greek manuscripts written before the sixth century only one reads as the Majority text does. Bruce Metzger argued that "on the surface, the [early] texts appears to limit the four hundred fifty years to the time that passed between the division of the land by Joshua and the institution of the judges. It was probably in order to prevent the reader from drawing such an erroneous conclusion that scribes transposed the temporal clause to the following sentence, producing the reading of the *Textus Receptus*."[468]

The real problem is not one of a textual error, but of the various translations and interpretations which have arisen out of this. How we translate and interpret the passage is what is of critical importance. No help is to be found in textual criticism.

View # 2 : Translation Difficulties
There are three main streams of translations. The older version usually follow the *Textus Receptus* which clearly marks the four hundred and fifty years as belonging to what follows, but even then the translations vary. Here are the three main threads and the translations which follow them in some fashion.

KJV, Tyndale, Webster, Darby, Geneva	NIV, NLV, NRSV, ESV, Wycliff, Douay-Rheims	NAS, RSV, RV, ASV
Utilizes the *Textus Receptus* to associated with the period of Judges.	Fitting with both the *Textus Receptus* and ancient texts it is placed in verse 20 but taking a more literal, and ambiguous, translation.	Follows the ancient texts placing it after verse 19 and generally assuming it refers to what precedes (but some are ambiguous).
E.g. At the end of verse 20 is read "after that he gave *unto them* judges about the space of four hundred and fifty years."	E.g. At the beginning of verse 20 is read, "all this took about 450 years"	E.g. At the end of verse 19 is read "*all of which took about four hundred and fifty years.*"

Now before examining the various interpretations, let us examine strictly the translations themselves. Of these three the first clearly restricts the years to the time of the judges. This creates far more difficulties than it solves and is based on late Greek manuscripts. "The correct reading continues with ως (there is no και before it) and places the dative of time in v. 19 and not, as the A.V. does, in v. 20 by placing the dative after the μετα phrase."[469] To shift years to the time of the judges neither solves the problem, as we shall see, nor is it supported in the ancient manuscripts.

The second translation actually utilizes the same manuscripts as the first, but deliberately chooses a more literal, and ambiguous, reading. One might almost call it a compromise between the *Textus Receptus* and the ancient

Greek texts. Its apparent ambiguity is actually its strength since it does not restrict the reading to a particular interpretation.

The last reading is based on the ancient Greek manuscripts. Although it appears to restrict the years to the period preceding the judges, this is not necessarily so as we shall see. Nonetheless, the fact that this is the seeming meaning is doubtless why so many later manuscripts tried to shift the years to the period of judges as Metzger suggested.

View # 3 : From Slavery to Joshua

In an attempt to fit the ancient textual reading with the Bible, some have argued that this could be translated as "after those transactions [which lasted] 450 years ..."[470] Stanley Toussaint argued that the years count from "oppression in Egypt (400 years), the wilderness sojourn (40 years), and the Conquest of Canaan under Joshua (10 years)."[471] This view, however, has many problems. First, how he gets 10 years for Joshua is beyond me. The division of lands was thirty years after Joshua crossed the Jordan (compare Joshua 14:7, 10, and 24:29), and many decades later Canaan could still not be said to have been conquered (compare Number 11:28 with Joshua 5:6 and 24:29)! Second, the period of oppression was four hundred and thirty years (Exodus 12:40), not four hundred. If Toussaint wishes to dismiss the period of the sojourn before they actually became slaves then he would have to prove that they became slaves only thirty years after the sojourn began, which is hard to argue given the testimony of Exodus 1:8 which suggests some passage of time and/or a significant change in power structure (such as the overthrow of the Hyksos, which took far more than thirty years – but see *Controversies in the Pentateuch* for more on this issue). If we correctly added the sojourn to the wilderness wandering and the conquest we would have five hundred years, not four hundred and fifty. This view arises from a strict interpretation of the third translation, but is suspect. Although it does have appeal, the numbers do not fit, and a closer examination of the passage indicates that this is not the best view.

View # 4 : From Isaac to Joshua

Matthew Poole takes a similar stance to Toussaint, except that he counts these years from the birth of Isaac to the distribution of the land, saying it is exactly 447 years,[472] thus the four hundred and fifty years is rounded off. Now Poole's dates arise from the belief that the sojourn in Egypt began with Abraham's entry into Egypt, a theory which is not without strong Scriptural support (see discussion on Genesis 15:13-16; Exodus 6:16, and 12:40 in *Controversies in the Pentateuch*). Now Archbishop Ussher placed Isaac birth 405 years before the Exodus,[473] so Poole's estimations are close to those of Ussher's. I personally agree that the sojourn dates back to Abraham's time, as I have defended in a lengthy debade in my previous volume, and so this is theory is preferable to Toussaint's, but it nevertheless has problems. For one thing, if the four hundred and fifty years go back to Isaac, then why does Paul not mention Isaac and why does he mention the forty years in the desert, if the forty years are a part of the four hundred and fifty? Moreover, the numbers still do not add up for like Toussaint's theory, whether we begin with the enslavement of Jews or the sojourn under Abraham, we still get four hundred and thirty years until the Exodus (Exodus 12:40). Add another forty years in the desert and the time of Joshua's conquest, and we are much closer to five hundred than four hundred and fifty. Although a viable option, a better solution should be sought before deciding.

View # 5 : From Joshua to the End of the Judges

Since the most natural reading of the Majority text (followed by the King James bible and others) is that Paul is referring solely to the period of Judges Matthew Henry proposes a unique solution. He argues that the period of Judges totals 330 years, but he then adds 111 years under which the Jews were under the servitide of the nations, e.g. Philistines.[474] These 111 years are deemed to be concurrent with the 330 years, but added together to equal 441 which is rounded up. This unique solution obviously appeals to King James only advocates but it seems to be grasping at straws for why would Paul have added concurrent years together? If the period of Judges was 330 then it was 330! Why would he add 111 years of servitude to the 330 years of Judges? This solution seems contrived to offer a solution which ironically arose from some scribes desire to present a solution! It is best to leave the text as is and seek a better solution elsewhere.

View # 6 : From the Exodus to Solomon

Ironically, since the *Textus Receptus* has shifted the passage from verse nineteen to verse twenty, and some translations, such as the King James, have polished the English by then moving the passage to the end of verse twenty, there are now some who argue that it should properly go at the beginning of verse twenty-one![475] This however, is completely unfeasible, for even if the *Textus Receptus* is the correct one, it is placed at the beginning of verse twenty and not at the end as it appears in the King James bible. Moreover, this would not be particularly helpful since placing it close to verse twenty-one would only take us to the time of Samuel, and not the Temple.[476] Finally, 1 Kings 6:1 explicitly states that it was four hundred and eighty years from the Exodus to the beginning of Solomon's temple. Why would Paul round such a precise and well documented number down to four hundred and fifty?

View # 7 : From Joshua to the Conquest of Jerusalem

Some have noted a very close parallel between this passage and the history of Josephus written decades later.[477] In *Antiquities of the Jews* Josephus recorded that:

> "The whole time from the warfare under Joshua our general against the Canaanites, and from that war in which he overcame them, and distributed the land among the Hebrews, (nor could the Israelites ever cast the Canaanites out of Jerusalem until this time, when David took it by siege), this whole time was five hundred and fifteen years."[478]

In other words, Jewish tradition did not consider that Canaan was completely conquered until King David finally took the city of Jerusalem over five hundred years later. Jerusalem, of course, is the Holy City of David and the capital of Israel. The fact that the Jews had never been able to conquer it was a stain upon Israel until David brought honor to Israel and claimed the Holy City. It is therefore argued that this passage is parenthetical and takes us up to conquest of Jerusalem by David.[479]

This theory is the most intriguing of all, but there are questions that must be answered before it can be accepted. First, what is the difference between the four hundred fifty years of Acts and the five hundred and fifteen years of Josephus? Second, how does this fit grammatically and exegetically with the passage in Acts?

In regard to the first question, Josephus dates the five hundred and fifteen years from "the warfare under Joshua"[480] whereas Acts dates this from "when He had destroyed seven nations in the land of Canaan, [and] distributed their land as an inheritance" (13:19). Thus Josephus begins with the beginning of the conquest whereas Acts would presumably begin with the end of the conquest. Nevertheless, sixty-five years is too long for the conquest. Moreover, five hundred and fifteen years after the crossing of the Jordan by Joshua would take us all the way to the ninth century B.C. toward the end of King Solomon's reign! It would seem then that Josephus was following the errant *Septuagint* chronology which was the common chronology utilized by Josephus.[481] Thus the relevance is over the dating from Joshua to David, rather than an agreement in chronology *per se*. This still leaves us with the problem of how we can fit four hundred and fifty years into this same time period. Solomon's Temple was begun four hundred and eighty years after the Exodus. If we eliminate the forty years of wandering in the desert then we are left with four hundred and forty years between Joshua's crossing the Jordan and the foundations of the Temple! Clearly, four hundred and fifty years does not seem to fit.

The second question is the grammatical one. How does the conquest of Jerusalem fit into the context of Paul's statement here? An argument can be made that this chronology is an aside, referring to the conquest of Canaan, which technically was not completed until David's time. This argument is possible, but by no means certain. When we combine this with the fact that four hundred and fifty years actually overshoots David's conquest by several decades, we must again consider this option tenuous.

Romanovich Rejtern – Abraham Brings Isaac as a Sacrifice – 1849

The *Terminus A Quo*

We know that the *terminus a quem*, or ending point, of Paul's remark properly refers to when Joshua " distributed their land as an inheritance" (13:19), but without knowing the exact *terminus a quo*, or starting point, to which Paul refers, it is impossible to know for certain which theory is correct. All have problems because none can agree on the *terminus a quo* or even the *terminus a quem*. Clearly Paul is making a generic statement with which the Jews were familiar. I believe the fourth and seventh views are the strongest, but neither is perfect because neither one establishes a clear *terminus a quo*. In researching this issue, I found that the only way to arrive at a solution was to determine what the exact starting point Paul was referencing. When I examined all the possibilities, I arrived at what I believe is an exact solution.

It is clear that wherever we begin it begins with these words: "the God of this people Israel chose our fathers and made the people great during their stay in the land of Egypt" (13:17). The solution is to be found in the word "chose." If "chose" is our *terminus a quo* then we must determine when that choice was made. Obviously there are several possibilities.

The possibility might be the calling of Abraham from Ur of the Chaldeans, but this possibility is eliminated immediately for Abraham did not even enter Canaan until many years later at age seventy-five (Genesis 12:4). Based on the "short chronology" of Genesis 15:13-16 and Exodus 12:40 (cf. Exodus 6:16 and Galatians 3:17), this would probably be the beginning of the sojourn five hundred years before Joshua divided the land.

Some have argued that because Isaac was the child of the promise, it is his birth to which Paul refers, but Abraham was seventy-five when he first entered Canaan (Genesis 12:4) and a hundred when Isaac was born (Genesis 21:5), so this was four hundred and seventy-five years before the division of land.

One other possibility remains. All Jews honor and revere that moment when Abraham's faith was tested on Mount Moriah. Christians too see the sacrifice of Isaac as a foreshadowing of Christ, the only begotten Son of God! Now according to Josephus, tradition says that Isaac was twenty-five years old when he was to be sacrificed by Abraham.[482] This would then be *exactly* four hundred and fifty years before the division of the land by Joshua!

Conclusion

It is clear that Paul was referring to something that the Jews would instinctly have known and understood. The chosing of Israel began with Abraham, but more specifically with his test upon Mount Moriah, upon which Solomon's Temple would be build over that very sacrificial rock. This event is revered to this very day by both Jews and Christians. Paul did not have to elaborate for all Jews knew this instinctively. It was exactly four hundred and fifty years from the testing of Abraham to the division of land by Joshua.

8

The Circumcision Debate and the Council of Jerusalem

We have already seen that Christianity was being pushed out of Jerusalem and that an increasing number of gentiles were converting to the faith. Peter had received a vision which confirmed to him that God is not partial, but Peter had not yet come to grapple with what this meant. Circumcision is the seal of the Jewish covenant. A covenant is a contract. It is a contract with God. In His covenant with Abraham God commanded that all the descendants of Abraham all of their servants are to be circumcised (Genesis 17:10-14). If a Jew is not circumcised then this means that the father has broken the covenant. However, gentiles had no such covenant and so were never circumcised. What were the apostles to do with gentiles? Should gentile converts to Christ be circumcised or not? This debate was the culminate in the Council of Jerusalem; a council which would have far reaching impacts too often overlooked by exegetes and the common reader.

The Apostle to the Gentiles
Acts 13:44-52

> "Paul and Barnabas spoke out boldly and said, 'It was necessary that the word of God be spoken to you first; since you repudiate it and judge yourselves unworthy of eternal life, behold, we are turning to the Gentiles.'"

Paul was the first to minister far beyond the bounds of ancient Israel. His first missionary journey took him into Cyprus and western Turkey where no missionary is recorded to have gone before. In his epistles Paul declared that he was called to preach the gospel to the gentiles (cf. Galatians 1:16) and even called himself an "apostle to gentiles" (Romans 11:13). Many times in his epistles the issue of circumcision is brought up, and many times he makes it clear that God is no respecter of persons. The Jews were called by God and chosen for a reason; but not to the exclusion of gentiles. It is through the Jews that God revealed Himself on account of the faith of Abraham. It is through the Jews that Jesus the Messiah came. It is through the Jews that the gospel originated, but this gospel is for all men; Jew or gentile. So it was that when Paul heard of the debate he returned to Jerusalem to settle the matter with the apostles and elders (Acts 15:2). Although they did not know it then, this was to set the stage for world missions.

Acts 14:11-18 – See Acts 17:23

The Council of Jerusalem
Acts 15:1-29

It was in writing my history of the apostles that I first discovered the vast historical significance of this council. It takes up but a small part of the book of Acts during which the apostles agree that circumcision should not be an obstacle to gentiles who want to come to Christ. However, the council actually did far more than this, for it was at this time that the apostles themselves began to leave Israel and minister to gentile nations. To be sure they continued to go to Jewish communities first, but they also preached to gentiles and established churches as far away as India and west Africa, and possibly even England![483]

Here it is my intention to take a fuller look at the council, at the major figures in the council, at the results of the council, and whether or not the council was intended to be a blueprint to deal with future problems in the church. By look at these issues we can gain a more deep understanding into the nature of the early church and its transition from a "Jewish cult" to a world wide religion of Christ.

Date of the Synod
The date of the Council of Jerusalem has variously been given between 48 and 50 A.D. Giving the council a more precise date is a little more difficult. I have given a full debate upon the chronology of Acts in Appendix A. Here I shall only briefly state the issue.

According to Galatians it was three years after his conversion that Paul when up to Jerusalem (1:18). "Then after an interval of fourteen years I went up again to Jerusalem" (2:1). This second incident is the council of Jerusalem, so most argue that it was 17 years after Paul's conversion, or 50 A.D. However, some argue that the fourteen years includes the three years of 1:18, making the council as early as 47 A.D. Both are wrong.

Paul conversion was either in 33 or 34 A.D. Because of the situation in Jerusalem and the close proximity of Stephen's martyrdom to the Pentecost, I believe that Paul was converted sometime in 33 A.D. Now according to Jewish idiom, "after X years" is synonymous with the English "in the Xth year." So that when Paul says he returned to Jerusalem "three years later" it could have either been 35 or 36 A.D. "After" another interval of fourteen years would then take us to either 48 or 49 A.D. Such was the common reconning of the Hebrew language.[484]

At this point it is impossible to Biblically narrow the council down further. However, from my study of the apostles I am inclined to believe that the council was toward the end of 48 A.D. in the Fall. This I make based on the apparent dissemination of the apostles from Israel. As early as 49 A.D. we see evidence that Matthew was in Egypt,[485] that Thomas had reached India as early as 50 A.D., and certainly by 52 A.D. when he reached South India.[486] Based on these facts, it would seem then that the evidence favors late 48 or early 49 A.D. as the date for this council.

Paul's Confrontation with Peter
Before the actual Synod Peter came to Antioch to meet Paul and later escorted him down to Jerusalem (compare Galatians 2:11 with Acts 14:26-15:2). Paul was considered important because he had been ministering to gentiles for well over a decade and a half. He was to give his testimony regarding the ministry to the gentiles, but it is important to note that Paul was not entering friendly territory so to speak. According to Paul, James was the leader of the party of circumcision and had managed to influence even Peter and Barnabas (Galatians 2:12-13). Paul also says that he chastised Peter "before them all" on account of this issue. Who were those before whom Peter was chastised, and what does the rebuke say regarding the relationship between Peter and Paul?

Now according to Paul, he was actually in the middle of his first missionary journey when he received a relevation from God, tell him to return to Antioch (Galatians 2:2). Because Paul had made a name for himself on account of his miraculous conversion and ministry to the gentiles the apostles were intrigued. Although Peter and Philip and others had ministered to gentiles in Judah, Syria, and the nearby areas, their ministries were still focused on Jews. Paul, however, moved out into western Turkey in predominantly gentile lands. Although he went "to the Jew first" (Romans 1:16; 2:9-10) there is no doubt that his ministry was predominantly to the gentiles (Romans 11:13; 1 Timothy 2:7). Consequently, Peter went up to Antioch to meet Paul (Galatians 2:11).

Both Acts and Galatians agree that the initial meeting with Peter and other disciples was one of confrontation. Acts says that there was "great dissension and debate" with the result that "*the brethren* determined that Paul and Barnabas and some others of them should go up to Jerusalem to the apostles and elders concerning this issue" (Acts 15:2). In Galatians Paul gives further details saying, "when Cephas [Peter] came to Antioch, I opposed him to his face, because he stood condemned" (Galatians 2:11). More than this, he publicly humiliated Peter, saying to him, "If you, being a Jew, live like the Gentiles and not like the Jews, how *is it that* you compel the Gentiles to live like Jews?" (Galatians 2:14). This was nothing less than a personal insult. To accuse a Jew of living like a gentile is akin to a modern racial slur. Jews were proud of being different from the gentile world. They were the "chosen race" and many looked down upon gentiles, which was part of the reason for this entire debate. Paul then called Peter out on the issue, noting that "prior to the coming of certain men from James, he used to eat with the Gentiles; but when they came, he *began* to withdraw and hold himself aloof, fearing the party of the circumcision" (Galatians 2:12).

Now two things can be said of this confrontation. First, Peter is to be commended for his change of heart. Too many take rebuke as a personal attack and become more stubborn, but Peter repented of his previous stance, and became the spokesman for the gentile party (Acts 15:7-11). Second, Paul does not appear to have revered Peter as the vicar of Jesus. Nowhere does Paul even pretend that Peter speaks for Jesus, although Peter had lived and worked with Jesus throughout his ministry! For Paul the only issue was what the Scriptures taught and he saw no grounds for denying the grace of Christ to those who were gentile. Circumcision was a sign of the covenant with the Jewish people. Gentiles were not Jews. Christ died for all, not just Jews. Therefore, gentiles should not be required to be circumcised. Paul's reasoning was simple, logical, and above all else, Biblical. As Paul concluded in Galatians 2:21, "I do not nullify the grace of God, for if righteousness *comes* through the Law, then Christ died needlessly."

The argument convinced Peter and others who decided "that Paul and Barnabas and some others of them should go up to Jerusalem to the apostles and elders concerning this issue" (Acts 15:2). There they told their story and eventually convinced even James that circumcision was an unnecessary stumbling block to gentiles and against the Will of God.

James the Pillar

James, Peter, and John "were reputed to be pillars" of the church (Galatians 2:9). Note that it is James, Peter, and John in that order. Also note that James the Great had died under Herod Agrippa four years earlier (Acts 12:2). Who then is this James, who was apparently the head of the Synod and one time proponent of the "party of circumcision" (Galatians 2:12)?

Protestants have traditionally argued that James the Just was the brother of Jesus who was converted after the Resurrection. Catholics usually believe that James the Just was the same as James the Less, the apostle. In unusual form I will state my conclusion first. Catholics are right, and yet in being right, they have fractured their belief in the primacy of the papacy. Let us look at the issues carefully.

Who Was James the Just?

History calls the first bishop of Jerusalem James the Just. This James is usually agreed to have been the author of the epistle of James. Of him the apostle Paul says that he was "the Lord's brother" (Galatians 1:19). Note that this is the only passage in which James the Just is referred to as the "Lord's brother." Now Catholics usually argue that this is simply the Hebrew word for "cousin" as well as brother, but this is not so for the Hebrew word for cousin is *dodan* (דּוֹדָן) and the Hebrew word for aunt is *dodah* (דּוֹדָה), found in Exodus 6:20, Leviticus 18:14, and 20:20. However, if James was Jesus's "brother" then most Protestants believe he could *not* have been an apostle for John declares that Jesus's step-brothers were not believers (John 7:5). Consequently, Protestants deny that James the Just was an apostle whereas Catholics deny that he was Jesus's brother. Both are wrong, and yet both are right as well.

In *Apostles After Jesus* I give a lengthy discussion upon this issue, so I will merely repeat the important facts. First, a careful examination of Matthew 13:55-56, 27:56, Mark 6:3, 15:40 (cf. Mark 16:1), Luke 24:10, and John 19:25 will demonstrate that James the son of Alphæus was one and the same as James the Less. Second, although there is a distinct Hebrew word for "cousin" in Hebrew, and Greek, there is also a distinct word of "step-brother." Consequently, Paul's use of the term "brother" must be seen affectionately, and not in its most strict meaning.

Second, this James the Less appears to be that mentioned in Galatians 1:19, where Paul associates him with the apostles. Thus James the Less, the apostle of Jesus, was also James the Just of history, the first overseer of Jerusalem. So James the Just was an apostle who apparently rose to great prominence after the death of James the Greater. This is apparent not only by history's record of him as overseer, but also by Paul in Galatians, and here in Acts as well. Let us take a closer look at James's prominent role in the affairs of the church, and the council of Jerusalem.

James, the Head of the Jerusalem Council?

The record of church history at this point does not concern us. If the Bible contradicts the church fathers, then the fathers were wrong. Of course, I am not denying they were wrong, but rather demonstrating from the Bible that James was indeed the head of the Council of Jerusalem, and apparently the church there as well.

Paul himself calls James a "pillar of the church" and places his name *first* before even Peter and John (Galatians 2:9)! Based on Paul's asertions in Galatians 2:12 Peter was not only influenced by James, but even intimidated as evidenced by the fact that he is said to have been "fearing the party of the circumcision" of which James then appears to have been associated. Moreover, it was James who appears to have had the final argument and read the council's final decision (Acts 15:13-21). All this implies that James's position was above even that of Peter and John. If the record of the church fathers is correct, then James was the head, or overseer (later called bishop), of the church in Jerusalem. This is supported by the fact that when Paul returned to Jerusalem many years later, only James appears to have still be residing in Jerusalem (cf. Acts 21:18), indicating that his work remained with the church there even after the other disciples ventured out into missions. This fits well with his position here at the council, but it doesn't fit well with those who hold the supremacy of the Roman church.

Even if we accepted that there was to be an unending line of apostles (see notes under Acts 1:21-26), then why would Rome supercede Jerusalem and why would James have superceded Peter's authority here? This is the same Peter who was publicly rebuked by Paul not long before (Galatians 2:11; cf. Acts 15:2). Now I do not mean to say that Peter was not one of the greatest of the apostles, but rather that this synod demonstrates that there was no central authority figure to whom the church turned. Jesus alone was the authority. The inner circle of apostles had been Peter, James the Greater, and John (cf. Matthew 17:1; Mark 9:2, 13:3, 14:33; Luke 8:51, 9:28), but now it appears that it had become James the Less, Peter, and John (Galatians 2:9; cf. Acts 21:18). So we may conclude that while the apostles obviously had greater authority than the elders or disciples, there was no clear individual leader among them. Even here in this debate, it was the entire church, lead by both apostles and elders, who met to decide the issue. This was the first synod, and it later became a pattern for many later synods, but were such synods what the apostles intended?

Was the Synod a Pattern to Follow?
The short answer is "yes and no." The Catholic church have prided themselves in following the pattern of the church council whereas most Protestants pride ourselves on our rule of following the Bible alone. However, this is somewhat disingenuous on both churches' parts. First, all churches, included Protestant denominations, have "conventions" in which issues relating to the church are discussed. Second, the Catholic church may have had synods, but traditionally, excluding the First Council of Nicaea, the Catholic church only invites Catholic churches to participate. This would be the equivalent of James inviting only church members who were of the party of circumcision to the Council of Jerusalem. So both Catholics and Protestants are here being a little dishonest with themselves.

In theory we all agree that the Bible is to be our guide, and not some council of humans making random decisions. Nevertheless, while circumcision was obviously a Biblical issue, its application to gentile converts was not so clear cut that the apostles themselves were not divided on the issue. The Bible is our final authority, but the world provides new challenges to the application of God's word. Can a man divorced before becoming a believer be a pastor? Is such-and-such a war acceptable in the sight of God? At what stage does submission to the government become disobedience to God (e.g. "Obamacare" and its Abortion Mandate)? Obviously these issues involve Biblical principles, but the application of those principles is debated among even many like-minded theologians. Consequently, councils, synods, and conventions are a common ways of airing these issues in virtually all churches. The real question is whether or not this was a pattern established by the apostles for the purpose of future church government. That is a question which is not so easy to answer.

Let us consider the circumstances of the Council of Jerusalem. The church was itself divided and in danger of a schism. The outpouring of the Holy Spirit upon gentiles was itself a subject of surprise (compare Acts 8:15-17 with 15:8), if not controversy. The purpose for the council was to avoid schism and bring the church together in accordance with the Will of God. Furthermore, it is apparent that all the apostles and elders were present at the council. Since there are no more apostles (see notes on Acts 1:21-26) the authority of any church council today is suspect. Historically speaking church councils have increasingly drifted away from the unity which they were intended to insure. The Council of Jerusalem was obviously a resounding success. The next council was that of Nicaea, called by Constantine to resolve the divisions which had taken place over the centuries since the apostles' demise. It is the only council in which mainstream Protestants, Catholics, and Eastern Orthodox *all* agree. With each successive council the church seems to have increasingly become divided rather than unified. This itself testifies to a pattern reminiscent of ancient Israel. As Israel moved from faithfulness to God to rebellion, so also the church of God moved from the faithfulness of the early church, to the rebellion of the Middle Ages and the modern age. Church councils are therefore a means for the church to attempt to resolve issues important to the day, but they have no lasting authority in the church. It is the Word of God to which we are accountable, and the Word of God alone. Only our faithfulness to Jesus will matter in the end.

The Results of the Council
The immediate results of the council recorded in Acts 15:13-31 was two fold. First, it was agreed that no unneccessary obstacles were to be placed before the gentiles. Circumcision was not to be required, but only an admonition to "abstain from things contaminated by idols and from fornication and from what is strangled and from blood" (15:20).

The second result of the council was "to choose men from among them to send to Antioch with Paul and Barnabas – Judas called Barsabbas, and Silas" (15:22). This action is significant because it marks the first official sanctioning of Paul's ministry to the gentiles.

This was followed soon after by a third result which may or may not have been a specific issue before the council, but was certainly a result of the council. Not only did the apostles send out Barsabbas and Silas, but the apostles themselves soon left for various mission fields around the world, fulfilling the Great Commission. According to Eusebius the apostles' mission fields were chosen by lot.[487] It appears from history that the earth was to be divided into four section, and the apostles were to take the Word of God out into these four quarters of the earth. Counting James the Greater, who died in Judah, the land appears to have been divided as follows:

The Four Quarters of the Earth Divided

Northern Africa	Europe/Asia Minor	Israel	The Eastern World
Matthew	Peter	James the Greater	Thomas
Philip	John	James the Less	Bartholomew
Simon the Zealot	Andrew	Matthias	Judas Thaddæus

The evidence of this is not only from church history, but indirect evidence from the Bible as well. It is not without significance that we read nothing else of Peter in the book of Acts, nor John, nor any other apostles except for Paul and James, who appears alone to have remained in Jerusalem where he was apparently the overseer (cf. Acts 21:18). This silence in regard to the other apostles can only be explained by the fact that they had each left for their own mission fields, and Luke's record was of what transpired in Jerusalem and with Paul, his companion and associate. With the apostles venturing out and away from Jerusalem the book of Acts begins to focus on Paul alone.

So the final result of the Council of Jerusalem was the fulfillment of the Great Commission and the beginning of the great mission fields beyond Israel. There is no question that the apostles reached as far as Rome, western Africa, and possibly even Spain and England in the west, and as far as India in the east.[488] The Great Commission was finally being fulfilled.

Conclusion

Although the Council of Jerusalem occupies just a single chapter in Acts, it was one of the most significant events in the early church. It opened the door for gentile converts to come to Christ unobstructed, and it paved the way for Christian missions around the world. In short, it began to fulfill the Great Commission of Jesus Christ (Matthew 28:19).

9

Paul's Second Journey

With the apostles moving out into their respective mission fields, the book of Acts now turns it attention to the mission of the apostle Paul. The rest of Acts deals exclusively with Paul's ministry. His first journey took Paul to western Turkey and Cyprus. After the Council of Jerusalem Paul sought to return to revisit the churches he had established, but also to expand further. In his second missionary journey he would venture as far as Greece.

Forbidden to Preach?
Acts 16:6-7

> "They passed through the Phrygian and Galatian region, having been forbidden by the Holy Spirit to speak the word in Asia, and after they came to Mysia, they were trying to go into Bithynia, and the Spirit of Jesus did not permit them."

Here is a seemingly strange aside in Acts. Luke records that Paul was forbidden by the Holy Spirit, also called the Spirit of Jesus, from witnessing the gospel in Asia (the country), Mysia, and Bithynia. Why? The answer is not to be found in Scripture, but may be found in history for Asia, Mysia, and Bithynia are believed to have been the mission fields of the apostles Andrew and John. It is significant that this took place shortly after the Council of Jerusalem, which again indicates that the apostles left for their mission fields soon after the council. Thus God's forbidding Paul to enter these lands was because John and Andrew were already asigned to take the gospel to those lands. Although Paul would later help and support John's churches in Asia, the Lord did not want Paul to infringe upon the initial missions of John and Andrew.

While this theory cannot be born out conclusively from Scripture, it fits the facts of history and of the events taking place in the Bible at this time. Asia, Mysia, and Bithynia were not being punished for some sin, but were being preserved for the missions of John and Andrew. Paul was to go on toward Greece, where he would be the first to bring the gospel.

Prophecy and Motives
Acts 16:16-19

> "It happened that as we were going to the place of prayer, a slave-girl having a spirit of divination met us, who was bringing her masters much profit by fortune-telling. Following after Paul and us, she kept crying out, saying, 'These men are bond-servants of the Most High God, who

are proclaiming to you the way of salvation.' ... Paul was greatly annoyed, and turned and said to the spirit, 'I command you in the name of Jesus Christ to come out of her!' ... when her masters saw that their hope of profit was gone, they seized Paul and Silas and dragged them into the market place before the authorities."

Here Paul is harassed by a demon possessed woman who appears on the surface to have been doing nothing more than confirming to the people that Paul was an apostle from Christ! Paul's reaction to her and the fact that she was possessed have been a source of great dissension among scholars throughout the centuries.

A Python Spirit?
Acts 16:16 says that this woman had a "spirit of divination." However, this is not without controversy in itself for the usual word for divination was μαντεια (*manteia*),[489] but here is found the rare word πυθωνος (*pythonos*) from which we get the word "python." This is because the Python snake was named after the mythical serpent (or dragon) of the god Apollo which was named Python.[490] According to the myth it was the Guardian of Delphi[491] until Apollo himself killed it.[492]

Now it is important to note that etymologically, the name Python does not originate with Greek mythology but rather the opposite, for in the story of the Python, the oracle of Delphi was named after the serpent. Hence, the oracle was a Pythia which practiced fortune-telling.[493] In other words, πυθωνος (*pythonos*) is a form of fortune-telling. This is clear from the Biblical use of the word, for it is said that she was "bringing her masters much profit by fortune-telling" (16:16). Despite this, some argue that πυθωνος (*pythonos*) should be translated as "ventriloquist" (see notes below)![494] Nonetheless, the proper translation is "divination" or "fortune telling" as found in all Greek Lexicons.

The Various Theories
The story itself is peculiar to some for the woman is saying nothing but "These men are bond-servants of the Most High God, who are proclaiming to you the way of salvation" (16:17). Is this not true? Why was the apostle so distraught by her actions? To answer this question countless theories have been put forth over the years. Of these four stand out and have garnered favor over the years. In addition to these four (debated below) are a handful of other hypotheses passed out over time. Some believe that the woman was looking for reward from the apostle while others argue that she was trying to appease them.[495] Both of these, however, play into a greater question. Why was she trying to appease them? What was the true motive of the spirit? Most important is why the apostle Paul reacted so angrily, even endangering his own life to silence her!

The Ventriloquist Theory

The rationalist, or liberal, reject miracles and the spiritual realm. They naturally tend to read psychology or natural phenomenon into the text. Here it is argued that in Plutarch εγγαστριμυθοι (*engastrimuthoi*), or ventriloquists, were called πυθωνες (*pythones*),[496] nevermind that this is not the *exact* word used in the Bible. They therefore completely ignore all other possibilities and translations, disregarding the context, and argue that the slave practiced ventriloquism![497] How does this fit the "fortune-telling" of the passage? According to the rationalist theory the woman used her "power of ventriloquism"[498] to fool the people into believing that she had a spirit. They then go on to say that after Paul's rebuke, the woman, "supposing her powers were due to such a spirit, was unable to ventriloquize any longer."[499]

Now logically this argument not only fails exegetically, but even psychologically, for one breath they claim that she was a fraud who used ventriloquism while at the same time claiming that she was so psychologically traumatized by the thought of loosing a spirit she did not possess she could no longer ventriloquize! The ingenuity of the theory is almost enough to compensate for its frivolity.

In order to justify this theory Parsons claims that "nowhere in the story is the 'Python spirit' labeled unclear or evil or demonic"![500] He then suggest that Paul only did this to "get a little peace and quiet."[501] Obviously, this theory is an illustration of the desperation to which the rationalist will go to remove the spiritual world from the Bible. It fails both the test of exegesis and logic.

The Forced Confession Theory

Another argument compares this passage to verses like Matthew 8:29, Mark 3:11, and Luke 4:41.[502] In each of those verses the demons recognize and acknowledge Jesus as the Christ and Son of God. However, the context is very different. In Mark 3:11 and Luke 4:41 the demons were told to keep silent by Jesus because His time (for crucifixion) had not yet come. They were not to reveal who He was until the time was right. The demons were acknowledging Christ, but they acknowledged Him out of fear. In this way some have argued that Jesus "forced her to confess"[503] in Acts 16:17, but the argument doesn't hold up by itself. For one thing, the advocate "seems to forget that the cry [in the gospel account] expressed nothing but agony and alarm."[504] The demons were fearful whereas here in Acts the woman shows no fear, but appears to be patronizing them.

The Mockery Theory

One suggested answer is that the demon was mocking Paul as a way of belittling him.[505] The theory is intriguing but once again fails to answer the fundamental questions. Why would a demon appear to advocate the ministry of Paul? If the demon were simply mocking Paul, then it is unlikely that she would have followed Paul for the Bible declares that she did this for "many days."

Surely there must have been some other motive involved to have pursued Paul for so long.

The Theory of the Cult
Very early in the history of the church Satan began to disguise himself as an angel of light (2 Corinthians 11:14). The gnostic cult was arguably the first ancient cult to attach itself to label of Christianity. Its doctrines were a lethal venom to its followers, denying the physical incarnation of Jesus, His death, and His Resurrection! Such cults not only lead people astray but also give the entire church a bad image, for unbelievers rarely distinguish between the true church and church cults. To this day many unbelievers associate Christianity with the Inquisition, despite the fact that the Inquisition was created to eradicate evangelical Christainity![506]

Here many believe "Satan essayed a new means of mischief, not assailing the gospel but patronizing it."[507] John MacArthur calls this "a bold attempt to infiltrate a deadly tare among the wheat, because what the demon-possessed girl was saying was absolutely true."[508] Baumgarten even suggests the spirit of the slave girl was assuming the place of the Holy Spirit and thus had to be silenced.[509] This argument makes the most sense.

Even in antiquity church fathers, such as Chrysostom, argued that by admitting Paul was a servant of God men, the demon was making itself accepted by naive followers as well so he could then deceive them. This is why Paul cast it out.[510] To this day the doctrine of demons (cf. Ephesians 4:14; 1 John 4:1) permeates the world, posing as Christian teachings. So, as Calvin said, Satan "pretends to be a friend of the Word and creeps in underground."[511] Another says that "through this cunning demon Satan tried to hinder the work by assuming a friendly relation towards the servants of the Lord Jesus Christ."[512]

So the reason for Paul's reaction and the context of the passage seems to best support the fact that the demon was seeking "to make it appear they were confederate with them."[513] By pretending to be an "angel of light" (cf. 2 Corinthians 11:14) the demon hoped to lead people astray from the truth. This is the best method by which demon deceive and this passage indicates that it was also one of the first methods.

Conclusion
To this day some occultists argue that their "arts" are perfectly consistent with the Bible. They make fortune-telling synonymous with prophesy or argue some similar grounds to justify their practices, which are condemned in the Bible. Here Paul encounters one such woman who was making herself out to be a prophetess and ally of the apostles, when her craft was really at odds with them. It was one of the first clear instances in Acts of Satan masquerading as an "angel of light" (2 Corinthians 11:14). Paul's rebuke and his casting of the demon from

her nearly led to his death. Such is the dark truth hidden behind these masquerading heretics who continue to deceive to this very day.

To An Unknown God – The Sermon on Mars Hill
Acts 17:23

> "For while I was passing through and examining the objects of your worship, I also found an altar with this inscription, '*To an Unknown God.*' Therefore what you worship in ignorance, this I proclaim to you."

The history of missions has seen two fundamental heresies over the centuries. The first heresy is to compel people to believe by force, in violation of conscience. Martin Luther objected to this saying, "the mind convinced by force is a mind not convinced at all." God judges by the heart so that no man can be compelled to believe against his will. The second heresy on the other extreme. It is compromise. We change Jesus to make Him more acceptable to those we seek to convert, but in changing Jesus we create only a cult which has few sincere believers anyway, and those few converts who are "won" are now deceived although they would have converted nevertheless had we just spoken the truth.

What then is the "correct" way of missions? Obviously, it is speaking the truth, but most missions now teach something called "contextualization." What is "contextualization"? It comes from the word "context" and means that we are to put the gospel in "context" to the culture to which we are witnessing, but what does *that* mean? Is the gospel different from one culture to another? Does context change the meaning of the gospel? This is the difficulty, for most who teach "contextualization" are really teaching compromise, and yet this is not necessarily so. Here in Acts Paul provides the consumate example of witnessing the gospel to a different culture unfamiliar with Judaism. In fact, as Paul had previously witnessed "to the Jew first, but also the Greek" (Romans 1:16; 2:9-10), this is the first instance in the Bible where Paul is clearly teaching to a different culture disassociated from Judaism and the Bible (but see notes on Acts 14:11-18 below). Consequently, it is important to look at Paul's speech, Paul's purpose, and the result of his preaching. Both sides of the arguments may be surprised at what we find.

Which Unknown God?
The first controversial words we encounter here are those of the altar to an "unknown God." Here Paul begins his discourse by referencing a pagan altar. Some have been very quick to note that "it is no unknown God but a Risen Christ with whom we have to deal."[514] Indeed this is so, and such Paul proclaimed, but the crux of the problem is that Paul begins with a pagan altar. How are we to understand Paul's use and the people's understanding? Is this "contextualization"?

Rothermel Peter – Paul Preaching at Mars Hill – 1860

Let us start by looking at the Greek. It is not "the" unknown God but "an" unknown God.[515] When Greek lacks the definite article, as it does here, is always indefinite,[516] meaning that if could refer to *any* god whom they did not know. This was done because the Greeks believed in a pantheon of gods and did not wish to offend any unknown god. The Greek word for "unknown God" is Αγνωστω Θεω (*Agnostoi Theoi*). Now αγνωστως (*Agnostos*) is the word from which we get "agnostic." Obviously Paul was not endorsing agnosticism.

What then are we to make of Paul's use of the altar? Clearly Paul used the altar as a starting point, but no sooner did he start with common ground than he immediately diverged. "What you worship in ignorance, this I proclaim to you" (17:23). From here on out there is not a hint of compromise, nor "contextualization." It is therefore his starting point which is at issue and nothing else. Were they on equal ground?

If we begin with a false concept, we will necessarily end with a false concept. It is vitally important to begin on firm ground. Paul was therefore looking for common ground. The altar existed because the Greeks knew that there was at least one god whom they did not know. Paul does not support the notion of multiple gods, nor endorse their worship of false gods (see "Blasphemy Against Artemis" below). He simply begins with a true concept. There is a God they did not know. Paul was there to preach that God. Such an example is but one where God plants seeds over time which take fruit centuries later. The case of Cortez, no missionary to be sure, is one such example. The Aztecs had a prophesy of a white god who would come and liberate them from the barbaric empire under which they suffered. The seeds were thus planted centuries before (see below for more on this).

Acts 14:11-18
The dangers of to much "contextualization" are obvious in passages like Acts 14:11-18 where Greeks witnessed the healing of a man. They instantly "began calling Barnabas, Zeus, and Paul, Hermes" (14:12) and attempted to offer sacrifices to them (14:14-18). Now none of this was through any fault of Paul or Barnabas, but it displays how dangerous compromise can be, and why religious cults thrived. Men would often seize upon the name of Jesus to make themselves out to be a great prophet or leader. In this case, just by observing a miracle, the pagan Greeks were ready to offer sacrifices to Paul as the god Hermes and Barnbas as Zeus! Paul did not "contextualize" here but resisted in every way possible.

The Blasphemy Against Artemis
That Paul did not compromise the gospel or risk perverting the gospel into something less than what it is, is apparent in Acts 19:24-41. There some merchants were enraged that the apostle was preaching against idolatry and charged Paul and Barnabas with blasphemy against the gods (Acts 19:26). A riot nearly ensued. This was not unusual, for those who oppose the truth will

always hate us. It is not our job to "make" someone love Jesus. Either they do or they do not. Changing Jesus does not change a sinner's heart. Jesus changes the sinner's heart.

So it is not a question of whether it is good or bad to offend someone, but whether or not that offense is Jesus. If we offend someone then the offense must be Jesus, and Jesus alone. It is not useful to purposely offend someone, as some do, but neither is it useful to avoid offense if that offense is the gospel itself. This leads to the real question. Does the gospel need to be "contextualized" at all?

"Contextualization"
The gospel transcends culture. Jesus speaks to all people. This is the beauty of the truth. It is not bound by a particular culture. Consequently, we might asks immediately of what value is "contextualization"? Surpirsingly, it does have some merit, but only some. Let us look at examples to help us understand the issue better.

Examples in Indian Missions
India's culture is so different from that of the west that when we speak of God the Indian often hears something quite different from what we mean. One Christian missionary in India, and not a conservative one, once stated that "there is a danger that Hindus may desire to adopt Christ in the same way and lower Him to the level of their gods."[517] This danger has two sides; like a double edged sword. On the one hand there is the danger of compromise, for in trying to make Jesus presentable to the Hindu, they accept Jesus only as an inferior god among many. On the other hand there is the danger that the Hindu will misunderstand our very concept of God because he hears even the name "god" in a differen *context* than us. For us God is a personal being and Creator of the universe. For most eastern religions nature and god are one. It is not without merit to note that in Paul's speech he *begins* by stating that God "made the world and all things in it" (17:24). The next words out of his lips were "does not dwell in temples made with hands" (17:24). Hence his first two statements have been perceived by some as an attack on Greek philosophy.[518] Paul began with common ground, but immediately started to *distinguish* the differences. It is common to hear Hindus say that "all religions are one." A beautiful Bollywood actress said, "all religions are the same," to which it should be replied, "sometimes the differences are more important than the similarities." In preaching the gospel, we must understand that it is what makes Jesus different that makes him special.

Cortez and the Aztecs
Cortez was no missionary. Let us be clear on this. He was a conqueror. Nonetheless, the conquest of old Mexico opened the door for the Aztec people. The history of Cortez is an important one for many reasons.

Some revisionist historians have claimed that the stories of human sacrifice among the Aztecs cannot be trusted, but it is the Aztecs themselves who recorded these rituals. Their own annals even boasted that in celebration of the victory of the king Ahuitzotl, 80,000 victims were sacrificed in four days.[519] Human sacrifice was, in fact, practiced almost everywhere in antiquity. The Jews were actually among the earliest in the near east to have halted the practice. That is the very context behind the story of Abraham's testing, and the reason that Jews did not continue the practice which was common place in Canaan at that time.

Now according to the legends of the Aztecs there was a white, bearded, god named Quetzalcoatl who once ruled Mexico. He left on the shores of Veracruz (the very place where Cortez had landed) and promised to return someday.[520] When Cortez arrived the people sent reports to the Aztec emperor of pale white men who "had weapons that thundered flame and smoke and killed at a distance; and they were mounted on strange beasts like deer."[521] The people themselves were eager for a deliverer. The barbarity of the Aztec empire was beyond measure, but when Cortez heard the legends he acted wisely in that he did not claim to be a god. On the contrary, he cut himself and showed them the blood, saying, "I am flesh and bone, the same as you."[522] Thus while he was more than happy to use the legend to his advantage, he was not stupid enough to claim deity which could easily have come back to haunt him (and get him excommunicated back home).

The point is that long before Cortez arrived God had planted seeds. The "prophecy" of Quetzalcoatl prepared the people of Mexico to receive the conquerors not as enemies, but as liberators. Certainly Cortez did not bring the gospel with him, but Christianity came to the shores of the New World nevertheless. The "context" was provided by God, but it was a "context" that could easily have been destructive. Had Cortez made himself out to be a god, he would have not only blasphemed Jesus Christ, but failed in his conquest, for once they saw his men die, they would have known he was lying. By telling the *truth*, the "prophecy" remained at the back of their minds, but the truth was before them. So also we must never forsake the truth for some perceived "context." What makes Jesus so great is the fact that His truth transcends culture. Jesus is the context.

The American "Contextualized" Gospel

"Contextualization" happens to everyone whether we know it or not. No one is immune. Often times we do it without even thinking, but that is usually when "contextualization" becomes compromise. One subtle example I will use is from evangelical Christians in America. We are use to hearing, "I am not religious, I just love Jesus," or some similar phrase. Now there is nothing wrong with this statement *per se*, but those who use it do not really even know what they are saying. It is true that faith in Jesus is all that God will look to for our salvation, but the statement itself stems from the modern secular movement in the West which deems religion evil. We are constantly told about how many people are killed in the name of religion, but are never told that more people have been slaughtered by "secular" governments in the past hundred years than people killed by religion in the history of planet earth! Also bear in mind that most westerners have been brainwashed into believing that "secularism" is the same thing as "religious neutrality." This is not so. Secularism literally means "without religion." Atheism is secular. Stalinism was secular. Hitler's Germany was secular. Mao Tse Tung was secular. America was religiously tolerant and neutral. America was about religious freedom. Note *religious* freedom. Freedom of religion stems from Christianity because it leaves the mind free to seek God.

"But religion is an obstacle" say many. This is both true and false. Religion is in theory (and I agree it is not so in practice) a means of seeking God. We agree that one can only find God through Jesus, but if we know and love Jesus then, whether we want to admit it not, we *are* religious. Why deny it? Because we are told over and over again that religion is an obstacle and bad. Nonetheless, what was Paul's remark? The very *first* words out of his lips were, "I observe that you are very religious in all respects" (17:22). Notice that he did not chastize them or criticize them for their religious devotion. It was good, because it meant they were seeking God. He then went on to tell them how they could find God! It was their love of religion that was the common ground upon which Paul began his speech. He then referred to the unknown God, and began to tell them how they could know that God. It is at this point only that he began to tell them what they were doing wrong.

The point is that when we say "I love Jesus, not religion," we must understand that we are ministering to a secular people. This is fine in the West, but when you go to the East (where I have ministered) such a remark sounds atheistic and contemptuous of God. Imagine if Paul had begun this sermon by saying how stupid religion was. If we are going to criticize "contextualization" then we must first understand when *we* are contextualizing the gospel.

Let me clarify my position here. I do not have a problem with westerners saying that loving Jesus is not a religion. I do have a problem when people do not realize what they are saying, when they think this is Scriptural rather than cultural, and when they take this cultural spin and attempt to apply it in another culture or "context." It is necessary to understand *when* we are contextualizing the gospel, before we can criticize those who do contextualize the gospel.

Paul and the Athenians

The *context* with which we are most concerned is that of the Bible. Without consideration of the context of Paul, nothing else matters. To begin with "the Athenians had been worshiping an object, not a personal God, a 'what,' not a 'whom.'"[523] They had idols to pagan gods and to unknown gods. "The very existence of the later is a palpable proof that a need of worshipping him was felt."[524] Paul begins with two positive remarks, concerning their religious nature in seeking God, and in the acknowledgement of a God unknown to them. He then immediately diverges and tells them where they have gone wrong. Arno Gaebelein saw this speech as an attack on Greek philosophy.[525] Far from compromising the gospel, he made clear that "we ought not to think that the Divine Nature is like gold or silver or stone, an image formed by the art and thought of man" (17:19). This was an assault upon the sin of idolatry. It was an attack upon one of their most sacred religious beliefs.

So was this a "hell fire and brimstone" sermon? No, it was neither compromise nor hell-fire. It was the truth. Let us break down his sermon into each main point, and see if those points would be perceived as "negative" or "positive" by the people.

"Positive" Aspects	"Negative" Aspects
He observed their religious devotion (17:22)	He rejected their concept of the gods (17:24)
He appealed to their acknowledgement of a God unknown to them (17:23)	He rejected the need of God to be served by man (17:25)
He appealed to God as being the God of all nationalities and races (17:26)	He rejected idolatry (17:29)
He appealed to their desire to find God (17:27)	He calls men ignorant and stresses the need for repentance (17:30)
	He warns of judgment day through Christ Jesus (17:31)

So we see that Paul's speech cannot be defined strictly as an offensive or non-offensive sermon. It was both. It was the truth. He neither offered them honey, nor threw mud. He merely spoke the truth. He began with what they could agree upon, but he quickly moved to what made Christ different. This is what I tell my Hindu friends. It is what makes Christ different that makes Him special.

The reaction to Paul's speech is important. "Some *began* to sneer, but others" were intrigued (17:32). The truth is *always* divisive, because some people will aways reject and hate the truth. This is why we have been persecuted, fed to lions, burned at stakes, and sent to concentration camps. Some will always hate the truth. To make the truth "acceptable" to these men, is to make it a lie.

Conclusion
Some like to compromise, thinking it will lead to more converts. Others like to offend, thinking it will lead to repentance. The truth is that neither is particularly beneficial. People are different. Some need a little "hell-fire and

brimstone" while others need a "big hug." We must not be so naive as to believe that the means of communication is what matters. What matters is whether or not the substance of the sermon is the truth, and the *whole* truth. A partial truth is a half-truth and a half-truth is as bad as a lie.

Understanding a culture is useful, but only to a point. We should not be trying to make the gospel "acceptable" to people, but only to find a proper starting point at which to communicate. If I say "god" to a Buddhist he will hear "impersonal force." If I understand this, then I can explain the difference to him. Then I am preaching the gospel. Context is only a starting point, not an ending point. It is what makes Jesus different that makes Him special great. Jesus *transcends* culture. This is why He has changed the world. Let us not demean Jesus by lowering Him to someone's cultural understandings. Let us be faithful to the Word of God which speaks to all people and all nations and all cultures, but truth transcents all these things, and He is the Way, the Truth, and the Life (John 14:6).

Why Did Claudius Expel the Jews?
Acts 18:2

"Claudius had commanded all the Jews to leave Rome."

Acts 18:2 says that "a Jew named Aquila, a native of Pontus ... recently come from Italy with his wife Priscilla, because Claudius had commanded all the Jews to leave Rome." This incident, the expulsion of Jews by Claudius, is recorded by Sutonius, the ancient Roman historian, who states that "the Jews at Rome caused continuous distrubances at the instigation of Chrestus, [and so] he expelled them from the city."[526] Who was this Chrestus? This question has become a contentious one in recent years. Many believe that it is a references to Christians. Others that it is the name of Christ in Latin. Still others argue that it is another man, then living, who was in no way associated with Christianity. Finally, some have suggested that it was a false Christ or Messiah that stirred the Jewish community.

This issue is an intriguing one for many reasons. First, if this does relate to Christianity, as it appears, then it shows how rapidly Christianity was spreading, and it shows how the division between Christianity and Judaism was increasing. The Romans did not at first distinguish between Christians and Jews, but that would change by the time of Nero, not long after Claudius. Second, this issue shows the fear that some radicals have of even admitting to *anything* in history related to Christianity. What in this brief statement of Sutonius is there that makes the secularist so afraid? Even the secular translator of Sutonius placed a footnote indicating his believe that Chrestus was Latin for Christ,[527] so why are so many troubled by this possibility? Let us examine the theories and evidence.

Until relatively recently few denied that Chrestus was in some way related to Christ and/or the Christians. John Calvin echoed the seemingly universal belief that Chrestus was Latin for Christ.[528] Neither Jews, nor secularists, nor the liberal rationalist Emil Schurer denied this. The later believed that the expulsion "was occasioned by the disturbances, which arose within Judaism in consequence of the preaching of Christ."[529] However, in modern times criticism of anything related to Christianity has led even many Christians to question this.

Lenski thought that Chrestus was a Greek name,[530] but if it is the name of a Greek man, then why were *the Jews* expelled from Rome? Clearly, this Chrestus was related to the Jews, not the Greek. Nonetheless, even men like Baumgarten argues that the ancient historians knew the difference between Chrestus and Christians[531] and would not have confused them. He thus infers that Chrestus was a "Greek and Roman name"[532] but offers no proof of any such man in history. If it was a Greek or Roman name, it is one that is missing from history books, save here in Sutonius. The fact is that Chrestus is not a name, but a title. Christ is the Greek word for Messiah. It is a title, not a name. Consequently, some have argued that the "Jews were excited to rebellion by" a false Christ then living at that time.[533]

Owing to the number of false Christs or Messiahs in that day, this is a possibility except that *false* Christs were always rebels. They had a history of rebellion against Rome, believing that the Messiah was to overthrow the Roman empire. This is why Jesus was falsely accused of treason against Caesar. Caiaphas was interested in playing upon the Roman fear of false Christs. Logically then, if this was a riot caused by a false Christ then it is Chrestos himself who would have been arrested and tried, not the Jewish population which opposed him! This argument does not work for the history records the Jews were expelled over an internal conflict, not an exterior threat against Rome.

This leaves us with two possibilities. Either Chrestus was a reference to Christians or to Christ Himself. MacArthur argued that Sutonius, "writing seventy years after the fact, wrongly assumed Chrestus (Christ) to have been in Rome."[534] Baumgarten objects to this argument saying that the historians were not so ignorant.[535] However, some argue that "it is most probable that those riots were among the Jews in Rome on account of Christianity, and that when the Roman authorities ask the cause, they were told it was 'Christos,' thus leading Sutonius to hink that 'Chrestus' was the name of the leader of the riots."[536] Read Sutonius's account carefully. He suggests that the disturbances were at the "instigation of Chrestus" which obviously infers Chrestus was present, but this is not necessarily true. If these were "the results of conflicts in synagogues between Messianists and non-Messianists"[537] then Christ could be said to have instigated the conflicts, even though He was not present. Certainly Sutonius was writing seventy years after the fact and using court records which only reflected what the Roman authorities were *told*. Since no arrest of this Chrestus is recorded, it is logical to assume that Claudius was unconcerned with the specifics. Remember that Jews and Christians were not distringuished at this time. As a result, Claudius saw this as a problem among Jews which was harming the harmony of Rome. He therefore expelled all the Jews, not just the followers of Chrestus.

Orosius places this in 49 or 50 A.D.[538] Despite the recent cries against the traditional interpretation, no evidence of a Greek or Roman Chrestus exist. It appears by all rights to be a Latinization of the title Christ. It is, as Gaebelein delcared, "undoubtebly" a reference to Christ,[539] and an indication that Christianity had already spread among the Jewish synagogues to Rome. This was doubtless one of many reasons that Paul was so eager to go to Rome.

10

Paul's Third Journey

Acts 18:23 begins Paul's third and final journey before he returns to Jerusalem. The other apostles, save James and probably Matthias, had already left for the missionary field. Antioch remained the most significant Church center outside of Jerusalem and is thus considered the beginning and end of each of Paul's missionary journeys. It was as close to home as Paul could get until he returned one final time to Jerusalem at the end of this journey, setting the stage for his arrest, trial, and appeal to the new Caesar, Nero.

The Ancient Prescript
Acts 19:0

What is verse 19:0? Obviously there is no such passage, but two ancient manuscripts contain a prescript to verse 19 which is not found in any Bibles, as it was not a part of the original text. Nonetheless, the verse is of interest as it relates to Acts 19:21.

Two ancient Greek texts replace the phrase, "it happened that while Apollos was at Corinth" with the statement, "although Paul wished, according to his own plan, to go to Jerusalem, the Spirit told him to return to Asia."[540] These are Papyrus 38 ($\mathfrak{P}^{38}$) and the Codex Bezae (or Cantabrigiensis). The former dates to the end of the third century. This prescript is also found in many Syrian manuscripts and some Italian ones as well. Now while it is agreed that this was apparently an addition, the question as to why the addition was made has intrigued many. One scholar claims that this statement is "neither in the character of Paul nor of Luke, who brings expressly into prominence how Paul allows all his decisions to be made by the will of God made known to him through the Spirit."[541] However, this author seems to miss the point, for in 19:21 there is a controversial passage which similarly reads, "Paul purposed in the Spirit to go to Jerusalem after he had passed through Macedonia and Achaia, saying, 'After I have been there, I must also see Rome.'" Many believe that it was "his spirit" and not God's.[542] This debate is reserved for the discussion on Acts 19:21 (cf. Acts 20:22-21:4 – Acts 25:11 – Acts 26:32), but it is of importance to draw the reader's attention to this ancient prescript before 19:1 which indicates that many believed, even in antiquity, that Paul was wrong to have wanted to return to Jerusalem. The prescript establishes immediately the notion that Paul should never have returned to Jerusalem but should have continued his mission to the gentiles uninterrupted. The debate is therefore an ancient one and one which discussed below.

Baptism of the Spirit
Acts 19:1-6 – See also Acts 8:15-17

"He said to them, 'Did you receive the Holy Spirit when you believed?' And they *said* to him, 'No, we have not even heard whether there is a Holy Spirit.'"

One of the most controversial passages in Acts is here where Paul encounters supposed Christian believers who had not received the Holy Spirit. This passage, like Acts 8:15-17, is used by some Pentecostals and Charismatic sects as proof that the baptism of the Spirit is a separate event from the rebirth. In Acts 8, however, we saw the "Samaritan Pentecost" in which God validated gentile converts without the need for circumcision. The event was unique in that the Jews had formerly believed that gentiles had to convert to Judaism before becoming believers. This matter was eventually settled at the Council of Jerusalem. Here, however, is a different situation.

Long after both the Pentecost and the "Samaritan Pentecost" were a group of disciples who had never received the Holy Spirit. Indeed, by their own words they had not even heard of the Holy Spirit (19:2)! This is the key. How could a disciple of Christ not have even heard of the Holy Spirit? To get an answer to this Paul asked, "into what then were you baptized?" (19:3). To this they replied, "into John's baptism" (19:3). Thus most believe that these were not truly disciples of Christ, but of John.[543] Still, some Pentecostals object to this saying that Paul's initial inquiry was "Did you receive the Holy Spirit *when* you believed?" (19:2). It was not *did* you believe, but *when* you believed. Some translations even read "since you believed" (KJV, Duoay-Rheims, Geneva), which appears to negate any doubt that they were true believers.[544] Therefore they maintain that this baptism is distinct from conversion. Which is true?

Beginning with the translation itself, "the Greek verb Paul used in his question to the twelve Ephesian disciples of John is πιστευσανες, an aorist participle meaning 'having believed' ... There is no hint or approximation of the meaning '*since* ye believed.' Paul wanted to know if there were truly converted or not."[545] The old English Wycliffe translations rendered the passage, "whethir ye that bileuen han resseyued the Hooli Goost?" In other words, it was a question, not a statement. Paul clearly wanted to know "whether" or not they truly were believers, for something was amiss.

However, Pentecostals are not alone in believing that Paul was not so much asking about their faith as about the Holy Spirit specifically. John Calvin argued that the Holy Spirit here refers only to "the visible graces God had given to the kingdom"[546] or rather the spiritual gifts.[547] In this sense he seems to agreed with those who say that "'the Holy Spirit' seems to mean primarily not the person or the hypostasis of the Holy Spirit in the Trinity, but 'the gift of the Holy Spirit', which 'fell'" on them.[548] Is it the "miraculous influences of the Holy" Spirit with which Paul was concerned?[549]

The answer to Paul's question negates any possibility that they truly knew Christ. They had not even been baptized into Jesus's name (19:3)! "They were not, therefore, even on the ground of Christian profession."[550] One scholar compared this to "swearing an oath of allegiance to a queen in a country and he neither knows the queen or country."[551] Erasmus held that they did not know the gospel but had heard only of John. He said, "the teaching of John was not an end in itself, but only witness to Jesus."[552]

Now some argue that these discipled may have thought John was the Messiah.[553] Luke 3:15 certainly implies that there were those who believed he may have been the Christ, and the Zabian sect is alleged to be one of these groups.[554] Could these have been Zabians? Could it be that Paul had heard of these men and this is why he approached the subject so delicately? Regardless of this idle speculation, one thing is beyond doubt. "They were in reality disciples of John,"[555] not Christ. "They knew nothing whatever of Christianity"[556] and "were ignorant of the effects of His sufferings" and Resurrection.[557] It is for this reason that Paul delicately made inquiry into their conversion. It was clear to Paul that they did not have the Holy Spirit. The question is, what did this mean to Paul. Did it mean that they were saved but did not yet have the Holy Spirit as some sects believe? Obviously, it is apparent that they were not followers of Christ at all. Paul was being polite in his inquiry. We cannot use this passage to support the notion that baptism of the Spirit is a distinct acts from conversion (and it is the receiving of the Holy Spirit of which is spoken here, not the "filling" of the Spirit). Consequently, these men had never been baptized into Christ because they had not previously known Christ.

The Name of Jesus
Acts 19:13-17

> "Jewish exorcists ... attempted to name over those who had the evil spirits the name of the Lord Jesus, saying, 'I adjure you by Jesus whom Paul preaches.' ... and the evil spirit answered and said to them, 'I recognize Jesus, and I know about Paul, but who are you?' And the man, in whom was the evil spirit, leaped on them and subdued all of them and overpowered them, so that they fled out of that house naked and wounded."

There are a number of people who attach a mystic power to the name of Jesus. This teaching has been criticized by some as a form of Christian magic[558] while others consider it nothing short of blasphemy to deny the "power of the name." Here then is a perfect passage to put this in context.

The Jews, who did not believe Jesus was the Messiah, saw and understood that demons were being cast out in Jesus's name. Perhaps believing that Jesus was a prophet, but not God, they began to cast out demons using the name of Jesus, but here the demon responds by saying, "I recognize Jesus, and I know about Paul, but who are you?" (19:15). It then attacks them and humilates them before all. The message is clear. It is not the *name* of Jesus, but *Jesus* who cast out demons. His name has no magic power in itself. In all cases it is Jesus who commands the spirits. We are but vessels and weak vessels cannot hold water. If the vessel is broken or cracked the water will invariably leak out. Jesus cannot be used. Prayer in Jesus name is of great effect, but the focus must always be Jesus and *His* will.

Gustsave Dore – Paul at Ephesus (Acts 19:19) – 19th Century

Jerusalem or Rome? – Was Paul Disobeying God?
Acts 19:21 – Acts 20:22-35 – Acts 21:4, 10-15

"Paul purposed in the Spirit to go to Jerusalem after he had passed through Macedonia and Achaia, saying, 'After I have been there, I must also see Rome.'"

The sequence of events which transpire in these last chapters of Acts begin with Paul's decision to return to Jerusalem before heading to Rome. Two vastly differing perspectives on this choice have been offered by commentators throughout history. The one compares Paul to Jonah. The other insist that Paul was obeying God's command exactly.

Among the former, Sir Robert Anderson said, "when Paul was bidden to go to Rome, and yet turned to Jerusalem, he was brought to Rome as a prisoner, discredited by a chain: when Jonah was bidden to go to Ninevah, and yet took ship for Tarshish, he ended by entering Ninevah."[559] Others, however, rebuke this teaching, saying, that it was the Holy Spirit. John Calvin held that Paul was "compelled by the Spirit" and "freely or calmly followed the leading or inspiration of the Spirit."[560] This conflict is exasperated by the seeming ambiguity of the language in Acts. Indeed, the evidence both for *and* against are compelling.

Beginning here in Acts 19:21, there are a total of four passages throughout Acts that bear upon this debate. It would be folly to propose a solution without having examined all these passages. The verses in question are Acts 19:21, 20:22-35, 21:4, 21:10-15. Beginning here with Acts 19:21, it is prudent to examine the text and translations of this passage. What was meant by "purposed in the Spirit" and whose spirit was it that did the purposing?

In Whose Spirit?
The Greek phrase εν τῳ πνευματι (*en to pneumati*) "may mean 'by his human spirit' and is thus included in the translation 'decided' or 'resolved' (so NEB, JB, TEV, NIV), or it may refer to direction 'by the Holy Spirit' (so RSV)."[561] Without the adjective "Holy" it is subjective as to whose spirit is intended here. A comparison to the parallel passages in 20:22-35, 21:4, and 21:10-15 may yield a better answer, but first let us examine the various translations and their approach.

The NIV takes an interpretive stance, translating this as "Paul decided to go to Jerusalem." No hint of God's will is present. On the other extreme is the New Living Translation which reads that Paul was "compelled by the Spirit." This too leaves no question as to the translation's interpretation. The RSV and ESV also favor the Holy Spirit, reading "resolved in the Spirit." The best translations, however, are somewhat ambiguous. The King James, RV, Tyndale, Webster, Wycliffe, ASV, Darby, and Duoay-Rheims all read "purposed in the spirit" with a little "s," The NAS and Geneva read the same but with a capital "S." Both are effectively neutral in their translations, but whether there is a captial or small "s" betrays the translator's opinions.

Is there anything in the immediate context to tell us whether it should be a little "s" (i.e. Paul's spirit) or a big "S" (i.e. the Holy Spirit)? Unfortunately, the immediate context gives little in the way of an answer. Matthew Poole compared this verse to Daniel 1:8 in which Daniel made up his own mind that he would not defile himself, but then declares that "yet in this his determination he had the influence and guidance of the Holy Ghost."[562] Still the comparison is weak for the Hebrew על-לבו (al-levo) literally means "in his heart" so there is no direct correlation to Luke's εν τω πνευματι (en to pneumati) meaning "in the spirit."

So we are again left with the unanswered question, was it his *own* spirit as many believe?[563] Was it, as Horatio Hackett said, "not in order to fulfill any revealed purpose of God, but to satisfy his own feelings"[564] or was it "a secret impulse of the Spirit" as Paton Gloag believed?[565] Perhaps the parallel passages can give us the answer that is so elusive here.

The Ominous Warnings
Arno Gaebelein declared that "it could not have been the Spirit of God who pointed him to go once more to Jerusalem, for we find that during the journey the Holy Spirit warned him a number of times not to go to Jerusalem."[566] Even Gleason Archer, who believes he was obeying the Holy Spirit, acknowledged that "the Holy Spirirt did everything to warn Paul of the danger and suffering that awaited him if he went back to Jerusalem."[567] So the question now becomes was Paul being told not to go, or was he being strengthened by warnings of what awaited him? Were the warnings intended to be a deterrent to his return to Jerusalem or to strengthen his resolve in the sufferings to come?

The first of these ominous warnings comes in Acts 20:22-23. It says, "now, behold, bound by the Spirit, I am on my way to Jerusalem, not knowing what will happen to me there, except that the Holy Spirit solemnly testifies to me in every city, saying that bonds and afflictions await me." Now Paton Gloag notes that "the Holy Spirit is mentioned in the next verse, and is apparently distinguished from τω πνευματι in this verse by the epithat το αγιον."[568] Hackett argues that "bound in Spirit" should be read as "his own, in his mind, feelings"[569] because the adjective "Holy" is not present in 22, but only in 23.[570] Thus many take this as Paul's first warning. If he goes "bonds and afflictions await me." Interestingly enough, the NIV, which formerly said "Paul decided to go to Jerusalem," here reads that Paul was "compelled by the Spirit."

One of the strongest arguments in favor of the Holy Spirit here is Paul's discourse which follows.

> "I do not consider my life of any account as dear to myself, so that I may finish my course and the ministry which I received from the Lord Jesus, to testify solemnly of the gospel of the grace of God. And now,

behold, I know that all of you, among whom I went about preaching the kingdom, will no longer see my face ... I know that after my departure savage wolves will come in among you, not sparing the flock; and from among your own selves men will arise, speaking perverse things, to draw away the disciples after them." (Acts 20:24-31).

So Paul knew even before he went that he would probably not see these men again. This seems to fit much better with Christ in Gethsamane than with Jonah on the ship to Tarshish. Nonetheless, two more warning are yet to come.

In Acts 21:4 disciples "kept telling Paul through the Spirit not to set foot in Jerusalem." Interestingly enough, all agree that here the Holy Spirit is intended. Naturally, some argue that this "proves conclusively that Paul purposed in his own spirit,"[571] but the alternative explanation is that "the Spirit's message was the occasion for the believers' concern rather than that their trying to dissuade Paul was directly inspired by the Spirit."[572] In other words, their attempt to dissuade Paul was motivated by the relevation, but not the Spirit's intention.[573] "They had foreknowledge of all his sufferings from the Spirit; and knowing but in part, being ignorant of that special command Paul had had to go to Jerusalem."[574]

Now deciding between these two options is not easy. A straightforward reading of the text would tend to lead to the assumption that "the Spirit was ordering Paul not to continue with his plans."[575] Nevertheless, Paul's speeches and determination make it clear that he believed he was following God's will. To this end Ironside suggested that Paul "may have erred" in his decision.[576]

If Paul was erring, the last warning should have set him straight, for the prophet Agabus, who was mentioned in 11:28, later appears to Paul, having come from Judea. "Coming to us, he took Paul's belt and bound his own feet and hands, and said, 'This is what the Holy Spirit says: "'In this way the Jews at Jerusalem will bind the man who owns this belt and deliver him into the hands of the Gentiles"'" (21:11). This prophesy has been compared to Jeremiah 27:2 wherein he prophesied the bondage of Israel to Babylon. Yet again, however, it is Paul's response that leaves us pause, for Paul said to them, "What are you doing, weeping and breaking my heart? For I am ready not only to be bound, but even to die at Jerusalem for the name of the Lord Jesus" (21:13).

Matthew Henry believed that "Paul had this express warning given him of his troubles, that he might prepare for them."[577] Like Jesus, he knew what was coming. This is a far different situation from Jonah. Longenecker believes that Holy Spirit was behind Paul's determination and that this is "supported by the use of the impersonal verb *dei* ('must'), which in Luke's writings usually connotes the divine will."[578]

So here we see that Paul had received no fewer than three warning at the behest of the Spirit, but the intent of those warnings is questioned. Was he being warned not to go to Jerusalem, but to Rome instead? Or was he being prepared for what was to come, giving him strength and resolve? Whatever the case, God's will prevailed, as it always does. Let us therefore look at the circumstances of the events which followed Paul's return to Jerusalem.

The Results of Paul's Decision
Whether it was the Holy Spirit or Paul's spirit, it was still Paul's decision to follow that inspiration. Therefore, let us briefly examine what happened as a result of his decision.

As a result of the riots which followed Paul's arrival, Paul was first taken prisoner and allowed to speak to the people, to whom he delivered the gospel (Acts 21:30-22:22). Then he stood before the Sadducees and Pharisees and gave his testimony (23:1-10), followed by testimony to both Jews and gentiles, and even the emperor himself! The political savvy with which Paul displays throughout these encounters is enough to say that Paul, were he not a man of high moral character, would have been a great politician. He waits until he is about to scourged to tell them he is a Roman citizen (22:25), he sets the Sadducees against the Pharisees while they were accusing him (23:6), he appeals to Caesar when no appeal was needed (26:32), and a great many other incidents which all set the stage for the gospel's confrontation with its most infamous enemy; Nero.

This is why Archer said, "as Paul stood before the Sanhedrin, before Felix and Festus, and even before Herod Agrippa II he enjoyed opportunities for witness that would never have come to him had he not become a *cause celebre*."[579] Indeed, "it certainly looks as if Paul's arrest and trials at Caesarea, and his later appeal before Nero Caesar at Rome, were God's means of bringing to pass the purpose He announced to Ananias so many years before."[580]

Could this have been Paul's (and the Lord's) plan all along? As we read the events which take place at Paul's trial it is obvious that Paul appealed to Caesar when it wasn't truly necessary (Acts 26:32). Did Paul panic? Was Paul premature in his appeal? Or perhaps Paul realized that there was no greater way to get the ear of Rome herself, and her emperor, than to appeal to Caesar, to whom he would have to give an account of his very religion; the religion of Christ! Whether this was truly Paul's plan or not, it was God's plan.

Conclusion
Even in antiquity there were some who viewed Paul's return to Jerusalem as a defiance and disobedient act. An ancient prescript found before 19:1 states that "although Paul wished, according to his own plan, to go to Jerusalem, the Spirit told him to return to Asia."[581] This belief was spawned by the idea that Paul did not heed the warning given to him, but in Act 23:11 "the Lord stood at [Paul's] side and said, 'Take courage; for as you have solemnly witnessed to My cause at Jerusalem, so you must witness at Rome also.'" Paul never seemed to doubt that this was all part of God's will, and the events which transpired only set the stage for Christianity to take center stage in the theater of Rome.

The honest historian can truly say that had Paul not returned to Jerusalem, been arrested and brought back to Rome in chains, Nero might never have known much about Christians, might not have persecuted us, and the world might very well have been different. Of course there are no accidents in history. God is the author of history and our sufferings have served as a testimony to our faith and to God's love for us. Despite all the persecutions we have persevered, we spawned modern democracy, build universities and hospitals, created the abolitionist movement, wrote great literature, sent missionaries around the world, and have shown the light of Christ unto all nations. Today that light is being doused and history is coming to its fruition. May we all stand as bravely as Paul in our hour of trial to come.

Acts 19:24-41 – See Acts 17:23

Worshipping on Sunday?
Acts 20:7 – See also 1 Corinthians 16:2

> "On the first day of the week, when we were gathered together to break bread, Paul *began* talking to them, intending to leave the next day, and he prolonged his message until midnight."

There has been a long standing debate among Christian sects and among Jews as to whether or not the apostles worshipped on Saturday or Sunday. This issue is even addressed by Paul to some extent in Romans 14:5-6. When one considers that many Christians are oblivious to basic facts regarding Sabbath, the answer is even more difficult.

To begin with, Sabbath comes from the Hebrew word שַׁבָּת (*Shabbath*) which is the seventh day of the week, from the Hebrew word for seven, שֶׁבַע (*sheba*). It is the day upon which God rested from creation (Exodus 20:8-11). Sunday is then the *first* day of the week, and the day upon which Jesus was resurrected from the dead (Matthew 28:1; Mark 16:2; Luke 24:1; John 20:1). This was "after the Sabbath, as it began to dawn toward the first *day* of the week" (Matthew 28:1). Consequently, Sunday is resurrection day, the first day of the week immediately after the Sabbath.

The question then is whether or not the apostles worshipped on Saturday or Sunday. Here we are told that it was "on the first day of the week, when we were gathered together to break bread" (Acts 20:7). Thus many argue that the apostles were now worshipping on Sunday rather than Saturday. Others that this was a memorial in addition to Sabbath worship. Still others argue that this was nothing more than dinner, and their worship continued to be on Saturday. The divisions break traditional lines and has been a source of divisiveness among some Christian sects. The arguments of each view are lengthy and by no means strictly exegetical. An examination of each view is prudent before making a decision.

The Sabbath View (Saturday Only)
A number of Christians believed that the early Christians continued to worship on Saturday as did their Jewish predecessors. To explain the breaking of the bread here in Acts one of two explanations is usually offered. The first is that this was not the Lord's Supper, but merely an ordinary dinner. The second is that Jewish Sabbath overlapts the beginning of Roman Sunday and hence it was both Sabbath and Sunday.

Breaking Bread as an Ordinary Dinner
Acts 2:46 states that they broke bread "day by day." The question has, therefore, become whether or not "breaking bread" is a daily memorial of the Lord's Supper or whether or not it was just an idiom for eating in general. One scholar believes that of the five "breaking bread" references in the book of Acts "at least one and perhaps as many as three of these [are] a noneucharistic sense."[582] However, there are no fewer than eleven references to breaking bread in the New Testament.

In Matthew 26:26, Mark 14:22, and Luke 22:19 Jesus establishes the Lord's Supper in memorial to Himself. In Luke 24:30-35 the disciples broke bread with the Lord and only them recognized Him as the risen Christ. Although it possible that this was an ordinary meal, it was Jesus who broke the bread and it was then that "He was recognized by them in the breaking of the bread" (24:35). This leaves four references in Acts, plus 1 Corinthians 10:16 in which Paul asks, "is not the bread which we break a sharing in the body of Christ?" What then of Acts?

Here in Acts breaking bread is mentioned four times. The first instance is in Acts 2:42 in which the breaking of the bread is coupled with prayer. A few passages later the apostles are said to have been "day by day ... breaking bread from house to house." The third passage is the one here in 20:7, followed by 20:11 which continues the story. The last reference is in 27:35 where Paul is fed as a prisoner, and yet even here it is said, "he took bread and gave thanks to God in the presence of all." So even here the breaking of the bread is accompanied by giving thanks.

What does all this mean? At best it means that every meal should be a Lord's Supper, but in the context of 20:7 it is clear that they were gathered together for this reason. As a result it is apparent that this was a memorial service of the Lord's Supper. One author calls the argument that this was a mere dinner "superficial" and insist it was the Lord's Supper.[583] I am inclined to agree given that they were "gathered together" for this purpose. John Calvin believed that the presence of so many was proof that this was no "private" dinner.[584] We must, therefore, acknowledge that is taking place is the Lord's Supper.

The Overlap Argument
As I discuss in *Controversies in the Gospels*, the Jewish day begins at sundown, not midnight as in the Roman method. This is the reason that Christ was taken down from the cross (John 19:21), because they did not want to defile the Sabbath by having someone on a cross after sundown. However, some Jews counted the new day at sunrise, as mentioned by Josephus.[585] Consequently, Lenski believed that the Jewish Sabbath overlapped Sunday by six hours.[586] Nevertheless, even if Luke and Paul were using the latter method, there are two problems with this theory.

First, according to the Jewish *Mishnah* Judaeans were allowed to work until afternoon on Friday, but shops had to be closed by sundown. Galileans, however, did not work on Friday at all.[587] This is because the Galilean's Sabbath began Friday at 6 A.M. and continued until Saturday at 6 A.M. whereas the Judaeans counted as Israel today with Sabbath beginning at 6 P.M. Friday and continuing until 6 P.M. Saturday. Lenski is thus assuming that the Galilean Sabbath did not begin until 6 A.M. Saturday, but this cannot be true for Jesus had his Last Supper on Thursday, not Friday and it was clearly a Passover meal (see *Controversies in the Gospels* for more on this issue). So there could be no overlap between Sabbath and Sunday at all.

Second, even if we assume, as Lenski does, that the Sabbath continued until 6 A.M. Sunday then the only overlap would be between midnight and sunrise. Lenski assumes that they were eating after midnight, as did John Calvin,[588] but what the text actually says it that Paul "prolonged his message until midnight" (20:7). So if Paul's message, which was after supper, was "prolonged," then this was clearly *before* midnight on the *first* day of the week. This deliniates the supper as taking place Sunday evening, some time before midnight. Consequently, it is impossible that this supper overlapped the Jewish Sabbath.

The facts make it abundantly clear that whether the apostles worshipped on Saturday or not, they were also practicing the Lord's Supper on Sunday. The question is therefore whether or not they had moved the Sabbath to Sunday or whether this was an *additional* service which did not effect their Saturday Sabbath worship.

The Lord's Day View (Sunday Only)
Having established that this was the Lord's Supper and that it took place on Sunday evening, we must then ask whether or not this established a pattern for worship on Sunday. Did the apostles observe traditional Jewish Sabbath or was this a new Sabbath?

In addition to this passage, 1 Corinthians 16:2 establishes that Christians did assemble together on Sunday to honor the Resurrection of Christ. Some argue that "the observance of Sunday as the Lord's day began when the

Lord appeared at least twice on Sundays to disciples after the resurrection"[589] and that this was a pattern to be followed. "Such a day was consecrated by the resurrection of Christ."[590] Indeed, there is no doubt that Sunday was a day of remembrance for Christians and has been ever since, but this does not negate Saturday in itself. Is there any evidence to prove that Sunday was now "the Christian sabbath"?[591]

One argument is made by Warren Wiersbe. He says that "nine of the Ten Commandments are repeated in the church epistles, but the Sabbath commandment is not repeated."[592] He suggest then that Sabbath worship was no longer required under Christ. This is, however, a weak argument. For one thing, if Sunday were the new "Sabbath-day" as William Tyndale translated it, then it would still be *Sabbath*. Interestingly enough, Thomas Cramner translated this "upon one of the Sabbath-days."[593] Was he implying that there were two Sabbath days? Probably not, but the idea of a double Sabbath is negated by the law itself. Matthew Poole believes that Sunday must have replaced Saturday because, "being part of the command, *six days shalt thou labour*, they could not in ordinary have rested the last day of the week and the first day too, without sinning against the law of God."[594] Now this sounds logical at first, except that Stanley Toussaint has noted that "the church met at night because most people had to work during the day."[595] The same sentiment is echoed by Richard Longenecker and many others.[596]

Thus there could not have been two Sabbaths, nor could Sunday have replaced the Sabbath since Jewish law still required them to work on Sunday. The fact that they were meeting at night proves this. This leaves us with only one possibility.

The Memorial View (Sunday Service in Addition to Sabbath)
They met Sunday evening after work "in memory of the Resurrection."[597] "Already it had been customary apparently for the disciples of the Lord Jesus Christ to gather together ... to break bread."[598] This was obviously a "Holy time"[599] during which Christians gathered together to honor the resurrection and pray.

We have no reason to believe that the apostles did not continue to honor the Saturday Sabbath if for no other reason than that it was the law. Why would the apostles so blatantly defy a law that had been around since the time of Moses? Did their worshipping on Sunday negate the traditional Sabbath? Of course not. Is there any evidence that Sunday had, at this time, replaced Saturday as the Sabbath? No, or else they would have been meeting in the mornings as we do today. Moreover, Acts 18:4 makes it clear that Paul was meeting "in the synagogue every Sabbath." Note "every" Sabbath. The memorial service found here was held on the day of resurrection, in addition to their normal Sabbath worship.

William Barclay believes that "we have here one of the first accounts of what a Christian service was like."[600] In one respect he is correct. This service was distinctly Christian. Sabbath worship was still conducted in the synagogues on Saturday and the apostles were constantly seen to attend these services (Acts 9:20; 13:5, 14-15, 43; 14:1; 17:1, 10, 17; 18:4, 8, 19, 26; 19:8; 22:19). Logically, there is no reason to believe that the early Christians replaced Saturday synagogue services. In order to understand what was happening we need to understand the synagogues and the prayer meetings like that we have encountered in this passage.

Synagogues in those days were not subdivided as they are today. Sadducees, Pharisees, Essenes, and other Jewish sects all met together in the same synagogue. The services were divided in different parts with worship, the reading of the Torah, and even open debate. It is during those debates that things sometimes became heated. This is probably why Claudius expelled Jews out of Rome (see Acts 18:2), for the Christians were meeting in the synagogues with the unbelieving Jews and many Jews felt that their services were being disrupted by non-Jews. Neither Paul nor the other apostles abandoned these services. Rather they used them as a means to spread the gospel. This is also why there was often such a violent reaction to the gospel. It was deemed heresy by many who felt as if the synagogue was being violated. Consequently, these private meetings in the home of believers on Sunday evening were the first distinctly *Christian* meetings. Eventually as time passed and Judaism broke with Christianity, the Sunday memorials became the normal time for meetings and Christians (most of whom would be gentile in the years to come) stopped attending synagogues.

Conclusion
I met with an Orthodox Jew once who was friendly with evangelical Christians, but he had one problem with us. He asked how we can worship on Sunday in violation of the fourth commandment. In answering him I realized that the answer was more historical than Biblical. I have heard the arguments on both sides, and neither seems to be taken solely from the Scripture. Saturday worshippers are accused of legalism and called heretics, while Sunday worshippers are accused of libertinism and called heretics just the same. Many Christians are confused over the Sabbath day. Even the great Erasmus called Sunday "a certain Sabbath"[601] and another author inexplicably justified Sunday as Sabbath by quoting Revelation 1:10,[602] but when when you read Revelation 1:10 is says only, "I was in the Spirit on the Lord's day." Nothing in the passage gives even the tiniest hint as to what day was the Sabbath.

Historically speaking Sunday service replaced Sabbath worship as the gentile Christians were driven out of the synagogues. Sunday, the day upon which Christians met privately to honor the resurrection, was naturally taken up as the day of worship, but based strictly on the Bible it seems apparent that the early Christians continued to meet in the synagogues with both believing and unbelieving Jews. This created an atmosphere that was sometimes hostile and the cause of many of the outbreaks of violence. Thus it is only logical that as time passed the gentile Christians expanded their church services on Sunday and abandoned the synagogues. This is history. It is not necessarily Biblical.

As to my own opinion on this overly divisive issue, I refer to Paul in Romans 14:5-6. "One person regards one day above another, another regards every day *alike*. Each person must be fully convinced in his own mind. He who observes the day, observes it for the Lord, and he who eats, does so for the Lord, for he gives thanks to God; and he who eats not, for the Lord he does not eat, and gives thanks to God." In other words, God commands that we honor Him and that we set aside a Holy Day. Technically that day *is* Saturday, but it was on Sunday that our Lord Jesus was resurrection. If someone wishes to worship on Saturday, let him. If someone wishes to worship on Sunday, let him. God judges by the heart so He will look to our conscience to see if we have honored him, not to external debates.

Acts 20:22-21:11 – See Acts 19:21

11

Paul's Trial and the Journey to Rome

It was no surprise that Paul's appearance in Jerusalem would stir up a hornet's nest. Three times Paul had been warned that he would end up in chains (Acts 20:22-35, 21:4, 21:10-15). The events which follow result in Christianity taking center stage in the world theater called Rome. From here on out Christianity would no longer be looked upon as a small Jewish cult but as a religion which was to change the face of the world.

Paul in Jerusalem
Acts 21:18 – 26:32

> "All the city was provoked, and the people rushed together, and taking hold of Paul they dragged him out of the temple, and immediately the doors were shut."

The first question which might be asked is why Paul's very appearance stirred such anger and emotion in Jerusalem. To understand this let us look as James's comments. When he greeted Paul he informed him that "there are many thousands among the Jews of those who have believed, and they are all zealous for the Law; and they have been told about you, that you are teaching all the Jews who are among the Gentiles to forsake Moses, telling them not to circumcise their children nor to walk according to the customs. What, then, is *to be done?* They will certainly hear that you have come" (Acts 21:20-22). These were the same Jewish-Christian sects to which James and Peter had once belonged, but now they viewed the apostles, and particularly Paul, as heretics who were allegedly teaching gentiles to defy the law of Moses.

To this very day there remain a small sect of Jewish-Christians (and I refuse to call them Messianic Jews, for most Messianic Jews have nothing to do with these men) who believe that Paul was a cult leader and heretic. They claim to follow Jesus but revile Paul and all he did. To these men Paul was teaching that Moses must be renounced. One of these sects was called Ebionites who probably murdered the apostle Philip over these same false charges.[603] Thus it is important to understand that while the Jews were the ones who sought Paul's life, it was actually a pseudo-Christian cult which stirred up the Jews with false accusation!

In Act 21:28 Paul was falsely accused of bringing gentiles into the inner court of the temple, which is punishable by death. This incited the first riot which led to his arrest for protective custody. The commander of the Roman soldiers was then forced to decide how to best handle the situation.

Before the People
If Paul had not been a decent human being, he would have made an excellent politician. Throughout these passages Paul carefully manipulates the events.

Immediately after Paul's arrest the commander was curious to know whether or not he was the Egyptian revolutionary who had caused a riot earlier. This Egyptian is mentioned in Josephus. According to him this man was a false prophet who sought to overthrow the Roman garrison in Jerusalem with 30,000 men (Acts 21:38 only refers to the Assassins who numbered 4000 in total, and not the entire army), but the governor Felix and his soldiers were able to disperse him and his followers.[604] The leader was never apprehended.[605] So the commander's concerns were well founded, fearing that the Egyptian may have returned, but after assuring the commander that he was not this man, Paul was given permission to address the crowd. Paul then reminded them that he had once persecuted Christians and gave his testimony. When the crowd reacted angrily the commander ordered Paul to be scourged in an attempt to appease the crowd (21:24).

It is at this point that Paul first employs his mastery of politics, for he waits until immediately before the scourging is to take place to ask, "is it lawful for you to scourge a man who is a Roman and uncondemned?" (21:25). Of course Paul knew the answer. He had waited knowing that the commander would become fearful that he had violated Roman law regarding Roman citizens (22:26-29). Under the Valerian and Porcian laws it was illegal to question a Roman citizen under torture. The emperor Augustus later strengthed these laws to protect citizens, which was a very small and highly prized right.[606] Thus the commander was now more favorably disposed toward Paul, not out of concern for his well being, but in order that he might not be accused of abusing a Roman citizen unlawfully, for the punishment for such a crime was severe indeed. So the next day he called the Jewish priests to explain what Paul's crime had been.

On the day of the trial Ananias slapped Paul. Paul immediately responded with what some believe may have been a prophecy. "God is going to strike you!" (23:3). Now while this was probably not intended as a direct prophecy by Paul, it is prophetic that the wicked will often die by their own deeds, and Ananias was such a corrupt high priest that he allowed his servants to steal tithes.[607] Even after he was deposed, shortly before Felix left office,[608] he continued to rule as a despot.[609] So corrupt was he that in the early days of the revolt Ananias was captured and slain by the Jewish revolutionaries as a traitor to Israel and the Jews.[610] God had indeed smote him.

Despite Ananias's wickedness, when Paul realizes that Ananias was the high priest he makes an apology of sorts, saying, "I was not aware, brethren, that he was high priest; for it is written, *'You shall not speak evil of a ruler of your people'*" (23:5). Now there is some debate as to why Paul would not have recognized Ananias. Some argue that Paul was suffering from an eye disease and appeal to Galatians 4:13-14 as proof of this,[611] but Galatians does not say what the illness was and there is no reason to believe that blindness was the illness. There are more likely reason that Paul did not recognize him. Ananias had become high priest in the eight year of Claudius (probably in 49 A.D.)[612] but was later arrested and sent to Rome shortly before Felix was appointed governor (probably 51 or 52 A.D.).[613] Paul may not have known of Ananias's return to Judaea. More importantly, they did not the internet back then, so it is likely that Paul had never met Ananias and did not know what he looked like.

Once again Paul carefully manipulates the situation to his advantage. As the Jews were gathered together Paul stated that "I am on trial for the hope and resurrection of the dead" (23:6). He did this knowing that the Pharisees, who believe in the resurrection of the dead, would immediately be confronted by the Sadducees who deny a resurrection or afterlife (23:8). The resulting turmoil was so severe that the commander needed troops to protect Paul. When a plot to assassinate Paul was revealed, the commander decided it was safest to send Paul to the governor/procurator Felix (23:9-35). So Paul was now being taken to the governor to be heard. This was but the first step in the ladder that would take him to Rome, and to the emperor Nero.

Before Felix
Felix was a slave who eventually became a freeman.[614] The exact circumstances are unknown, but we do know that his first wife was the grand-daughter of Marc Anthony and Cleopatra.[615] We can only speculate as to whether he acheived some fame somehow in battle, or if he had been a slave in her court and won her affection and love. However he came to it he was rewarded not only with his freedom but Claudius also bestowed him the governorship of Judaea.[616]

Nikolai Bodarevsky – The Apostle Paul On Trial –1875

Despite such humble beginnings Felix is said by Tacitus to have ruled with the cruelty and lust of a royal tyrant but with the spirit of a slave.[617] He was also an opportunists. He was married three times, and according to Sutonius all three were queens.[618] The last of these wives was the Jewish princess Drusilla (sister of Herod Agrippa II) whom he had married with the assistance of Simon the Sorcerer.[619] Although some doubt that this was the same Simon as confronted by Peter in Acts 8:9-24 there is no real reason to deny that they were the same. The facts, circumstances, and character, as well as the name and occupation, all fit. Only the question as to his place of birth lends doubt and the Bible does not actually identify Simon's birthplace, so it is probably that are the same.

In any case, he became procurator, or governor, of Judea probably around 52 or 53 A.D.[620] He took Drusilla as his wife some time before Paul's arrest as she was present at his trial (24:24). This establishes the trial of Paul sometime between 57 and 58 A.D. (also see Appendix A).

Now Felix was known to take bribes and Paul's unusually long imprisonment without having been convicted of anything was in part because Felix was hoping to receive bribe money for his release (Acts 24:26). However, he was also seeking to appease the Jews (cf. Acts 24:27). What is intriguing here is that Felix was clearly curious about this new faith. Acts says that Felix sought to have "a more exact knowledge about the Way" (or Christianity as it is known today) and this gave Paul an opportunity to witness the gospel to both him and Drusilla for two years (24:27)![621] It is not without merit to point out that many of these conversations were cut short by Felix's conscience, for "as [Paul] was discussing righteousness, self-control and the judgment to come, Felix became frightened" (Acts 24:25) and sent him away.

It was during this time that Caesarea, where Paul was imprisoned (23:33), was besieged by mass chaos and riots between the Jews and Syrians.[622] Judea was increasingly become a rebellious state and sometime between 59 and 60 A.D. Nero recalled Felix to Rome.[623] He left with his wife Drusilla and may have been followed by Simon the Sorcerer as tradition claims. In any case, Paul was left imprisoned in hopes of appeasing the high priests, possible in return for favorable reports by them of his administration (cf. Acts 24:27).

Before Festus and Agrippa
Josephus says little about Festus except that his brief rule was spent attempting to correct the problems created by his predecessors.[624] Agrippa, however, is another case. The young Agrippa II was strongly favorably disposed toward Rome throughout his life. He spent most of his life living together with his sister Berenice of whom rumor alleged an incestuous relationship. She had been married several times, once to her uncle, and would later have an affair with the same emperor Titus who destroyed Jerusalem.[625] He had no interest in Judaism

except as it related to politics. It is before these three rulers that Paul now appeared to offer his testimony.

After Festus arrived in Judea he naturally went down to the capital of Jerusalem. There the high priests requested that Paul be brought to Jerusalem for trial (25:3). The reasoning was probably that it was easier to gather witnesses together in Jerusalem than to transport them all up to Caesarea, but the real reason was that they were planning an ambush to assassinate Paul (25:3). Now although Felix had not allowed Paul to see his friends, it is possible that this had changed at some point. We do not know for certain, but we do know that Paul did want to be transferred to Jerusalem. Either by word of mouth or by common sense he knew that they would lay a trap for him in some way, and so he requested an appeal to Caesar (Acts 25:11). Later Agrippa remarked to Festus, "this man might have been set free if he had not appealed to Caesar" (26:32).

Vasily Surikov –Paul Explains the Christian Before King Agrippa and Festus – 1875

This appeal to Caesar is intriguing. Did Paul panic? Was Paul afraid of going to Jerusalem despite God's promise that he would witness in Rome (23:11)? Or perhaps Paul planned this all along as he means to get to Rome with the ear of the emperor? In any case, before departing for Rome he presented the gospel one more time, before Festus, Agrippa II, and Berenice.

Because Festus had only just arrived from Rome, King Agrippa and Berenice went up to Caesarea to pay their respects. In their meeting Festus mentioned Paul and his opinion that the dispute with Paul was not really over any crime but rather because "they had some points of disagreement with him about their own religion and about a dead man, Jesus, whom Paul asserted to be alive" (25:19). This intrigued Agrippa who requested to hear Paul himself (25:22). The next day Festus, Agrippa, and Berenice sat before Paul as he presented his testimony. It is the reaction of both Festus and Agrippa II which is most fascinating. Festus reacts emotionally, crying out, "Paul, you are out of your mind! *Your* great learning is driving you mad" (26:24). One can imaging the crowds reaction to this comment, but in responding to Festus Paul appeals to Agrippa who says, "in a short time you will persuade me to become a Christian" (26:28). Although the comment was probably somewhat tongue-in-cheek, there was a certain amount of sincerity in it as well. One might consider it a back-handed compliment.

Interestingly enough the words of Agrippa have been variously translated, with different significance attached to the meaning of those translations. The King James most infamously translates Agrippa's words as "Almost thou persuadest me to be a Christian," indicating a sincerity in Agrippa's words. On the other extreme is the NIV which reads, "Do you think that in such a short time you can persuade me to be a Christian?" In this case it is more of a chastising remark. The difference in interpretation is because of the difficulty of the Greek phrase, εν ολιγω με πειθεις Χριστιανον ποιησαι (*en oligo me peitheis Xristianon poihsai*).[626] Word for word this would say "in little persuade me Christian make." Obviously, the first question is whether or not "little" modifies "persuade" or indicates time. Without getting into Greek linguistics, the question boils down to the insertion of "me" between "little" and "persuade." It seems to cut off and isolate "little" which is left without anything to modify. Thus many take it mean "little time" (ESV, NAS, NIV). Other translations prefers "little persuasion" (ASV). The next question is then context. Was Agrippa being sincere or sarcastic?

Obviously the King James and others indicate that Agrippa is sincere whereas many other translation indicate a lack of sincerity. Perhaps ambiguity would be the best translation, but one thing is clear. Nothing in Agrippa's life indicates that he ever repented or was a man of religious devotion. In reality there are three kinds of people in this world. There are those who love the gospel. There are those who hate the gospel. Finally, there are those who are apathetic towards the gospel. Agrippa fell into the third category. He had no animosity towards the faith, but neither did he care. Stanley Toussaint argues that Paul had put Agrippa in a corner by his question, "do you believe the Prophets? I know that you do" (26:27). Considering Agrippa's seeming apathy towards religious matters, it may be that Agrippa did not believe in the prophets at all, so "it was probably a joking rebuttal of Paul."[627]

Whatever conviction Agrippa may or may not have had, Paul had presented the gospel before two governors, a king, a princess, and before the people of Jerusalem and Caesarea. Now it was his turn to take the gospel before the emperor himself in Rome. It is no small irony that Agrippa said, "this man might have been set free if he had not appealed to Caesar" (26:32), but this was not in God's plan.

Acts 22:1-6 – See Acts 9:1-9

Supplementary Additions?
Acts 24:6-8

"We wanted to judge him according to our own Law. But Lysias the commander came along, and with much violence took him out of our hands, ordering his accusers to come before you."

In these passages the lawyer for the high priests recounts what has already transpired. Since that was already recorded Luke apparently abbreviates his speech, not wanting to repeat unnecessary information. However, here is a passage that extends that dialogue. The problem is that some Bibles do not have this passage all.

Because the information is simply repetitive of what already took place the issue is of no real relevance save those King James only advocates and Bible critics who believe that modern translations are altering the Bible. In fact, while the verse is found in those translations which follow the *Textus Receptus* (King James, Tyndale, Webster, Wycliffe, ASV, Duoay-Rheims, Geneva), it is omitted not only in the modern NIV, RSV, RV, and ESV translations (NAS, NLT, and Darby place it in brackets) but also in the Latin Vulgate which almost always agrees with the *Textus Receptus*.

The reason should be obvious from the fact that the support for this text among ancient manuscripts is almost non-existent. It is found only in the sixth century Codex Laudianus 35 (E), the eighth century Athous Laurae (Ψ), and the tenth century Miniscule 1739 which bears a marginal note claiming to be transcribed from a fourth century manuscript. It is omitted in the papyrus 74 ($\mathfrak{P}^{74}$), the codices Sinaiticus (א), Alexandrinus (A), Vaticanus (B), Mutinensis (H), Regius (L), and Porphyrianus (P).[628]

In any examination of the verse it becomes readily apparent that some scribe added a marginal note to expand the discourse and remind himself of what had occurred. Some took the note to be a part of the passage itself, but whether we believe the text is original or not, it offers no information which is not already in the bible and absolutely nothing of any doctrinal importance or theological significance. There is no tampering with the text here.

Acts 26:9-19 – See Acts 9:1-9

The Shipwreck
Acts 27:1 – 28:15

"Striking a reef where two seas met, they ran the vessel aground; and the prow stuck fast and remained immovable, but the stern *began* to be broken up by the force of *the waves*."

The cynic would ask, "why did they have so much trouble and danger getting to Rome if God wanted Paul in Rome?" The answer is found in the surrounding events and the results of these troubles. Sometimes it is hard to understand God's plan unless we are looking backwards. When looking forward we cannot always understand, but when we realize that God always has a plan we will realize that there is an answer. Here is a perfect example. It is because of the troubles and dangers which Paul and the crew went through that Paul became greatly esteemed by his own captors. More than this, the gospel came even to a small tribal island and the centurion doubtless presented a favorable report to Seneca, the advisor of Nero.

It is not insignificant that Paul originally advised against setting sail from Lasea (27:8-10). The centurion, Julius, however, may have that Paul was making an excuse to delay the trip and, being advised by the captain that it was okay, they continued on only to find that Paul was right. The waters became more dangerous until the crew were in fear of their life. At this point it is Paul who assures them that God will protect them (27:21-26). In this same speech he prophesies that would shipwreck upon a small island. All of this would prove the crew that Paul was an apostle of God. It also appears that Julius had developed some level of trust in Paul for he prevented the soldiers from killing Paul and the others, for they feared that if they ran away they would all be crucified for letting prisoners escape.

After the shipwreck Jesus's controversial prophecy in Mark 16:18 came to pass as Paul was bitten by a deadly snake but no harm came to him. The natives then began to think of him as some kind of god (28:3-6). Later Paul healed the father of the island leader and many others (28:7-9). All these things not only brought the gospel to Malta but created a respect for Paul among the Romans so that Julius not only reported favorably to Seneca but Paul was given extensive freedoms during his house arrest in Rome (28:16-21). So God had a plan.

The Appeal to Caesar
Acts 28:16-31

"He stayed two full years in his own rented quarters and was welcoming all who came to him, preaching the kingdom of God and teacing concerning the Lord Jesus Christ with all openness, unhindered."

Many are intrigued by the ending of Acts, for Paul spends two years under house arrest in Rome and yet he had still not been heard by Caesar. What happened? What was the result of the trial? Why does Luke end Acts in this manner? I reserve that argument for the next section, because it is a highly debated one. Nevertheless, what happened to Paul is not a complete mystery. History provides us with strong clues as to Paul's fate.

Now the post-Biblical history of the apostles can be divided into three sources. These are historical records, traditions, and legends. Legends are of little value, and traditions may or may not be of value depending on how far removed they are from the original source. Like gossip around a table, the further removed the gossip from its origin the less likely it is to be true. Fortunately there are a plethora of sources for Paul so that the remainder of his life is no mystery, although some of the details may be in doubt. Additionally, and perhaps most importantly, the epistles of Paul give us some vital clues as well.

Most scholars are agreed that Paul was at first acquitted of charges.[629] This is based in part upon clues in the epistles. For example, Titus 1:5 mentions Paul's visit to Crete and yet nowhere in Acts does Paul stop in Crete. Additional, other passages indicate that Paul had only recently been to Troas (2 Timothy 4:13), but the only instance recorded in Acts would have been about six years earlier (Acts 20:6, 17). These and other passages imply that Paul did make some travels after his imprisonment in Rome. Furthermore, the earlier epistle of Philemon suggest that Paul anticipated his release (v. 22), but later epistles indicate that Paul knew he was going to die (e.g. 2 Timothy 4:7). Given the favorable circumstances surrounding Paul's imprisonment in Acts 28:16-31 and the political situation at that time, this seems likely.

Based on the Biblical chronology (see Appendix A) the book of Acts ends in approximately 62 A.D. At this time Seneca, the great Stoic advisor to Nero, was still in power.[630] He largely ruled in Nero's name was greatly respected as a noble Roman. Later legends (probably untrue) have Seneca and Paul exchanging letters discussing theology and philosophy. Some even try to make Seneca out to be a convert. Although such legends probably have little basis in fact, they do illustrate the Seneca was one who would have defended Paul against any charges of *superstitio illicita*.[631] It was not until Nero forced Seneca to retire (and eventually forced him to commit suicide) that the real Nero became apparent to the people. His reign of tyranny would be unparalled in history, but that did not happen until two years later in 64 A.D. So we are left with a choice. Either Paul remained in prison for another three to five years until his execution, or he was freed in 62 or 63 A.D., after Seneca's recommendations and possibly before his forced retirement, only to be later arrested again after the fire in Rome.

In addition to the Biblical evidence there is strong evidence that Paul had a fourth journey. Clement of Rome was on of the earliest overseers (bishops) of Rome who lived in the first century and is probably the same Clement mentioned in Philippians 4:3. If so he knew Paul personally. He recorded that Paul "came to the extreme limit of the west" before suffering martyrdom in Rome.[632] The extreme limit of the west would be Spain, to which Paul had desired to minister (Romans 15:24, 28). Hippolytus also records that Paul went to Spain.[633] It seems then that Paul fulfilled that wish after his release.

The next question then is when did Paul return to Rome, and why did he return to Rome, for it is clear that by the time of his second imprisonment Nero was already persecuting and killing Christians, most without trial. The evidence, discussed in my book *The Apostles After Jesus*, favors that Peter had arrived in Rome around 63 or 64 A.D. The fire in Rome broke out on July 19, 64 A.D. Nero wanted to make scapegoats of the Christians whom he hated and we were not only falsely accused of setting the fire to usher in the destruction of the world but we also accused of such crimes as cannibalism, atheism, and homosexuality.[634] Peter was arrested shortly thereafter and held prisoner where he was probably tortured for nine months before his execution (see Appendix B, C, and also *The Apostles After Jesus* for a defense of this view). This execution took place approximately June 29, 65 A.D, almost a year after the fire in Rome.

Now Paul's return to Rome is more questionable. Some believe that Paul died in the mass executions of June 29, 65 A.D, thus being martyred on the very same day as Peter.[635] Others believe he was not killed until the end of Nero's reign as late as 68 A.D.[636] In *The Apostles After Jesus* I concluded that the evidence best favors that Paul returned to Rome not long after hearing of the plight of the church, seeking to render whatever aid and comfort he could provide. Not realizing the depth of the problem as of yet, he arrived only to be arrested early during the persecutions. Like Peter he was kept in prison, without trial, until the day of mass execution upon which Nero would make a spectacle of the Christians.[637] As a citizen of Rome, a rare honor even among Rome's populous, Paul was mercifully spared the cruelties inflicted upon most Christian martyrs and beheaded on the same day as Peter in 65 A.D. leaving behind a legacy as one of the greatest of apostles and the man who first brought Jesus to the gentile world at large.

Missing Text?
Acts 28:29

"When he had spoken these words, the Jews departed, having a great dispute among themselves."

The book of Acts is unique in that while there are more questions as to the original text than all four gospels and more than the entire epistles, none of these textual disputes are of any significant importance. This passage, for example, is found in the King James and other ancient translations which follow the Majority Text or *Textus Receptus*. It is either omitted or placed in brackets in modern translations. The text was probably a marginal note mistaken for an actual text by later scribes, but that it was not part of the original is fairly evident by the fact that it appears in no Greek text until the middle ages. It is found in some Italian, Latin, and Syrian manuscripts,[638] but no ancient Greek text contains the passage. It is missing from papyrus 74 ($\mathfrak{P}^{74}$), the codices Sinaiticus (ℵ), Alexandrinus (A), Vaticanus (B), Codex Laudianus 35 (E), and Athous Laurae (Ψ). So while King James only advocates give fuel to the Bible critic to claim that the Bible has been altered there is neither evidence of intentional alteration nor is the passage of any significance whatsoever in theology, doctrine, or even exegesis. The United Bible Society Committee believes that the note was added because of "the abrupt transition from ver. 28 to ver. 30."[639] Regardless of whether this is true or not, it in no way effects the reliablity of the Scriptures or of our copies as the passage has no significance.

Was Acts Finished?

Given the world famous stories of the deaths of Peter and Paul in Rome and the infamous circuses of Nero, many have asked why Acts ends with Paul sitting under house arrest in Rome, apparently at peace. Opinions have varied. The Bible critics often have the hardest time explaining this ending, for they believe that Acts was written long after Paul's martyrdom. Why then did the author not include it? In short, is the book of Acts finished?

This may seem like a strange question to ask indeed, for the book of Acts was obviously finished in a technical sense of the word, but it *seems* unfinished to many eyes because it leaves off in much the same way as a cliffhanger. The apostle Paul is sitting in prison awaiting trial from Nero, arguably the most vile evil emperor in the history of one of the most vile empires in history.

To answer this question some have made various attempts to explain the ending in a theological sense. For example, Arno Gaebelein said that "the Book begins with Jesus and ends with Rome. It is a prophecy ... the book closes in an unfinished way, because the acts of Christ, the Spirit of God, and Satan, recorded in this book, are not finished."[640] Longenecker made a similar argument saying "in seeming to leave his book unfinished, he was implying that the apostolic proclamation of the gospel in the first century began a story that will continue until the consummation of the kingdom of Christ (Acts 1:11)."[641] While these remarks sound quaint they really evade the issue, for Acts ends with the simple words, "he stayed two full years in his own rented quarters and was welcoming all who came to him, preaching the kingdom of God and teaching concerning the Lord Jesus Christ with all openness, unhindered" (28:30-31).

Indeed, because of the seeming abruptness of the end of Acts some ancient copiests added to their Bibles the closing phrase "this is Jesus the Son of God, through whom the whole world is to be judged, amen."[642] This is not original and not found in any translations, but contained in some ancient manuscripts as scribal notes. It only illustrates that even in antiquity Acts *feels* unfinished to many. Why?

Sometimes the most obvious answer is the best. Because the Bible is a sacred text many want it to be "finished," but the reality is that if I am writing a history of America I will end it on the date of publication even if the Obama administration is not yet finished. I may not know how the "story ends" because my life has not ended. So also Luke was commissioned by a Theophilus (Luke 1:3; Acts 1:1) to write a history of Jesus and the apostles. Luke ends with Paul in prison because that is when he had finished writing. It is that simple. It is probable that Acts was written during this two year imprisonment while he resided at Rome. The gospel of Luke may also have been written at this time, although it may have at least been started years earlier when Paul was in prison at Caesarea. This would have been the opportune time for Luke to have interviewed Mary and other eyewitnesses to the life and events of Jesus. Upon finishing the gospel of Luke, he sent this to Theophilus, and began working on his second volume, the Acts of the Apostles which was finished at Rome around 62 A.D. while Paul was still awaiting trial. Such a simple answer may not fit our own desires, but it is reality. A history book ends when the author is ready to publish. So the history of Acts ends with Luke and Paul in Rome awaiting trial.

Appendix A

The Chronology of the Acts of the Apostles

"Chronology is the backbone of history."[643] This famous quotation lays at the heart of good scholarship and research. Quite often Bible critics, either through ignorance or deliberance, begin with a false chronology and then set out to prove the Bible wrong based on that chronology. For example, liberal scholars claim that the Exodus took place under Ramses II and then procede to demonstrate how all the archaeology contradicts this claim. Of course, so does the Bible! Nowhere does it say that Ramses II was the Pharaoh of the Exodus. Rather 1 Kings 6:1 states that the Exodus was 480 years before the dedication of Solomon's temple, which would place the Exodus about 150 years *before* Ramses II![644] See then how faulty chronology can be used to demolish history whereas good chronology can used to verify and authenticate history, and the accuracy of the Bible.

Now the book of Acts obviously takes place between the crucifixion of Christ and the persecutions of Nero. All agree on this. However, the exact time of certain events is under debate. Its importance varies and is not of as much significance as the Exodus date, but it does occasionally bear impact upon the circumstances and context of many of the apostles' lives and deeds. For example, when we get our chronology right we realize that Paul could easily have been released by Nero before the removal of Seneca, but if more than a year had passed after Seneca's departure Paul would almost certainly have been executed. The fact thus support the Biblical story, whereas poor chronology is sometimes used to cast doubt upon the record.

How does one arrive at a solid chronology when no specific chronology is given? The job of a chronologer is not unlike that of an archaeologist. In archaeology there are two types of dating; "absolute dating" which is fixed,[645] and "relative dating" which means that said object is older or young than another.[646] These relative dates can be set between different points of reference and in turn give clues to the true date, but cannot be fixed with certainty. This is also true for the historian. Certain events in Acts can be fixed in relation to history, while others are relative to those fixed points.

There are several fixed reference points in Acts, and about two dozen relative dating points. We must first establish the fixed reference points and then fit the relative dates around those. Of the fixed points, the first two are the Ascension (Acts 1:3) and Pentecost (Acts 2:1) which fall respectively on May 14 and 24, 33 A.D. Another reference point is found in Acts 18:2 where it says that "a Jew named Aquila, a native of Pontus ... recently come from Italy with his wife Priscilla, *because Claudius had commanded all the Jews to leave Rome.*" This event is recorded in secular history by Sutonius.[647] Yet another reference point is in Acts 25 where Festus replaces Felix as procurator of Judea. Such "fixed" references points allow us to place the events of Acts within the confines of world history, and to tie together relative dates. Let us therefore look at the specific passages, their chronology, and how they can be tied together.

Fixed References Points
There is some dispute as to the exact year of Jesus's crucifixion. Although some reject the traditional 33 A.D. crucifixion, the evidence is overwhelmingly in its favor. We know that Passover only fell on a Friday in the years of 27, 30, 33, and 36 A.D.[648] Since Luke 3:1 says that Jesus was "about" thirty, but not exactly thirty (or else the word 'ωσει would never have been used), in the fifteenth year of Tiberius (27 or 29 A.D.) we can reject 27 and 36 A.D. outright. This leaves us with 30 and 33 A.D. Now since Jesus's ministry was at least three and a half years, we can also reject 30 A.D. Moreover, the prophecy of Daniel 9:27 points to the very day of the crucifixion in 33 A.D. (see notes under *Controversies the Prophets*).[649] The resurrection would therefore have taken place on April 5, 33 A.D. This is then our first true reference point.

Acts 1:3 – The Ascension
After the resurrection we are told that Jesus "presented Himself alive after His suffering, by many convincing proofs, appearing to them over *a period of* forty days." It was then that He ascended to heaven before their very eyes (1:9). This took place on May 14, 33 A.D. This is then our first chronological marker within the book of Acts.

Acts 2:1 – Pentecost
Pentecost is actually the Hebrew Feast of Weeks. It takes place fifty days after Passover when Moses delivered the Law to the people of Israel on Mount Sinai. Pentecost comes from the Greek word for fiftieth. So Pentecost took place on May 24, 33 A.D.

Acts 11:8 – The Famine
The prophet Agabus prophesied that there would be a great famine throughout the Roman empire during the reign of Claudius. Both Tacitus and Josephus record this famine. It is Josephus, however, who gives a more precise history. He indicates that it began during the procurator Fadus's reign shortly after Joseph was appointed High Priest.[650] This took place in 44 A.D., not long after the death of Herod Agrippa, which is mentioned in Acts 12:21-23. Bear in mind that Acts 11:8 is about the prophecy of Agabus. Thus the famine itself did not begin until the end of 44 A.D. or even 45 A.D. This prophecy was given shortly before the death of James the Great and Herod Agrippa I.

It is of interest to note that this famine created some political intrigue for according to Josephus Helena and Izata of the Parthian empire supported

Israel and the Jews during the famine.[651] The famine itself is believed to have lasted three to four years.

Acts 12:1-2, 21-23 – The Death of James and Herod Agrippa I

The death of James the Greater took place shortly before the Feast of Unleavened Bread (12:2-3) which precedes Passover. Shortly thereafter Herod Agrippa I had Peter arrested and imprisoned (12:3) but when Peter escaped the very next day Herod searched for him to no avail. We are then told that Herod went down to Caesarea (12:19). Although we do not exactly how long he was at Caesarea it is apparent that this was a relatively short time after the martyrdom of James and the escape of Peter during Passover week (12:19). It is there in Caesarea where we are told of Herod Agrippa's death (12:19-23). This event is recorded by Josephus. According to him:

> "Now when Agrippa had reigned three years over all Judea, he came to the city Cesarea, which was formerly called Strato's Tower; and there he exhibited shows in honor of Caesar, upon his being informed that there was a certain festival celebrated to make vows for his safety. At which festival a great multitude was gotten together of the principal persons, and such as were of dignity through his province. On the second day ... his flatterers cried out, one from one place, and another from another, (though not for his good,) that he was a god ... Upon this the king did neither rebuke them, nor reject their impious flattery ... A severe pain also arose in his belly, and began in a most violent manner ... he was carried into the palace, and the rumor went abroad every where, that he would certainly die in a little time. ... And when he had been quite worn out by the pain in his belly for five days, he departed this life, being in the fifty-fourth year of his age."[652]

Now this event is dated to 44 A.D.[653] although at least one scholar argues it should be 43 A.D. based on the assumption that Caesarean games took place every four years, rather than five years,[654] but Josephus also says that Agrippa had ruled three years over all Judea which would clearly place this in 44 A.D. As to the exact date Josephus is only clear that this was about a week after the festivities for Caesar began. Acts places this some time after Passover, but is not precise. According to Wieseler the games took place in August, and he places Agrippa's death on August 5, 44 A.D.[655] While it may not be possible to date Agrippa's death this precisely, it is clear that James was executed shortly before Passover in 44 A.D. This is our fourth fixed reference point in Acts.

Acts 13:7 – The Proconsul Sergius Paulus

A proconsul of Paphos in Cyrpus is mentioned as having been converted by the Apostle Paul. In 1887 archaeologists recovered a boundary stone from the time of Claudius which confirmed his existence as proconsul. According to the stone Sergius Paulus was appointed proconsul in 47 A.D.[656]

Although we do not know the exact time of Paul's visit, this can be "fixed" after 47 A.D. and before the Council of Jerusalem. Most likely this was either 47 or 48 A.D. although early 49 A.D. is also a possibility.

Acts 18:2 – *Claudius Expels the Jews*

Aquila and Priscilla we are told arrived "recently" from Italy after being evicted by Claudius. This was discussed previously under Acts 18:2. Here the relevance is that the date for this expulsion is fixed between 49 or 50 A.D. by Paulus Orosius, the ancient historian.[657] Thus we have another reference point fixed sometime between 49 and 50 A.D.

Acts 18:12 – *Proconsul Gallio*

We are told that Paul arrived in Achaia (in modern Greece) during the proconsulship of Gallio. This Lucius Junius Gallio Annaeanus was the brother of Seneca, the famed stoic philosopher, senator, and teacher of the young Nero (at which he failed miserably). The Delphi Inscription is a collection of nine fragments of an imperial letter by Claudius. In it Gallio is mentioned as procunsul and this inscription is dated to approximately 52 A.D[658] Most scholars therefore place Acts 18:12 sometime between 52 and 53 A.D.[659]

Acts 23:24 / 24:27 – *Felix and Festus*

Paul was originally brough to trial during the procuratorship of Felix, but "after two years had passed, Felix was succeeded by Porcius Festor" (24:27). This established a date for Paul's imprisonment, but only inasmuch as we can establish and exact date for the succession. On this there is some debate.

The ancients only say that Festus was appointed by Nero (or rather Seneca who was acting in the emperor's name until 62 A.D.). Josephus does not say how long transpired between the death of Claudius and the appointment of Festus under Nero,[660] so many assumed that this must have taken place early during Nero's reign. Merrill Tenney, for example, places Festus around 57 A.D.[661] Most scholars tend to support a later date of 60 A.D.[662] The reasonings are as follows.

Advocates of the early date note that Josephus mentioned the death of Claudius only a few chapters before Festus's appointment. Since Claudius died in 54 A.D. they find it very unlikely that six years could have passed.[663] However, Josephus is interested only the history of Judea, and not Rome. Emil Schurer remarked that "Josephus puts almost everything that that he relates of the proceedings of Felix under the reign of Nero (*Antiq.* xx.9.1-9; *War of the Jews*, ii.12.8-14, 1). Felix must therefore have exercised his office for a least some years under Nero."[664] Secondly, we know that Albinus, the later successor for Festus, arrived in 62 A.D.[665] Although Festus's reign was short, it lasted at least 18 months before his death. Almost all scholars therefore agree that the appointment of Festus should be placed some time between 58 and 60 A.D. with the vast majority tying the events to other specifics in Nero's reign closer to 60

A.D.[666] Thus without getting into a protracted debate, it is best to say that late 59 or early 60 A.D. is the best attested date for the arrival of Festus. This in turn places the original trial of Paul under Felix around 58 A.D.

Acts 28:30 – Paul of Rome

Finally, we are told that Paul stayed in Rome two years after his arrival. Although the journey to Rome was prolonged because of the shipwreck, they stayed only three months there before securing new passage (28:11). It is doubtful that the trip took more than five or six months at the most. Hence our final fixed reference point appears to be in late 62 A.D. or early 63 A.D. with the close of the book of Acts.

Piecing Together the Chronology of Acts

Now we have approximately eleven "fixed" reference points. While some of these "fixed" points are only "fixed" within a year or two, they still serve their purpose of establishing points to which we can tie the rest of Acts. Within these passages are some events which indicate time, but not precise time. These are relative reference points. For example, we know that the Eunuch had come up from Ethiopia to worship (8:27). We do not exactly what feast he had come to observe, but know that it took place close to a Jewish Feast. We can then tie this event to the fixed reference point is some degree of accuracy. Let us then look at the rest of Acts and see where they fit into the picture.

Acts 2:2–6:6 – From Pentecost to the Appointment of the Seven Deacons

We are not given a timeline for these events, but it is clear that the events of chapters two to four all take place immediately after Pentecost as there is no indication of any lapse of time. The events of chapter five do assume that a period of months had passed as the church was now trying to settle upon how to take care of the poor and needy. This could not have been too greatly long after Pentecost for the issue would have been brought forward relatively soon. It most likely took place a few months after Pentecost at the latest.

It is with chapter six that we now see a new issue arising in the church. This concerned the treatment of Hellenistic Jews and widows. Once again some time appears to have passed but it is unlikely that this these issues had gone unresolved for a great period of time. Once again it is best to place this chapter no more than six months after Pentecost. However, Acts 6:7 does indicate a lapse of some time, although the exact amount of time is unknown.

Consequently, Acts 2:2 - 6:6 should be tentatively placed in the first six months after Pentecost, in the spring and summer of 33 A.D.

Acts 6:7–8:1 – The Martyrdom of Stephen

It is hard to place the martydom of Stephen into an exact timetime. There is no indication of any significant time transpiring between 6:6 and 6:8. Acts 6:7 is a summary of the events which had taken place since Pentecost. It does serve as a transitional passage from the election of the deacons to the story of Stephen and may or may not imply any significant passage of time. However, due to the correlation between Stephen's martyrdom, the conversion of Saul, and the events which follows most agree that this took place within a year of Pentecost. Merrill Unger believes it took place in 34 A.D.,[667] a date with which many agree. I am inclined to believe that it either took place toward the end of 33 A.D. or early in 34 A.D.

Acts 8:2-26 – The Scattering of the Disciples and the Samaritan Pentecost
We know that the scattering of the disciples and the persecution of Saul took place immediately after the stoning of Stephen. The journey of Philip into Samaria also appears to coincide with this persecution. It is therefore dated to the early part of 34 A.D.

Acts 8:27-40 – The Ethiopian Eunuch
It is unclear how long Philip preached in Samaria but is it clear that this is a continuation of Philip's story and his ministry. Although there is no specific timeline it is interesting to note that an Ethiopian Eunuch had come all the way from his home country to worship in Jerusalem. Such a journey for "worship" implies that he had come to attend one of the Jewish Feasts or Festivals that year. The question is, which one?

There are seven Hebrew Feasts which are celebrated in Israel. These are Passover, the Feast of Unleavened Bread, the Feast of First-Fruits, Pentecost, Rosh Ha-Shannah, Yom Kippur, and Sukkot. In addition to these Jews also began to commemorate Purim and Hannukah. Of course there are other festivals as well, but we expect that for a men to make such a long journey for the purpose of worship, he must have come for one of these nine holidays. This may also be supported by the fact that the apostles were in Jerusalem despite the threats upon their lives (8:14, 25). Although the apostles probably remained behind to support the church in Jerusalem, it was clearly a danger for them. Eventually many of the apostles were found working out of Antioch, Syria and Saul ventured out to Damascus, Syria to hunt Christian there. It thus seems that most Christians relocated to Syria, but the apostles remained, or perhaps they had returned to celebrate the Feast of Passover? This is conjecture to be sure. Nevertheless, it is true that the Ethiopian had participated in some religious worship.

If we have thus far been accurate in our chronology then we are already in the early part of 34 A.D. It so then there are only two major holidays which he could have been observing. The first is Purim which falls in February-March of the Gregorian calendar. The second is, of course, Passover which is usually in March or April. If Passover had passed it would be odd indeed that the Bible does not mention it. Since it is no particular interest to the story this remains a possibility, but more than likely it was Purim that the Eunuch may have come to commemorate. While we cannot be sure of this, or even that he was celebrating a holiday, it appears to make the most logical sense. Coming all the way from Ethiopia must have been a special occasion, thus this event probably took part in the early days of March, 34 A.D. This is a tentative suggestion.

Acts 9:1-18 – Saul's Conversion

The conversion of Paul followed these events in close proximity. It is likely that he wished to bring Christians back to Jerusalem before the start of Passover. However, some scholars believe that Paul's conversion did not take place until much later. Merrill Unger argues that it took place in 37 A.D.[668] apparently based on the "short" chronology of Galatians 1:18; 2:1. In other words, he counts backwards from the Council of Jerusalem using a faulty chronology and then places Paul's conversion in 37 A.D. However, I demonstrated that the most likely scenario is that Galatians 1:18 and 2:1 are different reconnings, whose last and first year overlap, thus it is not seventeen full years, but closer to sixteen years. As the reader will see, these numbers fit perfectly with the fixed chronological markers and with our relative markers. Thus a conversion in 34 A.D. not only fits with a proper reading of Galatians 1:18 and 2:1 but also with the narrative of Acts. His conversion could then be set with a relative degree of accuracy in mid-March 34 A.D.

Acts 9:19-30 – The Return of Paul

As aforementioned, Acts 9:19 indicates a break in time. The Greek phrase "εγενετο δε μετα" (*egeneto de meta*), which is found in the middle of 9:19 may literally be translated as "it happened afterwards." The conjuction δε (*de*) can also mean "a change in temporal setting."[669] Clearly Paul was not "proving Jesus was the Christ" (9:22) only days after his conversion. Galatians 1:17-18 makes this clear, for Paul states that "I went away to Arabia" to study the Word of God "and returned once more to Damascus ... three years later." Luke omits this interim, but makes the time shift obvious, even though most translations do not bring this out lucidly enough. The question then is the exact date of this return to Damascus.

Paul says that he returned "after three years," but repeated in the study of antiquity we find that the Hebrews (and Greeks) understood the word "after" to include the start of a time frame, not its end. In otherwords if I say "after Tuesday" in English it means anytime after Tuesday *ends*. In Greek and Hebrew (and other near east languages) the idiom meant anytime after Tuesday *begins*. This unspoken assumption exist in all languages, but translators do not always bring it out. This same issue occurs in the gospels (see *Controversies in the Gospels*). In short, after three years literally means "after the third year began." We do not know exactly how long after, but we know that it was *during* the third year, and not following it, for such is the idiom of Hebrew. Consequently, Paul's return to Damascus took place sometime in 36 A.D. as did his visit to Jerusalem and his first meeting with Peter.

Acts 9:31–10:48 – From Aeneas and Tabitha to Cornelius
There is no indication of the exact time frame during which these events took place, but 9:32 again uses the phrase "ἐγένετο δέ" *(egeneto de)* indicating a passage of time. 10:1 probably also implies a shift in time and temporal use of δέ *(de)* so we can only place these events between our other time markers. In so doing it is apparent that these passages take place over a number of years, from 36 A.D. to as late as 43 A.D.

Acts 11:1-30 – Agabus and the Famine Relief Effort
It is at this point that the gentile debate begins to arise. Again, we do not know the time frame but it appears to be close to the prophesy of Agabus. 11:26 implies that was at least one year before Agabus's prophecy. Although there may be a time break between 11:26 and 11:27, the flow of the narrative may suggests otherwise. The question is when did the relief for Jerusalem begin? The events of Acts 12:1-23 take place before the famine began, but after the prophecy of Agabus. Some have assumed that this is an anachronistic aside, but the narrative does not indicate such. Rather it appears that the believers in Jerusalem were anticipating the coming famine and preparing for it in advance. This is supported by Acts 12:25 which mentions the return of Paul from his duty immediately after the death of Herod. So these events tie directly to the fixed marker of Agabus and the prophecy of the famine. We may then place these events between 43 and 44 A.D.

Acts 12:3-19 – The Imprisonment of Peter
Obviously the arrest of Peter took place during the Feast of Unleavened Bread within a week (or less) of James's execution. While we do not known how long he was in prison, it is apparent that Herod Agrippa sought to bring him to trial immediately after the Feast was over. Thus Peter's imprisonment was sometime in March, possibly early April, 44 A.D.

Acts 13:1-13 – The First Journey of Paul Begins
Here marks the beginning of Paul's first journey. Since their first stop was the island of Cyprus and since the reign of Sergius Paulus is one of our fixed reference points (13:7) it is apparent that Paul's journey began at the earliest in the first part of 46 A.D. but probably sometime in 47 A.D., the year Sergius was appointed proconsul in Cyprus.

Acts 13:14–14:26 – Paul's First Journey Completed
The First Journey of Paul takes him through Asia Minor and the countries then called Lycia and Galatia. This was the shortest of Paul's missionary journeys, probably lasting between one and two years. One year seems a little short considering the number of cities in which they ministered, so it is probable that it was closer to two years. What is certain is that they returned

to Antioch not long before the Council of Jerusalem. Although this council is not a "fixed" reference point *per se*, it is a rubicon the history of the apostles and can be set (if not fixed) with a relative degree of certainty. Given the comment that they had spend "a long time" with the disciples in Antioch it is logical to assume that they returned home at least six months before the council, possibly even earlier.

Acts 15:1-32 – The Council of Jerusalem
In some respects the Council of Jerusalem is a rubicon for the book of Acts and for church history. Although it is not recorded by secular history it can be tied to world history with a fair degree of accuracy. Most historians variously date this council between 47 and 51 A.D. However, the early date cannot properly reconcile with Galatians unless Paul's conversion was before 33 A.D. That is based on the erroneous dating of the crucifixion before 33 A.D. Likewise, the late date may be rejected as well. It is based solely upon a western reading of Galatians 1:18, 2:1 in which they count seventeen full years beyond Paul's conversion. This is not acceptable either. As aforementioned, in Acts 9:19-30 a proper understanding of the Hebrew idiom puts the return of Paul to Jerusalem in 36 A.D., not 37 A.D. When we then add Galatians 2:1 to this, we should be again counting by Hebrew reckoning from 36 A.D. Thus sometime in the fourteenth year would be between 49 and 50 A.D. Depending on the exact dates involved, it is possible that the council took place in the earliest part of 49 A.D.

There are two reasons to believe that this took place in the early part of 49 A.D. First, there is evidence that the apostles were already beginning missions in far away countries by late 49 and early 50 A.D. For example, it is apparent that by 52 A.D. Thomas had already arrived in India via a land route (see Appendix C). Likewise we see some evidence that Matthew had already arrived in Egypt by 49 A.D. Second, during Paul's Second Missionary Journey he meets Aquila and Priscilla who had "recently" been expelled from Rome. This is one of our fixed reference points, and it occurred in either 49 or 50 A.D. Given that Paul's second journey had already been in progress for some time it is highly unlikely that this council could have take place after 49 A.D.

Acts 15:33–18:1 – Paul's Second Journey Begins
Paul's Second Missionary Journey began soon after the Council of Jerusalem. After some time, probably at least six months, he comes to Corinth where he encounters Aquila and Priscilla. This is fixed as being "recently" after Claudius's expulsion of Jews from Rome. Since that took place in either 49 or 50 A.D., Paul's second journey must have embarked no less than six months are so before this. Obviously, the second journey began sometime near the first half of 49 A.D.

Acts 18:2-11 – Paul in Corinth
After arriving sometime in 50 A.D. the Bible tells us that "he settled *there* a year and six months" (18:11). This takes us to the last months of 51 A.D.

Acts 18:12-22 – Paul's Second Journey Completed
Acts 18:12 is another fixed reference point as Gallio was apparently proconsul from 52 to 53 A.D. Since Paul had stayed six months in Corinth and left there probably in the later months of 51 A.D. we must assume that his arrival in Achaia was shortly after Gallio's appointment in 52 A.D. The question is how long did he remain there? Acts 18:18 says that Paul remained there "many days." This can be idiomatic for months or even years, but it is generally agreed that the events of Acts do not require anything more than a few months at most. It is soon after that he leaves Achaia and returns to Antioch, ending his Second Missionary Journey, probably in 52 or 53 A.D. at the latest.

Acts 18:23–21:16 – Paul's Third Journey
Acts 18:23 begins with the words "after having spent some time there." Obviously this is an indeterminate period of time. Scholars have debated as to when this journey began. Some place it as early as 51 A.D. while others put is as late as 54 A.D. Merrill Unger argues that Paul arrived in Ephesus around October 53 A.D., although he gives no specific reasons for such a precise date.[670]

Paul first passed through Galatia and Phrygia and spent some time "strengthening all the disciples" there (18:23). Paul then came first to Ephesus where he spent three months preaching in synagogues (19:8). Then he began to preach for two years in the Greek schools of Ephesus (19:10). It is at this point that Paul begins to plan a return to Jerusalem after visiting Macedonia and Achaia (19:21). Having arrived in Greece sometime later he spent another three months (20:3). In verse 20:6 we now hear of the Feast of Unleavened Bread, and that Paul was in hurry to arrive in Jerusalem before Pentecost (20:16). Let us then pause and look at the events which have thus far expired. All these events took a minimum of three years. Consequently, Merrill Unger argues that Paul arrived in Jerusalem on May 20, 57 A.D.,[671] but this is unlikely for two years. First, the arrest of Paul was only two years before the appointment of Festus (24:27) which is "fixed" at 60 A.D. (but see notes on Acts 23:24 / 24:27 above). That would make Paul's arrival at Pentecost in 58 A.D. Second, Acts 20:31 implies that Paul spent three years in Ephesus alone. If we then add the travels to other regions, we arrive a four years rather than the *minumum* assumed three. Certainly the events of Acts 18:23 and 20:3-17 took some time. So the minumum three year journey should be expanded to at least four years. Finally add the journey time and circumstances from 21:1-16 and it becomes more readily apparent that Paul's third journey took at least four full years, and probably a little longer.

So it appears that Paul most likely left on his third journey either toward the end of 53 A.D. or the early part of 54 A.D. It ended when he stepped foot in Jerusalem near Pentecost in May 58 A.D.

Acts 21:17–23:23 – Paul's Arrest

Acts 21:27 indicates that a week had passed before Paul's arrest. That means he was arrested at the end of May. The initial inquiry took no more than a few days, and the military caravan to Caesarea may have taken a couple of days to arrive. So his appearance in Caesarea probably occurred in the first days of June 58 A.D.

Acts 23:24–24:23 – Paul's Trial

The high priests did not arrive in Caesarea until almost a week later (24:1), but Paul states that it was "no more than twelve days ago I went up to Jerusalem to worship" (24:11), indicating that this five days dates back to his arrest. This trial thus began less than two weeks after his arrival, and five days after his arrest.

Acts 24:23-27 – Paul's Imprisonment at Caesarea

According to Acts 24:27 Paul remained in prison for two years until Festus arrived. That arrival is a "fixed" date which most place in 60 A.D. So Paul remained imprisoned at Caesarea from 58 to 60 A.D.

Acts 25:1–26:32 – Paul's Hearing Before Festus and Agrippa

Approximately two weeks after Festus's arrival (cf. Acts 25:1; 25:6) Paul appealed to Caesar. Then "after many days" (25:14) he stood for Herod Agrippa II, Berenice, and Festus and delivered the gospel. Soon thereafter he left for Rome. Now the exact length of Luke's "many days" (25:14) cannot be determined but inasmuch as he had appealed to Caesar it is not likely that Festus would have unnecessarily delayed his removal to Rome. It is probable that they simply waited until the next prison ship bound for Rome. We should probably assume a month or two at the most, sometime in 60 A.D.

Acts 27:1-44 – The Journey to Rome Begins

We are told that after a "good many days" (27:7) and a "considerable time" (27:9) they began to encounter troubled waters. For two weeks they had drifted at sea (27:18-20, 27, 33). Finally they shipwrecked on Malta island south of Italy. Owing to travel time and the description of the problems they had sailing to Italy, these events probably took between one and two months, but probably closer to two.

Acts 28:1-14 – The Shipwreck

Although we do not exactly when the shipwreck occured, it is clear that the natives were cold and set a fire. This indicates that it was already close to winter. This is confirmed by Acts 28:11 which states that there was "an Alexandrian ship which had wintered at the island." Given our previous chronology it is safe to place this shipwreck in the winter months of 60 A.D. Later they met with Publius, the leader of the island, for three days (28:7). It was after three months that they finally found charter to Italy (28:11). Staying in Syracuse for three days (28:12) they then set out again and arrived at Puteoli two days later (28:13) where they remained for seven days (28:14). At this point they finally arrive in Rome.

Gustave Dore - The Shipwreck - 19th Century

Putting together all the pieces here it was just over fourteen weeks between the shipwreck and their arrival at Rome, or around three and a half months. If they wrecked in November or December then they arrived in Rome somewhere around March 61 A.D.

Acts 28:15-30 – Paul in Rome

Acts closes with Paul in Rome awaiting trial. Acts 28:30 summarizes this saying, "he stayed two full years." Since this is "full years" we must assume that this takes us to the spring of 63 A.D.

Below is a full chart showing the apparent chronology of Acts as outlined above. Fixed dates are shown in bold. The following page is a larger chart showing all the primary figures of history at the time side by side.

Passage	Event	Date
Acts 1:3	The Ascension	**May 14, 33 A.D.**
Acts 2:1	Pentecost	**May 24, 33 A.D.**
Acts 2:2 - 6:6	From Pentecost to the 7 Deacons	Spring and Summer 33 A.D.
Acts 6:7 - 8:1	The Martyrdom of Stephen	Late 33 to early 34 A.D.
Acts 8:2-26	The Samaritan Pentecost	Early 34 A.D.
Acts 8:27-40	The Ethiopian Eunuch	Early March (?) 34 A.D.
Acts 9:1-18	Saul's Conversion	Mid-March (?) 34 A.D.
Acts 9:19-30	Paul Returns to Jerusalem	36 A.D.
Acts 9:31 - 10:48	Tabitha and Cornelius	Between 36 and 42/43 A.D.
Acts 11:1-27	The Gentile Debate Arises	Late 42 to early 43 A.D.
Acts 11:28-30	Agabus Prophesies the Famine	**Early 44 A.D.**
Acts 12:3	James the Great Executed	**March 44 A.D.**
Acts 12:3-19	Peter's Imprisonment and Escape	March-April 44 A.D.
Acts 12:21-23	Herod Agrippa I Dies	August **44 A.D.**
Acts 13:1-6	Paul's First Journey Begins	Late 46 to early 47 A.D
Acts 13:7	Paul Before Sergius Paulus	**47-48 A.D.**
Acts 13:13	John Returns to Jerusalem	47 A.D.
Acts 14:26	Paul's First Journey Ends	Late 48 A.D.
Acts 15:1-30	The Council of Jerusalem	**Early 49 A.D.**
Acts 15:33 - 18:1	Paul's Second Journey Begins	Early 49 A.D.
Acts 18:2	Jews Expelled from Rome	**49-50 A.D.**
Acts 18:1-11	Paul in Corinth	From 50 to late 51 A.D.
Acts 18:12	Paul Before Proconsul Gallio	**52-53 A.D.**
Acts 18:12-22	Paul Second Journey Ends	Late 52 A.D. to 53 A.D.
Acts 18:23	Paul's Third Journey	Early 54 A.D. to May 58 A.D.
Acts 21:17 - 23:24	Paul's Arrest	May to June 58 A.D.
Acts 23:24	Paul Tried Before Felix	The first week of June **58 A.D.**
Acts 23:25 - 24:27	Paul's Imprisonment	58 to 60 A.D.
Acts 24:27	Festus Arrives from Rome	**60 A.D.**
Acts 25:1 - 27:44	Paul Is Sent to Caesar	Late 60 A.D.
Acts 28:1-14	The Shipwreck	Late 60 A.D. - March 61 A.D.
Acts 28:15-30	Paul in Rome - Close of Acts	March 61 to Spring **63 A.D.**

Chronological Chart on the Acts of the Apostles

Date (A.D.)	Emperor	Governor of Judea	High Priests	Kings	Acts of the Apostles
33	Tiberius	Pontius Pilate	Annas - Caiaphas (acting High Priest)	The Tetrarchy	Pentecost
34					Martyrdom of Stephen
35					Conversion of Saul
36					
37		Marcellus	Jonathan		Paul Meets Peter
38	Caligula	Marullus	Theophilus	Herod Agrippa I	
39					
40					
41					
42	Claudius		Simon Mattathias & Elioneus		
43					James the Great Executed
44		Cuspius Fadus			Peter Imprisoned
45			Joseph		
46					Paul's 1st Journey Begins
47		Tiberius Julius Alexander			
48					Paul's 1st Journey Ends
49					Council of Jerusalem
50		Ventidius Cumanus			Paul's 2nd Journey Begins
51			Ananias		
52					
53					Paul's 2nd Journey Ends
54					Paul's 3rd Journey Begins
55	Nero	Antonius Felix		Herod Agrippa II	
56					
57					Paul's 3rd Journey Ends
58			Joseph		Paul Arrested in Jerusalem
59					
60			Ishmael		
61		Porcius Festus			Paul's Journey to Rome
62					
63		Albinus	Joseph Cabi Ananus		Paul is Acquitted
64			Joshua & Mattathias		Paul's Fourth Journey Fire in Rome
65		Florus			Peter and Paul executed

Appendix B

Peter and Rome

Because Acts ends with Paul in prison nothing is said of Peter's end. Traditionally both Catholics and Protestants accepted, and sometimes altered, the ancient tradition that Peter died in Rome, being crucified upside. However, a number of Protestants have questioned whether or not Peter was ever even *in* Rome.[672] Although the Bible does speak to this issue, it only speaks cursorily. There is no explicit evidence as to what happened to Peter after the Council of Jerusalem. He is never mentioned in Acts after this council and his epistles only give clues. We can piece together certain facts, but to draw broad conclusions based on these facts, as some on both sides of the fence have done, is poor exegesis. I will therefore dedicate this entire appendix to the history of Peter. In this history I count the Bible first and foremost as our main authority. After that come ancient epistemology, followed by ancient historians. Next comes tradition, with legends being of little or no merit.

Can history sync with the Biblical record? Obvious if it is truly history, then it will sync. If it is legend then it will not. Consequently, it is best to look at individual aspects of Peter in both history and the Bible. After evaluating those aspects we can then, and only then, piece together all the pieces of the puzzle.

Was Peter Ever In Rome?

Too many have assumed that if Peter was in Rome, he was bishop of Rome. This assumption naturally stems from Catholic tradition, but logically there is no connection between his possible residence in Rome and his alleged bishopry in Rome. After all, Paul was in Rome. Was he pope? No, the issues are separate and will be addressed separately. To assume that the two are connected is to demolish your own arguments, for you have created a bond and link between two events that may or may not be linked at all. Consequently, both Catholics and Protestants in their presuppositions have created an invisible barrier that only detracts from the truth. It is best to start solely with the question of Rome itself.

In examining the evidence we should start with the source; Peter. Although he does not give us any specific information about his history after the Council of Jerusalem there are many clues in his epistles which provide our first pieces of the puzzle. These are the fixed pieces. All other pieces of the puzzle must be fit around these pieces. If they do not fit with them, then they must be rejected. The Bible itself is thus our first source.

The Biblical Evidence
The Biblical evidence can itself be divided into several parts. Obviously Peter's epistles give us clues, as we would be expect. Some believe that Paul's epistles may also yield clues. Although we might expect to start with Peter, I prefer to start with Paul in hopes of removing some subliminal assumptions that many have. Then starting with a clear slate, we can approach the Biblical evidence more fresh.

Peter in Paul's Epistles
John Calvin made an infamous argument from silence in order to prove that Peter was never in Rome. He ask why, if Peter was in Rome, did Paul never even mention Peter? Did not Paul refer to numerous contemporaries who were with him in Rome? This argument seems powerful at first glance, but upon close examination it falls apart on several levels.

There is a collection of Paul's epistles that are called the "Prison Epistles" since they were written when Paul was in prison. It is true that in those epistles he mentioned Mark, Aristarchus, Demas, Luke, Epaphras (Philemon 23-24), Artemas, Tychicus (Titus 3:12), and many others. The omission of Peter in these epistles would indeed seem odd if he were in Rome *at that time*. The problem is that we have already established that there were two imprisonments of Paul. When Paul wrote Titus and Philemon he was already making plans for what to do after his release from prison (Titus 3:12; Philemon 22).[673] In many of these letters it seems apparent that Paul had high hopes of being released. However, when he wrote 2 Timothy he had no such hopes. He was resigned to martyrdom. In 2 Timothy he said, "I have fought the good fight, I have finished the course, I have kept the faith in the future there is laid up for me the crown of righteousness" (4:7-8). Moreover, he explicitly says that "Luke is with me" (4:11) and ask that Mark be sent to him. As will become clear in this appendix, Paul was not being permitted many visitors. It is probable that 2 Timothy is the only epistle he was even permitted to send (and may have been smuggled out by Luke) while he was in prison, for the persecutions of Nero had already begun and Paul himself knew that his fate was sealed.

Let us now look at these epistles. The first prison epistles were clearly written during his first imprisonment sometime between 60 and early 63 A.D. In those epistles he was free to meet and receive people (Acts 28:30-31). Thus between 60 and 63 A.D. Calvin's argument has great merit, and we see no evidence in the Bible of Peter visiting Rome at this time. Note, however, that Mark was with Paul between 60 and 63 A.D.

Now during the second imprisonment things had clearly changed. Since there is debate as to exactly when Paul was rearrested our conclusions are limited but the following facts can be ascertained. First, he was not permitted to receive many visitors. Only Luke was permitted to see him, probably because he was a physician. Second, he requested that Mark come from Ephesus. Third, tradition (as we shall see) claims that Peter died in 65 A.D. so depending on when Paul was rearrested, Peter may already have died, making it hard for Paul to have met him even if he had been permitted to do so.

Personally I believe that Paul was arrested in 65 A.D. as I discussed in *The Apostles After Jesus*. Nonetheless, no one was being permitted to see Peter and only Luke had seen Paul. The weakness of the argument from silence is thus magnified at this stage. What is not weak is the fact that Paul explicitly places Mark in Rome between 60 and 63 A.D. and in Ephesus in 65 A.D. Apparently Mark returned to Rome that same year. This is relevant because Mark is mentioned as Peter's companion in his own epistle. Let us then look at his own words.

Clues from Peter's Epistles

Peter's first epistle was written to those in "Pontus, Galatia, Cappadocia, Asia, and Bithynia" (1 Peter 1:1). All these ancient countries reside in modern day Turkey, or Asia Minor. It is thus apparent that after the Council of Jerusalem, we cannot say how long after, Peter was ministering in Asia Minor and working with the churches therein. The intriguing thing is that this epistle appears to have been written from "Babylon" (1 Peter 5:13). If this is the famous Babylon in Iraq, as some Protestants believe, then this would place Peter a thousand miles from the churches to whom he was writing and ministering. More significant is the fact that Mark was with him at that time!

There are two interpretations of "Babylon" in this passage. The first is that Babylon is a "code word" for Rome itself. Just as we call Las Vegas "Sodom" so Babylon had become a byword for those who oppress Israel. Given that the War of the Jews had already begun, this is a possibility. The second view is that Peter was in the literal Babylon of history in Iraq, and therefore nowhere near Rome.

The debate over Babylon has been an extensive one. It involes the Bible, prophecy, and history. Some believe that Babylon will be reborn while others believe that the Bible *forbids* Babylon's resurrection (cf. Jeremiah 51:64). Many see Babylon was symbolic for Rome (including a great many are evangelical "literalists") while others see it as nothing short of the literal Babylon, even arguing that it can be nothing else but. This debate is so extensive that I am forced to deal with in both *Controversies the Prophets* and *Controversies in Revelation*. It is therefore hard to succinctly repeat all the evidence in a few pages, but I shall endeavor to do just that nonetheless.

Babylon in the Bible, in Prophecy, and in History

Let us begin with Babylon in prophecy. Jeremiah 51:64 says that "Babylon shall sink down and not rise again." Isaiah 13:19-20 declares that "Babylon, the beauty of kingdoms, the glory of the Chaldeans' pride, will be as when God overthrew Sodom and Gomorrah. It will never be inhabited or lived in from generation to generation." Some have attempted to link these prophecies with those of *"Mystery"* Babylon in Revelation 17-18. However, the problems with linking literal Babylon to *Mystery* Babylon are much harder than some might think. While men like Charles Dyer insist that literal Babylon is the only "literal" interpretation possible,[674] he must in fact take much more of Revelation 17-18 allegorically than literally, for the Babylon of Revelation is located by a great Sea Port, not a desert (18:17-19). Additionally, Dyer takes the "gold, silver, precious stones, pearls, fine linen, silk, citron wood, ivory, costly wood, bronze, iron, marble, cinnamon, spice, incense, perfume, frankincense, wine, olive oil, fine flour, wheat, cattle, sheep, horses, chariots, and slaves" of 18:11-13 almost exclusively as oil. More significant, however, is the fact that the prophecy of Jeremiah is that Babylon would "sink down" (51:64), whereas *Mystery* Babylon is destroyed by fire in a single instance (17:16 - 18:9). The greatest problem, however, is the fact that the prophecies of Isaiah and Jeremiah have been literally fulfilled in the past, and thus Jeremiah's prophecy that it shall "not rise again" (51:64) must also hold true.

According to Isaiah and Jeremiah several things are to happen to Babylon. The two most important ones are that, "It will never be inhabited or lived in from generation to generation" and that "Desert creatures will lie down there, and their houses will be full of owls." Let us then take a closer look a these prophecies. Babylon first began to "sink down" with the conquest of Babylon by Cyrus and the Medes. After that conquest Alexander the Great took the city in 331 B.C. Since then history records no fewer than ten conquest of Babylon. The city "changed hands several times"[675] in the next few years alone. Perdiccas was the first regent until he was killed by Seleucus in 321 B.C.[676] Seleucus then lost the city to Antigonus five years later,[677] but recaptured the city four years after that.[678] Still Antigonus would not give up and "a fierce and bitter war brought terrible suffering upon Babylon."[679] So great was the destruction and terror that the Babylonian chronicles themselves describe "weeping and mourning in the land."[680] The eventual victory of Seleucus over Antigonus would not end Babylon's woes. Assyriologist Georges Roux speaks about the "half-ruined city"[681] of this time and says that "it was already partly deserted, a great number of its inhabitants having been transferred to Seleucia."[682] Babylon was "no longer the seat of royal government"[683] but it was a prize which conquerors still sought. As Jeremiah prophesied Babylon was slowly sinking down (cf. Jeremiah 51:64). In the wars that would ensue between the Parthians and the Greeks, and later the Parthians and Romans, Babylon would again trade hands many times. In the year 126 B.C. the Parthians took control of Babylon[684] although war between Crassus of Rome and the Parthians continued over Babylon. By the time Cassius Dio entered the city he was able to say that Babylon was "nothing but mounds and stones and ruins."[685] When the Roman Emperor Septimus Severus entered Babylon he found it deserted.[686] Most importantly, Pliny, who lived at the time of the apostles, said "the Great City has become a great desert."[687]

So it would seem that the prophecies of Isaiah and Jeremiah were fulfilled literally. Babylon sank down over time so that it was neither "inhabited or lived in from generation to generation" (Isaiah 13:20). Moreover, "desert creatures will lie down there, and their houses will be full of owls, Ostriches also will live there, and shaggy goats will frolic there. And hyenas will howl in their fortified towers and jackals in their luxurious palaces" (Isaiah 13:21). Yet this last prophecy also refutes those who equate Babylon with Mystery Babylon. These scholars point out that Babylon is compared to Sodom and Gomorrah, as if this proves that Babylon must be destroyed in the same manner as Sodom and Gomorrah,[688] but they ignore the fact that Moab, Ammon, Ninevah, and Assyria are also compared to Sodom in prophecy. For example, Zephaniah 2:9 declares "surely Moab will be like Sodom, and the sons of Ammon like Gomorrah – A place possessed by nettles and salt pits, and a perpetual desolation." These cities, like Babylon, are "a perpetual desolation" (Zephaniah 2:9) just "like Gomorrah" and "like Sodom." Nowhere in the Old Testament is there a declaration that they will fall in ball of fire from heaven. On the contrary, the imagery is one of "sinking" (cf. Jeremiah 51:64) down over time. Mystery Babylon is, by definition, a *mystery*. It cannot be the ancient Babylon of Iraq for "the curse that Babylon would never come to be settled in and inhabited again ... proved itself an effectual one."[689]

Now let us look specifically at Babylon in the time of the apostle Peter. Here Pliny is the only contemporary of the apostle, and Pliny declared that "the Great City has become a great desert."[690] At the time it was under the control of Parthia, the dreaded enemies of the Romans. As far as we can tell it was deserted and had no population, certainly no population significant enough to warrant such a long and treacherous journey by Peter.

Summary Conclusion

There are approximately seven primary reasons to reject the notion of Peter's presence in the ancient Babylonian city. The first is, of course, the fact that the prophesied fall of Babylon had already taken place and the city is said to have been deserted by Peter's contemporary Pliny. There seems then no reason to believe that there was any significant population there, let alone a large Jewish community.

Second, Babylon lay in Parthia. This creates several problems. To begin with travel between two waring countries would not be easy and it is unlikely that Peter would have been allowed to travel freely back and forth between Rome and Parthia. Moreover, the distance and travel time make it virtually impossible to believe that Mark could have traveled from Rome to Babylon and back to Ephesus and Rome in the narrow time frame which our history allows. This leads to the third and fourth points.

If Peter's ministry was to the churches of Asia Minor, to whom he wrote his epistle (1 Peter 1:1) then how could he have ventured so far in the opposite direction. They did not have air plane or cars back then, so when the apostles' mission fields were meted out, it is likely that they never expected to return home. When Thomas and Bartholomew moved out eastward (past Babylon) they never returned to Israel (see Appendix C). Logically, an apostle's mission fields should be located in a central area and not be darting back and forth across thousands of miles. Paul was one of the more well traveled apostles and his missions never took him beyond the countries of Mediterranean.

Fourth, if Peter was in Parthia then the backdrop of 1 Peter becomes null and void. All agree that "the Neronian persecutions apparently furnish the background" for 1 Peter.[691] However, Nero had no authority over Parthia, nor would Peter's life be threatened by Nero in Parthia and yet every ancient father records that Peter died under Nero.[692]

Fifth, even those who believe Peter was in Iraq admit that Babylon had become a byword for Rome. The War of the Jews had already begun and the term was in common verbage at that time. Just as we speak of "Sodom" in Las Vegas or Hollywood, so Babylon referred to those empires that oppressed God's people.

Sixth, not a single ancient historian, church father, or even legend places Peter in Parthia. This would be astounding indeed, for if Peter had ventured to Babylon of Iraq surely those who lived there would have honored and commemorated the event. It is true that many legends sometimes claim the apostles went where they did not go, but this would be the first time in history that an apostle traveled somewhere and left *no* tradition!

Finally, and most importantly, the Bible itself seems to forbid this interpretation, for Mark was in Ephesus when Paul wrote his last epistle (2 Timothy 4:7-8) and presumeably traveled to Rome shortly thereafter. This was probably around 65 A.D. We also know that Mark was in Rome between 60 and 63 A.D. as he is referred to by Paul in Philemon 23 and Colossians 4:10. Astoundingly he is also mentioned as Peter's companion in Babylon (1 Peter 5:13) in an epistle generally dated around 65 A.D![693] This is only possible if Peter's "Babylon" was the idiomatic usage common at that time.

In short, the epistles of Peter and Paul yield sufficient proof, through the appearance of Mark, that Peter's "Babylon" was but a byword for Rome. The Biblical evidence, although not conclusive, supports the notion that Peter visited Rome. To what extend Peter was involved in Rome we cannot say, but that he at least visited Rome somewhere close to 65 A.D. seems to be supported by the Bible.

Historical Evidence from Antiquity
All agree that the ancient historians universally believed that Peter died in Rome. Evangelical Protestants scholar Harold Ironside summarized it saying simply that Peter died in Rome "if we can trust early Church History."[694] Can we? Better yet, can we not? This really cuts at the heart of the issue. Catholics

argue that the Catholic church goes back to Peter while Protestants deny this, and yet at the same time some Protestants reject the early church fathers based on the subliminal belief that they support Catholicism! In fact, if the early church fathers were living today I think the honest historian would say that they would be split between Catholicism and Protestantism, but probably none of them would be thoroughly happy with either. This is therefore a mute point. Those who lived closest to the events would probably have a better idea of what happened. The discussion of Peter's martydom and his alleged papacy is addressed below. Here I discuss only the histroral evidence of Peter's *presence* in Rome during the time of Nero.

Dionysius, the overseer (or bishop) of Corinth died in 170 A.D. but wrote in the mid-second century. He places Peter and Paul's martyrdom in Rome.[695] Irenaeus, one of the earliest and most important of church fathers, lived from 130 to 202 A.D.[696] He is apparently the first to call Peter and Paul the founders of the church in Rome,[697] although it seems apparent that they were only its spiritual founders, for the Roman church clearly existed before Paul ever arrived in Rome (cf. the book of Romans and Acts). Other ancients who place Peter in Rome include the second century bishops Clement of Alexandria[698] and Hippolytus,[699] as well as Gaius (or Caius) of Rome[700] and Tertullian.[701]

In addition to these witnesses is the apocryphal Acts of Peter dated to the middle of the second century. This work has been described as a work of historical fiction[702] and was actually declared heretical by pope Gelasius I in the fifth century.[703] Nevertheless, it provides one of the earliest sources of tradition in which Peter is said to have traveled to Rome to confront Simon the Magician. Because the apostle Paul was no longer in Rome, it is said that the church requested an apostle to deal to Simon the Magician. After coming to Rome Peter was eventually arrested after the famous story of the *Quo Vadis* on the Appian Way and crucified upside down.[704]

Of all these sources Hippolytus provides us with the most thorough information, part of which can be confirmed in the Bible. He said, "Peter preached the Gospel in Pontus, and Galatia, and Cappadocia, and Bithynia, and Italy, and Asia, and was afterwards crucified by Nero in Rome with his head downward, as he had himself desired to suffer in that manner."[705] The first part of this can be confirmed in 1 Peter 1:1. The second part fits with later sources and with Mark's presence in Rome (cf. 2 Timothy 4:7-8; 1 Peter 5:13). It is also important to note that Irenaeus was a second generation disciple. Polycarp had been trained by the apostle John who in turned trained Irenaeus, who in turn tutored Hippolytus. If these men did not know what happened to Peter then who would? So Irenaeus and Hippolytus provide strong support to the idea that Peter had at least been to Rome in the mid-60s.

All these sources are second century sources within one to three generations of the original apostles. Later sources become more suspect as we drift further and further from the original source, but if none of these men knew what happened to Peter, then we could not know at all. Furthermore, if Peter did not die in Rome, then we have *no* information about the later years of Peter's whereabouts at all!

Conclusion
The evidence, both Biblical and historical, supports that Peter had at least been to Rome and died there under Nero's persecution. If Mark was with Peter and Paul during the same general time frame, then they must have both been in the west somewhere near Italy. There is no plausible way to explain how Mark could be in both the east and west within a year or two, particularly with war raging in the east. With no historical evidence placing Peter outside the Roman empire it is best to accept that Peter ventured to Rome late in his life and became one of the first victims of the awful persecution of Nero.

Was Peter Ever the Bishop of Rome?

Now if we accept that Peter resided in Rome for a time late in his life, does it follow that he was the Bishop of Rome? On this point Protestants and Catholics will never agree. The Catholic Church claims that the papacy was established in Matthew 16:18 and that the church fathers all hailed Peter as the first pope while some Protestants argue that none of the earlies church fathers believed Peter was bishop and that Matthew 16:18 doesn't even refer to Peter! Obviously, finding the truth between these extreme positions is not easy to do, but I shall endeavor to do so anyway looking, as we did before, at the Biblical and historical evidences.

Biblical Evidence
Matthew 16:18 is the passage which is cited by Catholics as Biblical support for a papacy. In it Jesus said to Peter:

> "You are Peter, and upon this rock I will build My church; and the gates of Hades will not overpower it. I will give you the keys of the kingdom of heaven; and whatever you bind on earth shall have been bound in heaven, and whatever you loose on earth shall have been loosed in heaven."

Now Catholics note that the word for "rock" here in Matthew is the same word from whence Peter derives his name. With equal vigor some Protestants claim that Jesus alone is the rock. Since I dealt with this in *Controversies in the Gospel* I will only summarize my own conclusion. Jesus is, in Greek, the *lithos* (λιθος) or cornerstone, but not the *petra* (πετρα) or rock. It is Jesus Himself who gave Peter his nickname (cf. John 1:42) and it is obviously a wordplay on his name, "You are *Petros* (Πετρος) and on this *petra* (πετρα) I will build my church." This is parallel to Paul's statement in Ephesians 2:20

where the apostle Paul declares that the universal Church is "built upon the foundation of the apostles and prophets, Jesus Christ himself being the chief corner *stone*." Peter is an apostle, and a "rock," but Jesus is the cornerstone.

So having established that Jesus was indeed talking about Peter, the next question is what the "keys to kingdom" represent. If I antagonized my Protestant friends with my answer to the first question then I shall antagonize my Catholic friends with this answer.

According to the official *Catechism of the Catholic Church* article 553, the keys of the kingdom represent "supreme authority"; not just authority, but *supreme* authority. However, as Matthew Henry pointed out, "the Old Testament promises relating to the church were given immediately to particular persons, eminent for faith and holiness, as to Abraham and David, which yet gave no supremacy to them, much less to any of their successors."[706] The question is not one of authority but *supreme* authority.

Many may be surprised to learn that this is not the only passage which speaks of the power to bind on heaven and earth. This exact same phrase is found, for in Matthew 18:18 except that it refers to *all* the disciples. Some even argue that Jesus was speaking to *all* believers. Certainly Peter is not the only one to whom this authority was given.

Furthermore, it is clear that while Peter was a member of the inner circle and one of the most important apostles, he did not have supreme authority over the other apostles. This is most obvious by the Apostle Paul's public rebuke, even humiliation, of Peter in Galatians 2:11-14. As discussed previously, James the Greater and even James the Less may also have been considered superior to Peter at one time or another, but I will leave this judgment to the reader.

What is most evident is that even if we accepted the theory that Peter was some sort of pope, there is not the slightest hint of any unending succession of apostles in this passage or anywhere else in the Bible. Under "The Thirteenth Apostle Acts 1:21-26" I discussed the theory of apostolic succession and rejected it as unbiblical. Nothing in Matthew 16:18 even touches upon a succession of apostles. If God did not have an unending succession of prophets in the Old Testament it is indeed odd that in a dispensation were we have the Holy Spirit God now believes we need an unending succession of apostles! And that when we have the Words of Sacred Scripture to help guide us as well.

While Peter and Paul are considered the spiritual founders of the church of Rome it is clear that neither were its material founders. In the book of Romans Paul, who was the "apostle of gentiles" (Romans 11:13), does not address his Roman epistle to Peter but rather greets Timothy, Lucius, Jason, Sosipater, Tertius, Gaius, Erastus, and Quartus (Romans 16:21-23). Nowhere is Peter's name even mentioned, and Paul had not yet been to Rome. This would be odd indeed of Peter had been in Rome and was a material founder of the church.

Two more arguments remain from the Bible. According to the apostle Paul "God has appointed in the church, first apostles, second prophets, third teachers, then miracles, then gifts of healings, helps, administrations, *various kinds of tongues*" (1 Corinthians 12:28). Where are the overseers (or bishops) in this list? Are they "teachers" or "administrators"? In either case, had Peter desired to be the bishop of Rome it would be a step *down* from apostle! Why would Peter demote himself? Think about the job of an overseer or bishop. They are shepherds of the local church community. The apostles were missionaries and evangelists. They serve the church at large, but a bishop serves the local church. You *cannot* do both. Moreover, according to 1 Timothy 3:10 a bishop must first serve as a deacon to prove his worthiness. Nowhere is the office of the overseer or bishop equated with the apostleship, nor could it be. This would be the equivalent of the President of the United States attempting to serve as governor and mayor or New York at the same time! These are different duties and offices. The apostles are far above the bishops. In fact, if we ignore the debate over Peter for a second, we find that in church history only James the Just is ever called a bishop, and that being bishop of Jerusalem. He was one of the only apostles who never left Judah, because he had to stay with and care for the *local* church in Jerusalem.

Finally, if we were to believe that an apostle was to serve as the bishop of Rome, then logically would not Paul have made a better option? After all, if Peter were the supreme apostle, should he not have served in Jerusalem? Was Paul not the the "apostle to the gentiles" (1 Timothy 2:7)? Did Peter not have an "apostleship to the circumcised" (Galatians 2:8)? Would not the "apostle to the gentiles" be a better "pope" for the pagan city of Rome? Would not Peter then be better suited to Jerusalem?

Biblically there is no support for the doctrine of the papacy and some strong evidence against it. The apostles were just that, apostles. They were not bishops and there was no provision for any succession of apostles. Bishops are the serve their local church communities and not to place themselves above other bishops. They begin as deacons and prove themselves worthy (1 Timothy 3:10). In most cases their duties and function are far different from that of the apostles.

Early Church History
Although early tradition does equate Peter with the founder of Rome (along with Paul) the first indication that Peter was a bishop does not appear until the early third century when the bishop of Carthage, Cyprian, spoke of the primacy of Peter in a matter of fact manner.[707] Before this time there is no church father who clearly refers to the primacy of Peter or any succession of apostles. In fact, the earliest church fathers all make Linus the first bishop of Rome, and not Peter.

Irenaeus, the second generation disciple of John, states in the mid-second century that "the blessed apostles, then, having founded and built up the Church, committed into the hands of Linus the office of the episcopate. Of this Linus, Paul makes mention in the Epistles to Timothy."[708] Note two things. First, Peter was obviously still alive when Linus became bishop. Second, it was both Peter and Paul who appointed him to the bishopry, showing that the early church did not hold Peter supreme over Paul.

More than this Hegesippus and others from the second century also affirm that Linus was the first pope. Such is acknowledged even by Catholic scholars.[709] Nonetheless, it is to be admitted that by the third century Peter became uniformly identified as the first pope. Still, there are some very interesting anomalies omitted by those who appeal to this "unanimity" of the post-second century bishop lists. In the days of Constantine there was a famed "chronography" which lists the popes from Peter to the then pope Liberius. What is interesting is that while this chronography of popes does list Peter as the first pope, it claims that he held that office from the Pentecost until "the time of Nero, from the consulate of Saturninus and Scipio."[710] This would be 55-56 A.D. Interestingly enough this is the approximate time that most believe Paul wrote his epistle to the Romans.[711] Moreover, we know for a fact that Peter never left Palestine until after the Council of Jerusalem around 49 A.D. as his whereabouts are explicitly described in the book of Acts. It seems the height of absurdity to claim that Peter was the bishop of Rome in 33 A.D. when the church of Rome did not even exist yet! Nor can we believe with credibility that Peter travelled to Rome at this time. On this I am backed up by Catholic scholars who reject the chronology of this document, but the interesting part is not that its chronology is in error, but in the manner of its error.

The "Chronography of 354" bears all the marks of inserted Peter before Linus without amending Linus's tenture. In other words, papal list before the third century place Linus as the first bishop of Rome. The church of Rome is universally believed to have been founded sometime in the early to mid-fifties. Thus the "Chronography of 354" may actually provide us with a copy of the earliest list with the only difference being the insertion of Peter as "pope" from 33 to 55 A.D., which all acknowledge is a mistake and impossibility. Later Catholics shifted Linus's term until after Peter's death, and yet more intriguing is the fact that early martyrs lists claim that Linus died in the persecutions of Nero along with Peter![712] Consequently, modern day Catholics reject Linus's martyrdom and shift papal dates to accomodate Peter's rule.

We can see then that the tradition that Peter was the bishop of Rome developed probably sometime in the late second century. Even as early as the fourth century accomodations were being made to properly place Peter in the bishop lists. However, the earliest sources all agreed that Linus was the first bishop and that he was martyred under Nero. The historical support for Peter as the first bishop of Rome is therefore suspect.

Conclusion

The belief that the bishop of Rome was a successor to the apostle Peter began to develop in the late second and early third centuries. There is no firm belief for such an office in the Bible, and certainly no indication of any succession thereof. The earliest papal lists omit Peter and the earliest church fathers all refer to Linus as the first bishop. The standard papal lists of today appear to conform to lists developed in the third and fourth centuries, long after Peter.

Biblically the office of bishop is incompatible with the office of the apostles which was far above that of bishops. Only James the Just appears to have served as a bishop and he was thus the only apostle who did not serve as a missionary and evangelist. A bishop serves a local community. An apostle is sent out to the whole world. It is only because of an apparent vacuum left by the absence of the apostles that the bishops of Rome began to assert their authority in such matters. Historically speaking the supremacy of the papacy was never even accepted by all European churches until well into the Middle Ages and even then pockets of resistance continued until the Reformation.[713] The sheer terror which such an institution created should itself be evidence that it is not from God whose true apostles spread the truth of the gospel and never persecuted those who rejected them.

Peter's Martyrdom

If I angered Protestants in the first section and infuriated Catholics in the second, then perhaps I will appease both here ... or more likely neither. I have already affirmed by belief that Peter visited Rome and died in Rome under Nero, but that he was never the bishop of Rome nor did any claim it to be so for nearly a century afterwards. The critic will ask how I can accept one tradition while rejecting another. A fair question. I have weighed each against the Biblical evidence, however peripheral, but I have also weighed earlier traditions to be of more value than later ones.

What then of Peter's death? How did he die? How trustworthy are the early church fathers and tradition? Is there any Biblical evidence to support his martyrdom? To this last question it is stated in John 21:19 Jesus "signif[ied] by what kind of death [Peter] would glorify God." He said, "when you grow old, you will stretch out your hands and someone else will gird you, and bring you where you do not wish to *go*" (John 21:18). This is universally accepted as an indication that Peter would be apprehended and led to a place of execution. This indicates a "lawful" arrest and execution. Beyond this we cannot say strictly from the Bible what happened to Peter, but not more than a generation from Peter we have testimony of this death and martyrdom; the first being that of Clement of Rome who probably witnessed his death.

This same Clement is sometimes believed to have been the same Clement mentioned in Philippians 4:3. Although his testimony is meager he does validate the belief that Peter was martyred.[714] Dionysius believed that Peter and Paul died "at the same time."[715] Clement of Alexandria related the tradition that "the blessed Peter, on seeing his wife led to death, rejoiced on account of her call and conveyance home, and called very encouragingly and comfortingly, addressing her by name, 'Remember thou the Lord.' Such was the marriage of the blessed and their perfect disposition towards those dearest to them."[716] He also said that Peter left behind at least one child.[717] Some traditions say that the child was a daughter, named Petronilla, who was born after Christ, and crippled in childhood.[718] Hippolytus said that "Peter preached the Gospel in Pontus, and Galatia, and Cappadocia, and Bithynia, and Italy, and Asia, and was afterwards crucified by Nero in Rome with his head downward, as he had himself desired to suffer in that manner."[719] Likewise, Tertullian stated that Peter was under Nero[720] in Rome "where Peter endures a passion like his Lord's."[721] The apocryphal *Acts of Peter* is probably our earliest source, and relates traditions that may date to the first century. It is in this document that the *Quo Vadis* story is first related:

> "And as he went forth of the city, he saw the Lord entering into Rome. And when he saw him, he said: Lord, where are you going? [*quo vadis?* in Latin] And the Lord said unto him: I go into Rome to be crucified. And Peter said unto him: Lord, are you being crucified again? He said unto him: Yea, Peter, I am being crucified again. And Peter came to himself: and having beheld the Lord ascending up into heaven, he returned to Rome, rejoicing, and glorifying the Lord, for that he said: I am being crucified: that which was about to befall Peter."[722]

Peter is then said to be taken to be crucified, but he begs to be crucified upside down in deference to Christ of whom he is unworthy.[723] All these witnesses are from the first century after the apostolic age. What then are we to make of this?

That Peter was martyred was prophesied by the Lord Jesus Himself (John 21:18-19). That it was Nero who ordered the death of Peter is attested by every church historian from the earliest of church fathers. The method of execution is also agreed to have been crucifixion. Not a single tradition, or even legend, has Peter in Parthia or elsewhere, which would be incredible if he had truly been there. The sheer unaninimity of the traditions attest to the fact that Peter was crucified under Nero in Rome. However, there is some debate as to the detail; especially the timing and the events which preceded his martyrdom.

Traditions variously place Peter's martyrdom in 65 or 67 A.D., and between June 29 and July 4.[724] In the first century Clement of Rome said that Peter suffered "not one but many labors" before meeting his death.[725] This may be a reference to the belief that Peter was held in a dungeon for nine months, chained to a column, before being led away to execution.[726] This is quite possible for Tacitus tells us that Nero tortured several Christians into confessing to the fire in Rome.⁷²⁷ All agree that Nero sought to deflect suspicion from himself for the fire in Rome. If Nero knew that he had an apostle prisoner, it only makes sense that he would have tried to torture Peter into "confessing" to the fire in Rome. It would surely have been a boon to have a leader of the church renounce Jesus, and it is only logical to assume that Nero spent at least nine months attempting to do just this.

Caspar de Crayer – The Martyrdom of St. Peter – 1650s

Furthermore, most believe that 1 Peter was written in anticipation of coming persecution.[728] Merrill Unger believed that "the Neronian persecutions apparently furnish the background."[729] This fits with the fact that Peter knew he was going to die and that Nero would soon begin to persecute Christians in a way never before known at that time. Like Paul's second epistle to Timothy, probably written around the same time, he knew his death was impending. Why?

Regardless of whether or not we accept the *Quo Vadis* tradition, there appears to be some truth to this story. If Peter was arrested shortly after the fire in Rome, in either the Fall or Winter of 64 A.D. the nine months later would be in 65 A.D. which some hold to be the correct date for Peter's death.[730] It likely that Peter, after hearing Christians were being blamed for the fire, had either tried to leave afterwards or was among the first apprehended. I have debated the chronology of Peter and Paul's death more fully in *The Apostles After Jesus*, so here I will merely state my belief that he died in 65 A.D. on a day which Nero set aside to make a spectacle of all the Christians prisoners. Some were crucified, some beheaded, some were lit afire as human torches, and others made a spectacle of in the Circus Maximus. That Peter chose to be crucified upside down is not unusual. There was no single method of crucifixion[731] and it fits the character of Peter that he chose this method, declaring himself unworthy to die like Christ.

In short, the fire in Rome broke out on July 19, 64 A.D. Within a month or two Nero was circulating rumors that the Christians were responsible for the fire. Peter may have tried to escape Rome, but for whatever reasons he either returned (as per the *quo vadis* vision) or was discovered and arrested. This probably took place in September. Nine months later, after failing to extract a "confession" from Peter, Nero decided to make an example of the great apostles Peter and Paul (who I believe was already in prison by this time), ordering Paul beheaded (as he was a Roman citizen) and Peter crucified. At his request, the soldiers inverted the cross, knowing it would cause much agony. The traditional date of Peter's death is June 29.

Jean Leon Gerome – The Christian Martyrs' Last Prayer – 1860

Edward Armitage – The Christian Martyr – 1863

Appendix C

The Lives of the Apostles

Because the book of Acts ends with Paul's first imprisonment in Rome, the Scripture itself says nothing of how the apostles, save James the Greater, died. Nor do we read of their missions after leaving Jerusalem, except for Paul and a few scant hints in regard to Peter's whereabout found in his epistles. History, however, has said a great deal. The problem is that much of that history has become muddled by tradition and even legend.

Some stories appear hopelessly confused and even contradictory. Some stories place the apostle Philip in Asia while others place him in Africa. Some place Simon's death in the Middle East while others have him dying in England. What are we to make of such confusion? When faced with such evidence, I look at several things. First, were the names of different men conflated? Often the problems resolve themselves. Philip, for example, was the name of one of the elders in Acts, but it was also the name of an apostle. When these two became confused, so also the traditions became muddled. Second, how early or late were these traditions? Obviously medieval legends do not have as much merit as a first century tradition. Third, what is the source of the story? Legends differ significantly from history and even tradition. Some sources are far more reliable than others. Most importantly, does the tradition fit with the Bible? By examining all of these the lives and ministry of the apostles become more clear.

Here then is a brief summary of the apostles' lives after the Council of Jerusalem. Some are disputed, and rightly so, but in examining the evidence, a reasonable conclusion may be reached for all.

* When I began to write this appendix I soon found the wealth of material was far too vast to place in a single appendix, nor could I find a book which I felt sufficiently and fairly addressed all the evidences. To that end this appendix grew into my book, *The Aposltes After Jesus*. In this appendix I will summarize the evidence and conclusions that I made in that book, but for a thorough defense of my history please consult that book.

The Apostles After Christ

Not including Paul, the book of Acts records the acts and ministries of the apostles up until the Council of Jerusalem. After this council the lives of the other apostles grows silent. Only Paul is followed thereafter, and even then only up until his first imprisonment in Rome. Here then, presented in the likely order of their death, is the history of the apostles after they ventured out from Jerusalem.

James the Greater (44 A.D.)
James was the brother of John, and surnamed one of the "sons of Thunder." Some believe that he was the father of James the Less,[732] but there is neither Biblical support for this nor any historical support. He is the only apostle mentioned as having died in the Bible (Acts 12:1). He was a member of the "inner circle" and may have been the leader, if not spokesperson, for the apostles as he was singled out for execution. Herod Agrippa sought to strike at the church by hitting the apostles. Logically, he went after the leaders first. James was executed by decapitation, and Peter was arrested. This took place shortly before Passover, likely in March 44 A.D.

A fanciful, late, and unreliable legend claims that James was beckoned by a vision of the virin Mary to come to Spain sometime between Pentecost and his death.[733] Given that Mary was still living at this time, the late date of the legend, the lack of historical support, and the Biblical record itself (it was Paul who first ventured to the gentile lands) the story can be rejected out of hand. There is one interesting tradition regarding James's death, however. The second century church father Clement of Alexandria recorded that the man who had falsely accused James was so moved by his testimony and courage in the face of death that he converted to the faith himself and was executed alongside James, having received his forgiveness.[734] Whether the story is true or not cannot be said. We only know that James became the first apostle to be martyred sometime in March 44 A.D.

Philip (Circa 54 A.D.)
The history and traditions of Philip are the most confused of all the apostles. Some traditions place his ministry and death in Asia while others place him in Africa. The reasons for this will become clear.

Philip is scarcely mentioned in the first three gospels, but has a role in John's gospel. John says that he was from Bethsaida, from whence Andrew and Peter also came (John 1:44). Many believe that he was also a fisherman and a follower of John the Baptist,[735] although the Bible is not specific on either point. What is specific is that it was Philip who told the apparently skeptical Nathaniel Bartholomew about Jesus.

In the book of Acts a man named Philip is seen converting many Samaritans and the Ethiopian Eunuch (Acts 8). The problem is that many believe the Philip of Acts is a different Philip from Philip the apostle. This is in part because Acts 21:7 describes Philip the Evangelist as one of the seven deacons (Acts 21:7) who were appointed to oversee the welfare of the Church (Acts 6:3-5), but why would an apostle be called by the inferior title of deacon? If he were the apostle he would not be designated as "one of the seven" (Acts 21:9), but one of "the Twelve" (Acts 6:2).

If there were two Philips then the traditions of Philip found in history are clearly conflated. This fact allows us to trace common threads in these histories and separate them. For example, the traditions of Philip in Asia declare that the graves of his virgin daughters rest there to this day, but in the Bible it is Philip the Evangelist who had four virgin daughters, not Philip the Apostle (Acts 21:9). Other evidence led me to the conclusion that the Apostle Philip should be identified with the African tradition. The fact that he died early in the history of the apostles also explain the relative silence of him in tradition, for his missions were cut short.

Apparently Philip left Israel not too long after the Council of Jerusalem. I believe that he ventured to Carthage, Africa (in modern day Lybia). There he began to establish his mission in north-central Africa (Matthew was assigned north-eastern Africa and Simon north-western Africa). It is there that he encounted trouble with the Ebionites. The Ebionite sect was a cult which grew out of the Judaizers mentioned in Galatians 2 and elsewhere (cf. Acts 15:1). They believed that salvation was afforded through the law of Moses and that one could not be saved without circumcision. Consequently they rejected the results of the Council of Jerusalem and considered the apostles to be heretics. They accused Philip of requiring Jews to renounce Moses,[736] and stoned him to death sometime around 54 A.D.[737]

Nathanael Bartholomew (62 A.D.)
Bartholomew (בַּר-תַּלְמַי) is Aramaic for the Son of Tal'may. *Bar* (בַּר) means "son" in Aramaic (in Hebrew it is *ben* [בֵּן]). Bartholomew is, therefore, not his given name. John calls him Nathanael, which is another common name among the Jews, so it is natural that they might prefer to call him Bartholomew. With the possible exception of Philip there is no apostle whose post-Biblical history is so confusing and conflated as that of Bartholomew. He has been associated with Philip in Turkey, with a mission in Armenia, and even with India. Additionally, his martyrdom has been variously ascribed to crucifixion, flaying (skinning), and decapitation. Even the country of his death is variously attributed to Armenia or India.

In *The Apostles After Jesus* I gave my reasons for rejecting the association with Philip. I believe that Bartholomew headed east to Armenia, which lay between the Black Sea and the Caspian Sea. It is little wonder that Bartholomew became their parton saint. In fact, it is for that very reason that the later missions of Bartholomew were transferred by tradition back to Armenia. The evidence that the apostle died in Armenia is simply lacking. It is my opinion that because of his position as the father of the Armenian church the eastern church transplanted the deeds and martyrdom of Bartholomew to Armenia. However, it is clear that Bartholomew eventually left Armenia to minister in central India, perhaps intending to meet with Thomas (Thomas was the first to enter India – see notes below).

Like Armenia, the evidence that Bartholomew visited India is ancient and strong. In fact, the names of kings and governors of which are spoken in the apocryphal writings do correspond to India rulers of that time,[738] showing an intricate knowledge of local central Indian history which western traditions could not have had.[739] In any case, the evidence supports the fact that Bartholomew visited India, in what was the Satavahan empire,[740] on the west coast of central India, near modern day Mumbai (Bombay). He arrived around 60 A.D.[741] but his mission was relatively short lived as I concluded that Bartholomew incurred the wrath of king Aristakarman who was angered when he heard that the governor Pulumayi granted this new religious sect the freedom to criticize their gods. He apparently ordered the execution of both Pulumayi and Bartholomew in 62 A.D.[742] The manner of his execution was cruel and in accordance with eastern execution. Bartholomew was probably beaten, skinned (flayed), and then had his head placed on a pole to serve as a warning.[743]

James the Less (62 or 63 A.D.)
James the Less is called James the Just in history (see Acts 15:1-29 for a defense of this). He rose to prominence following the death of James the Greater and assumed the role of overseer of the church in Jerusalem. He was apparently the head of the Council of Jerusalem and at one time was a leader of the party of circumcision. Having repented of the error he delivered the final decision against requiring circumcision. After the council most of the apostles left for the mission field, but James remained in Jerusalem to oversee the church. He remained there (cf. Acts 21:18) until his martydom.

The Jewish rebellion which would result in the destruction of the Temple in 70 A.D. began in 66 A.D., but the atmosphere and tensions around Jerusalem had heightened significantly in the years before the actual revolt began. James is the only apostle explicitly described in Josephus, who records his death.[744] Other ancient chronologers and historians have also recorded what happened to James.[745] It is said that during the week of Passover Feast Jewish radicals ordered James to renounce Christ before all the people. James was placed atop the parapet walls of the Temple where all could see and hear, but instead of renouncing Jesus, he boldly proclaimed the gospel. In a rage they threw James down from the Temple walls, but he did not die so people immediately began to stone him to death, but the fatal blow came from a strike to the head with a club. Thus James was mercifully spared the War of the Jews, giving his life in testimony to Jesus. This took place during Passover week in either 62 or 63 A.D.

Simon Peter (65 A.D)
The life and death of Peter were treated in Appendix B because of its controversial nature. Thus I shall only repeat as much as it prudent in this context. Peter was a member of the inner circle and one of the spokesmen for the apostles. Tradition claims that after leaving Jerusalem he lived in Antioch Syria for seven years.[746] One thing is clear. From the Bible we know that Peter ministered the the churches in modern day Turkey; specifically the churches of Pontus, Galatia, Cappadocia, Bithynia, and the country called Asia (1 Peter 1:1).

Later Peter appears to have ventured to a place he called "Babylon." This "Babylon" was also the residence of John Mark (1 Peter 5:13) whom we know was in Rome at that time (cf. 2 Timothy 4:11; Philemon 1:24). The term "Babylon" had long been a byword for the decadence of Rome and the evidence is overwhelming that Peter traveled to Rome after Paul's first imprisonment ended, but not long after his arrival the infamous fire broke out in Rome on July 19, 64 A.D. Christians were falsely blamed and accused of crimes ranging from cannibalism to atheism and homosexuality.[747] Peter was arrested shortly thereafter and held prisoner where he was probably tortured in an attempt to exact a phony confession, as had been done to other Christians. During this time Paul too had been re-arrested. Nine months after Peter's arrest Nero decided to make a spectacle of his captives. Paul, being a citizen of Rome, was beheaded whereas Peter and his wife were dragged out to the Appian Way. Peter bid his wife farewell (she may have been executed before his very eyes) and was crucified upside down. This probably took place on June 29, 65 A.D.

Paul (65 A.D.)
As with Peter I addressed Paul's life and death previously (see notes under "The Appeal to Caesar - Acts 28:16-31"). Thus I will offer a brief summary and conclusion here.

Paul was the most influential of all the apostles, and yet he was not an apostle in the beginning. In fact, he persecuted Christians and condoned their executions. With all the zeal and fervor of a fanatic he hunted down Christians until he himself became a convert. From that day forward Paul used all the zeal he once used to hunt Christians and diverted it to spreading the gospel. The book of Acts recounts most of his journeys but ends with Paul still in prison and awaiting trial. He was later released, but some might wonder why the demonic Nero would have released Paul at all. The answer is found in heistory for Nero first became emperor he was still a boy of sixteen years.[748] His chief advisor was a famed stoic philosopher named Seneca who had been appointed the young emperor's tutor. It was Seneca who handled all the affairs of state until 62 A.D. when Nero forced Seneca to retire.[749] It was after Seneca's forced retirement that Nero became the tyrant of history.

Now of Paul's post-imprisonment life there is more said than perhaps even of Peter. As I attested previously, I believe that Paul spend the next two years building up the churches of Asia Minor and fulfilling his wish to visit Spain. It probably in Spain where Paul first hear of the fire in Rome and of the plight of the Roman church. Perhaps as a father loves his son, so Paul desired to return to Rome to help the church. There he was arrested and imprisoned a second time. This time there would be no acquittal.

Most all agree that Paul was decapitated by Nero just outside Rome on the road to Ostia. Although there is debate as the exact year of his death, I concluded in *The Apostles After Jesus* that he died the same year, and even the same day, as Peter just as the most ancient tradition recounts.[750] This was June 29, 65 A.D.

Matthias (69 or 70 A.D.)
Although the traditions of Matthias are conflated with those of Matthew and perhaps another disciple, I have concluded that he was one of the few apostles who remained in Jerusalem and most probably served as an elder at the Church of Jerusalem until the seige of Jerusalem by Rome when Jewish rebels martyred him and tightened their grip upon the beseiged city.[751]

Andrew (69 or 70 A.D.)
Andrew served in Asia minor near the Black Sea. He most probably traveled in a circle around the Black Sea, thus becoming the first apostle to venture into the southern portions of modern day Ukraine and Russia outside the bounds of the ancient Roman empire. For that reason he is honored as the patron saint of Russia. However, he moved back down south of the Black Sea and continued his ministry in Asia Minor.

Eventually he moved to modern day Greece where he ministered in cities like Corinth, Philippi, Sparta, and Megara.[752] Presumeably Andrew was in Philippi when the Neronian persecutions began in Rome.[753] Despite what some revisionist historians claim, the persecutions were not restricted to Rome, although the majority of persecution was concentrated there. Nero was not popular with the regional governors, but most killed some Christians in order to appease the emperor, lest they be accused of neglecting their duty. Peter and Paul were not the only apostles to die under Nero, but they were the only ones to die in Rome. Andrew, however, appears to have escaped death under Nero, although just barely. History records that he died only a year (some say two years) after Nero's suicide.

Finally Andrew made his way down to southern Greece in the city of Patrae (or Patras), in what was then the country of Achaia. There he converted the wife and brother-in-law of the regional governor Ægeates. This much seems certain as the story is repeated often by various different sources. When we discount the normal embellishments of the various stories, we are left with the same basic facts which no serious historians have rejected. Ægeates, in revenge for the conversion of his wife, ordered Andrew to recant his teachings or suffer upon the cross.[754] Refusing to do so, Andrew was fastened upon a cross with ropes, so that he would not bleed to death. This was done to prolong the agony and give wild animals a chance to feast upon him while he yet lived. The cross itself was of the "X" shape, thus it has become known as "St. Andrew's cross."[755] It is said that he lingered on the cross for three and a half days before dying on the night of November 30.[756] His last words are said to have been, "O cross, most welcome and long looked for,"[757] thus embracing his martyrdom.

Thomas (70 A.D.)

Thomas has been called the "Apostle to the Orient."[758] He traveled more extensively than any other apostle, even to south India where he is to this very day considered the father of the Indian church. The dominant Christian sect in India is even called the *Mar Thoma* Church, from the Hebrew *Thoma* (Thomas). Although there is debate as to some of the traditions of Thomas, there is no doubt in my mind that he founded the church in Kerala, South India.

With the exceptions of Peter, Paul, and possibly John, there is more said of Thomas than other apostle. The wealth of information is doubtless because he was so well traveled. I refer to the reader to my *Apostles After Jesus* for an extensive debate. Nonetheless, if my conclusions are accurate then Thomas was assigned the land east of Jerusalem. He set out first to the tiny kingdom of Osroene in ancient Mesopotamia and moved into Parthia.[759] The ancient countries of Carmania, Hyrcania, Bactria, Media, and Persia all reside in modern day Iraq and Iran. Each of these Thomas stopped in en route to India. Although he probably did not spend more than four to six months in any of those countries, he planted the seeds of the faith and founded churches before resuming his journey. Eventually he found his way into parts of Afghanistan and Pakistan in ancient northern India.

If traditions are the believed then Thomas converted a king Gundaphorus of ancient Indo-Parthia. One thing is certain. The historicity of king Gundaphorus was verified in the nineteenth century when ancient first century coins bearing his name were discovered.[760] Moreover, history records that the Kushan empire overran Indo-Parthia in the early 50s, conquering much of northern India.[761] This is the same time that Thomas would have left to venture into south India. It would also explain the erroneous legends that Thomas brought the gospel to Peking, China for the Kushans were Chinese and had doubtless heard the gospel from Thomas's disciples whom he left behind in Indo-Parthia.

The strongest evidence revolves around Thomas's arrival in Kerala, South India in 52 A.D. He embarked on a ship from a northern India port in modern day Pakistan and bypassed central India, heading to Malabar, Kerala where a Jewish trade community resided. This was Thomas's ultimate destination and he was to spend the rest of his life in south India. That Thomas did indeed minister in Kerala is strongly supported not only by a multitude of traditions and histories, but also to an extent in archaeology. For example, it is well known that Pallivaanavar, a mid-second century king of Kerala, was a Christian.[762] Since Christian missionaries (aside from Thomas) did not arrive in India until the end of the second century, it is apparent that the gospel had already been brought sometime before the Pallivaanavar. Moreover, when the second century the missionary Pantaeus arrived in India, expecting to be the first to bring the gospel he was shocked to find a large Christian community there who had a copy of Matthew's gospel, but no other. This again fits perfectly with Thomas for at the time the apostles left Israel only the gospel of Matthew had been written.[763] So Thomas would have brought the gospel of Matthew with him, but no other New Testament book. The appearance of that gospel and no other then supports a missionary who had left Israel before the other New Testament writings had been produced.

Now Thomas served in south India until his death. According to various sources was working in what is today Mylapore, Chennai, in the state of Tamil Nadu, India. Being advanced in age he finally settled down there. Various traditions and legends surround his death near a cave in what is today called "St. Thomas Mound" in Chennai, India.[764] Although there are three differing accounts of his martyrdom they all share some things in common which may be taken as true. In all accounts Thomas dies by spears in modern Chennai, India. This took place in 70 A.D.

Thus Thomas has often been called the "Apostle to the Orient." He is credited founding the church in India and to this very day the church of *Mar Thoma* is named after him. Surely "Apostle to India" is a more fitting title than the unfair epithet "Doubting Thomas" for the man who ventured further than any apostle.

Matthew Levi (70 or 71 A.D.)
The traditions of Matthew are among the most conflated and confusing of the apostles, but at the same time there is a strong indication in all that Matthew became the apostle to Egypt and Ethiopia.[765]

After completing the first gospel in Hebrew while in Israel, Matthew was sent out to minister in northeastern Africa. Clement of Alexandria said that Matthew left Israel fifteen years after Pentecost.[766] Allowing for a year error, this means that Matthew moved to Egypt the same year as the Council of Jerusalem in 49 A.D. While ministering in Egypt it is also believed that he later translated his own gospel into Greek for the African people. Eventually, he ventured down to Ethiopia presumeably to visit with the Ethiopian Eunuch of Acts 8. Tradition says that the eunuch served under Queen Candace, which is probably the historical Queen Kandake who ruled Ethiopia from 40-50 A.D.[767] Having been set free after her death, the eunuch ministered in and around Ethiopia. It is probable that he and Matthew met many times and worked with one another over the years.

In time Christianity fell out of favor in the court of Ethiopia. After working in Egypt and Ethiopia for twenty-three years Matthew was apparently assassinated around 70 or 71 A.D.

Judas Thaddeaus (72 A.D.)
Judas Lebbæus was surnamed Thaddæus to distinguish him from the other Judas. As with some other apostles tradition conflates different disciples, creating conflicting stories. However, it does appear that the following can be said with a fair degree of certainty.

Thaddæus was one of three apostles sent east beyond the borders of the Roman empire. He first ventured to Edessa in ancient Mesopotamia, in the kingdom of Osroene, where he allegedly converted the king Abgar (V) the Black. The legends surrounding this are unreliable, but it does seem that Abgar favored Christianity in his kingdom which led to the hostility and hatred of his son Abgar VI. In any case, Thaddæus left a thriving church behind in Edessa as he set out to preach the gospel throughout Mesopotamia and parts of Parthia.

Now Abgar VI became king in 71 A.D.[768] According to tradition "there arose one of [Abgar the Black's] contumacious sons, who was not favorable to peace" and began to persecute the church.[769] The evidence clearly make this son Abgar VI who persecuted Christians in his kingdom. He had writen the king of Parthia and warned him of the intrusion of a "foreign" religion in his land.[770] That religion was that of Christ. Apparently, Thaddæus was one of his first victims. We do know the circumstances of Thaddæus's arrest and differing accounts have been presented as to his manner of death, but it would seem that he was crucified.[771]

Simon the Zealot (74 A.D.)
The first part of Simon's history is very well established. The last part of his history is anything but. What is established with credibility is that Simon was one of the three apostles assigned to Roman Africa. Since Matthew was minsitering in northeastern Africa and Philip had gone to northcentral Africa, Simon set out as far as modern day Morocco. He traveled across north Africa to Cyrene (Libya), the country called Africa, and Mauritania. It was probably in the mid to late 50s that Simon had to face a choice. Where was he to go next?

It is at this point that various traditions emerge. Conflating Simon the Zealot with Simon Cleopas and others (Simon was a very common name), traditions variously have Simon returning to Israel, venturing into Parthia with Thaddæus, or being the first to bring the gospel to the isle of Great Britain.

Now most scholars automatically reject the Great Britain tradition. This is because the historic struggle of Christianity in Britain is well documented. The pagan Druids and later Saxons, among others, barbarically persecuted Christians and at various times drove it from the island except for small pockets.[772] Of course this does not mean that missionaries never went there. On the contrary, archaeology has confirmed that there were churches in Britain as early as the second century, and possibly even earlier.[773]

Having outlined the evidence and my conclusions in another book,[774] I will again state my conclusions. I reject the stories of Simon in the east as a conflation with other disciples named Simon. Simon the Zealot was at the far west of Africa and the known world. If he did not go back to Israel, there was only one place for him to go and that was the Roman colony of Britain. It would be a journey from which Simon would never return.

Not long after Simon arrived in Britain and began to establish churches Britain was in revolt against Rome. Around 60 A.D. Nero seized Queen Boadicea's land and had her daughters raped and tortured.[775] The Queen then started a revolt which was to begin a war which would last for more than two decades after her death. Simon had a choice. He could leave or he could stay, but if he stayed he would be considered a traitor to Rome. He could never go home. I believe he chose to stay with his flock in Britain and there he remained for almost fifteen years until he was apprehended and crucified by Romans as an enemy of Rome around 74 A.D.[776]

John (101-106 A.D.)

The "beloved" apostle is the only apostle who did not die a martyr's death, although he did not escape torture. Of him more has been said than almost any other apostle and yet some modern scholars attempt to rewrite his post-Biblical history for suspect theological reasons.[777]

There seems no doubt that John went to Asia minor and nursed all the churches therein. He resided at Ephesus, which he made his home, and traveled to the nearby churches in Asia minor to oversee their care and instruction. According to his second generation disciple Irenaeus, he resided there until the time of Trajan,[778] with the exception of his exile to Patmos during the reign of Domitian. Some credit him with founding of the churches in Smyrna, Pergamos, Sardis, Philadelphia, Laodicea, and Thyratira,[779] but others say he merely took over the "orphaned" churches that Paul had established.[780] Given the allusion in Acts 16:6 (see notes there) I believe it is possible that John founded many of these churches. In any case, he certainly served them until the time of Domitian in the late 90s.

It is the *universal* opinion of the ancients that it was Domitian, and no other, who exiled John to Patmos. The circumstances as to how this came to be are also quite credible. When Domitian began to persecute Christians he sought out the only living apostle, John. John was arrested and brought to Rome where Domitian set in boiling oil, but John survived. Now according to ancient Roman custom, no prisoner who had survived a failed execution could be executed, for he was deemed to have been favored by the gods. Consequently, John was sent to exile in Patmos where he wrote the book of Revelation (so says the apostle himself, Revelation 1:9).

After Domitian's death John was released and returned to Ephesus. There he stayed until his death at a ripe old age. Some legends claim that John was raptured like Elijah of old.[781] Another legend relates the story that John, though buried, is but asleep awaiting the day that he would be awakened before the Second Coming in Last Days.[782] Thus John, it is said, is like a sort of ancient Rip Van Winkle who will awaken centuries later and will thus be alive when Jesus returns. These theories arise from John 21:23 in which ironically John makes clear that he did not believe the legends that he was not to die.

The year of John's death is disputed. Some place it in 101 A.D. while others place it 106 A.D.[783] He was probably over ninety years of age when he died at peace in Ephesus.[784]

The Apostles' Companions

There are many companions and disciples left behind by the apostles. We know that many died martyrs in the early persecuted church. It is said that their blood was the seed of the church.[785] Here is a brief summary of what we know about twenty-five of the apostles' companions who are mentioned in the Bible. Countless more died for their faiths and bear the crown of life (Revelation 2:10).

Andronicus was a prisoner along with Paul, probably during his imprisonment and trial before the proconsul Sergius Paulus of Cyprus around 47 or 48 A.D. Hippolytus, the early church father, calls Andronicus one of the seventy (Luke 10:1),[786] and a bishop of Pannonia,[787] which was a region corresponding to the area where Hungary, Croatia, Bosnia, and Serbia meet. According to the early martyrologists Andronicus died under Nero's persecution.[788]

Antipas is mentioned by the apostle John, wherein the Lord Himself calls him "My witness, My faithful one, who was killed among you" (Revelation 2:13). This testimony alone is strong enough. From this we know that Antipas served in the chuch of Pergamum, which is modern day Aeolis, Turkey. We also know that he died a martyr's death worthy of the Lord's mention in Revelation. According to the early martyrologists his manner of death was particularly cruel. It is said that he was sealed in a bronze idol and cooked to death. This took place approximately 95 A.D. during the early phase of Domitian's persecution,[789] probably about the same time John was arrested and brought to Rome.

Aquila and Priscilla (or Prisca) were a husband and wife team mentioned six times in the Bible They were Jews expelled from Rome during the time of Claudius (Acts 18:2). Having traveled to Greece from there they met and became close friends and associates of Paul. Apparently they returned to Rome by the time of Paul's epistle (Romans 16:1). Early sources are conflicted in whether or not they died under Nero[790] or survived to accompany Luke on his journeys.[791] Personally, I believe that as leaders in the church of Rome they did not escape Nero's wrath and died in Rome under Nero's terrible persecution as many traditions hold.

Aristarcus was one of Paul's "traveling companions from Macedonia" (Acts 19:29) who was a prisoner with Paul on the journey to Rome (27:2; cf. Colossians 4:10). Tradition ascibes to him the title of overseer at Thessalonica for some time after this,[792] and he is also called one of the seventy by

Hippolytus.[793] Later he is said to have been found in Rome, captured by Nero's men and fed to the lions in the arena.[794]

Barnabas, who real name was Joseph (Acts 4:36) is probably the most famous of Paul's associates. It was he who defended Paul before the apostles (9:27) and accompanied him on his first missionary journey. However, because of the fallout between Mark and Paul, Barnabas chose to accompany Mark rather than Paul when he set out on his second missionary journey (15:38-39). From there they set out to Cyprus. There Barnabas and John Mark ministered the gospel for some years. According to tradition they received copies of the newly written gospel of Matthew,[795] probably around 48 A.D. Some time after this a wicked man named Barjesus "was enraged, and brought together all the multitude of the Jews; and they having laid hold of Barnabas ... took Barnabas by night, and bound him with a rope by the neck; and having dragged him to the hippodrome from the synagogue, and having gone out of the city, standing round him, they burned him with fire, so that even his bones became dust."[796] John Mark is said to have escaped along with Timon (cf. Acts 6:5) and fled to Egypt.

Barsabbas, whose given name was Joseph, also had another nickname, being Justus. This Joseph Justus Barsabas has often been confused with Barnabas by some church fathers, but they are clearly different individuals. This Barsabbas was one of the two put forward as a replacement for Judas Iscariot (Acts 1:23). He was probably one of the seventy (Luke 10:1) and acording to Hippolytus he served as the overseer of Eleutheropolis,[797] twenty miles southwest of Jerusalem, and about ten miles west of Hebron. Beyond this we know nothing of Barsabbas save Papias's matter of fact statement that he was forced to drink poison but suffered no harm (cf. Mark 16).[798]

Next we come to Carpus who is found in 2 Timothy 4:13. He was allegedly was one of the seventy who served as the bishop or overseer of either Troas[799] or Berytus in Thracia.[800] Given that his only appearance in the Bible is when Paul asks Timothy to "bring the cloak which I left at Troas with Carpus" (2 Timothy 4:13) it seems more likely that Carpus was overseer there in Troas, on the coastal city of modern day Turkey. We do not know any specifics about his death save that he died a martyr in Troas, quite probably during the Neronian persecutions.[801]

Indich, or Fudich, is the name tradition ascribes to the Ethiopian Eunuch.[802] According to tradition he was a court official under Queen Candace which corresponds to Queen Kandake of history who reigned from 40-50 A.D.[803] Upon her death Indich probably became a free man due to his prominent position and set out to preach the gospel in Arabia Felix (Saudi Arabia) and one of the many tiny islands off the coast of Ethiopia in the Red Sea, called Caprobano or Ceylon. Today it called the Dahlak Archipelago in the country of Eritrea. There he is said to have been martyred in circa 110 A.D.[804]

John Mark originally sailed to Cyprus with his cousin Barnabas. However, after the martyrdom of Barnabas he fled the island and went to Alexandria Egypt. There he is credited with founding the church of Alexandria[805] and ministering to "the whole of Inner Egypt."[806] By this time Matthew had probably already moved into Ethiopia. In any case Mark eventually left the church of Alexandria in the hands of a certain Eumenes,[807] and returned to work with Peter, with whom he is said to have written the gospel of Mark,[808] probably around 60 A.D. Eventually he appeared in Rome with Paul during his first imprisonment. Although some traditions say that Mark died in the eighth year of Nero, others place his death many decades later under the persecutions of Trajan in the early second century. Since the eighth year of Nero would actually be before the persecutions began, I concluded, for various reasons, that the alternate traditions are true. Namely, that Mark eventually returned to Alexandria and served there until the time of Trajan when he was fastened with hooks and dragged to his place of execution where he was to be burned alive.[809]

Jude, the brother of James, is sometimes confused with the apostle or a brother of Jesus. In fact, he was probably neither and most likely the brother of James the Less. His epistle was probably among the last to be written after the death of many of the apostles. We know little of his life except that he resided in Jerusalem until the War of the Jews forced him to relocate to Lebannon where he would die of old age decades later.

Linus is mentioned in 2 Timothy 4:21 as a companion of Paul in Rome. It is he whom all the ancient church fathers call the first overseer, or bishop, of Rome. As discussed in the previous appendix, I am of the opinion that he too died a martyr under Nero in 67 A.D. as early traditions claim.

Along with Barnbas and Mark, no companion is as well known as Luke the physician (Colossians 4:14) and historian who wrote the gospel of Luke and the book of Acts. He probably wrote both during the four years of Paul's first imprisonment in both Jerusalem and in Rome. He alone was with Paul at the end of his life (2 Timothy 4:11). If tradition is to be believed then he began his own ministry in Macedonia after the death of Paul.[810] He is also said to have minstered in Byzantium and Thrace,[811] although his later tradition is not as certain. In any case, he was preaching in Greece when the persecution of Domitian began and an edict against Christians was passed throughout the whole empire. Then, at age eighty-four, in 93 A.D., Luke was hung by the neck upon an olive tree until dead.[812]

Nicanor was one of the seven deacons of Acts 6:5. We know that he died a martyr, but no early traditions give specific information. Later tradition claims that he died under the persecution of Paul which followed.[813]

Onesimus, mentioned in Philemon, became an overseer at Ephesus and was stoned to death under Trajan in 111 A.D.[814]

Onesiphorus is mentioned as a friend of Paul who was not ashamed to be seen with the prisoner when he was awaiting his execution (2 Timothy 1:16). Hippolytus called him a bishop, overseer, of Corone,[815] or Colophon, not far from Ephesus in Asia. Apparently his affection for Paul in chains did not escape the eyes of Rome. Sometime after returning to Asia he was arrested by the governor who had him scourged and then tied to wild horses which were unleashed. Thereupon he was dragged to death.[816]

Parmenas was another of the seven deacons (Acts 6:5). Of him we know almost nothing except that he is alleged to have been overseer in a city called Soli,[817] whose location today we can only guess. It is further said that he died a martyr, although the time and manner of his death also remain a mystery.[818]

Philip the Evangelist has often been confused with the apostle, but this Philip was one of the seven deacons (Acts 6:5; 15:2, 4, 6, 22-23; 16:4) and probably the one who converted the Ethiopian Eunuch.[819] He appears to have settled in Hierapolis of Asia with his four prophetess daughters (Acts 21:9).[820] Having separated the various conflated traditions I believe that Philip lived and worked in Asia Minor until the time of Domitian. Then, about the same time that John was arrested and brought to Rome, Philip was crucified upside down.[821]

Prochorus was another of the seven deacons of Acts 6:5. He is counted as one of the seventy and called an overseer of the church in Nicomedia, Bithynia[822] which is about fifty miles east of modern day Istabul, Turkey. Curiously though, Hippolytus says that he "was the first that departed, believing together with his daughters."[823] Perhaps he meant that Prochorus was among the first to leave for foreign missions. Prochorus is also said to be a nephew of Stephen and a companion of the apostle John.[824] He is said to have died under the persecutions of Nero in Antioch.[825]

Rufus is mentioned in Romans 16:13 as being at Rome. It is probable that this Rufus is the same son of Simon of Cyrene (Mark 15:21), as his mother was dear to Paul (Romans 16:13). Polycarp mentions Rufus, and a certain Zosimus, along with Ignatius and Paul as leaders of the church in Asia.[826] Hippolytus calls him one of the seventy and the overseer of Thebes, Greece near Corinth.[827] The evidence leads me to believe that both Rufus and Zosimos were beheaded in Philippi during the persecution of Trajan around 109 A.D.[828]

Silas, the prophet (Acts 15:32), travelled with Paul in his second journey. He had been chosen by the apostles to accompany Paul along with a Judas Barsabbas (Acts 15:22). Tradition says that Silas was scourged and suffered many other tortures before finally meeting his death, which was apparently either at the very end of Nero's persecutions or shortly thereafter.[829]

Simon Cleopas was a brother of James the Just (Mark 6:3) and probably one of Jesus's cousins. Early testimony makes him the second overseer of Jerusalem after the death of James the Just, his brother.[830] However, he must have spent the first part of his bishopry in exile, as Jerusalem was under seige by Rome. After the fall of Jerusalem, however, he was allowed to return to the occupied city where he lived a long and fruitful life until the reign of Trajan. This Trajan sought not only to erradicate Christians, but also Jews and specifically the entire lineage of King David. As a member of all three, Simeon was a prime target by Atticus, the Roman procurator, and crucified[831] about 109 A.D.[832]

Timon was another of the seven deacons (Acts 6:5) and one of the seventy. According to the *Acts of Barnabas*, considered largely historical, he joined Barnabas and Mark in Cyprus where he was taken ill. Soon after recovering they began to distribute Matthew's gospel. When Barnabas was martyred, he fled Cyprus along with Mark and went to Alexandria.[833] From there he appears to have moved to Nabatæa, which was a country then engulfing all of the Arabian peninsula, most of Jordan, and southern Syria of today. There he appears to have become the overseer of Bostra, in southern Syria, east of Israel.[834] According to Dorotheus, he was burned alive, becoming one of the six deacons known to have died a martyr.[835]

Timothy whom Paul called one like a son (1 Timothy 1:18; 2 Timothy 1:2) accompanied Paul on his second and third missionary journeys and was the last man Paul wrote before his death. Tradition claims that Timothy served as overseer at Ephesus for fifteen years,[836] but give conflictings dates for his death. All we know for certain is that he was stoned to death for the faith.[837]

Finally we come to Trophimus who is Trophimus is mentioned three times in the Bible (Acts 20:4; 21:29; 2 Timothy 4:20). He is considered to be among the seventy and is said to have been beheaded alongside Paul.[838]

These are the companions of the apostles of whom we know the most. Many others left a legacy which the Lord will honor in heaven, and whose fruits laid the groundwork for the church. The following pages offer concise charts on the apostles and their companions and where they ministered and died.

The Apostles

Apostle	Ministry	Modern Equivalent	Death
James the Greater	Judea	Israel	Executed in 44 A.D.
Philip	Carthage	Tunisia & Northern Africa	Stoned in 54 A.D.
James the Less	Overseer of Jerusalem	Jerusalem, Israel	Thrown from temple parapet and stoned, on Passover 62 or 63 A.D.
Simon Peter	The greater Roman Empire including Italy	Turkey, Greece, and Italy	Crucified upside down in Rome in 65 A.D
Paul	Throughout the Roman Empire	Turkey, Greece, Italy, & Spain	Beheaded near Rome under Nero in 65 A.D.
Matthias	Judea	Israel	Martyred in 69 or 70 A.D.
Matthew	Egypt and Ethiopia	Egypt and Ethiopia	Assassinated circa 70 A.D.
Thomas	Moved eastward into Parthia, Carmania, Hyrcania, Bactria, Media, Persia, Indo-Parthia, and India	Iran, Turkmenistan, Afghanistan, Pakistan, Kashmir, and India	Martyred in Chennai, India around 70 A.D.
Andrew	Bithynia, Pontus, Thracia, Moesia, Scythia, Armenia, Cappodocia, Greece, & Achaia	Turkey, Greece, and all countries by the Black Sea	Crucified in 70 A.D.
Bartholomew	Armenia, Mesopotamia, Parthia, and India	Syria, Turkey, Armenia, Azerbaijan, Iran, and India	Martyred in Mumbai, India around 70 A.D.
Judas Thaddæus	Syria, Osroene, Mesopotamia, and Persia	Syria, Armenia, Iraq, and Iran	Crucified in 72 A.D.
Simon the Zealot	Cyrenaica, Africa, Mauretania, & Britainnia	North Africa and Great Britain	Crucified in England around 74 A.D.
John	Asia Minor	Turkey	The only apostle to die a natural death in Ephesus in 101 or possibly 106 A.D.

The Apostles' Companions

Disciple	Ministry	Modern Equivalent	Death
Barnabas	Syria, Lycia, Galatia, & Cyprus	Syria, Turkey, and Cyprus	Burned alive in Cyprus around 55 A.D.
Epaphas	Unknown	Unknown	Slain under Nero around 65 A.D.
Trophimus	Unknown	Unknown	Beheaded alongside Paul in 65 A.D.
Andronicus	Pannonia	Hungary, Croatia, Bosnia, and Serbia	Slain under Nero between 65 and 68 A.D.
Aquila	Italy, Greece, and Macedonia, and Asia Minor	Italy, Turkey, Greece, and Macedonia	Slain under Nero between 65 and 68 A.D.
Aristarchus	Greece, Italy, and possibly Macedonia	Greece, Italy, and possibly Macedonia	Fed to lions between 65 and 68 A.D.
Carpus	Thracia and Asia Minor	Turkey and possibly Bulgaria or even Romania	Slain under Nero between 65 and 68 A.D.
Prochorus	Asia Minor	Turkey	Slain under Nero between 65 and 68 A.D.
Priscilla (Prisca)	Italy, Greece, and Macedonia, and Asia Minor	Italy, Turkey, Greece, and Macedonia	Slain under Nero between 65 and 68 A.D.
Linus	Italy	Italy	Probably martyred under Nero in 67 A.D.
Onesiphorus	Asia Minor	Turkey	Dragged to death under Nero
Silas	Asia Minor, Greece, and Macedonia	Turkey, Greece, and Macedonia	Scourged and martyred under Nero's reign before 68 A.D.
Timothy	Asia Minor, Greece, and Macedonia	Turkey, Greece, and Macedonia.	Stoned to death.

The Apostles' Companions cont.

Disciple	Ministry	Modern Equivalent	Death
Jude	Judea, Samaria, Galilee, and Lebannon	Israel and Lebannon	Probably died of natural causes at a ripe old age.
Justus Barsabbas	Judea	Israel	Unknown
Timon	Cyprus, Egypt, and Nabataea	Cyprus, Egypt, Jordan, and Syria	Burned alive.
Luke	Asia Minor, Greece, Macedonia, and Thracia	Turkey, Macedonia, Greece, and possibly Bulgaria	Hung on an olive tree around 93 A.D.
Antipas	Asia Minor	Turkey	Sealed in a bronze idol and cooked alive about 95 A.D.
Philip the Evangelist	Asia Minor	Turkey	Crucified upside down, probably under Domitian.
John Mark	Asia Minor, Cyprus, Egypt, Italy, and possibly Illyricum	Turkey, Italy, Cyprus, and Egypt, with the possibly of Albania and Greece	Possibly dragged and burned in Alexandria in Trajan's time.
Rufus	Italy, Greece	Italy, Greece	Beheaded in 109 A.D. under Trajan.
Simeon Cleopas	Judea	Israel	Tortured and martyred about 109 A.D.
Indich (aka Fudich)	Ethiopia, the Arabia Felix, and Ceylon	Ethiopia, Saudi Arabia, and Eritrea	Martyred circa 110 A.D.
Dionysius	Unknown	Unknown	Martyred, possibly under Trajan circa 111 A.D.
Onesimus	Asia Minor	Turkey	Stoned around 111 A.D.

Appendix D

The Authenticity of the New Testament

Having established that the New Testament is based on historical fact, the next logical question is whether or not the New Testament is a faithful transmission of the followers of Jesus or whether or not they are either late forgeries or alterations of the original texts.

Having addressed the issue of authenticity in the introduction of each gospel it is not my intention to repeat what all but the most liberal or atheistic of critics deny; that the disciples of Christ were indeed the authors of the gospels which bear their name. Rather I will discuss whether or not the original writings of the authors have been changed or altered and the formation of the Canon of the New Testament.

* This Appendix is the same as that found in *Controversies in the Gospels* and *Controversies in the Epistles*. It is reproduced here for those who do not have or have not read those volumes.

The Canon of the New Testament

The internet and books like *The DaVinci Code* have served to promote some absurd myths about the Bible and Christianity. One of those myths is the idea that the Bible somehow relates to the time of Constantine the Great. In fact, nothing could be further from the truth. The Bible had long been established, accepted, and canonized before Constantine was ever born. In fact, "the Council of Nicea did not address the issue of canonicity"[839] for that issue had long been settled.

The "canon" is a term used to represent those books which have been recognized as the authoritative Word of God. Other books, while they may be instructive, useful, or historical, are not considered canon. Only those books in the canon are considered to be the infallible Word of God. So the question is, how did the canon come to be? As aforementioned, the Council of Nicea had *nothing* to do with the canon, because it was accepted centuries earlier. Let us look at the debate and the facts.

The Acceptance of the Canon
The primary questions concerning the canon are "when" and "how." We will begin with "when." As already mentioned, some attempt to argue that the canon was never settled until the time of Constantine. Even some evangelical publishers have blindly published books by "scholars" who argue for a late canon date based on suspect arguments. Lee Martin McDonald, for example,

sites ancient authors who may have rejected part of the canon (even as some do today) or perhaps even accepted other books (even as the Mormons and others do today).[840] Furthermore, if a church father quoted from an apocryphal book (see below) he *assumes* that the church father accepted it as canon.[841] He nowhere proves this assumption. Others argue that it was the Council of Laodicea in 363 A.D. which settled the canon.[842]

Now some might wonder how this is a controversy at all. Either the books are in the Bible or they are not! Right? Wrong. "Books" was we know them today did not exist in antiquity. They used scrolls which were kept separate. A scroll could obviously be only so large. No one denies that all twenty-seven books of the New Testament existed in the early church, but so did many other books. Since "books," in the traditional sense of the word, did not exist until Constantine's time, it is easy for some to dishonestly argue that the canon did not exist until Constantine's time. However, the facts invalidates these claims.

As early as the second century we have a list of the canonical books. The discovery of the Muratorian canon in the nineteenth century demonstrated that the canon had most likely been accepted by the time of its composition, circa 170 A.D.[843] Nevertheless, there are some problems with the Muratorian canon. For one thing the manuscript is damaged and so the first two books of the canon are not visible. However, the gospel of Luke is explicitly said to be the third gospel, indicating that Matthew and Mark were the first two gospels.[844] Additionally, Hebrews, James, 1 and 2 Peter, and 3 John appear to be omitted.[845] Still, some believe that they may have been in the document; its fragmentary nature being evidence that the books *could* have been listed.[846] Alternately, the Muratorian canon includes the Wisdom of Solomon (an apocryphal Old Testament book) as among the canon of the New Testament.[847] Consequently, some critics use these discrepancies as evidence that the canon was not settled.

The irony of the critics is their inate ability to contradict themselves. Consider that one author admits that there was "wide agreement"[848] on the Scriptures under Diocletian's persecutions, but then goes on to claim that the canon dates to the time of Eusebius[849] (a contemporary of Constantine). Of course, how could he deny that the Scriptures were not already "widely" agreed upon, for the emperor Diocletian not only persecuted Christians but actively sought to find and destroy "all copies of the Bible."[850] To this end Christians were tortured until they revealed where their copies were hidden. Obviously, one cannot search out and destroy copies of the Scriptures if there was no Biblical canon!

The fact is that from earliest time the church fathers refer to the "Scripture"[851] of New Testament authors. All twenty-seven books of the New Testament are cited *as* Scritpure by one or more of the fathers. The following chart shows all the major Uncials (complete "books" of the Bible, as opposed to individual scrolls popular in the early days of Christianity), apostolic fathers, and ante-Nicean church fathers (those who preceded Constantine and the Council of Nicea) who quote a specific book *as* Scripture. It is noteworthy that just because a church father did not quote a book does not mean that the book was not a part of Scripture. I, for example, did not quote from Titus in this book, and yet it is a part of Scripture. Nevertheless, the citations should prove that there was uniformity upon the canon from the earliest of times. I have also included those apocryphal books which are not a part of Scripture, but appear to be quoted as such from a few fathers (this will be explained in a section below). A more detailed explanation of the chart and its implications will follow.

Biblical Book	Primary Uncials	Books Quoted as Scripture Apostpolic Fathers	Ante-Nicean Church Fathers
Matthew	ℵ / A / B / C / D	Cl / Ba / Δ / Ig P / Ir / CA / M	J / Hp / Cy / N / M / T / L Mu
Mark	ℵ / A / B / C / D	Cl / Δ / Ig / P / Ir CA / M	J / Hp / Cy / N / M / T / L Mu
Luke	ℵ / A / B / C / D	Cl / Δ / Ig / P / Ir CA / M	J / Hp / Cy / N / M / T / L Mu
John	ℵ / A / B / C / D	Cl / Ba / H / Ig Ir / CA / M	J / Hp / Cy / N / M / T / L Mu
Acts	ℵ / A / B / C / D	Cl / Δ / H / Ig / P Ir / CA / M	J / Hp / Cy / N / M / T / L Mu
Romans	ℵ / A / B / C / D	Ba / Δ / Ig / P / Ir / CA / O / M	J / Hp / Cy / N / M / T / L Mu
1 Corinthians	ℵ / A / B / C / D	Di / Δ / H / Ig P / Ir / CA / O / M	J / Hp / Cy / N / M / T / L Mu
2 Corinthians	ℵ / A / B / C / D	Di / P / Ir / CA O / M	Hp / Cy / N / M / T / L Mu
Galatians	ℵ / A / B / C / D	Ig / P / Ir / CA O / M	J / Hp / Cy / N / M / T / L Mu
Ephesians	ℵ / A / B / C / D	Di / Ig / P / Ir CA / O / M	Hp / Cy / N / M / T / L Mu
Philippians	ℵ / A / B / C	Di / H / P / Ir CA / O / M	Hp / Cy / N / M / T / L Mu
Colossians	ℵ / A / B / C / D	Ig / Ir / CA / O / M	Hp / Cy / N / M / T / L Mu
1 Thessalonians	ℵ / A / B / C	P / Ir / CA / O / M	Hp / Cy / M / T / L / Mu
2 Thessalonians	ℵ / A / B / C	P / Ir / CA / O / M	J / Hp / Cy / M / T / L Mu
1 Timothy	ℵ / A / C / D	Di / P / Ir / CA O / M	Hp / Cy / N / M / T / L Mu
2 Timothy	ℵ / A / C / D	P / Ir / CA / O / M	Hp / Cy / T / L
Titus	ℵ / A / C / D	Di / Ir / CA / O / M	Hp / Cy / N / M / T / L Mu
Philemon	ℵ / A / C / D	Ir / O / M	L
Hebrews	ℵ / A / B / C / D	Δ / Ir / CA / O	J / Hp / Cy / M / T / L
James	ℵ / A / B / C / D	Ig / Ir / CA / M	J / Hp / Cy / M / T / L
1 Peter	ℵ / A / B / C / D	H / Ig / P / Ir CA / O	J / Hp / Cy / M / T / L Mu
2 Peter	ℵ / A / B / C / D	P / Ir / CA / O	J / Hp / Cy / M / T / L Mu
1 John	ℵ / A / B / C / D	Δ / H / P / Ir / CA O / M	J / Hp / Cy / M / T / L Mu
2 John	ℵ / A / B / C / D	Ir / O / M	Cy / T / Mu
3 John	ℵ / A / B / C / D	O	T
Jude	ℵ / A / B / C / D	Δ / CA / O / M	Hp / Cy / M / T / Mu
Revelation	ℵ / A / C / D	H / Pa / Ir / CA / O / M	J / Hp / Cy / M / T / L Mu

Table
Primary Uncials
ℵ = Sinaticus / A = Alexandrinus / B = Vaticanus / C = Ephraemi / D = Claromontanus (Bezae)

Table cont.
Apostolic Fathers
Cl = Clement of Rome / Ba = Epistle of Barnabas / P = Polycarp / Ig = Ignatius / Δ = Didache / Ir = Irenaeus / Pa = Papias / H = Shepherd of Hermas / CA = Clement of Alexandria / Di = Diognetus / O = Origen / M = Muratorian canon

Ante-Nicean Church Fathers
J = Justin Martyr / Hp = Hippolytus / Cy = Cyril / N = Novatian / M = Methodius / T = Tertullian / L = Lactantius / Mu = Muraturian fragment

Apocryphal Books

Apocryphal Book	Primary Uncials	Apostpolic Fathers	Ante-Nicean Church Fathers
Hermas	ℵ / D	Ir	-
Barnabas	ℵ / D	Cl	-
Apoc. Peter	D	Cl	-
Acts of Paul	D	-	-
1 Clement	A	-	-
2 Clement	A	-	-
Didache	-	Cl	-

Looking at the preceding charts, several things should be apparent. First, every book in the New Testament was accepted as Scripture by one or more of the earliest church fathers. Second, the books which have the fewest citations are the smallest books, indicating that the lack of citations is not because they were not accepted was Scripture but because there was not as much material to quote (even as I have not quoted from 3 John in this book). Third, of the five earliest Uncials no book from the New Testament is found in fewer than four of them. Also note that some of these Uncials are damaged meaning that the missing books could have been there, although we cannot prove it. Four, no apocryphal book from the New Testament has more than three major sources! Five, the "Gospel is Thomas," which the "Jesus Seminar" placed alongside the four true gospels, is not cited by a single author, father, or Uncial! *No one* believed the "Gospel of Thomas" to be anything but a forgery.[852]

Another intriguing proof that the canon had been settled long before Constantine is the fact that critics appeal to the heretic Marcion who compiled a canon of Scripture which omits some of the current twenty-seven books of the Bible, but neglect to mention that "Marcion formed his Bible in declared opposition to the holy scriptures of the church from which he had separated."[853] In other words, Marcion's canon demonstrates only that he was in opposition to the canon which already existed!

In short, there can be no doubt that the twenty-seven books which comprise the New Testament were accepted as canon from the earliest of times. By at least the second century, the majority of Christians agreed upon the sacred scriptures, and some books were accepted from the time of their writing (cf. 2 Peter 3:16). Attempts to date the canon to Constantine's time or later are naive at best, and dishonest are worst. Modern day "books" date to that era, but the scrolls which comprise the Bible were accepted as Scripture from the time of the apostles and their disciples.

How Was the Canon Formed?
A fair question is "how was the canon formed?" The fact that this is not an easy question to answer should in itself refute those who claim that some church council formed the canon. Were this true the evidence would be undeniable. The problem is that before Constantine's time there was no unified church government throughout the land. This fact alone demonstrates that the acceptance of the canon (as shown above) was not the work of some council or church authority, but the work of the Holy Spirit.

It has been argued that the writings of the apostles were accepted from the very beginning as they were written.[854] This is partially true, but not entirely. It is possible that Paul wrote more letters than have become a part of the Bible, and it is certain that some writings of the apostles, notably John's *Revelation*, were debated for some time before becoming accepted. The early church was not naive and were cautious to insure that no false or heretical forgery made it into the canon. Because there were no chuch councils or popes to rule on these issues, there was occasional division as evidenced by the church father's writings. This, however, only further substantiates that the guiding force was the Holy Spirit, for it seems certain that at least twenty-five of the twenty-seven New Testament books were accepted as canon by the end of the second century, and probably much earlier.

Entire books have been written upon the question of "how." Consequently, I will refer to reader to Randall Price's *Searching for the Original Bible* or similar work. For the purposes of this appendix I will merely summarize my conclusions. First, apostolic authority was the primary requirement for canonization, and no book which could not be demonstrated to have been either written by an apostle, or by a close associate of an apostle, would be accepted. Second, the book had to be inspired and instructive. As Paul stated, "All Scripture is inspired by God and profitable for teaching, for reproof, for correction, for training in righteousness" (1 Timothy 3:16). Finally, the church was careful to insure that nothing contrary to the teachings of Jesus (as indicated by those gospels accepted *from the beginning*) would enter into the canon. As a result, some books were held to be instructive and useful but *not* Scripture (see below). In other words, the Holy Spirit guided the early church and insured that only those works inspired by the Holy Spirit and by witnesses and disciples of the apostles would enter into the canon.

Apocryphal Books
The term "lost books of the Bible" is a term floated around by people with suspect motives and agendas. Some, like the sham "Jesus Seminar", count the fraudulent "Gospel of Thomas" as one of "five gospels" in order to cast doubt

on the four authentic gospels, but none tell you that *no one* other than the gnostic cults has ever accepted the Gospel of Thomas. Nevertheless, books entitled "the Lost Books of the Bible" imply that there are indeed "lost books" which did not make into the Bible. Why? What are these books?

Many books are written today. It was no different in the days of the early church, but what comprised a Biblical book and a non-Biblical book? As discussed above, the first criteria is whether or not it was written by a disciple of Christ or someone connected to the apostles who had first hand knowledge of either Jesus or His apostles. *No* book could be accepted to the canon which did not meet this criteria, no matter how good a book it might be.

It is true that religious cults have always existed, and to that end there were cults which attempted to create their own Scriptures and their own "gospels." Nevertheless, *none* of these books were ever accepted by mainstream churches. Despite what the critics imply, there are only six books excluded from the canon which were ever truly considered for the canon. No other book, especially those of the gnostics, were ever even debated in the mainstream church. What of those seven books?

Of all the so-called "lost books" only six appear in any early Uncials, and only four are quoted among the apostolic fathers. These are the *Shepherd of Hermas, the Epistle of Barnabas, the Apocalypse of Peter, the Acts of Paul,* the epistles *1 & 2 Clement,* and the *Didache* or *"Teachings of the Apostles."*

The Shepherd of Hermas

The *Shepherd of Hermas* is essentially a long parable. It uses allegory to tell moral Christian messages and to represent the church. It is certainly of early Christian origin although probably not from the first century. Those few who did accept it as authoritative argue that the author was the Hermas mentioned in Romans 16:14, thus connecting the author to the apostle Paul.[855] However, most of the church fathers believe it was written by the brother of the bishop of Rome, Pius I, in the second century.[856] This fact alone would exclude it from the canon although it did engender respect from many. Athantasius, for example, considered *Hermas* to be "a most profitable book"[857] but most definitely "not belonging to the canon."[858] This widespread respect has often been used to imply its controversy, but in fact only Irenaeus quotes *Hermas* as "scripture." The book can be found in the Codex Sinaiticas and the Codex Bezae, but nowhere else is placed alongside Scripture. Considering how widespread the church had become by the time of Irenaeus it is apparent that very few accepted *Hermas* as scripture. Since there are those, to this very day, who differ on the Biblical canon (religious cults and "liberal" theologians, for example), the fact that Irenaeus seems to stand alone is a testament to the uniformity of the early church fathers.

The Epistle of Barnabas

After the *Shepherd of Hermas,* only the *Epistle of Barnabas* comes close to eliciting real controversy. The epistle is supposed by many to be the writing of the apostle Paul's long time companion, but the epistle nowhere makes this claim for itself.[859] Most believe that the epistle was written sometime between 70 A.D. at the earliest and 132 A.D. at the latest.[860] This makes the epistle among the earliest non-Biblical books, and explains why it is so popular, but like the *Shepherd of Hermas*, respect for its antiquity and content does not lend support to any claim for canonicity. It is found in both the Codex Sinaiticas and the Codex Bezae alongside *Hermas* but quoted only by Clement of Rome as possible scripture. Again, considering how widespread the church and the scriptures were at this time, this is meager support to argue against an established canon. The *Epistle of Barnabas* is a book indicative of early Christian thought, but not a part of scripture, nor does its author even make this assertion.

The Apocalypse of Peter

The *Apocalypse of Peter* was not written by Peter, but is acknowledged to be a forgery written in the second century. Nonetheless, because of its proximity to the early church it was popular among some in the early church. It obviously draws its inspiration from the book of Revelation, but differs from it in numerous ways. A great deal of *Peter's Apocalypse* is a vision of hell and a description of the punishments bestowed on people for various sins. Those punishments often correspond to their crimes. For example, unrepentant mothers of abortion must wade in the blood and corpses of dead children. This book is found only in the Codex Bezae and quoted as scripture only by Clement of Rome. No other church father calls its scripture, nor is there any real support for its inclusion in the canon.

The Acts of Paul

First mentioned by Tertullian in the second century, but not as a canonical work, the *Acts of Paul* is a collection of traditions about Paul as well as containing the "third epistle" to the Corinthians (see below). The traditions include the story of Peter being crucified upside down. The Acts is dated to the middle of the second century and is nowhere cited as scripture by any church father. Nevertheless, it is found in the Codex Bezae. It has never been accepted as a part of the canon.

The 1st and 2nd Epistles of Clement

Clement is generally believed to be Clement of Rome. Various traditions make him either the second of fourth bishop of Rome.[861] Some church fathers believe that this Clement was Flavius Clemens, the emperor Domitian's cousin and former consul, who was martyred by the emperor around 96 A.D.[862] Others argue that he was the Clement mentioned in Philippians 4:3, but this is less likely.[863] If it were the Clement of Paul's epistle then he would be from Philippi, not Rome. It also seems unlikely that this Clement was Clemens who died in 96 A.D. since tradition, if it to be accepted, makes Clement the pope from 91 A.D. to 101 A.D.[864] In any case, his proximity to the apostles and the tradition that he learned from the apostles themselves have made the epistles very popular among the early church, but despite this fact, they are nowhere cited as scripture, nor do the epistles make claim to spiritual authority.[865] Of the texts cited above, they are found only in the Codex Alexandria. It is also worth noting that some church fathers rejected 2 Clement as genuine.

The Didache or "Teachings of the Apostles"

The *Didache* has been described as "a church-manual of primitive Christianity."[866] It is divided into two sections. The first is considered a "moral treatise" while the second "gives directions affecting church rites" such as baptism, prayer, and fasting.[867] The author is unknown and the *Didache* is nowhere called canonical by the early church except via Clement of Rome's extensive quotations from it.

One may have noticed that Clement of Rome factors into five of these seven "lost books." Clement, of course, was not an apostle, but allegedly tutored under one of the apostles. Two of the seven were his epistles (actually the second may not have been his at all) and it is in those epistles that he alone refers to three other books as Scripture. If we reject Clement's opinions then only the *Shepherd of Hermas* is cited by any apostolic father as scripture. No other apocryphal book is quoted as anything more than "a profitable" but non-canonical book.[868]

Other books which have been presented as "lost books" include the *Third Epistle of Paul to the Corinthians*, the *Epistle of Paul to the Laodiceans*, the *Gospel of Thomas*, and even the *Gospel of Judas*!

The Third Epistle of Paul to the Corinthians

The *Third Epistle of Paul to the Corinthians* is an extract taken out of the *Acts of Paul* (see notes above). It is suggested that it may be a letter referred to in 1 Corinthians 5:9 or even 2 Corinthians 7:8. Certainly it is an indication that not everything written by Paul was made a part of Scripture. This is not troublesome since only those books inspired by the Holy Spirit are to be considered canon. *If* this epistle is genuine, and many doubt it, it is a useful epistle and instructive, but not inerrant or inspired, and therefore is not a part of the canon.

The Epistle of Paul to the Laodiceans

Colossians 4:6 says, "When this letter is read among you, have it also read in the church of the Laodiceans; and you, for your part read my letter *that is coming* from Laodicea." Like the missing letter to the Corinthians, it is clear that not everything Paul wrote became a part of Scripture, nor should they have. The epistle here is alleged to be one of those missing letters, although most all agree that this letter is a forgery. Not only is it not accepted by any mainstream church father but they actively oppose it. This is because the letter is believed to be a forgery used to promote false and heretical doctrines. This is also why it is listed as Scripture by a few early gnostic cults and by the heretic Marcion. The Muratorian canon explicitly rejects the epistle as a forgery.[869]

The Gospel of Thomas

The gnostics were one of the earliest Christian cults in Christendom. This "gospel" was attacked as a gnostic forgery and as heretical by Hippolytus and other church fathers, even including the "liberal" allegorist Origen.[870] It has never been included in any list of canons discovered. There is no question as to its late gnostic origin. Depite this it has been hailed as a "lost gospel" by modern Bible critics and cults, even being the basis for some of the conspiracies in books and movies like the *DaVinci Code*. In fact, no serious scholar believes this "gospel" was written by Thomas or even that it dates to the first century as some critics claim.[871] The irony is that the same critics who will date Thomas to the first century without a shred of evidence, reject the true gospels as dating to the first century. Such dishonesty would not even be worthy of mention were it not for the rise of gnosticism popularized by secular Hollywood.

The Gospel of Judas

Another gnostic "gospel," this forgery dates to the late second century or possibly much later. Containing a dialoque between Jesus and Judas, who betrayed Christ, it is apparent that the "gospel" is used to promote heresies about Jesus, and sympathizes with the traitor of Jesus. No one has ever accepted it as authentic or canonical. Once again, it would not be worth mentioning at all were it not for the National Geographic channel airing gnostic propaganda disguised as new.[872]

Conclusion

The Biblical canon was closed and complete by sometime in the second century. Although there were dissenters and hold-outs who did not agree completely on the canonitical books, all twenty-seven books of the New Testament were accepted by most mainstream churches, and long before Constantine the Bible was as it is now so that when the emperor Diocletian sought to eradicate the Bible, he knew exactly what books to look for. The uniformity of the Biblical canon from early church is itself a testament to the fact that it was the Holy Spirit, and not some church council, that moved men to accept the inspired works of the New Testament.

The Authenticity and Transmission of Text

Critics claim that the Bible has been substantially altered since it was originally written, and even deny that the Bible was written in the early dates to which it is credited. In short, they claim that the Bible cannot be trusted in what it says. They ask, without wanting an answer, "how can we know what is authentic and what is not?" Many of these critics subscribe to what is called "higher criticism," but contrary to their claims it is the "higher critics" who disregard facts for unsubstantiated theories. *Textual criticism* is the *science* or study of the transmission of ancient texts. Textual criticism relies on *facts* such as the findings of the Dead Sea scrolls and witnesses to ancient scribal practices. Textual criticism is the science by which we can say with confidence that the Bible is authoritative in that it faithfully transmits the original authors words in all substantive and important matters, as the reader will see.

Having said this, it is true that all scholars, whether liberal or conservative, agree that scribes make occasional mistakes in the transmission and copying of texts. The issue is not whether or not any errors can be found in the texts, but whether or not we can determine what errors exist and whether or not these errors have become incorporated into our modern text.

It is easy for the skeptic to mislead people into believing that we are left to ponder what the original texts said with phony numbers, dishonest representations, and lies about antiquity, but by studying the facts it becomes easily and readily apparent that with very few exceptions, scribal errors are not only easy to detect but the original remains faithfully recorded elsewhere, for there were many scribes and many texts made. We do not rely on a single scribe or a single document but the works of many men from different places in different times. Moreover, the scribes were not the only people to see or read the texts, thus the work of the scribes would be exposed to outside examination and scrutiny. While the critic portrays the scribes as dishonest and unethical men, history shows to the contrary. The scribes believed that what they were doing was sacred, and hence they tried faithfully, with fear and trembling, to reproduce copies without error. The proof of this follows.

Surviving Texts
Critics will make a point of saying that we do not have any of the original manuscripts the apostles wrote. They deliberately ignore that we do not have the original manuscripts from *any* book in antiquity, nor could you prove it if we did. Can anyone reading this tell me what the apostle Paul's handwriting looks like? If not, then you could not prove we had the original even if we did! Moreover, even after the invention of the printing press one could easily asks, "do we have the original plates?" The answer would probably be "no."

How then can we know what was originally written. Obviously, as copies are spread out across the world, it becomes harder and harder to "forge" or alter the original without making it vastly different from other copies distributed elsewhere. Even a vast conspiracy would not be able to co-ordinate alterations of copies across the east and west, across multiple countries and continents, or across different language translations. Consequently, the more copies one has, the easier it is to determine if mistakes or alterations were made, and how series these alterations may have been made. It may even be possible to determine which is the original and which is the alteration by comparing the different texts (see next section).

In regard to the New Testament there has been what some have called "an embarrasment of riches"[873] and an "abundance of textual evidence"[874] unparralleled in antiquity. The riches are composed of two parts. First is the sheer number of ancient manuscripts from all over the various parts of the known world and in many different languages and translation. Second is the antiquity of the manuscripts. In fact, while we cannot honestly claim to have any "original autographs" we can say with fair certainty that we have at least one manuscript (probably two or three) which date to a time when apostle John, and probably John Mark, were still living!

The oldest manuscripts known to exist are papyri 32 ($\mathfrak{P}^{32}$), 45 ($\mathfrak{P}^{45}$), 46 ($\mathfrak{P}^{46}$), 52 ($\mathfrak{P}^{52}$), 64 ($\mathfrak{P}^{64}$), 66 ($\mathfrak{P}^{66}$), and 75 ($\mathfrak{P}^{75}$).[875] All of these manuscripts are dated to before 200 A.D. However, scholars are reluctant to date most of these before then because of the difficulty in proving such a date. Nonetheless, there is good evidence to date at least three to the early second century, or even before then.

Papyrus 46 ($\mathfrak{P}^{46}$) is formally dated to around 200 A.D.[876] as are most all papyri which are suspected to be second century, but which cannot be proven with certainty. Nevertheless, paleographer Young Kyu Kim argued that based on the style of Greek lettering (which changes over time, just the modern letter "s" used to be written as "ʃ") it should be dated to "Later First Century."[877] The only arguments used against this dating is that "$\mathfrak{P}^{46}$ is a perfectly ordinary copy"[878] and that "it must have taken some time for the nine Epistles that are preserved in $\mathfrak{P}^{46}$ to have been collected."[879] On this basis Metzger rejects a date of 80 A.D. for the manuscript, but nowhere does he provide evidence for dating it later than the first part of second century. If we then accept Metzger's silent admission that Kim's thesis is sound save the time needed for preservation, and we acknowledge that such collections are found in the early second century, then we would have no reason to reject $\mathfrak{P}^{46}$ as dating somewhere between 100 and 115 A.D.

Papyrus 52 ($\mathfrak{P}^{52}$) is among "the oldest copy of any portion of the New Testament known to be in existence today."[880] It dates to at least 125 A.D. if not before.[881] Additionally, Papyri 66 ($\mathfrak{P}^{66}$) is yet another second century document which Herbert Hunger, director of the papyrological collections at the National Library in Vienna, dates to the early second century.[882]

Now if tradition is to be believed the apostle John died in the time of emperor Trajan at age one hundred.[883] Traditional also makes John a teenager at the time of Jesus' ministry. Since Trajan ruled from 98 to 117 A.D. and because Jesus died in 33 A.D. we may conclude that John was no more than twenty at this time. Eighty years later would be around 113 A.D. Of course one tradition or another have both John and John Mark dying in 106 A.D.[884] Although I do not suppose that John wrote $\mathfrak{P}^{46}$, $\mathfrak{P}^{52}$, or $\mathfrak{P}^{66}$ is apparent that the New Testament can make a closer claim to the autographs than any other writing of antiquity in history. It is of interest to note, however, that both $\mathfrak{P}^{52}$ and $\mathfrak{P}^{66}$ are papyri of John's gospel. It is inconceivable that forged and/or altered copies of John's gospel would be circulating at a time when John still lived without his raising a hand in objection! Surely, the manuscripts we have lend credibility to the fact that we have authentic replicas.

The chart below compares the Biblical texts with all other major works of antiquity (none of which the critics doubt to be authentic).[885]

Ancient Manuscripts

Author/Book	Oringally Written	Earliest Existing Copy	Difference	# of Copies
Homer's *Iliad*	900 B.C.	400 A.D.	500	643
Euripedes	5th Cent. B.C.	Circa 1000 A.D.	1500	9
Herodotus	5th Cent. B.C.	1st Cent. A.D.	400	75
Sophocles	5th Cent. B.C.	Circa 1000 A.D.	1400	100+
Thucydides	5th Cent. B.C.	900 A.D.	1300	20
Aristotle	4th Cent. B.C.	Circa 1000 A.D.	1400	5
Demostenes	4th Cent. B.C.	900 A.D.	1300	200
Plato	4th Cent. B.C.	900 A.D.	1200	7
Julius Caesar	1st Cent. B.C.	900 A.D.	1000	10
Lucretius	60 B.C.	1550 A.D.	1600	2
Livy	59 B.C.-17 A.D	350 A.D.	400	27
Tacitus	Circa 120 A.D.	1100 A.D.	1000	20
Suetonius	Circa 140 A.D.	950 A.D.	800	200+
The New Testament	40-95 A.D.	100-150 A.D.	25-50	5700+

Obviously the wealth of textual data belongs to the Bible before any other book of antiquity. Ironically this has become a double edged sword for critics will count the number "errors" by scribes at around 200,000 while neglecting to mention that of 5700 manuscripts and the 7958 verses (averaging very roughly 25 words per verse) in the New Testament (totalling over one billion words in all) these "errors" not only represent a tiny percentage of the New Testament, but, as we shall see, only around 40 verses are truly in doubt, and less than a dozen make any real difference to the texts, two of which are here in the gospels which I have addressed (see notes on Mark 16:9-20 and John 8:2-11).

Analysing the Scribal Errors
How can I say that 40 of the 7958 verses in the New Testament are in doubt? Actually, I believe the number is far fewer, but not all scholars are as conservative as I am, so in fairness it is worth examining how we arrive at these conclusions. It has already been demonstrated that there is a wealth of information about the New Testament from various countries, languages, and people very early in Christian history. Copies do not get disseminated quickly or easily in antiquity. *If* the Bible were altered then we would expect to find one of several things. First, we might expect a passing of centuries before copies are discovered such as implied in the *DaVinci Code* and other anti-Christian conspiracies. Since this is not the case, and far from it, we can discount this. A second thing we might look for would be substantial differences in various copies of a certain country or region as opposed to those of another (the same might be true of translations into other languages). In this case, it is argued that there are differences, but as we shall see the differences are linguistic, minor, and easy to distinguish.

The four major textual designations are the Byzantine textual tradition, the Alexandrian textual tradition, the Western textual tradition, and the

Caesarean textual tradition.[886] Nonetheless, contrary to the what the critic wishes, these textual "traditions" are extremely close. The greatest differences between these arise from linguistic and educational differences. For example, the Alexandrian tradition has a tendency to alter quotation of the Old Testament from the author's translation to conform to the famed Greek *Septuagint* translation so well known in Alexandria.[887] The modern day equivalent would be if an author quoted the New American Standard Bible translation, but a copy distributed in England changed the quotations to all be from the King James Bible. Another example of alterations made by one of these "traditions" is the use of synonyms for outdated words.[888] For example, a famous verbal spar erupted once in Eusebius' time over a priest who substituted the then modern word for "bed" or "pallet" for the antiquated Biblical word found in John 5:8.[889] Such fights, however, only show how great was the desire to be faithful to the original text. Moreover, an examination of the types of errors and mistakes found in these manuscripts also serves to demonstrate how easy it is to spot the errors from the original text!

Errors of Sight

There are various kinds of errors of sight, all of which are easy to catch. For example, the Greek letters Λ and the Δ look very similar. Sometimes a scribe may mistake one letter for another as in Acts 15:40 where the Greek word ΕΠΙΛΕΞΑΜΕΝΟΣ (*epilaxamenos*) meaning "having chosen" is mistakenly taken for ΕΠΙΔΕΞΑΜΕΝΟΣ (*epidaxamenos*) meaning "having received" in the Codex Bezae.[890] Other examples are when a scribe sees the same word in close succession and accidentally skips over the first appearance of the word. In these instances a short sentence or clause may have been omitted, but it is, once again, easy to catch the mistake in the manuscript.

Errors of Writing

These errors could be summarized simply as ancient *typos*. Misspelled words or poor penmanship which might then be mistaken for something else typify these types of errors. Obviously there are the easiest to spot and of no significance.

Errors of Hearing

Sometimes scribes would have a copy read to them rather than reading it themselves. On occasion there will be words which sound very similar or have similar endings. Various diphthongs, for example, may be confused for one another. Again, these are usually pretty obvious and easy to catch. One example is from papyrus 46 ($\mathfrak{P}^{46}$) in which νεικος (*neikos*) meaning "conflict" is mistaken for νικος (*nikos*) meaning "victory."[891]

Errors of Memory

A common error is when a reader looks at the text and then begins to write the copy from his mind he may forget trivial things like word order (particularly if he is tired). A common error found is the fact that some texts often read "Jesus Christ" while others read "Christ Jesus." Most of these errors make no difference in the meaning or translation of a text, and are easy to recognize.

Misunderstanding

Misunderstandings can fit in with some of the errors listed above but can also include things such as misunderstanding common abbreviations which were often used by scribes. For example, θεος (*theos*) meaning "God" is sometimes abbreviated simply as θς (*ths*), which can easily be mistaken for ος (*os*) which is a relative pronoun.[892] Thus "God" is mistakenly replaced with the pronoun "He."[893] Such instances are again obvious and insignificant.

Grammatical Changes

Another common change is the substitution of words or grammar for more modern (for the time of the writing) ones. The use of synonyms to replace words was common. As mentioned above, John 5:8 is an example of where a later Greek word for "bed" or "pallet" was substituted for the more antiquated one used by Jesus.[894] A modern day parallel is the updating of English grammar in newer translations. Since no one uses "ye" or "thou" anymore, "you" is used to replace those words. The same thing took place with Greek copies. Nevertheless, by looking at textual traditions and using a basic knowledge of *Koine* Greek, these instances are also quite easily recognizable and insignificant.

Intentional Changes

All of the changes or errors listed above are either accidental errors or minor changes in grammar and vocabulary. Here, however, we come to those changes which are of importance for these would be deliberate changes to the text. Note that of all the "errors" and "changes" to which the critic appeals, these actually represent the tiniest of percentage of the discrepancies. Moreover, these alterations are often even easier to spot because of the plethora of diverse manuscripts, textual traditions, and translations available. Any serious alterations to the original apostles' manuscripts would have to have been done while the apostles were still living, and they would surely have objected! Indeed, as aforementioned, we have at last two manuscripts which date to the time when two of the gospel authors were still alive![895] Consequently, this tiny percentage of alterations among the hundreds of thousands of verses known to exist in ancient manuscripts is insignifact; particularly in light of the fact that no doctrine of the Christian faith rest upon a single passage, but many passages!

So it should be obvious that the claims that we cannot know what the original texts of the apostles contained are frivolous. Only forty verses are seriously contested by any but the most atheistic or liberal of critics. Of these forty only four are of any real significance; two of which are here in the gospels (see notes on Mark 16:9-20 and John 8:2-11).

Summary

The wealth of textual copies available of the New Testament is unparalleled in history. No book in antiquity compares to the "embarassment of riches"[896] available for the New Testament. It is for this very reason that critics attempt to exploit textual variants ("errors") found in these texts while neglecting to mention that the sheer volume of information available to us makes it easy to detect well over 99% of these mistakes, and no information leads us to believe that the Bible handed down to us today was intentionally altered. Let us compare the Biblical debate to that of other works of antiquity.

Homer's *Iliad* is among the most famous works of antiquity. No scholar denies that we have is a faithful copy of what he wrote. However, of the 15,600 lines that make up Homer's classic, 764 lines are in question[897] whereas "of the approximately 20,000 lines that make up the entire New Testament, only 40 lines are in question. These 40 lines represent one quarter of one percent of the entire text and do not in any way affect the teaching and doctrine of the New Testament."[898] Consider that "these 764 lines [in Homer's *Iliad*] represent over 5% of the entire text, and yet nobody seems to question the general integrity of that ancient work."[899] The 40 lines of the New Testament represents less than on half of one percent of all the verses in the New Testament or .005%. No serious person can deny that we have faithful reproductions of what the apostles wrote.

Conclusions

There has been much talk about the "historical Jesus" among so-called "liberal scholars" but how can we discover the true "historical Jesus" if we reject the historical documents written by those who actually knew and lived and worked with Jesus? These "scholars" claim to want to know the "real" Jesus by rejecting the writings of those who did know the real Jesus. They attempt to replace true history with their own imagination. They make Jesus into their image without any witnesses, while scorning the witnesses and testimony of the apostles left to us in the New Testament.

Former Chief Inspector for Scotland Yard, Sir Robert Anderson, said of the "higher critics" who reject the gospels, "if the case could be brought before any serious judicial tribunal it would be 'laughed out of court.'"[900] He noted that, "as usual with experts, the critics look only at one side of the question."[901] When examining the Bible from a legitimate critical viewpoint Anderson said, "I am not assuming that the Evangelists were *inspired*, but merely that they were competent and trustworthy witnesses."[902] He did believe that the Bible was inspired, but his *faith* in the inspiration of the Bible was not based on ignorance, but knowledge.

Sir Anderson said that "our belief in God tends to a belief in the existence of a written revelation."[903] The Bible is that written revelation.

History proves this. What we have are what the disciples wrote. What we read is what Jesus taught to His followers. What we *know* about the Bible is why we have *faith* in what it says. No man's beliefs are 100% fact nor 100% faith. This is the great lie that insecure agnostics and critics present. They *assume* miracles cannot happen and declare this to be a fact. They then reject all facts that do not fit this assumption. They operate on faith but claim to operate on facts. The honest Christian knows that his faith is a question of trust. Every man has a different level of trust. Certainly God will reward those who have a higher level of trust in Him, but this does not make our faith in Him contrary to the facts, but in accordance with them.

A man has *faith* that his wife is not cheating on him. He does not *know* this, but his faith is based on what he does know about his wife. If his wife slept around a lot before their marriage, his faith might be misplaced, but if his wife was a virgin on their wedding night he has good cause to believe in her faithfulness. Fidelity before marriage is a good indicator of faithfulness after marriage. Yes, we can sometimes misplace our faith, but that faith is not based on ignorance. Because we know the Bible is true and accurate in all that can be examined, we have faith that it is true and accurate when it speaks of what cannot be examined. I *know* that Moses led the Jews out of Egypt (a fact even admitted by the pagan Egyptian priest Manetho).[904] I have *faith* that Moses parted the Red Sea. I *know* that Jesus was crucified, dead, and buried under Pontius Pilate and that His body disappeared on the third day. I have *faith* that He was resurrected from the dead. Faith is what pleases God, ignorance displeases God. The two are at odds with one another. Our faith is based on God's faithfulness and the truth of His word, for "without faith it is impossible please God" (Hebrews 11:6).

ENDNOTES

1 catholic-resources.org/Bible/NT-Statistics-Greek.htm
2 John Wesley, for example, participated in the Great Awakening movement in America in the 1730s before returning to England to found the Methodist Church.
3 Sir Robert Anderson, *The Critics Criticized* Pickering & Inglis (London, England) 1904 pg. 153
4 Merrill Tenney, *New Testament Survey* Wm. B Eerdmans Publishing (Grand Rapids, Mich.) 1985 pg. 232
5 Robert Gundry, *A Survey of the New Testament* Zondervan Publishing (Grand Rapids, Mich.) 1994 pg. 295
6 See notes on Luke in David Criswell, *Anonymous : Who Wrote the Book of Hebrews* Fortress Adonai (Dallas, TX) 2013
7 George Holley Gilbert, *Acts* MacMillian Co. (New York, NY) 1908 pg. 26
8 John Calvin, *Acts* Crossway Books (Wheaton, Ill.) 1995 pg. 16
9 John Lightfoot, *Commentary on the Acts of the Apostles* J.F. Dove (London, England) 1823 pg. 22
10 R.C.H. Lenski, *The Interpretation of the Acts of the Apostles* Warburg Press (Columbus, OH) 1944 pg. 29
11 Albert Barnes, *Notes on the Acts of the Apostles* Harper & Brothers (New York, NY) 1854 pg. 10
12 Paton Gloag, *Acts of the Apostles* Vol. 1 Klock & Klock Christian Publishers (Minneapolis, MN) 1870 pg. 47
13 Joseph Alexander, *Commentary on the Acts of the Apostles in One Volume* Zondervan Publishers (Grand Rapids, Mich.) 1956 pg. 10
14 Desiderius Erasmus, *Paraphrase on the Acts of the Apostles* University of Toronto Press (Toronto, Canada) 1995 pg. 7
15 Chrysostom, *Ancient Commentary on the Scritpures : New Testament Vol. V : Acts* Thomas Oden, ed., InterVarsity (Downers Grove, Ill.) 2006 pg. 7
16 Ephraem the Syrian, *Ancient Commentary on the Scritpures : New Testament Vol. V : Acts* Thomas Oden, ed., InterVarsity (Downers Grove, Ill.) 2006 pg. 8
17 Richard Longenecker, "Acts of the Apostles," *The Expositor's Bible Commentary* Vol. 9 Zondervan Publishing (Grand Rapids, Mich.) 1981 pg.256
18 H.A. Ironside, *Lectures in the Book of Acts* Loizeaux Brothers (New York, NY) 1943 pg. 21
19 William Kelly, *An Exposition of the Acts of the Apostles* C.A. Hammond (London, England) 1952 pg. 11
20 Mikael Parsons, *Paideia Commentary : Acts* Baker Academics (Grand Rapids, Mich.) 2008 pg. 29
21 Ignatius, *Ante-Nicene Fathers* Vol. I Alexander Roberts & James Donaldson, eds., Charles Scribner (New York, NY) 1886 pg. 87
22 Tertullian, *Ante-Nicene Fathers* Vol. III Alexander Roberts & James Donaldson, eds., William B. Eerdmans Publishers (Grand Rapids, Mich.) 1999 pg. 687
23 Bede, *Ancient Commentary Vol. V* op. cit. pg. 11
24 Charles Spurgeon, *Treasury of the New Testament* Volume Two Zondervan (Grand Rapids, Mich.) 1950 pg. 733
25 Jonathan Edwards, *"The Blank Bible"* Part 2 Stephen Stain, Ed., Yale University Press (New Haven, CT) 2006 pg. 968
26 Cf. W.A. Criswell, *Acts in One Volume* Zondervan Publishers (Grand Rapids, Mich.) 1983 pg. 51
27 John MacArthur, *The MacArthur New Testament Commentary* Acts 1-12 Moody Bible Instituted (Chicago, Ill.) 1994 pg. 23
28 Jerry Falwell & Ed Hindson, eds., *Liberty Commentary on the New Testament* Liberty Press (Lynchburg, Virginia) 1978 pg. 221

29 Albert Barnes, *Barnes' Notes on the New Testament* One Volume ed. Kregel (Grand Rapids, Mich.) 1962 pg. 372
30 Robert Gundry, *Matthew* Wm. B. Eerdmaans (Grand Rapids, Mich.) 1982 pg. 553
31 Merill Unger, *Unger's Bible Dictionary* Moody Press (Chicago, Ill.) 1957 pg. 615
32 John MacArthur, *The MacArthur New Testament Commentary Matthew 24-28*   Moody Bible Institute (Chicago, Ill.) 1985 pg. 228
33 John Wesley, *Explanatory Notes Upon the New Testament* Abraham Paul (New York, NY) 1818 pg. 284
34 W.F. Albright & C.S. Mann, *The Anchor Bible : Matthew* Doubleday & Co. (Garden City, NY) 1971 pg. 340
35 *Liberty Commentary* op. cit. pg. 87
36 Warren Wiersbe, *Be Loyal* Victor Books (Wheaton, Ill.) 1987 pg. 199
37 Ibid.
38 www.tentmaker.org/Dew/Dew3/D3-JudasIscariot.html
39 Desiderius Erasmus, *The Collected Works of Erasmus*   Vol. 45 *Paraphrase on Matthew* Dean Simpson, trans., University of Toronto Press (Toronto, Canada) 2008 pg. 362
40 Ibid.
41 Wesley, *New Testament* op. cit. pg. 92
42 Alexander, op. cit. pg. 37
43 Ibid. pg. 37
44 Matthew Henry, *Matthew Henry's Commentary on the Whole Bible* Vol. 6 *Acts to Revelation* Hendrickson Publishers (Peabody, Mass.) 1991 pg. 10
45 Ibid.
46 Alexander, op. cit. pg. 37
47 Lawrence Browne, *Indian Church Commentaries - Acts of the Apostles* Diocesan Press (London, England) 1925 pg. 25
48 Ibid.
49 Erasmus, op. cit. pp. 12-13
50 Alexander, op. cit. pg. 37
51 Jaroslav Pelikan, *Acts* Brazos Press (Grand Rapids, Mich.) 2005 pg. 46
52 Alexander, op. cit. pg. 37
53 A.C. Gaebelein, *The Gospel of Matthew* Vol. 1 Our Hope (New York, NY) 1910 pg. 205
54 MacArthur, *Acts 1-12* op. cit. pg. 34
55 Gloag, op. cit. pg. 67
56 Browne, op. cit. pg. 25
57 J. Rawson Lumby, *Acts of the Apostles* Cambridge University Press (Cambridge, England) 1882 pg. 13
58 Thomas Abbott, *A Critical and Exegetical Commentary on the Epistles to the Ephesians and to the Colossians* T & T Clark (Edinburgh, Scottland) 1897 pg. 117
59 William Barclay, *The Letters to the Galatians and Ephesians* Westminister Press (Philadelphia, PN) 1954 pp. 171-172
60 Ibid.
61 Alexander, op. cit. pg. 37
62 Barnes, *Notes One Vol. Ed.* op. cit. pg. 23
63 Horatio Hackett, *Commentary on the Original Text of Acts of the Apostles*   Gould & Lincoln (New York, NY) 1859 pg. 50
64 Pelikan, op. cit. pg. 46
65 Calvin, *Acts* op. cit. pg. 25
66 Barnes, *Notes One Vol. Ed.* op. cit. pg. 23
67 Browne, op. cit. pg. 25
68 Erasmus, *Acts* op. cit. pp. 12-13
69 Merrill Unger, *Unger's Bible Dictionary* Moody Press (Chicago, Ill.) 1957 pg. 1129
70 Ibid.

71 Joseph Alexander, *Commentary on the Acts of the Apostles in One Volume* Zondervan Publishers (Grand Rapids, Mich.) 1956 pg. 37
72 Horatio Hackett, *Commentary on the Original Text of Acts of the Apostles* Gould & Lincoln (New York, NY) 1859 pg. 50
73 John Foxe, *Foxe's Book of Martyrs* Clarion Classics (Grand Rapids, Mich.) 1926 (abridged ed.) pg. 5
74 Thieleman J. van Braght, *Martyrs' Mirror* Herald Press (Scottdale, PN) 1950 ed. (1660 orig.) pg. 88
75 David Criswell, *The Apostles After Jesus* Fortress Adonai (Dallas, TX) 2113
76 Ibid.
77 Van Braght, op. cit. pg. 88
78 Ibid.
79 Ibid. pg. 91
80 John Foxe, *Acts and Monuments of the Church*   Vol. 1 Religious Tract Society (London, England) 1853 reprint pg. 97
81 Ibid. pg. 95
82 Van Braght, op. cit. pg. 90
83 Ibid. pg. 91
84 Ibid.
85 Ibid. pp. 91-92
86 James Ussher, *Annals of the World* Master Books (El Cajon, CA) 2003 pg. 843
87 Van Braght, op. cit. pg. 75
88 Criswell, *The Apostles After Jesus* op. cit.
89 Gloag, op. cit. pg. 67
90 Sir Robert Anderson, *The Bible or the Church?* can be found online at : http://www.newble.co.uk/anderson/biblech/biblech9.html
91 Barclay M. Newman, Jr., ed., *A Concise Greek-English Dictionary of the New Testament* United Bible Society (Stuttgart, Germany) 1971 pg. 55
92 William Genesius, *Gesenius' Hebrew and Cahaldee Lexicon to the Old Tesament* Samuel Tregelles, trans., Baker Books (Grand Rapids, Mich.) 1847 (1984 ed.) pg. 269
93 Pentecost, op. cit. pg. 1363
94 Anderson, *The Bible or the Church?* op. cit.
95 Sir Robert Anderson, *The Silence of God* Kregel Publications (Grand Rapids, Mich.) 1978 pg. 75
96 Mal Couch, *A Biblical Theology of the Church* Kregel Publications (Grand Rapids, Mich.) 1999 pg. 52
97 Ibid.
98 Mal Couch, *An Introduction to Classical Evangelical Hermeneutics* Kregel Publications (Grand Rapids, Mich.) 2000 pg. 182
99 H. A. Ironside, *Notes on the Prophecy and Lamentations of Jeremiah* Loizeaux Brothers (Neptune, NJ) 1906 pg. 163
100 Ibid. pg. 164
101 Charles Feinberg, *The Prophecy of Ezekiel* Moody Press (Chicago, Ill.) 1969 pg. 575
102 Sir Robert Anderson, *The Silence of God* Kregel Publications (Grand Rapids, Mich.) 1978 pg. 76
103 See A.C. Perumalil, *The Apostles in India* St. Paul Press (Bangalore, India) 1952
104 See Criswell, *The Apostles After Jesus* op. cit.
105 Randall Price, *The Coming Last Days Temple* Harvest House (Eugene, OR) 1999 pg. 72
106 Josephus, "War of the Jews," VII.viii.6 *The Complete Works of Josephus* Kregel Publications (Grand Rapids, Mich.) 1981 pg. 601
107 John Nelson Darby, *The Collected Writings of J.N. Darby Prophetic No. 1 Vol. 2* Bible Truth Publishers (Addison, IL) n.d. pp. 320-321
108 Gloag, *Acts Vol. 1* op. cit. pg. 85

109 Ibid. pg. 85
110 F.W. Farrar, *Texts Explained* F.M. Barton (Cleveland, Oh.) 1899 pg. 128
111 Gloag, *Acts Vol. 1* op. cit. pg. 83
112 Cassiodorus, *Ancient Commentary Vol. V* op. cit. pg. 24
113 Ibid.
114 Gloag, *Acts Vol. 1* op. cit. pg. 82
115 Lumby, op. cit. pg. 17
116 Gloag, *Acts Vol. 1* op. cit. pg. 82
117 Leo the Great, *Ancient Commentary Vol. V* op. cit. pg. 23
118 Cf. Laurence Browne, *Indian Church Commentaries - Acts of the Apostles* Diocesan Press (London, England) 1925 pg. 34
119 William Barclay, *Acts of the Apostles* Westminister Press (Philadelphia, Penn.) 1953 pg. 15
120 Ibid.
121 Ibid. pg. 16
122 Ironside, *Acts* op. cit. pg. 43
123 Bede, *Ancient Commentary Vol. V* op. cit. pg. 23
124 Cyril, *Ancient Commentary Vol. V* op. cit. pg. 24
125 Barnes, *Notes One Vol. Ed.* op. cit. pg. 378
126 Alexander, op. cit. pg. 44
127 Gloag, *Acts Vol. 1* op. cit. pg. 82
128 Parsons, op. cit. pg. 38
129 John Wesley, *Explanatory Notes Upon the New Testament* Abraham Paul (New York, NY) 1818 pg. 285
130 George Holley Gilbert, *Acts* MacMillan Co. (New York, NY) 1908 pg. 35
131 W.A. Criswell, *Acts in One Volume* op. cit. pg. 90
132 MacArthur, *Acts 1-12* op. cit. pg. 41
133 Charles Spurgeon, *Acts of the Apostles : Four Centuries of Baptist Interpretation*, Beth Barr, etc. eds. Baylor University (Waco, TX) 2009 pg. 116
134 Ibid.
135 W.A. Criswell, *Acts in One Volume* op. cit. pg. 90
136 MacArthur, *Acts 1-12* op. cit. pg. 41
137 Charles Spurgeon, *Four Centuries of Baptist Interpretation*, op. cit. pg. 118
138 John Gill, *Four Centuries of Baptist Interpretation*, op. cit. pg. 113
139 B.H. Carroll, *Four Centuries of Baptist Interpretation*, op. cit. pp. 126-127
140 Augustine, *Ancient Commentary Vol. V* op. cit. pg. 24
141 Lumby, op. cit. pg. 16
142 Leo the Great, *Ancient Commentary Vol. V* op. cit. pg. 23
143 George Halley Gilbert, *Acts* MacMillian Co. (New York, NY) 1908 pg. 39
144 David Wenham, "Unity and Diversity in the New Testament," *A Theology of the New Testament by George Eldon Ladd* Wm. B. Eerdmans (Grand Rapids, Mich.) 1974 pg. 698
145 Bede, *Ancient Commentary Vol. V* op. cit. pg. 29
146 Matthew Henry, *Matthew Henry's Commentary on the Whole Bible : Vol. 4* Hendrickson Publishers (Peabody, Mass.) 1991 pg. 956
147 Richard Longenecker, "Acts," *Expositor's Bible Commentary Vol. 9* Frank Gaebelein, ed., Zondervan Publishers (Grand Rapids, Mich.) 1986 pg. 276
148 John Lightfoot, *Commentary on the Book of Acts* J.F.Dove (London, England) 1823 pg. 58
149 Alexander, op. cit. pg. 62
150 Cyril, *Nicene and Post-Nicene Fathers Second Series Vol. VII* Philip Schaff, ed., Charles Scribner (New York, NY) 1892 pg. 129
151 Martin Luther, *Luther's Works Vol. 18* Concordia House Publishing (St. Louis, MS) 1958 pg. 107
152 John Calvin, *Calvin's Commetnaries Vol. XIV Commentary on The Minor Prophets Book 2*, Baker Books (Grand Rapids, Mich.) 1999 pg. 92

153 Wesley, op. cit. pg. 2500
154 John Lightfoot, *The Whole Works of the Rev. John Lightfoot Vol. II* J. F. Dove (London, England) 1822 pg. 239
155 Matthew Poole, *A Commetnary on the Holy Bible Vol. II* Hendrickson Publishers (Peabody, Mass.) n.d. pg. 893
156 John Gill, *Expositions of the Old Testament Vol. 4* William Hill Collinridge (London, England) 1852 pp. 648-649
157 Henry, *Vol. 4* op. cit. pg. 956
158 John Wesley, *Explanatory Notes Upon the Old Testament Vol. III Psalms LXIII – Malachi* Schmul Publishers (Salem, Ohio) 1975 pg. 2500
159 Calvin, *Minor Prophets Book 2*, op. cit. pg. 94
160 Alexander, op. cit. pg. 62
161 A.J. Rosenberg, ed., *The Books of Twelve Prophets Vol. I with Rashi Commentary* Judaica Press (New York, NY) 1986 pg. 239
162 John Walvoord, *Every Prophecy of the Bible* Chariot Victor Publishing (Colorado Springs, Co.) 1999 pg. 289
163 John Wesley, *Explanatory Notes on the New Testament* Abraham Paul (New York, NY) 1818 pg. 286
164 MacArthur, *Acts 1-12* op. cit. pg. 53
165 Ibid.
166 Alexander, op. cit. pg. 62
167 Heinrich Meyer, *Handbook to the Acts of the Apostles Vol. 1* T&T Clark (Edinburgh, Scotland) 1861 pg. 78
168 Browne, op. cit. pg. 40
169 J. Dwight Pentecost, *Things to Come* Zondervan Publishers (Grand Rapids, Mich.) 1958 pg. 486
170 William Estep, *The Anabaptist Story* Broadman Press (Nashville, TN) 1963 pp. 22-37
171 Justo Gonzalez, *The Story of Christianity Vol. 2* Harper & Row (San Francisco, CA) 1984 pg. 56
172 Philip Schaff, *History of the Christian Church Vol. 8* Hendrickson Publishers (Peabody, Mass.) 1996 pg. 67
173 Loraine Boettner, *Roman Catholicism* Presbyterian & Reformed (Phillipsburg, NJ) 1962 pg. 190
174 Joseph Thayer, *A Greek-English Lexicon of the New Testament* Baker Books (Grand Rapids, Mich.) 1977 pg. 94
175 Alexander, op. cit. pg. 84
176 http://www.catholic.com/quickquestions/was-jesus-baptized-by-immersion
177 http://www.thywordistruth.com/questions/Question-355.html
178 R.C.H. Lenski, *The Interpretation of the Acts of the Apostles* Wartburg Press (Columbus, Ohio) 1944 pg. 106
179 *Catechism of the Catholic Church* [1213] Online version available at the Vatican website : http://www.vatican.va/archive/ENG0015/__P3G.HTM
180 Sir Robert Anderson, "Misunderstood Texts of the Bible," *The Compete Works of Sir Robert Anderson Vol. 2* Fortress Adonai (Dallas, TX) 1916 (2010 ed.) pg. 291
181 Paton Gloag, *Acts of the Apostles Vol. 1* Klock & Klock (Menneapolis, MN) 1870 pg. 110
182 Is there such a thing as a "secret Christian"? I believe there can be, but this is *not* what the apostles desired or taught. They required a public profession of faith, which immediately put the believer's life in jeopardy.
183 MacArthur, *Acts 1-12* op. cit. pg. 73
184 Ibid.
185 Ibid.
186 Dale Moody, *Four Centuries of Baptist Interpretation*, op. cit. pg. 191
187 Ibid. pg. 190

188 Ibid.
189 Ibid.
190 George Halley Gilbert, *Acts* MacMillian Co. (New York, NY) 1908 pg. 45
191 Stagg, op. cit. pg. pg. 190
192 Cf. Stagg, op. cit. pg. 190
193 MacArthur, *Acts 1-12* op. cit. pg. 73, but MacArthur wrongly suggest that this was a public breaking with Judaism which is in error, for Christianity had not yet broken with Judaism and was rightly considered a Jewish sect at this time.
194 Barnes, *Acts* op. cit. pg. 53
195 H.A. Ironside, *Lectures on the Book of Acts* Loizeaus Bro. (New York, NY) 1943 pg. 69
196 John Calvin, *Acts* Crossway Books (Wheaton, Ill.) 1995 ed. pg. 45
197 John Wesley, *Explanatory Notes on the New Testament* Abraham Paul (New York, NY) 1818
198 Stanley Toissaint, "Acts," *The Bible Knowledge Commentary : New Testament* John Walvoord & Roy Zuck, eds., Victor Books (Wheaton, Ill.) 1986 pg. 359
199 Paton Gloag, *Acts of the Apostles Vol. 1* Klock & Klock (Menneapolis, MN) 1870 pg. 110
200 From *Our Faith and the Facts*, pg. 399 as cited by http://www.bible.ca/cath-baptism.htm
201 Longenecker, *Expositor's Bible Commentary Vol. 9* op. cit. pg. 284
202 Dale Moody, *Four Centuries of Baptist Interpretation*, op. cit. pg. 191
203 MacArthur, *Acts 1-12* op. cit. pg. 87
204 Ibid.
205 R.C.H. Lenski, *The Interpretation of the Acts of the Apostles* Wartburg Press (Columbus, Ohio) 1944 pp. 117-118
206 H.A. Ironside, *Addresses on the First Epistle to the Corinthians* Loizeaux Brothers (New York, NY) 1938
207 http://www.levitt.com/essays/luke
208 Ibid.
209 http://www.rwaynestacy.com/2011/03/was-luke-gentile.html
210 http://www.levitt.com/essays/luke
211 David Allen, *The Lukan Authorship of Hebrews* op. cit. pg. 266
212 George Milligan, *The New Testament Documents: Their Origin and Early History*, Macmillan and Co. (London, England) 1913 pg. 149
213 J.B. Lightfoot, *The Apostolic Fathers* Baker Books (Grand Rapids, Mich.) 1984 ed. pg. 567
214 Karl Marx and Frederick Engels, *The Communist Manifesto* Article II, Progress Publishers (Moscow, Russia) 1848
215 Karl Marx and Frederick Engels, *The Communist Manifesto* Article III, Progress Publishers (Moscow, Russia) 1848
216 Frederick Engels, *The Principles of Communism* Progress Publishers (Moscow, Russia) 1847 as cited by http://marxists.org/archive/marx/works/1847/11/prin-com.htm
217 Frederick Engels, *The Communist Confession of Faith* Progress Publishers (Moscow, Russia) 1847 as cited by http://marxists.org/archive/marx/works/1847/11/prin-com.htm
218 Marx and Engels, *The Communist Manifesto* Article III, op. cit.
219 Cited by W.A. Criswell, *Acts in One Volume* Zondervan (Grand Rapids, Mich.) 1983 pg. 113
220 Engels, *The Principles of Communism* op. cit. and Engels, *The Communist Confession of Faith* op. cit. as cited by http://marxists.org/archive/marx/works/1847/11/prin-com.htm
221 Criswell, *Acts in One Volume* op. cit. pg. 113
222 Marx and Engels, *The Communist Manifesto* Article II, op. cit.
223 Engels, *The Principles of Communism* op. cit. as cited by
 http://marxists.org/archive/marx/works/1847/11/prin-com.htm
224 John Dewey, *Experience and Education* Collier Books (New York, NY) 1938 pg. 54
225 Ibid.
226 John Dewey, *School and Society* Cosimo Classics (New York, NY) 1889 as cited by Samuel Blumenfeld, *N.E.A. Trojan Horse in American Education* The Paradigm Co. (Boise, Idaho) 1984 pg. 105

227 Blumenfeld, *N.E.A.* op. cit. pg. 112
228 Allan Bloom, "Has the Open University Closed the American Mind?" *Current Issues & Enduring Questions* Barnet & Dedas, eds., St. Martin's Press (Boston, MA) 1990 pg. 222
229 Socialist Union, *Twentieth Century Socialism* Penguin Books (New York, NY) 1956 pg. 38
230 Marx and Engels, *The Communist Manifesto* Article II, op. cit.
231 Criswell, *Acts in One Volume* op. cit. pg. 116
232 Gloag, *Acts Vol. 1* op. cit. pg. 163
233 Ibid.
234 Ironside, *Acts* op. cit. pg. 119
235 Barnes, *Notes One Vol. Ed.* op. cit. pg. 409
236 J. Rawson Lumby, *Acts of the Apostles* Cambridge University Press (Cambridge, England) 1882 pg. 52
237 Lenski, *Acts* op. cit. pg. 190
238 Browne, op. cit. pg. 81
239 Lightfoot, *Acts* op. cit. pg. 75
240 Ibid.
241 Marx and Engels, *The Communist Manifesto* Article II, op. cit.
242 Barnes, *Acts* op. cit. pg. 90
243 MacArthur, *Acts 1-12* op. cit. pg. 152
244 Gloag, *Acts Vol. 1* op. cit. 170
245 Lenski, *Acts* op. cit. pg. 194
246 William Kelly, *An Exposition of the Acts of the Apostles* C.A. Hammond (London, England) 1952 pg. 50
247 Erasmus, *Acts* op. cit. pg. 38
248 Calvin, *Acts* op. cit. pg. 72
249 Erasmus, *Acts* op. cit. pg. 38
250 MacArthur, *Acts 1-12* op. cit. pg. 153
251 A.C. Gaebelein, *Acts of the Apostles* Our Hope (New York, NY) 1912 pg. 103
252 Ironside, *Acts* op. cit. pg. 122
253 Cf. *Four Centuries of Baptist Interpretation*, op. cit. pg. 265
254 Jerry Falwell & Ed. Hindson, eds., *Liberty Commentary on the New Testament* Liberty Press (Lynchburg, Virginia) 1978 pg. 82
255 MacArthur, *Acts 1-12* op. cit. pg. 152
256 M. Baumgarten, *Acts of the Apostles Vol. 1* T&T Clark (London, England) 1854 pg. 112
257 John Wesley, *Explanatory Notes on the New Testament* Abraham Paul (New York, NY) 1818
258 Frank Stagg, *Four Centuries of Baptist Interpretation*, op. cit. pg. 263
259 Browne, op. cit. pg. 82
260 Chrysostom, *Ancient Commentary Vol. V* op. cit. pg. 91
261 John Pohill, *Four Centuries of Baptist Interpretation*, op. cit. pg. 265
262 Calvin, *Acts* op. cit. pg. 71
263 Cf. David Criswell, *Rise and Fall of the Holy Roman Empire* Fortress Adonai (Dallas, TX) 2014
264 Chaim Potok, *Wanderings* Ballantine Books (New York, NY) 1978 pg. 271
265 Martin Gilbert, ed. *Atlas of Jewish Civilization* Macmillan Press (New York, NY) 1990 pg. 49
266 Josephus, "Antiquity of the Jews," XX.v.1 *Complete Works* op. cit. pg. 418
267 Ibid.
268 Ibid. XX.v.2
269 Longenecker, "Acts," *Expositor's Bible Commentary Vol. 9* op. cit. pg. 322
270 Ibid.
271 Ibid.
272 Josephus, "Antiquity of the Jews," XX.v.3 *Complete Works* op. cit. pg. 419

273 John Lightfoot, *From the Talmud and Hebraica, Volume 4* Cosimo Classics (New York, NY) 2013 pg. 54 Cf. also Adam Clarke, *Commentary on the Bible* notes on Acts 5:36 CD version (E-Sword) 2010
274 Matthew Poole, *A Commentary on the Holy Bible Vol. III* Hendrickson Publishers (Peabody, Mass.) n.d. pg. 401
275 Barnes, *Acts* op. cit.
276 Emil Schurer, *A History of the Jewish People in the Time of Jesus Christ First Divsiion Vol. II* Hendrickson Publishers (Peabody, Mass.) 1890 pg. 168
277 James Ussher, *Annals of the World* 6098 Master Books (El Cajon, CA) 2003 pg. 783
278 Criswell, *Apostles After Christ* op. cit. pg. 117
279 John Gill, *Exposition of the Entire Bible* notes on Acts 5:36 CD version (E-Sword) 2010
280 http://www.jewishencyclopedia.com/articles/14369-theudas
281 Josephus, "Antiquities" XIII.xiv.2 *Complete Works* op. cit. pp. 285-286
282 Emil Schurer, *A History of the Jewish People in the Time of Jesus Christ First Divsiion Vol. I* Hendrickson Publishers (Peabody, Mass.) 1890 pg. 300
283 James Ussher, *Annals of the World* 6098 Master Books (El Cajon, CA) 2003 pg. 783
284 Josephus, "Antiquities" XVII.x.5 *Complete Works* op. cit. pg. 371
285 Philip Schaff, *History of the Christian Church Vol. 1* Hendrickson Publishers (Peabody, Mass.) 1996 pg. 732
286 Josephus, "Antiquities" XVII.x.5 *Complete Works* op. cit. pg. 371
287 Josephus, "War of the Jews" II.iv.1 *Complete Works* op. cit. pg. 473
288 F.F. Bruce, *Commentary on the Book Of Acts* Wm. B. Eerdmans (Grand Rapids, Mich.) 1954 pg. 124
289 Tacitus, *Histories* 5.9.2
290 Josephus, "Antiquities" XVII.x.6 *Complete Works* op. cit. pg. 371 Also compare with Josephus, "War" II.iv.2 *Complete Works* op. cit. pg. 473
291 http://www.haaretz.com/weekend/week-s-end/in-three-days-you-shall-live-1.218552
292 Schurer, *First Division Vol. II* op. cit. pg. 4
293 F.F. Bruce, *Commentary on the Book Of Acts* Wm. B. Eerdmans (Grand Rapids, Mich.) 1954 pg. 124
294 Josephus, "Antiquities" XVII.vi.2 *Complete Works* op. cit. pg. 364 Cf. Bruce, *Acts* Wm. B. op. cit. pg. 124
295 Josephus, "Antiquities" XVIII.i.1 *Complete Works* op. cit. pg. 376
296 Ibid.
297 Josephus, "War" II.viii.1 *Complete Works* op. cit. pg. 476
298 Josephus, "Antiquities" XVIII.i.6 *Complete Works* op. cit. pg. 377
299 Matthew Poole, *Commentary on the Holy Bible : Vol. I* Hendrickson Publishers (Peabody, Mass.) n.d. pg. 30
300 Ibid.
301 John Calvin, *A Commentary on Genesis* Banner of Truth Trust (London, England) 1965 ed. pg. 336
302 Ussher, op. cit. pg. 22
303 John Lightfoot, *The Whole Works of the Rev. John Lightfoot Vol. II* J. F. Dove (London, England) n.d. pg. 333
304 Matthew Henry, *Matthew Henry's Commentary on the Whole Bible : Vol. 1* Hendrickson Publishers (Peabody, Mass.) 1991 pg. 67
305 John Wesley, *Explanatory Notes Upon the Old Testament Vol. I Genesis – Judges XIV* Schmul Publishers (Salem, Ohio) 1975 pg. 51
306 John Gill, *Expositions of the Old Testament Vol. 1* William Hill Collinridge (London, England) 1852 pg. 72
307 Augustine, "City of God," *Nicene and Post-Nicene Fathers Second Series Vol. II* Philip Schaff, ed., Charles Scribner (New York, NY) 1894 pg. 320
308 Ibid. pg. 319

309 Abraham Ibn Ezra, *Commentary on the Pentateuch*   Vol. 1 Genesis Menorah Publishing Company (New York, NY) 1988 ed. pg. 96
310 Rashi, *Chumash with Rashi's Commentary : Beresith* A.B. Silbermann, ed., Feldheim Publishers (Jerusalem, Israel) 1934 pg. 48
311 Louis Ginzberg, *The Legends of the Jews*   Vol. 1 Genesis to Jacob   Jewish Publication Society (Philadelphia, Pennn.) 1909 pg. 206
312 Mikael Parsons, *Paideia Commentary : Acts* Baker Academia (Grand Rapids, Mich.) 2008 pg. 91
313 Alexander, op. cit. pg. 258
314 Ibid.
315 Henry Morris, *The Genesis Record* Baker Book House (Grand Rapids, Mich.) 1976 pg. 290
316 Alexander, op. cit. pg. 258
317 *The Midrash Rabbah   Vol. 1 Genesis* Soncino Press (New York, NY) 1977 ed. [XXVI-7] pg. 315
318 Lightfoot, *Works Vol. II* op. cit. pg. 333
319 Morris, *The Genesis Record* op. cit. pg. 289   Morris actually as 130 years, but I have corrected to contextually to 145.
320 Stanlet Toussaint, *Bible Knowledge Commentary : New Testament* Walvoord & Zuck, eds., Victor Books (Wheaton, Ill.) 1986 pg. 370
321 Lumby, op. cit. pg. 82
322 Lightfoot, *Acts* op. cit. pg. 112
323 *Discoveries in the Judaean Desert XII : Qumran Cave 4 VII*   Clarendon Press (Oxford, England) 1994 pg. 19
324 Lumby, op. cit. pg. 84
325 Calvin, *Acts* op. cit. pg. 115
326 Barnes, *Notes One Vol. Ed.* op. cit. pg. 426
327 Lenski, *Acts* op. cit. pg. 292
328 Kelly, *Acts* op. cit. pg. 96
329 MacArthur, *Acts 1-12* op. cit. pg. 213
330 *Criswell Study Bible*, W.A. Criswell, ed., Thomas Nelson Publishers (Nashville, TN) 1979 pg. 1023
331 Cf. Gesenius op. cit. pp. 586-587
332 Gleason Archer, *Encyclodpedia of Bible Difficulties* Zondervan Publisher (Grand Rapids, Mich.) 1982 pg. 381
333 Cf. A.T. Olmstead, *History of Assyria* Charles Scribners (New York, NY) 1923 & Robert Rogers, *A History of Babylonia and Assyria Vol. II* Eaton & Mains (New York, NY) 1901
334 Archer, op. cit. pp. 381-382
335 John Joseph Owens, *Analytical Key to the Old Testament*   Vol. 4 Baker Books (Grand Rapids, Mich.) 1994 pg. 814
336 Gesenius, op. cit. pg. 395
337 Cerinthus, *Ante-Nicene Fathers Vol. III* op. cit. pg. 651
338 Farrar, op. cit. pp. 137-138
339 Lumby, op. cit. pg. 93
340 Barnes, *Notes One Vol. Ed.* op. cit. pg. 427
341 Gloag, *Acts Vol. 1* op. cit. pg. 254
342 Calvin, *Acts* op. cit. pg. 122
343 Gloag, *Acts Vol. 1* op. cit. pg. 254
344 Wesley, op. cit.
345 Horatio Hackett, *Commentary on the Original Text of the Book of Acts of the Apostles* Gould & Lincoln (New York, NY) 1859 pg. 143
346 Tertullian, "Apology," *Ante-Nicene Fathers Vol. 3* Alexander Roberts & James Donaldson, eds., Charles Scribner (New York, NY) 1886 pg. 54
347 Pelikan, op. cit. pg. 110

348 Cf. Barnes, *Notes One Vol. Ed.* op. cit. pg. 430
349 Josephus, "Antiquities of the Jews," XX.vii.2 *Complete Works* op. cit. pg. 420
350 William Whiston, note on XX.vii.2 *Complete Works* op. cit. pg. 420
351 Hippolytus, "Refutation of All Heresies," VI.ii *Ante-Nicene Fathers Vol. 5* Alexander Roberts & James Donaldson, eds., Charles Scribner (New York, NY) 1886 pg. 74
352 Cf. Unger, op. cit. pp. 327-328
353 Schaff, *History of the Church Vol. 1* op. cit. pg. 566
354 Merrill Tenney, *New Testament Survey* Wm. B. Eerdmans (Grand Rapids, Mich.)1985 pg. 73
355 Justo Gonzalez, *The Story of Christianity Vol. 1* HarperCollins (San Francisco, CA) 1984 pg. 59
356 Ibid.
357 Kenneth Scott Latourette, *A History of Christianity Vol. 1* Harper & Row (New York, NY) 1953 pg. 123
358 Robert Gundry, *A Survey of the New Testament* Zondervan Publishers (Grand Rapids, Mich.) 1194 pg. 60
359 Merrill Tenney, *New Testament Survey* Wm. B. Eerdmans (Grand Rapids, Mich.)1985 pg. 74
360 Gonzalez, *The Story of Christianity Vol. 1* op. cit. pg. 60
361 Barclay Newman, *A Concise Greek-English Dictionary* United Bible Society Stuttgart, Germany) 1971 pg. 38
362 Robert Gundry, *A Survey of the New Testament* Zondervan Publishers (Grand Rapids, Mich.) 1194 pg. 61
363 Gonzalez, *The Story of Christianity Vol. 1* op. cit. pg. 59
364 Kenneth Scott Latourette, *A History of Christianity Vol. 1* Harper & Row (New York, NY) 1953 pg. 123
365 Barnes, *Notes One Vol. Ed.* op. cit. pg. 430
366 Schaff, *History of the Church Vol. 1* op. cit. pg. 566
367 Hippolytus, "Refutation of All Heresies," VI.ii-xv *Ante-Nicene Fathers Vol. 5* op. cit. pp. 77-81
368 Ibid. pg. 77-78
369 Criswell, *Apostles After Christ* op. cit. pg. 186
370 The full text of *the Acts of Peter* may be found at http://www.earlychristianwritings.com/text/actspeter.html
371 Hippolytus, "Refutation of All Heresies," VI.xv *Ante-Nicene Fathers Vol. 5* op. cit. pg. 81
372 Eusebius, *Eusebius, The Church History* 2.13-15 Paul Maier, trans. Kregel Publishers (Grand Rapids, Mich.) 1999 pp. 72-72
373 Justin Martyr, "The First Apology of Justin," *Ante-Nicene Fathers Vol. 1* op. cit. pg. 171
374 Note on Eusebius 2:13, op. cit. pg. 72
375 Coxe, *Ante-Nicene Fathers Vol. 1* op. cit. pg. 171
376 Mentioned by Tertullian, *Ante-Nicene Fathers Vol. III* op. cit. pg. 215
377 Parsons, op. cit. pg. 114
378 Joseph Thayer, *Greek-English Lexicon of the New Testament* Baker Books (Grand Rapids, Mich.) 1977 pg. 649
379 Ibid. pg. 385
380 Gaebelein, *Acts* op. cit. pp. 146-147
381 Gloag, *Acts Vol. 1* op. cit. pg. 278
382 Kelly, *Acts* op. cit. pg. 98
383 John Calvin, *Commentary on the Last Four Books of Moses* Baker Books (Grand Rapids, Mich.) 1999 pg. 149
384 John Wesley, *Explanatory Notes Upon the Old Testament Vol. I Genesis – Judges XIV* Schmul Publishers (Salem, Ohio) 1975 pg. 217
385 C. H. Spurgeon, *The Treasury of the Old Testament Vol. 1 : Genesis to 2 Kings* Zondervan (Grand Rapids, Mich.) 1951 pg. 200
386 Ironside, *Acts* op. cit. pg. 181

387 Josephus, "Antiquities of the Jews," XX.vii.2 *Complete Works* op. cit. pg. 420
388 Gloag, *Acts Vol. 1* op. cit. pg. 278
389 Irenaeus, *Ante-Nicene Fathers Vol. I* op. cit. pg. 347
390 MacArthur, *Acts 1-12* op. cit. pg. 239
391 Parsons, op. cit. pg. 116
392 Longenecker, *Expositor's Bible Commentary Vol. 9* op. cit. pg. 359
393 *Catechism of the Catholic Church* [1316] Online version available at the Vatican website : http://www.vatican.va/archive/ccc_css/archive/catechism/p2s2c1a2.htm
394 *Catechism of the Catholic Church* [1307-08] Ibid.
395 http://forums.catholic.com/showthread.php?t=199525
396 *Catechism of the Catholic Church* [1294] op. cit.
397 *Catechism of the Catholic Church* [1307] Ibid.
398 http://www.andrewcorbett.net/articles/subsequence.html
399 Ibid.
400 Tim Enloe, http://enrichmentjournal.ag.org/201002/201002_119_HS_Separate.cfm
401 David Petts, *The Holy Spirit: An Introduction* Mattersey Hall (Mattersey, England:) 1998
402 Longenecker, *Expositor's Bible Commentary Vol. 9* op. cit. pg. 359
403 Henry, *Commentary Vol. 6* op. cit. pg. 81
404 Poole, *Commentary Vol. III* op. cit. pg. 410
405 Gloag, *Acts Vol. 1* op. cit. pg. 288
406 Hackett, op. cit. pg. 150
407 George Halley Gilbert, *Acts* MacMillian Co. (New York, NY) 1908 pg. 94
408 Longenecker, *Expositor's Bible Commentary Vol. 9* op. cit. pg. 359
409 Chrysostom, *Ancient Commentary Vol. V* op. cit. pg. 93
410 Calvin, *Acts* op. cit. pg. 137
411 David Petts, *The Holy Spirit: An Introduction* Mattersey Hall (Mattersey, England:) 1998
412 Gaebelein, *Acts* op. cit. pg. 150
413 Browne, op. cit. pg. 132
414 Anthony Hoekema, *Holy Spirit Baptism* Wm. B. Eerdmans (Grand Rapids, Mich.) 1972 pp. 26-27
415 D.A. Carson, *Showing the Spirit* Baker Book (Grand Rapids, Mich.) 1987 pg. 144
416 Steven Waterhouse, *Not By Bread Alone* Westcliff Press (Amarillo, TX) 2007 pg. 244
417 Meyer, *Acts Vol. 1* pg. 230
418 Longenecker, *Expositor's Bible Commentary Vol. 9* op. cit. pg. 359
419 Toussaint, *Bible Knowledge Commentary* op. cit. pg. 373
420 Longenecker, *Expositor's Bible Commentary Vol. 9* op. cit. pg. 359
421 Gaebelein, *Acts* op. cit. pg. 151
422 Ethiopian Jews are often considered to be discriminated against in Israel because their heritage is suspect. The Hebrew word for Ethiopia is "Cush" and a "Cushite" is a person from Cush, but the term "Cushi" is a racial slur leveled against Ethiopian Jews.
423 Cf. Josephus, *Antiquities* op. cit. pp. 181-182
424 Ussher, op. cit. pg. 327
425 Thieleman J. van Braght, *Martyrs' Mirror* Herald Press (Scottdale, PN) 1950 ed. (1660 orig.) pg. 105
426 Gloag, *Acts Vol. 1* op. cit. pg. 310
427 Cf. Criswell, *Apostles After Christ* op. cit. pg. 100
428 Cf. Eberhard Nestle and Kurt Aland, *Nestle-Aland Novum Testamentum Graece* United Bible Society (Stuttgart, German) 1898 & 1979 pg. 690
429 Metzger, *Textual Commentary* op. cit. pg. 315
430 Hackett, op. cit. pg. 159
431 Barnes, *Acts* op. cit. pg. 146
432 A.T. Robertson, *Four Centuries of Baptist Interpretation*, op. cit. pg. 402
433 Ibid.

434 Lenski, *Acts* op. cit. pg. 348
435 Meyer, *Acts Vol. 1* pg. 241
436 Calvin, *Acts* op. cit. pg. 147
437 J.A. Bengal, cited in Meyer, *Acts Vol. 1* pg. 241
438 David Wenham, "Appendix," *A Theology of the New Testament* George Eldon Ladd, Wm B. Eedrmans (Grand Rapids, Mich.) 1974 pg. 704
439 http://www.harrington-sites.com/house1.html
440 http://www.ewtn.com/vexperts/showmessage_print.asp?number=367829&language=en
441 Cf. Thayer, op. cit. pp. 22-23 and Newman, *Concise* op. cit. pg. 6
442 Ibid.
443 Lenski, *Acts* op. cit. pg. 356
444 Gaebelein, *Acts* op. cit. pg. 170
445 Gloag, *Acts Vol. 1* op. cit. pg. 324
446 Ibid.
447 Ibid.
448 Ibid.pg. 323
449 Ibid.
450 Lenski, *Acts* op. cit. pg. 356
451 Gaebelein, *Acts* op. cit. pg. 170
452 Parsons, op. cit. pg. 128
453 Ironside, *Acts* op. cit. pg. 208
454 Ironside, *Acts* op. cit. pg. 201
455 http://www.harrington-sites.com/house1.html
456 Richard Young, *Intermediate New Testament Greek* Broadman & Holman (Nashville, TN) 1994 pg. 183
457 Warren Trenchard, *Complete Vocabulary Guide to the Greek New Testament* Zondervan Publishing (Grand Rapids, Mich.) 1992 pg. 70
458 Thayer, op. cit. pg. 173
459 Translation found in Logos Bible Software on the Nestle-Aland Greek text, by Libronix.com.
460 *Liberty Commentary* op. cit.
461 Gaebelein, *Acts* op. cit. pp. 198-199
462 Josephus, "Antiquities," xvii.6.5 *Complete Works* op. cit. pp. 365-366
463 Jean Marton, *Science and the Bible* Moody Press (Chicago, Ill.) 1978 pg. 261
464 Josephus, "Antiquities," xix.8.2 *Complete Works* op. cit. pp. 412-413
465 Edwin R. Thiele, *The Mysterious Numbers of the Hebrew Kings* Kregel Publications (Grand Rapids, Mich.) 1983 pg. 33
466 Barnes, *Notes One Vol. Ed.* op. cit. pg. 459
467 Sir Robert Anderson, "Bible and Modern Criticism," *Complete Works Vol. 2* op. cit. pg. 166 in original
468 Bruce Metzger, *A Textual Commentary on the Greek New Testament* United Bible Society (Stuttgart, Germany) 1994 pg. 359
469 Lenski, *Acts* op. cit. pg. 519
470 Barnes, *Acts* op. cit. pg. 195
471 Toussaint, "Acts," *Bible Knowledge Commentary* op. cit. pg. 390
472 Poole, *Vol III* op. cit. pg. 427
473 Ussher, op. cit. pp. 26 & 39
474 Henry, *Vol 6* op. cit. pg. 133
475 Gilbert, op. cit. pp. 135-136
476 Farrar, op. cit. pg. 147
477 Paton Gloag, *Acts of the Apostles Vol. 2* Klock & Klock (Menneapolis, MN) 1870 pg. 23
478 Josephus, "Antiquities," vii.3.1 *Complete Works* op. cit. pg. 151
479 *Liberty Commentary* op. cit.
480 Josephus, "Antiquities," vii.3.1 *Complete Works* op. cit. pg. 151

481 Cf. Barnes, *Notes One Vol. Ed.* op. cit. pg. 459
482 Josephus, "Antiquities," i.13.2 *Complete Works* op. cit. pg. 37
483 For a brief history of the apostles, see Appendix C, or my *Apostles After Jesus* for a full debate. My purpose here is to give a fuller history of the council by combining Acts with Paul's account in Galatians 2.
484 Think of it this way. After the 3rd year had *begun* or after it *ended*? In English it is usually "ended," but in Hebrew and Koine Greek it was always after it *began*.
485 Criswell, *Apostles After Jesus* op. cit. pp. 95-100
486 Criswell, *Apostles After Jesus* op. cit. pp. 71-78
487 Eusebius, 3.1 *Church History* op. cit. pg. 93
488 Evidence for this can be found in my *Apostles After Jesus*.
489 Thayer, op. cit. pg. 389
490 Ironside, *Acts* op. cit. pg. 374
491 Gloag, *Acts Vol. 2* op. cit. pg. 119
492 Calvin, *Acts* op. cit. pg. 280
493 www.theoi.com/Text/HomericHymns1.html
494 Gilbert, op. cit. pg. 159
495 S AB pg. 229
496 Thayer, op. cit. pg. 557
497 William Barclay, *Acts of the Apostles* Westminster Press (Philadelphia, PN) 1953 pg. 134
498 Browne, op. cit. pg. 266
499 Ibid. pg. 267
500 Parsons, op. cit. pg. 231
501 Ibid.
502 Hackett, op. cit. pg. 262
503 Lumby, *Acts* op. cit. pg. 208
504 M. Baumgarten, *Acts of the Apostles Vol. 2* T&T Clark (London, England) 1854 pg. 121
505 Cf. Lenski, *Acts* op. cit. pg. 665
506 Criswell, *Holy Roman Empire* op. cit. pp. 215-216, 255-269
507 Kelly, *Acts* op. cit. pg. 234
508 John MacArthur, *Acts 13-28* Moody Press (Chicago, Ill.) 1996 pg. 97
509 M. Baumgarten, *Acts of the Apostles Vol. 2* T&T Clark (London, England) 1854 pg. 121
510 Chrysostom, *Ancient Commentary Vol. V* op. cit. pg. 203
511 Calvin, *Acts* op. cit. pg. 280
512 Gaebelein, *Acts* op. cit. pg. 287
513 Gloag, *Acts Vol. 2* op. cit. pg. 120
514 Barclay, *Acts* op. cit. pg. 143
515 Lumby, op. cit. pg. 226
516 Alexander, *Acts* op. cit. pg. 614
517 Browne, op. cit. pg. 285
518 Gaebelein, *Acts* op. cit. pg. 307
519 Serge Grunzinski, *The Aztecs - Rise and Fall of an Empire* Harry Abrams (New York, NY) 1987 pg. 49
520 Michael Wood, *Conquistadors* University of Caolifornia Press (Berkley, CA) 2000 pg. 44
521 Hammond Innes, *The Conquistadors* Alfred A. Knoft (New York, NY) 1969 pg. 115
522 Ibid. pg. 137
523 Parsons, op. cit. pg. 246
524 Baumgarten, *Acts Vol. 2* op. cit. pg. 162
525 Gaebelein, *Acts* op. cit. pg. 307
526 Sutonius, *Lives of the Twelve Caesars* V.25 Robert Graves, trans. Welcome Rain (New York, NY) 1957 pg. 176
527 Robert Graves, note under Sutonius V.25, op. cit. pg. 176
528 Calvin, *Acts* op. cit. pg. 308

529 Emil Schurer, *A History of the Jewish People in the Time of Jesus Christ* Vol. IV (2nd Div. Vol. II) Hendrickson Publishers (Peabody, Mass.) 1890 pg. 238
530 Lenski, *Acts* op. cit. pg. 745
531 Baumgarten, *Acts Vol. 2* op. cit. pg. 129
532 Ibid.
533 Gloag, *Acts Vol. 2* op. cit. pg. 169
534 MacArthur, *Acts* op. cit. pg. 147
535 Baumgarten, *Acts Vol. 2* op. cit. pg. 129
536 Browne, op. cit. pg. 303
537 Parsons, op. cit. pg. 250
538 Gilbert, op. cit. pg. 172
539 Gaebelein, *Acts* op. cit. pg. 312
540 Metzger, *Textual Commentary* op. cit. pg. 415
541 Ibid. pp. 415-4176
542 Gaebelein, *Acts* op. cit. pg. 334
543 Lenski, *Acts* op. cit. pg. 782
544 Gaebelein, *Acts* op. cit. pg. 324
545 W.A. Criswell, *Four Centuries of Baptist Interpretation*, op. cit. pg. 406
546 Calvin, *Acts* op. cit. pg. 319
547 Ibid.
548 Pelikan, op. cit. pg. 84
549 Barnes, *Acts* op. cit. pg. 260
550 Kelly, *Acts* op. cit. pg. 275
551 Cf. Alexander, *Acts* op. cit. pg. 649
552 Erasmus, *Acts* op. cit. pg. 116
553 Hackett, op. cit. pg. 310
554 Ibid.
555 Browne, op. cit. pg. 312
556 Gaebelein, *Acts* op. cit. pg. 325
557 Gloag, *Acts Vol. 2* op. cit. pg. 196
558 Dave Hunt & T.A. McMahon, *The Seduction of Christianity* Harvest House (Eugene, OR) 1984
559 Anderson, *Bible and Modern Criticism* op. cit. pg. 152
560 Calvin, *Acts* op. cit. pg. 335
561 Longenecker, op. cit. pg. 500
562 Poole, *Vol III* op. cit. pg. 448
563 E.g. Lumby, op. cit. pg. 277
564 Hackett, op. cit. pg. 316
565 Gloag, *Acts Vol. 2* op. cit. pg. 211
566 Gaebelein, *Acts* op. cit. pg. 333
567 Archer, op. cit. pg. 384
568 Gloag, *Acts Vol. 2* op. cit. pg. 246
569 Hackett, op. cit. pg. 336
570 Ibid.
571 Gaebelein, *Acts* op. cit. pg. 334
572 Longenecker, op. cit. pg. 516
573 Toussaint op. cit. pg. 415
574 Poole, *Vol. III* op. cit. pg. 454
575 Longenecker, op. cit. pg. 516
576 Ironside, *Acts* op. cit. pg. 478
577 Henry, *Vol. 6* op. cit. pg. 222
578 Longenecker, op. cit. pg. 500
579 Archer, op. cit. pg. 384

580 Archer, op. cit. pg. 384
581 Metzger, *Textual Commentary* op. cit. pg. 415
582 Pelikan, op. cit. pg. 216
583 Gaebelein, *Acts* op. cit. pg. 343
584 Calvin, *Acts* op. cit. pg. 330
585 Josephus, "The Jewish War" VI.ix..3 *Complete Works* op. cit. pg. 588
586 Lenski, *Acts* op. cit. pp. 824-925
587 *Mishnah* Pesahim iv. 5. [Jacob Neusner, trans., *Mishnah* Yale University Press (London, England) 1988 as cited by Harold Hoehner, *Chronological Aspects of the Life of Christ* Zondervan Publishing (Grand Rapids, Mich.) 1977 pg. 88]
588 Calvin, *Acts* op. cit. pg. 330
589 Browne, op. cit. pg. 337
590 Gloag, *Acts Vol. 2* op. cit. pg. 234
591 Henry, *Vol. 6* op. cit. pg. 208
592 Warren Wiersbe, *Be Transformed* Victor Books (Wheaton, Ill.) 1987 pp. 131-132
593 Alexander, *Acts* op. cit. pg. 689
594 Poole, *Vol III* op. cit. pg. 451
595 Toussaint, op. cit. pg. 413
596 Longenekcer, op. cit. pg. 509
597 Lumby, op. cit. pg. 270
598 Ironside, *Acts* op. cit. pg. 462
599 Barnes, *Acts* op. cit. pg. 273
600 Barclay, *Acts* op. cit. pg. 162
601 Erasmus, *Acts* op. cit. pg. 121
602 Kelly, *Acts* op. cit. pg. 297
603 "The History of Philip," *Apocryphal Acts of the Apostles Vol. 1*, J. B. Lightfoot, D.D, trans. Williams & Norgate (London, England) 1871
604 Josephus, *War* II.xiii.5 op. cit. pg. 483
605 Ibid.
606 Longenecker, op. cit. pg. 528
607 Schurer, *First Division Vol. II* op. cit. pg. 189
608 Unger, op. cit. pg. 49
609 Emil Schurer, *A History of the Jewish People in the Time of Jesus Christ Vol. III (2nd Div. Vol. I)* Hendrickson Publishers (Peabody, Mass.) 1890 pg. 202
610 Josephus, *War* II.xvii.9 op. cit. pg. 492
611 Longenecker, op. cit. pg. 530
612 Josephus, *Antiquities* XX.v.2 op. cit. pg. 418
613 Josephus, *Antiquities* XX.vi.2 op. cit. pg. 420
614 Sutonius, V.28 op. cit. pg. 177
615 Schurer, *First Division Vol. II* op. cit. pg. 176
616 Sutonius, V.28 op. cit. pg. 177
617 Tacitus, *History* V.9 op. cit. as cited in Schurer, *First Division Vol. II* op. cit. pg. 176
618 Sutonius, V.28 op. cit. pg. 177
619 Josephus, "Antiquities of the Jews," XX.vii.2 *Complete Works* op. cit. pg. 420
620 Unger, op. cit. pp. 327-328
621 Longenecker offer an intriguing theory. He argues that it was during this two year period in which Luke began to write his gospel (Longenecker, op. cit. pp. 542-543). This could very well be the case for he had previously been busy travelling with Paul and working with him. If Theophilus commissioned the histories, we can imaging it would have taken Luke several years at least to compile these two histories (Luke and Acts). During this time he might have finished Luke and begun working on Acts, which would be finished during the two year imprisonment in Rome. But also see "Was Acts Finished?" for my own opinion on this matter.
622 Josephus, *War* II.xiii.7 op. cit. pg. 483

623 Schurer, *First Division Vol. II* op. cit. pg. 182
624 Josephus, *War* II.xiv.1 op. cit. pg. 483
625 Schurer, *First Division Vol. II* op. cit. pp. 195-206
626 Some manuscripts have "to become" rather than "to make."
627 Toussaint, op. cit. pg. 426
628 See Nestle-Aland, op. cit. Acts 24:6-8
629 Gloag, *Acts Vol. 2* op. cit. pg. 452
630 H.H. Scullard, *From the Gracchi to Nero* Routledge (New York, NY) 1959 pp. 306-307
631 "Religious superstition" for which Christians would later be killed. Cf. Marta Sordi, *The Christian and the Roman Empire* University of Oklohama (Oklahoma City, OK) 1986 pg. 31
632 1 Clement 5:5-6, Clement of Rome, *The Apostolic Fathers*, J.B. Lightfoot & J.R. Harmer, eds., Baker Books (Grand Rapids, Mich.) 1984 pg. 59
633 Hippolytus, "On the Twelve Apostles," *Ante-Nicene Fathers Vol. 8* Alexander Roberts & James Donaldson, eds., Charles Scribner (New York, NY) 1886 pp. 254-256
634 Cf. Sutonius, *Lives of the Twelve Caesars* VI Rains (Great Britain) 1957 & Cornelius Tacitus, *The Annals: The Reigns of Tiberius, Claudius, and Nero* XV.44 Oxford University (Oxford, England) 2008
635 Dionysius of Corinth, "Letter to the Roman Church," III, *Ante-Nicene Fathers Vol. 8* op. cit. pg. 765
636 Foxe, *Acts and Monuments Vol. 1* op. cit. pg. 104
637 See Criswell, *Apostles After Jesus* pp. 142-157
638 Metzger, *Textual Commentary* op. cit. pg. 444
639 Ibid.
640 Gaebelein, *Acts* op. cit. pg. 429
641 Longenekcer, op. cit. pg. 573
642 Metzger, *Textual Criticism* op. cit. pg. 445
643 Thiele, op. cit. pg. 33
644 C.f. David Criswell, *Controversies in the Pentateuch* Fortress Adonai (Dallas, TX) 2009
645 Colin Renfrew & Paul Bahn, *Archaeology: Theories, Methods, & Practice* Thames & Hudson Ltd. (New York, NY) 1991 p. 22
646 Bill McMillon, *The Archaeology Handbook* John Wiley & Sons, Inc. (New York, NY) 1991 pg. 114
647 Sutonius, *Lives of the Twelve Caesars* V.25 Robert Graves, trans. Welcome Rain (New York, NY) 1957 pg. 176
648 Harold Hoehner, *Chronological Aspects of the Life of Christ* Zondervan Publishing (Grand Rapids, Mich.) 1977 pg. 100
649 See David Criswell, *Controversies in the Gospels* Fortress Adonai (Dallas, TX) 2012
650 Josephus, "Antiquities," xx.1-2 *Complete Works* op. cit. pp. 414-416
651 Josephus, "Antiquities," xx.2.1-3 *Complete Works* op. cit. pp. 415-416
652 Josephus, "Antiquities," xix.8.2 *Complete Works* op. cit. pp. 412-413
653 Schurer, *First Division Vol. II* op. cit. pg. 163
654 Ibid.
655 Ibid.
656 Jack P. Lewis, *Historical Backgrounds of Bible History* Baker Book House (Grand Rapids, Mich.) 1971 pg. 153
657 Gilbert, op. cit. pg. 172
658 Jerome Murphy-O'Connor, *St. Paul's Corinth: Text and Archaeology* Liturgical Press (Collegeville, MN), 2002 pg.161
659 Tenney, op. cit. pg. 235
660 Josephus, *War* II.xiii.8 op. cit. pp. 483-484
661 Tenney, op. cit. pg. 235
662 Unger, op. cit. pg. 363
663 Schurer, *First Division Vol. II* op. cit. pg. 183

664 Ibid.
665 Ibid.
666 Ibid.
667 Unger, op. cit. pg. 1046
668 Unger, op. cit. pg. 832
669 Young, *Intermediate New Testament Greek* op. cit. pg. 183
670 Unger, op. cit. pg. 835
671 Ibid. pg. 836
672 Cf. Alexander Hislop, *The Two Babylons* Loizeaux Brothers (Neptune, NJ) 1916 pg. 209
673 Unger erroneously places the Epistle to Titus during his second imprisonment as do many others (Unger, op. cit. pg. 1104) but the express statement that he was expecting to winter in Nicopolis (3:12) defies logic if this was his second imprisonment. This can only be reconciled with his first imprisonment.
674 Charles H. Dyer, with Angela Hunt, *The Rise of Babylon : Sign of the End Times* Tyndale House (Wheaton, Ill.) 1991
675 Georges Roux, *Ancient Iraq* Penguin Books (New York, NY) 1992 ed. pg. 413
676 Ibid.
677 Ibid.
678 Ibid.
679 Ibid.
680 Ibid.
681 Ibid. pg. 416
682 Ibid.
683 Ibid.
684 Ibid. pg. 414
685 Even Charles Dyer quotes Dio on this matter (Dyer, *Rise of Babylon* op. cit. pg. 128).
686 Roux, op. cit. pg. 421
687 Cited in John Gill, *Expositions of the Old Testament* Vol. 3 William Hill Collinridge (London, England) 1852 pg. 794
688 Dyer, op. cit. pg. 19
689 Franz Delitzsch, *Biblical Commentary on the Prophecies of Isaiah* Vol. 1 William B Eerdmans (Grand Rapids, Mich.) 1949 pg. 304
690 Gill, *Vol. 3* op. cit. pg. 794
691 Unger, op. cit. pg. 850
692 Cf. Tertullian, "Scorpiace," *Ante-Nicene Fathers Vol. 2* Alexander Roberts & James Donaldson, eds., Charles Scribner (New York, NY) 1886 pg. 648
693 Unger, op. cit. pg. 850
694 Ironside, *John* op. cit. pg. 890
695 Dionysius of Corinth, "Letter to the Roman Church," III, *Ante-Nicene Fathers Vol. 8* op. cit. pg. 765
696 Cf. Coxe, *Ante-Nicene Fathers Vol. 1* op. cit. pg. 309
697 Irenaeus, "Against Heresies," 3:2, *Ante-Nicene Fathers Vol. 1* op. cit. pg. 415
698 Clement of Alexandria, "Miscellanies," 7.11.63-64 *Ante-Nicene Fathers Vol. 2* Alexander Roberts & James Donaldson, eds., Charles Scribner (New York, NY) 1886 pg. 541
699 Hippolytus, "On the Twelve Apostles," *Ante-Nicene Fathers Vol. 8* Alexander Roberts & James Donaldson, eds., Charles Scribner (New York, NY) 1886 pp. 254-256
700 Gaius of Rome, "Dialogue with Proclus," *Eusebius, The Church History* 2.25 Paul Maier, trans. Kregel Publishers (Grand Rapids, Mich.) 1999 pg. 86
701 Tertullian, "On Prescription Against Heretics," *Ante-Nicene Fathers Vol. 2* op. cit. pg. 260
702 Bernard Ruffin, *The Twelve : The Lives of the Apostles After Calvary* One Sunday Visitor (Huntington, IN) 1970 pg. 53
703 Criswell, *Apostles After Jesus* op. cit. pg. 186
704 The full text of *the Acts of Peter* may be found at

http://www.earlychristianwritings.com/text/actspeter.html
705 Hippolytus, "On the Twelve Apostles," *Ante-Nicene Fathers* Vol. 8 Alexander Roberts & James Donaldson, eds., Charles Scribner (New York, NY) 1886 pp. 254-256
706 Henry, *Vol. 5* op. cit. pg. 187
707 Cyprian, "Epistles of Cyprian," *Ante-Nicene Fathers Vol. 5* op. cit. pg. 377 & 394
708 Irenaeus, "Against Heresies," 3:3, *Ante-Nicene Fathers Vol. 1* op. cit. pg. 416
709 J.N.D. Kelly, *The Oxford Dictionary of Pope* Oxford University Press (Oxford, England) 1986 pg. 6
710 www.tertullian.org/fathers/chronography_of_354_13_bishops_of_rome.htm
711 Unger, op. cit. pg. 933
712 Kelly calls these "legends" (Kelly, op. cit. pg. 7).
713 Cf. David Criswell, *Rise and Fall of the Holy Roman Empire* op. cit.
714 Clement of Rome, "The First Epistle of Clement," 1 Clement 5:4, *Ante-Nicene Fathers Vol. 1* op. cit. pg. 6
715 Dionysius of Corinth, "Letter to the Roman Church," III, Ibid. pg. 765
716 Clement of Alexandria, "Miscellanies," 7.11.63-64 *Ante-Nicene Fathers Vol. 2* Alexander Roberts & James Donaldson, eds., Charles Scribner (New York, NY) 1886 pg. 541
717 Clement of Alexandria, "Miscellanies," 3.6.52 Ibid. pg. 390
718 Cf. Notes on the *The Acts of Peter* op. cit
719 Hippolytus, "On the Twelve Apostles," *Ante-Nicene Fathers* Vol. 8 Alexander Roberts & James Donaldson, eds., Charles Scribner (New York, NY) 1886 pp. 254-256
720 Tertullian, "Scorpiace," *Ante-Nicene Fathers Vol. 2* Alexander Roberts & James Donaldson, eds., Charles Scribner (New York, NY) 1886 pg. 648
721 Tertullian, "On Prescription Against Heretics," *Ante-Nicene Fathers Vol. 2* op. cit. pg. 260
722 *The Acts of Peter* op. cit.
723 Ibid.
724 Cf. Criswell, *Apostles After Jesus* op. cit. pp. 11-36
725 Clement of Rome, "The First Epistle of Clement," 1 Clement 5:4, *Ante-Nicene Fathers Vol. 1* op. cit. pg. 6
726 Ruffin, op. cit. pg. 57
727 Tacitus, *Annals*, op. cit. 15.44
728 Ruffin, op. cit. pg. 55
729 Merrill Unger, *Unger's Bible Dictionary* Moody Press (Chicago, Ill.) 1957 pg. 851
730 Robert Gundry, *A Survey of the New Testament* Zondervan Publishers (Grand Rapids, Mich.) 1994 pg. 437
731 Cf. David Criswell, *Controversies in the Gospels* Fortress Adonai Press (Dallas, TX) 2012
732 C. Bernard Ruffin, *The Twelve : The Lives of the Apostles After Calvary* One Sunday Visitor (Huntington, IN) 1970 pg. 72
733 Ibid. pg. 76
734 Clement of Alexandria, "Hypotyposes," *Ante-Nicene Fathers Vol. 2* op. cit. pg. 579
735 Ruffin, op. cit. pg. 103
736 "The History of Philip," *Apocryphal Acts of the Apostles Vol. 1*, J. B. Lightfoot, D.D, trans. Williams & Norgate (London, England) 1871
737 See *Apostles After Jesus* for my defense of this theory. Also compare Van Braght, op. cit. pg. 74 and Foxe, *Acts and Monuments Vol. 1* op. cit. pg. 97
738 A.C. Perumalil, *The Apostles in India* St. Paul Press (Bangalore, India) 1952 pp. 11ff
739 Also see the Indian kings lists discovered by archaeologists. Although there are problems with the dates, the names correspond very closely to tradition, unlike those of Armenia. http://www.ibiblio.org/britishraj/Jackson2/appendix04.html
740 Ibid.
741 Ruffin, op. cit. pg. 116
742 Perumalil, *The Apostles in India* op. cit. pp. 11ff
743 See Criswell, *Apostles After Jesus* pp. 81-94

744 Josephus, "Antiquities of the Jews," 20.9.1, *The Complete Works of Josephus* Kregel Publishers (Grand Rapids, Mich) 1981 pg. 423
745 Hegesippus, "Memoirs," *Eusebius The Church History*, 2:23 op. cit. pp. 81-82
746 Cited in Ruffin, op. cit. pg. 51
747 Cf. Sutonius, *Lives of the Twelve Caesars* VI Rains (Great Britain) 1957 & Cornelius Tacitus, *The Annals: The Reigns of Tiberius, Claudius, and Nero* XV.44 Oxford University (Oxford, England) 2008
748 H.H. Scullard, *From the Gracchi to Nero* Routledge (New York, NY) 1959 pg. 304
749 Ibid. pp. 306-307
750 See Criswell, *Apostles After Jesus* op. cit. pp. 142-157
751 See Ibid. pp. 137-141
752 Ruffin, op. cit. pg. 67
753 Ibid. pg. 68
754 Van Braght, op. cit. pg. 88
755 Unger, *Bible Dictionary* op. cit. pg. 52
756 See Criswell, *Apostles After Jesus* pp. 49-56
757 Ibid. pg. 97
758 See Criswell, *Apostles After Jesus* pp. 65-80
759 Hippolytus, "On the Twelve Apostles," *Ante-Nicene Fathers Vol. 8* op. cit. pp. 254-256
760 Ruffin, op. cit. pg. 128
761 John E. Hill, *Through the Jade Gate to Rome* BookSurge (Charleston, SC) 2009 pg. 29
762 Erwin Lueker, ed., *Lutheran Cyclopedia* Concordia Press (St. Louis, MI) 1975 pg. 406
763 Once again see my *Controversies in the Gospels* for evidence that Matthew was indeed the first gospel written, and that it was written before 49 A.D. when Thomas would have embarked on his journey.
764 Alexander Mar Thoma Metropolitan, *The Mar Thoma Church : Heritage and Mission* Puthethu Offset (Thiruvalla, Kerala, India) 1985 pg. 13
765 See Criswell, *Apostles After Jesus* pp. 95-102
766 Clement of Alexandria, "Stromata," iv.9, *Ante-Nicene Fathers Vol. 2* op. cit. pg. 422
767 Criswell, *Apostles After Jesus* pg. 100
768 http://www.nestorian.org/kings_of_edessa.html
769 "Teaching of Addæus the Apostle," *Ante-Nicene Fathers Vol. 8* op. cit. pp. 657-665
770 History records that the Parthians of this time viewed Christianity as a "western" or "foreign" religion at odds with they religions. This is indicated in "Teaching of Addæus the Apostle."
771 See Criswell, *Apostles After Jesus* pp. 117-128
772 C.f. H.P.R. Finberg, *The Formation of England 550-1042* Paladin Granada Publishing (London, England) 1976
773 G. H. R. Horsley, *New Documents Illustrating Early Christianity: a Review of the Greek Inscriptions and Papyri* William B. Eerdmans (Grand Rapids, Mich.) 1987 pg. 138
774 See Criswell, *Apostles After Jesus* pp. 129-136
775 Kenneth Morgan, ed., *Oxford Illustrated History of Britain* Oxford University Press (Oxford, England) 1984 pg. 19
776 See Criswell, *Apostles After Jesus* pp. 129-136
777 Some try to place his exile in Patmos under Nero despite the unanimous testimony of the ancient church fathers, including John's own second generation disiple Irenaeus! They reason for this is the fact that Revelation was written in Patmos and they want to attribute the prophecies of the anti-Christ to Nero. For additional discussion see my *Controversies in Revelation*.
778 Irenaeus, "Against Heresies," 3:4, *Ante-Nicene Fathers Vol. 1* op. cit. pg. 416
779 John Foxe, *Foxe's Book of Martyrs* Clarion Classics (Grand Rapids, Mich.) 1926 (abridged ed.) pg. 5
780 Ruffin, op. cit. pg. 94

781 "Acts of the Holy Apostle and Evangelist John the Theologian," *Ante-Nicene Fathers Vol. 8* op. cit. pg. 560-564   Also cf. Hippolytus, "On the Twelve Apostles," *Ante-Nicene Fathers Vol. 8* op. cit. pp. 254-256
782 Augustine, *Ancient Christian Commentary on Scripture New Testament IV B John 11-21* John Elowsky, ed., InterVarsity Press (Downers Grove, Ill.) 2006 pg. 395
783 Theodore of Mapsuestia, *Ancient Christian Commentary Vol. IV B* Ibid. pg. 395
784 See Criswell, *Apostles After Jesus* pp. 41-48
785 This is a classic paraphrase from Tertullian, "Apology," *Ante-Nicene Fathers Vol. 3* Alexander Roberts & James Donaldson, eds., Charles Scribner (New York, NY) 1886 pp. 54-55
786 Hippolytus, "On the Twelve Apostles," *Ante-Nicene Fathers Vol. 8* op. cit. pp. 254-256
787 Ibid.
788 Van Braght, op. cit. pg. 86
789 Hippolytus, "On the Twelve Apostles," *Ante-Nicene Fathers Vol. 8* op. cit. pp. 254-256
790 Van Braght, op. cit. pg. 86
791 "The Teachings of the Apostles," *Ante-Nicene Fathers Vol. 8* op. cit. pg. 671
792 Ibid. pg. 85
793 Hippolytus, "On the Twelve Apostles," *Ante-Nicene Fathers Vol. 8* op. cit. pp. 254-256
794 Van Braght, op. cit. pg. 85
795 "The Acts of Barnabas," *Ante-Nicene Fathers Vol. 8* op. cit. pg. 493-486
796 Ibid.
797 Hippolytus, "On the Twelve Apostles," *Ante-Nicene Fathers Vol. 8* op. cit. pp. 254-256
798 Papias, "Fragments of Papias," *Ante-Nicene Fathers Vol. 1* op. cit. pg. 154
799 Van Braght, op. cit. pg. 94
800 Hippolytus, "On the Twelve Apostles," *Ante-Nicene Fathers Vol. 8* op. cit. pp. 254-256
801 Van Braght, op. cit. pg. 94
802 Ussher, op. cit. pg. 327
803 Criswell, *Apostles After Jesus* pg. 100
804 Ibid.
805 "The Teachings of the Apostles," *Ante-Nicene Fathers Vol. 8* op. cit. pg. 670
806 Ibid. pg. 671 (Note that India here is conflated with Ethiopia due to the fact that Ethiopia was called "Cush" in antiquity whereas India was bordered by the Hindu-Kush mountains and part of India was occupied by the Kushans after 55 A.D.)
807 Eusebius, 4.11 op. cit. pg. 143 (Note that Eumenes actually means "Good Menes." Menes is held to be the name of the first king of Egypt, thus this bishop was probably a native of Egypt).
808 So says the early church father Papias, as cited by Eusebius, *Church History* II.16
809 Cf. Van Braght, op. cit. pg. 78 and Dorotheus, as cited by Foxe, *Acts and Monuments* op. cit. pg. 95
810 "The Teachings of the Apostles," *Ante-Nicene Fathers Vol. 8* op. cit. pg. 670
811 Ibid. pg. 671
812 The *Babylon Namebook*, as cited by Van Braght, op. cit. pg. 95
813 Dorotheus, as cited by Foxe, *Acts and Monuments* op. cit. pg. 95
814 Van Braght, op. cit. pg. 107
815 Hippolytus, "On the Twelve Apostles," *Ante-Nicene Fathers Vol. 8* op. cit. pp. 254-256
816 Van Braght, op. cit. pg. 87
817 Hippolytus, "On the Twelve Apostles," *Ante-Nicene Fathers Vol. 8* op. cit. pp. 254-256
818 Dorotheus, as cited by Foxe, *Acts and Monuments* op. cit. pg. 95
819 http://www.thebereancall.org/content/who-was-philip-evangelist
820 Polycrates & Papias, quoted by Eusebius, *The Church History*, 3.31 op. cit. pg. 119 & 3.39 pg. 127
821 Hippolytus, "On the Twelve Apostles," *Ante-Nicene Fathers Vol. 8* op. cit. pp. 254-256
822 Ibid.
823 Ibid.
824 Van Braght, op. cit. pg. 93

825 Ibid.
826 Polycarp, "The Epistle of Polycarp," *Ante-Nicene Fathers Vol. 1* op. cit. pg. 35
827 Hippolytus, "On the Twelve Apostles," *Ante-Nicene Fathers Vol. 8* op. cit. pp. 254-256
828 Van Braght, op. cit. pg. 105
829 Van Braght, op. cit. pg. 86
830 Eusebius, 4.5, op. cit. pg. 137
831 Hegesippus, *Memoirs,* as cited by Eusebius, 3:32 op. cit. pg. 121
832 Van Braght, op. cit. pg. 105
833 "The Acts of Barnabas," *Ante-Nicene Fathers Vol. 8* op. cit. pg. 493-486
834 Hippolytus, "On the Twelve Apostles," *Ante-Nicene Fathers Vol. 8* op. cit. pp. 254-256
835 Dorotheus, as cited by Foxe, *Acts and Monuments* op. cit. pg. 95
836 Van Braght, op. cit. pg. 98
837 Ibid.
838 Hippolytus, "On the Twelve Apostles," *Ante-Nicene Fathers Vol. 8* op. cit. pp. 254-256 Also see Van Braght, op. cit. pg. 94
839 Randall Price, *Searching for the Original Bible* Harvest House (Eugene, OR) 2007 pg. 156
840 Lee Martin McDonald, *The Biblical Canon* Hendrickson Publishers (Peabody, Mass.) 1995
841 Ibid.
842 Randall Price, *The Search for the Original Bible* Harvest House (Eugene, OR) 2007 pg. 154
843 Brian Edwards, *Nothing but the Truth* Evangelical Press (Webster, NY) 2006 ed. pg. 218
844 Ibid.
845 http://www.christian-history.org/muratorian-canon.html
846 Brian Edwards, *Nothing but the Truth* Evangelical Press (Webster, NY) 2006 ed. pg. 218
847 http://www.christian-history.org/muratorian-canon.html
848 McDonald, op. cit. pg. 314
849 Ibid. pg. 308
850 Philip Schaff, *History of the Christian Church Vol. 2* Hendrickson Publishers Peabody, Mass.) 1996 pg.
851 F.F. Bruce, *The Canon of Scripture* IVP Academic (Downers Grove, Ill.) 1988 pg. 121
852 The "Jesus Seminar" was a seminar of so-called theologians who met and voted on what portions of the gospels were true and what portions were legends. They called this book the "Five Gospels" and concluded that *only* "love your neighbor as yourself" was legimate, rejecting everything else in the gospels as suspect.
853 F.F. Bruce, *The Canon of Scripture* IVP Academic (Downers Grove, Ill.) 1988 pg. 144
854 Edwards, op. cit. pg. 226
855 J.B. Lightfoot, & J.R. Harmer, *The Apostlic Fathers* Baker Book House (Grand Rapids, Mich.) 1984 pg. 293
856 Ibid.
857 Bruce, op. cit. pg. 77
858 Ibid.
859 Lightfoot & Harmer, op. cit. pg. 239
860 Ibid.
861 J.N.D. Kelly, *The Oxford Dictionary of Popes* Oxford University Press (Oxford, England) 1986 pg. 7
862 Lightfoot & Harmer, op. cit. pg. 3
863 J.N.D. Kelly, *The Oxford Dictionary of Popes* Oxford University Press (Oxford, England) 1986 pg. 7
864 Ibid.
865 Clement is controversial among Protestants because he is the only early church father who appeals to the authority of bishops, but even this statement is a far cry from the doctrine of papal supremacy expressed later.
866 Lightfoot & Harmer, op. cit. pg. 215
867 Ibid.

868 Bruce, op. cit. pg. 77
869 Ibid. pg. 166
870 Ibid. pg. 201
871 http://en.wikipedia.org/wiki/Gospel_of_thomas
872 http://www.goarch.org/ourfaith/ourfaith9560
873 Price, op. cit. pg. 113
874 Ibid.
875 Nestle & Aland, *Nestle-Aland Novum Tetamentum Graece* op. cit. pp. 685-688
876 Ibid. pg. 686
877 Young Kyu Kim, "Paleographical Dating of $\mathfrak{P}^{46}$ to the Later First Century," *Biblica*, lxix (1988) pp. 248-257
878 Metzger, op. cit. pg. 265
879 Ibid.
880 Metzger, op. cit. pg. 38
881 Kurt & Barbara Aland, *The Text of the New Testament* trans. Erroll Rhodes Wm. B. Eerdmans (Grand Rapids, Mich.) 1989 69
882 Cf. Metzger, op. cit. pg. 40, footnote 1
883 Theodore of Mapsuestia, *Ancient Christian Commentary Vol. IV B* op. cit. pg. 395
884 Ibid & John Foxe, *Acts and Monuments of the Church* op. cit. Pg. 95
885 Compiled from Hunt, *Defense of the Faith* op. cit. pg. 71 & Price, op. cit. pg. 114
886 Greenlee, op. cit. pp. 81-87
887 Metzger, op. cit. pg. 217
888 Ibid. pg. 196
889 Ibid.
890 Ibid. pg. 187
891 Ibid. pg. 191
892 Greenlee, op. cit. pg. 58
893 It is interesting to note that King James only advocates often attack modern translations for "removing" the word "God." However, the reverse (ος mistaken for θς) also occurs. There is no grand conspiracy to remove God from the Bible. Such attacks are not only frivolous, but the King James only advocate would also be surprised to learn how many times modern translation use the word "God" where it is *missing* from the King James.
894 Ibid. pg. 196
895 Cf. John Foxe, *Acts and Monuments of the Church Vol. 1* Religious Tract Society (London, England) 1860s ed. pg. 95
896 Price, op. cit. pg. 113
897 Norman L. Geisler and William E. Nix, *A General Introduction to the Bible*, Moody (Chicago, Ill.) 1986 ed. pp. 366-67
898 Randall Niles, "Bible Manuscripts," http://www.allaboutthejourney.org/bible-manuscripts.htm
899 Ibid.
900 Anderson, *Bible and Modern Criticism* op. cit. pg. 47
901 Ibid. pg. 48
902 Ibid. pg. 223
903 Ibid. pg. 78
904 See David Criswell, *Controversies in the Pentateuch* Fortress Adonai (Dallas, TX) 2007

WORKS CITED

BOOKS

Thomas Abbott, *A Critical and Exegetical Commentary on the Epistles to the Ephesians and to the Colossians* T & T Clark (Edinburgh, Scottland) 1897

Kurt & Barbara Aland, *The Text of the New Testament* Erroll Rhodes, trans. Wm. B. Eerdmans (Grand Rapids, Mich.) 1989

W.F. Albright & C.S. Mann, *The Anchor Bible : Matthew* Doubleday & Co. (Garden City, NY) 1971

Joseph Alexander, *Commentary on the Acts of the Apostles in One Volume* Zondervan Publishers (Grand Rapids, Mich.) 1956

David Allen, *The Lukan Authorship of Hebrews* B&H Academic (Nashville, TN) 2010

Sir Robert Anderson, *The Bible or the Church?* Pickering & Inglis (London, England) 1902

Sir Robert Anderson, *The Compete Works of Sir Robert Anderson Vol. 2* Fortress Adonai (Dallas, TX) 2010

Sir Robert Anderson, *The Critics Criticized* Pickering & Inglis (London, England) 1904

Sir Robert Anderson, *The Silence of God* Kregel Publications (Grand Rapids, Mich.) 1978

Gleason Archer, *Encyclodpedia of Bible Difficulties* Zondervan Publisher (Grand Rapids, Mich.) 1982

William Barclay, *Acts of the Apostles* Westminister Press (Phaladelphia, Penn.) 1953

William Barclay, *The Letters to the Galatians and Ephesians* Westminister Press (Philadelphia, PN) 1954

Albert Barnes, *Barnes' Notes on the New Testament* One Volume ed. Kregel (Grand Rapids, Mich.) 1962

Albert Barnes, *Notes on the Acts of the Apostles* Harper & Brothers (New York, NY) 1854

M. Baumgarten, *Acts of the Apostles Vol. 1* T&T Clark (London, England) 1854

M. Baumgarten, *Acts of the Apostles Vol. 2* T&T Clark (London, England) 1854

Samuel Blumenfeld, *N.E.A. Trojan Horse in American Education* The Paradigm Co. (Boise, Idaho) 1984

Loraine Boettner, *Roman Catholicism* Presbyterian & Reformed (Phillipsburg, NJ) 1962

Lawrence Browne, *Indian Church Commentaries - Acts of the Apostles* Diocesan Press (London, England) 1925

F.F. Bruce, *The Canon of Scripture* IVP Academic (Downers Grove, Ill.) 1988

F.F. Bruce, *Commentary on the Book Of Acts* Wm. B. Eerdmans (Grand Rapids, Mich.) 1954

John Calvin, *Acts* Crossway Books (Wheaton, Ill.) 1995

John Calvin, *Calvin's Commetnaries Vol. XIV Commentary on The Minor Prophets Book 2*, Baker Books (Grand Rapids, Mich.) 1999

John Calvin, *A Commentary on Genesis* Banner of Truth Trust (London, England) 1965 ed.

John Calvin, *Commentary on the Last Four Books of Moses* Baker Books (Grand Rapids, Mich.) 1999

D.A. Carson, *Showing the Spirit* Baker Book (Grand Rapids, Mich.) 1987

Adam Clarke, *Commentary on the Bible* notes on Acts 5:36 CD version (E-Sword) 2010

Mal Couch, *A Biblical Theology of the Church* Kregel Publications (Grand Rapids, Mich.)

Mal Couch, *An Introduction to Classical Evangelical Hermeneutics* Kregel Publications (Grand Rapids, Mich.) 2000

David Criswell, *Anonymous : Who Wrote the Book of Hebrews* Fortress Adonai (Dallas, TX) 2013

David Criswell, *The Apostles After Jesus* Fortress Adonai (Dallas, TX) 2113

David Criswell, *Controversies in the Gospels* Fortress Adonai (Dallas, TX) 2012

David Criswell, *Controversies in the Pentateuch* Fortress Adonai (Dallas, TX) 2009

David Criswell, *Rise and Fall of the Holy Roman Empire* Fortress Adonai (Dallas, TX) 2014

W.A. Criswell, *Acts in One Volume* Zondervan Publishers (Grand Rapids, Mich.) 1983

John Nelson Darby, *The Collected Writings of J.N. Darby* Prophetic No. 1 Vol. 2 Bible Truth Publishers (Addison, IL) n.d.

Franz Delitzsch, *Biblical Commentary on the Prophecies of Isaiah* Vol. 1 William B Eerdmans (Grand Rapids, Mich.) 1949

John Dewey, *Experience and Education* Collier Books (New York, NY) 1938

John Dewey, *School and Society* Cosimo Classics (New York, NY) 1889

Charles H. Dyer, with Angela Hunt, *The Rise of Babylon : Sign of the End Times* Tyndale House (Wheaton, Ill.) 1991

Brian Edwards, *Nothing but the Truth* Evangelical Press (Webster, NY) 2006 ed.

Jonathan Edwards, *"The Blank Bible"* Part 2 Stephen Stain, Ed., Yale University Press (New Haven, CT) 2006

Frederick Engels, *The Principles of Communism* Progress Publishers (Moscow, Russia) 1847

Frederick Engels, *The Communist Confession of Faith* Progress Publishers (Moscow, Russia) 1847

Desiderius Erasmus, *The Collected Works of Erasmus* Vol. 45 Paraphrase on Matthew Dean Simpson, trans., University of Toronto Press (Toronto, Canada) 2008

Desiderius Erasmus, *Paraphrase on the Acts of the Apostles* University of Toronto Press (Toronto, Canada) 1995

William Estep, *The Anabaptist Story* Broadman Press (Nashville, TN) 1963

Eusebius, *Eusebius, The Church History* 2.13-15 Paul Maier, trans. Kregel Publishers (Grand Rapids, Mich.) 1999

Abraham Ibn Ezra, *Commentary on the Pentateuch* Vol. 1 Genesis Menorah Publishing Company (New York, NY) 1988 ed.

Jerry Falwell & Ed Hindson, eds., *Liberty Commentary on the New Testament* Liberty Press (Lynchburg, Virginia) 1978

F.W. Farrar, *Texts Explained* F.M. Barton (Cleveland, Oh.) 1899

Charles Feinberg, *The Prophecy of Ezekiel* Moody Press (Chicago, Ill.) 1969

H.P.R. Finberg, *The Formation of England 550-1042* Paladin Granada Publishing (London, England) 1976

John Foxe, *Acts and Monuments of the Church* Vol. *1* Religious Tract Society (London, England) 1860s reprint

John Foxe, *Foxe's Book of Martyrs* Clarion Classics (Grand Rapids, Mich.) 1926 (abridged ed.)

A.C. Gaebelein, *Acts of the Apostles* Our Hope (New York, NY) 1912

A.C. Gaebelein, *The Gospel of Matthew* Vol. *1* Our Hope (New York, NY) 1910

Norman L. Geisler and William E. Nix, *A General Introduction to the Bible*, Moody (Chicago, Ill.) 1986 ed.

William Genenius, *Gesenius' Hebrew and Cahaldee Lexicon to the Old Tesament* Samuel Tregelles, trans., Baker Books (Grand Rapids, Mich.) 1847 (1984 ed.)

George Holley Gilbert, *Acts* MacMillian Co. (New York, NY) 1908

Martin Gilbert, ed. *Atlas of Jewish Civilization* Macmillan Press (New York, NY) 1990

John Gill, *Expositions of the Old Testament* Vol. *1* William Hill Collinridge (London, England) 1852

John Gill, *Expositions of the Old Testament* Vol. *3* William Hill Collinridge (London, England) 1852

John Gill, *Expositions of the Old Testament* Vol. *4* William Hill Collinridge (London, England) 1852

Louis Ginzberg, *The Legends of the Jews* Vol. *1 Genesis to Jacob* Jewish Publication Society (Philadelphia, Pennn.) 1909

Paton Gloag, *Acts of the Apostles* Vol. *1* Klock & Klock (Minneapolis, MN) 1870

Paton Gloag, *Acts of the Apostles* Vol. *2* Klock & Klock (Menneapolis, MN) 1870

Justo Gonzalez, *The Story of Christanity* Vol. *1* HarperCollins (San Francisco, CA) 1984

Justo Gonzalez, *The Story of Christianity* Vol. *2* Harper & Row (San Francisco, CA) 1984

Robert Gundry, *Matthew* Wm. B. Eerdmaans (Grand Rapids, Mich.) 1982

Robert Gundry, *A Survey of the New Testament* Zondervan Publishers (Grand Rapids, Mich.) 1994

Serge Grunzinski, *The Aztecs - Rise and Fall of an Empire* Harry Abrams (New York, NY) 1987

Horatio Hackett, *Commentary on the Original Text of the Book of Acts of the Apostles* Gould & Lincoln (New York, NY) 1859

Matthew Henry, *Matthew Henry's Commentary on the Whole Bible : Vol. 1* Hendrickson Publishers (Peabody, Mass.) 1991

Matthew Henry, *Matthew Henry's Commentary on the Whole Bible : Vol. 4* Hendrickson Publishers (Peabody, Mass.) 1991

Matthew Henry, *Matthew Henry's Commentary on the Whole Bible Vol. 6 Acts to Revelation* Hendrickson Publishers (Peabody, Mass.) 1991

John E. Hill, *Through the Jade Gate to Rome* BookSurge (Charleston, SC) 2009

Alexander Hislop, *The Two Babylons* Loizeaux Brothers (Neptune, NJ) 1916

Harold Hoehner, *Chronological Aspects of the Life of Christ* Zondervan Publishing (Grand Rapids, Mich.) 1977

Anthony Hoekema, *Holy Spirit Baptism* Wm. B. Eerdmans (Grand Rapids, Mich.) 1972

G. H. R. Horsley, *New Documents Illustrating Early Christianity: a Review of the Greek Inscriptions and Papyri* William B. Eerdmans (Grand Rapids, Mich.) 1987

Dave Hunt, *Defense of the Faith* Harvest House (Eugene, OR) 1994

Dave Hunt & T.A. McMahon, *The Seduction of Christianity* Harvest House (Eugene, OR) 1984

Hammond Innes, *The Conquistadors* Alfred A. Knoft (New York, NY) 1969

H.A. Ironside, *Addresses on the First Epistle to the Corinthians* Loizeaux Brothers (New York, NY) 1938

H.A. Ironside, *Lectures on the Book of Acts* Loizeaus Bro. (New York, NY) 1943

H. A. Ironside, *Notes on the Prophecy and Lamentations of Jeremiah* Loizeaux Brothers (Neptune, NJ) 1906

Flavius Josephus, *The Complete Works of Josephus* Kregel Publications (Grand Rapids, Mich.) 1981

J.N.D. Kelly, *The Oxford Dictionary of Pope* Oxford University Press (Oxford, England) 1986

William Kelly, *An Exposition of the Acts of the Apostles* C.A. Hammond (London, England) 1952

George Ladd, *A Theology of the New Testament by George Eldon Ladd* Wm. B. Eerdmans (Grand Rapids, Mich.) 1974

Kenneth Scott Latourette, *A History of Christianity Vol. 1* Harper & Row (New York, NY) 1953

R.C.H. Lenski, *The Interpretation of the Acts of the Apostles* Warburg Press (Columbus, OH) 1944

Jack P. Lewis, *Historical Backgrounds of Bible History* Baker Book House (Grand Rapids, Mich.) 1971

J.B. Lightfoot, *The Apostolic Fathers* Baker Books (Grand Rapids, Mich.) 1984 ed.

John Lightfoot, *Commentary on the Acts of the Apostles* J.F. Dove (London, England) 1823

John Lightfoot, *From the Talmud and Hebraica, Volume 4* Cosimo Classics (New York, NY) 2013

John Lightfoot, *The Whole Works of the Rev. John Lightfoot Vol. II* J. F. Dove (London, England) n.d.

J. Rawson Lumby, *Acts of the Apostles* Cambridge University Press (Cambridge, England) 1882

Martin Luther, *Luther's Works Vol. 18* Concordia House Publishing (St. Louis, MS) 1958

John MacArthur, *The MacArthur New Testament Commentary Acts 1-12* Moody Bible Instituted (Chicago, Ill.) 1994

John MacArthur, *The MacArthur New Testament Commentary Acts 13-28* Moody Press (Chicago, Ill.) 1996

John MacArthur, *The MacArthur New Testament Commentary Matthew 24-28* Moody Bible Institute (Chicago, Ill.) 1985

Lee Martin McDonald, *The Biblical Canon* Hendrickson Publishers (Peabody, Mass.) 1995

Bill McMillon, *The Archaeology Handbook* John Wiley & Sons, Inc. (New York, NY) 1991

Jean Marton, *Science and the Bible* Moody Press (Chicago, Ill.) 1978

Karl Marx and Frederick Engels, *The Communist Manifesto* Progress Publishers (Moscow, Russia) 1848

Alexander Mar Thoma Metropolitan, *The Mar Thoma Church : Heritage and Mission* Puthethu Offset (Thiruvalla, Kerala, India) 1985

Bruce Metzger, *A Textual Commentary on the Greek New Testament* United Bible Society (Stuttgart, Germany) 1994

Heinrich Meyer, *Handbook to the Acts of the Apostles Vol. 1* T&T Clark (Edinburgh, Scotland) 1861

George Milligan, *The New Testament Documents: Their Origin and Early History*, Macmillan and Co. (London, England) 1913

Kenneth Morgan, ed., *Oxford Illustrated History of Britain* Oxford University Press (Oxford, England) 1984

Henry Morris, *The Genesis Record* Baker Book House (Grand Rapids, Mich.) 1976

Jerome Murphy-O'Connor, *St. Paul's Corinth: Text and Archaeology* Liturgical Press (Collegeville, MN), 2002

Eberhard Nestle and Kurt Aland, *Nestle-Aland Novum Testamentum Graece* United Bible Society (Stuttgart, German) 1898 & 1979

Barclay M. Newman, Jr., ed., *A Concise Greek-English Dictionary of the New Testament* United Bible Society (Stuttgart, Germany) 1971

A.T. Olmstead, *History of Assyria* Charles Scribners (New York, NY) 1923

John Joseph Owens, *Analytical Key to the Old Testament Vol. 4* Baker Books (Grand Rapids, Mich.) 1994

Mikael Parsons, *Paideia Commentary : Acts* Baker Academics (Grand Rapids, Mich.) 2008

Jaroslav Pelikan, *Acts* Brazos Press (Grand Rapids, Mich.) 2005

J. Dwight Pentecost, *Things to Come* Zondervan Publishers (Grand Rapids, Mich.) 1958

A.C. Perumalil, *The Apostles in India* St. Paul Press (Bangalore, India) 1952

David Petts, *The Holy Spirit: An Introduction* Mattersey Hall (Mattersey, England:) 1998

Matthew Poole, *Commentary on the Holy Bible : Vol. I* Hendrickson Publishers (Peabody, Mass.) n.d.

Matthew Poole, *A Commetnary on the Holy Bible Vol. II* Hendrickson Publishers (Peabody, Mass.) n.d.

Matthew Poole, *A Commentary on the Holy Bible Vol. III* Hendrickson Publishers (Peabody, Mass.) n.d.

Chaim Potok, *Wanderings* Ballantine Books (New York, NY) 1978

Randall Price, *The Coming Last Days Temple* Harvest House (Eugene, OR) 1999

Randall Price, *Searching for the Original Bible* Harvest House (Eugene, OR) 2007

Rashi, *Chumash with Rashi's Commentary : Beresith* A.B. Silbermann, ed., Feldheim Publishers (Jerusalem, Israel) 1934

Colin Renfrew & Paul Bahn, *Archaeology: Theories, Methods, & Practice* Thames & Hudson Ltd. (New York, NY) 1991

Robert Rogers, *A History of Babylonia and Assyria Vol. II* Eaton & Mains (New York, NY) 1901

A.J. Rosenberg, ed., *The Books of Twelve Prophets Vol. I with Rashi Commentary* Judaica Press (New York, NY) 1986

Georges Roux, *Ancient Iraq* Penguin Books (New York, NY) 1992 ed.

Bernard Ruffin, *The Twelve : The Lives of the Apostles After Calvary* One Sunday Visitor (Huntington, IN) 1970

Philip Schaff, *History of the Christian Church Vol. 1* Hendrickson Publishers (Peabody, Mass.) 1996

Philip Schaff, *History of the Christian Church Vol. 2* Hendrickson Publishers Peabody, Mass.) 1996

Philip Schaff, *History of the Christian Church Vol. 8* Hendrickson Publishers (Peabody, Mass.) 1996

Emil Schurer, *A History of the Jewish People in the Time of Jesus Christ First Divsiion Vol. I* Hendrickson Publishers (Peabody, Mass.) 1890

Emil Schurer, *A History of the Jewish People in the Time of Jesus Christ First Divsiion Vol. II* Hendrickson Publishers (Peabody, Mass.) 1890

Emil Schurer, *A History of the Jewish People in the Time of Jesus Christ Vol. III (2nd Div. Vol. I)* Hendrickson Publishers (Peabody, Mass.) 1890

Emil Schurer, *A History of the Jewish People in the Time of Jesus Christ Vol. IV (2nd Div. Vol. II)* Hendrickson Publishers (Peabody, Mass.) 1890

H.H. Scullard, *From the Gracchi to Nero* Routledge (New York, NY) 1959

Socialist Union, *Twentieth Century Socialism* Penguin Books (New York, NY) 1956

Marta Sordi, *The Christian and the Roman Empire* University of Oklohama (Oklahoma City, OK) 1986

C. H. Spurgeon, *The Treasury of the Old Testament Vol. 1 : Genesis to 2 Kings* Zondervan (Grand Rapids, Mich.) 1951

Charles Spurgeon, *Treasury of the New Testament Volume Two* Zondervan (Grand Rapids, Mich.) 1950

Sutonius, *Lives of the Twelve Caesars* Robert Graves, trans Welcome Rain (New York, NY) 1957

Cornelius Tacitus, *The Annals: The Reigns of Tiberius, Claudius, and Nero* Oxford University (Oxford, England) 2008

Joseph Thayer, *A Greek-English Lexicon of the New Testament* Baker Books (Grand Rapids, Mich.) 1977

Edwin R. Thiele, *The Mysterious Numbers of the Hebrew Kings* Kregel Publications (Grand Rapids, Mich.) 1983

Merrill Tenney, *New Testament Survey* Wm. B Eerdmans Publishing (Grand Rapids, Mich.) 1985

Warren Trenchard, *Complete Vocabulary Guide to the Greek New Testament* Zondervan Publishing (Grand Rapids, Mich.) 1992

Merrill Unger, *Unger's Bible Dictionary* Moody Press (Chicago, Ill.) 1957

James Ussher, *Annals of the World* Master Books (El Cajon, CA) 2003

Thieleman J. van Braght, *Martyrs' Mirror* Herald Press (Scottdale, PN) 1950 ed. (1660 orig.)

John Walvoord, *Every Prophecy of the Bible* Chariot Victor Publishing (Colorado Springs, Co.) 1999

Steven Waterhouse, *Not By Bread Alone* Westcliff Press (Amarillo, TX) 2007

John Wesley, *Explanatory Notes Upon the New Testament* Abraham Paul (New York, NY) 1818

John Wesley, *Explanatory Notes Upon the Old Testament Vol. I Genesis – Judges XIV* Schmul Publishers (Salem, Ohio) 1975

John Wesley, *Explanatory Notes Upon the Old Testament Vol. III Psalms LXIII – Malachi* Schmul Publishers (Salem, Ohio) 1975

Warren Wiersbe, *Be Loyal* Victor Books (Wheaton, Ill.) 1987

Warren Wiersbe, *Be Transformed* Victor Books (Wheaton, Ill.) 1987

Michael Wood, *Conquistadors* University of Caolifornia Press (Berkley, CA) 2000

Richard Young, *Intermediate New Testament Greek* Broadman & Holman (Nashville, TN) 1994

REFERENCE WORKS

Acts of the Apostles : Four Centuries of Baptist Interpretation, Beth Barr, etc. eds. Baylor University (Waco, TX) 2009

Ancient Christian Commentary on Scripture New Testament IV B John 11-21 John Elowsky, ed., InterVarsity Press (Downers Grove, Ill.) 2006

Ancient Commentary on the Scritpures : New Testament Vol. V : Acts Thomas Oden, ed., InterVarsity (Downers Grove, Ill.) 2006

Ante-Nicene Fathers Vol. 1 Alexander Roberts & James Donaldson, eds., Charles Scribner (New York, NY) 1886

Ante-Nicene Fathers Vol. 2 Alexander Roberts & James Donaldson, eds., Charles Scribner (New York, NY) 1886

Ante-Nicene Fathers Vol. 3 Alexander Roberts & James Donaldson, eds., Charles Scribner (New York, NY) 1886

Ante-Nicene Fathers Vol. 5 Alexander Roberts & James Donaldson, eds., Charles Scribner (New York, NY) 1886

Ante-Nicene Fathers Vol. 8 Alexander Roberts & James Donaldson, eds., Charles Scribner (New York, NY) 1886

Apocryphal Acts of the Apostles Vol. 1, J. B. Lightfoot, D.D, trans. Williams & Norgate (London, England) 1871

The Apostlic Fathers J.B. Lightfoot, & J.R. Harmer, eds., Baker Book House (Grand Rapids, Mich.) 1984

The Bible Knowledge Commentary : New Testament John Walvoord & Roy Zuck, eds., Victor Books (Wheaton, Ill.) 1986

Catechism of the Catholic Church

Complete Vocabulary Guide to the Greek New Testament Warren Trenchard, Zondervan Publishing (Grand Rapids, Mich.) 1992

The Complete Works of Josephus Kregel Publishers (Grand Rapids, Mich) 1981

Criswell Study Bible, W.A. Criswell, ed., Thomas Nelson Publishers (Nashville, TN) 1979

Discoveries in the Judaean Desert XII : Qumran Cave 4 VII Clarendon Press (Oxford, England) 1994

The Expositor's Bible Commentary Vol. 9 Frank Gaebelein, ed., Zondervan Publishing (Grand Rapids, Mich.) 1981

Eusebius, The Church History 2.25 Paul Maier, trans. Kregel Publishers (Grand Rapids, Mich.) 1999

Greek-English Lexicon of the New Testament Joseph Thayer, Baker Books (Grand Rapids, Mich.) 1977

Lutheran Cyclopedia Erwin Lueker, ed., Concordia Press (St. Louis, MI) 1975

The Midrash Rabbah Vol. 1 Genesis Soncino Press (New York, NY) 1977 ed. [XXVI-7]

Mishnah Jacob Neusner, trans., Yale University Press (London, England) 1988

Nestle-Aland Novum Testamentum Graece Eberhard Nestle and Kurt Aland, eds., United Bible Society (Stuttgart, German) 1898 & 1979

Nicene and Post-Nicene Fathers Second Series Vol. II Philip Schaff, ed., Charles Scribner (New York, NY) 1894

Nicene and Post-Nicene Fathers Second Series Vol. VII Philip Schaff, ed., Charles Scribner (New York, NY) 1892

PERIODICALS

Allan Bloom, "Has the Open University Closed the American Mind?" *Current Issues & Enduring Questions* Barnet & Dedas, eds., St. Martin's Press (Boston, MA) 1990

Young Kyu Kim, "Paleographical Dating of $\mathfrak{P}^{46}$ to the Later First Century," *Biblica*, lxix (1988)

MISCELANEOUS SOURCES

John Gill, *Exposition of the Entire Bible* CD version (E-Sword) 2010

Logos Bible Software

catholic-resources.org/Bible/NT-Statistics-Greek.htm

en.wikipedia.org/wiki/Gospel_of_thomas

enrichmentjournal.ag.org/201002/201002_119_HS_Separate.cfm

marxists.org/archive/marx/works/1847/11/prin-com.htm

www.allaboutthejourney.org/bible-manuscripts.htm

www.andrewcorbett.net/articles/subsequence.html

www.bible.ca/cath-baptism.htm

www.catholic.com/quickquestions/was-jesus-baptized-by-immersion

www.christian-history.org/muratorian-canon.html

www.earlychristianwritings.com/text/actspeter.html

www.ewtn.com/vexperts/showmessage_print.asp?number=367829&language=en

www.goarch.org/ourfaith/ourfaith9560

www.haaretz.com/weekend/week-s-end/in-three-days-you-shall-live-1.218552
www.harrington-sites.com/house1.html
www.ibiblio.org/britishraj/Jackson2/appendix04.html
www.jewishencyclopedia.com/articles/14369-theudas
www.levitt.com/essays/luke
www.nestorian.org/kings_of_edessa.html
www.newble.co.uk/anderson/biblech/biblech9.html
www.rwaynestacy.com/2011/03/was-luke-gentile.html
www.tentmaker.org/Dew/Dew3/D3-JudasIscariot.html
www.tertullian.org/fathers/chronography_of_354_13_bishops_of_rome.htm
www.thebereancall.org/content/who-was-philip-evangelist
www.theoi.com/Text/HomericHymns1.html
www.thywordistruth.com/questions/Question-355.html
www.vatican.va/archive/ENG0015/__P3G.HTM

www.ingramcontent.com/pod-product-compliance
Lightning Source LLC
Chambersburg PA
CBHW061633040426
42446CB00010B/1404